What Happened

Hillary Rodham Clinton

SIMON & SCHUSTER

NEW YORK   LONDON   TORONTO   SYDNEY   NEW DELHI

For the team who stood with me in 2016
and worked their hearts out for a better, stronger, fairer America.
Being your candidate was one of the greatest honors of my life.

Contents

Idealism and Realism

Frustration

Resilience

If you are tired, keep going.

If you are scared, keep going.

If you are hungry, keep going.

If you want to taste freedom, keep going.

—Harriet Tubman

Author's Note

This is my story of what happened.

It's the story of what I saw, felt, and thought during two of the most intense years I've ever experienced.

It's the story of what led me to this crossroads of American history and how I kept going after a shocking defeat; how I reconnected with the things that matter most to me and began to look ahead with hope, instead of backward with regret.

It's also the story of what happened to our country, why we're so divided, and what we can do about it.

I don't have all the answers, and this isn't a comprehensive account of the 2016 race. That's not for me to write—I have too little distance and too great a stake in it. Instead, this is *my* story. I want to pull back the curtain on an experience that was exhilarating, joyful, humbling, infuriating, and just plain baffling.

Writing this wasn't easy. Every day that I was a candidate for President, I knew that millions of people were counting on me, and

I couldn't bear the idea of letting them down. But I did. I couldn't get the job done, and I'll have to live with that for the rest of my life.

In this book, I write about moments from the campaign that I wish I could go back and do over. If the Russians could hack my subconscious, they'd find a long list. I also capture some moments I want to remember forever, like when my tiny granddaughter raced into the room while I was practicing my convention speech, and what it was like hours later to step onstage to deliver that speech as the first woman ever nominated by a major political party for President of the United States.

I write about people who inspired me, from a minister in South Carolina who talked with me about love and kindness, to residents who banded together in a town poisoned by lead, to tireless campaign volunteers giving everything they had for a better future. And I share my thoughts on big challenges I've grappled with for decades that have taken on new urgency, such as the roles that gender, race, and class play in our politics and the importance of empathy in our national life.

I've tried to learn from my own mistakes. There are plenty, as you'll see in this book, and they are mine and mine alone.

But that's not the end of the story. We can't understand what happened in 2016 without confronting the audacious information warfare waged from the Kremlin, the unprecedented intervention in our election by the director of the FBI, a political press that told voters that my emails were the most important story, and deep currents of anger and resentment flowing through our culture.

I know some people don't want to hear about these things, especially from me. But we have to get this right. The lessons we draw from 2016 could help determine whether we can heal our democracy and protect it in the future, and whether we as citizens can begin to bridge our divides. I want my grandchildren and all future generations to know what really happened. We have a responsibility to history—and to a concerned world—to set the record straight.

I also share with you the painful days that followed the election. A lot of people have asked me, "How did you even get out of bed?" Reading the news every morning was like ripping off a scab. Each new revelation and outrage made it worse. It has been maddening to watch our country's standing in the world plummet and to see Americans live in fear that their health care might be taken away so that the superrich can get a tax cut. There are times when all I want to do is scream into a pillow.

But slowly, on a personal level, it has gotten better—or at least less terrible. I did quite a bit of thinking and writing, some praying, some stewing, and, in time, a good deal of laughing. I went on a lot of long walks in the woods with my husband and our dogs, Tally and Maisie, who took all this much better than we did. I surrounded myself with friends and caught up on some of the shows that people have been telling me about for years, as well as a lot of HGTV. Best of all, I spent time with my wonderful grandchildren, making up for all the bedtime stories and songs in the bathtub I missed during my long months on the campaign trail. I believe this is what some call "self-care." It turns out, it's pretty great.

Now when people ask how I'm doing, I say that, as an American, I'm more worried than ever—but as a person, I'm doing okay.

This book is the story of that journey. Writing it has been cathartic. I got angry and sad all over again. At times, I've had to step away, lie down, close my eyes, and try to empty my mind. This book has been hard to write for another reason: I've lost count of the number of times that I've sat at my kitchen table working on these pages, been interrupted by a breaking news alert, hung my head and sighed, and then took out my red pen and started revising.

I've tried to make my peace with painful memories and recapture some of the fun that filled more days on the campaign than you might think. In the past, for reasons that I try to explain, I've often felt I had to be careful in public, like I was up on a wire without a net. Now I'm letting down my guard.

By the time I finished writing, I felt ready to face the future again. I hope that, by the final page, you'll be right there with me.

I will always be grateful to have been the Democratic Party's nominee and to have earned 65,844,610 votes from my fellow Americans. That number—more votes than any candidate for President has ever received, other than Barack Obama—is proof that the ugliness we faced in 2016 does not define our country.

I want to thank everyone who welcomed me into their homes, businesses, schools, and churches over those two long, crazy years; every little girl and boy who ran into my arms at full speed or high-fived me with all their might; and the long chain of brave, adventurous people, stretching back generations, whose love and strength made it possible for me to lead such a rewarding life in the country I love. Thanks to them, despite everything else, my heart is full.

I started this book with some words attributed to one of those pathbreakers, Harriet Tubman. Twenty years ago, I watched a group of children perform a play about her life at her former homestead in Auburn, New York. They were so excited about this courageous, determined woman who led slaves to freedom against all odds. Despite everything she faced, she never lost her faith in a simple but powerful motto: Keep going. That's what we have to do now, too.

In 2016, the U.S. government announced that Harriet Tubman will become the face of the $20 bill. If you need proof that America can still get it right, there it is.

What Happened

It's supposed to be hard. If it wasn't hard, everyone would do it. The hard is what makes it great.

—*A League of Their Own*

Perseverance

That which does not kill us makes us stronger.

—Friedrich Nietzsche (and Kelly Clarkson)

Showing Up

Deep breath. Feel the air fill my lungs. This is the right thing to do. The country needs to see that our democracy still works, no matter how painful this is. Breathe out. Scream later.

I'm standing just inside the door at the top of the steps leading down to the inaugural platform, waiting for the announcer to call Bill and me to our seats. I'm imagining that I'm anywhere but here. Bali maybe? Bali would be good.

It's tradition for Bill and me, as a former President and First Lady, to attend the swearing-in of the new President. I had struggled for weeks with whether or not to go. John Lewis wasn't going. The civil rights hero and Congressman said that the President Elect was not legitimate because of the mounting evidence of Russian interference in the election. Other members of Congress were joining him in boycotting a President Elect they saw as divisive. A lot of my supporters and close friends urged me to stay home, too.

My friends understood how painful it would be to sit on the platform and watch Donald Trump sworn in as our next Commander in

Chief. I had campaigned relentlessly to make sure that never happened. I was convinced he represented a clear and present danger to the country and the world. Now the worst had happened, and he was going to take the oath of office.

Plus, after the mean-spirited campaign Trump ran, there was a decent chance I'd get booed or be met with "Lock her up!" chants if I went.

Still, I felt a responsibility to be there. The peaceful transfer of power is one of our country's most important traditions. I had touted it around the world as Secretary of State, hoping that more countries would follow our example. If I really believed in it, I had to put my feelings aside and go.

Bill and I checked with the Bushes and the Carters to see what they were thinking. George W. and Jimmy had been among the first to call me after the election, which meant a lot to me. George actually called just minutes after I finished my concession speech, and graciously waited on the line while I hugged my team and supporters one last time. When we talked, he suggested we find time to get burgers together. I think that's Texan for "I feel your pain." Both he and Jimmy knew what it felt like to put yourself on the line in front of the whole country, and Jimmy knew the sting of rejection. He and I commiserated over that a bit. ("Jimmy, this is the worst." "Yes, Hillary, it is.") It was no secret that these former Presidents weren't fans of Donald Trump. He had been absolutely vicious to George's brother Jeb in particular. But were they going to the inauguration? Yes.

That gave me the push I needed. Bill and I would go.

That's how I ended up right inside the door of the Capitol on January 20, waiting to be announced. It had been such a long journey to get here. Now I just had to take a few more steps. I took Bill's arm and squeezed it, grateful to have him by my side. I took a deep breath and walked out the door with as big a smile as I could muster.

On the platform, we sat next to the Bushes. The four of us had caught up inside a few minutes earlier, trading updates about our daughters and grandchildren. We chatted like it was any other day. George and Laura gave us the latest news about the health of George's parents, former President George H. W. and Barbara, both of whom had been in the hospital recently but, happily, were now on the mend.

As we sat waiting for the President Elect to arrive, my mind wandered back to that incredible day twenty-four years earlier when Bill took the oath of office for the first time. It could not have been easy for George H. W. and Barbara to watch, but they had been extraordinarily gracious to us. The outgoing President left a letter for Bill in the Oval Office that is one of the most decent and patriotic things I've ever read. "Your success now is our country's success. I am rooting hard for you," he wrote. We did our best to show the same graciousness to George W. and Laura eight years later. At this moment, I was trying to summon a similar attitude about the incoming President. As I had said in my concession speech, he deserved an open mind and the chance to lead.

I also thought about Al Gore, who in 2001 sat stoically through George W.'s inauguration despite having won more votes. Five members of the Supreme Court decided that election. That must have been awful to bear. I realized I was inventing a new pastime: imagining the pain of past electoral losses. John Adams, our second Commander in Chief, suffered the indignity of being the first President ever voted out of office, losing to Thomas Jefferson in 1800, but he got a measure of revenge twenty-five years later when his son John Quincy was elected. In 1972, George McGovern lost forty-nine out of fifty states to Richard Nixon—Bill and I worked hard on McGovern's campaign and have indelible memories of that defeat. And let's not forget William Howard Taft, whom Teddy Roosevelt had groomed to succeed him. Four years later, in 1912, Teddy decided Taft wasn't doing a good enough job as President, so he ran as a third-party candidate, split the electorate, and Woodrow Wilson won. That had to hurt.

Then Bill touched my elbow, and I snapped back to the present.

The Obamas and the Bidens were in front of us. I imagined President Obama riding over in the presidential limo with a man who had risen to prominence partly by lying about Barack's birthplace and accusing him of not being an American. At some point in the day's proceedings, Michelle and I shared a rueful look. It said, "Can you believe this?" Eight years before, on the bitterly cold day when Barack was sworn in, our heads were full of plans and possibilities. Today was just about putting on a game face and getting through it.

The President Elect finally arrived. I had known Donald Trump for years, but never imagined he'd be standing on the steps of the Capitol taking the oath of office as President of the United States. He was a fixture of the New York scene when I was a Senator—like a lot of big-shot real estate guys in the city, only more flamboyant and self-promoting. In 2005, he invited us to his wedding to Melania in Palm Beach, Florida. We weren't friends, so I assumed he wanted as much star power as he could get. Bill happened to be speaking in the area that weekend, so we decided to go. Why not? I thought it would be a fun, gaudy, over-the-top spectacle, and I was right. I attended the ceremony, then met Bill for the reception at Trump's Mar-a-Lago estate. We had our photo taken with the bride and groom and left.

The next year, Trump joined other prominent New Yorkers in a video spoof prepared for the Legislative Correspondents Association dinner in Albany, which is the state version of the more famous White House Correspondents' Association dinner. The idea was that the wax figure of me at the Madame Tussauds museum in Times Square had been stolen, so I had to stand in and pretend to be a statue while various famous people walked by and said things to me. New York Mayor Mike Bloomberg said I was doing a great job as Senator—then joked about running for President in 2008 as a self-funder. When Trump appeared, he said, "You look really great. Unbelievable. I've never seen anything like it. The hair is magnificent. The face is beautiful. You know,

I really think you'd make a great President. Nobody could come close."
The camera pulled back to reveal he wasn't talking to me after all but to
his own wax statue. It was funny at the time.

When Trump declared his candidacy for real in 2015, I thought it
was another joke, like a lot of people did. By then, he'd remade himself
from tabloid scoundrel into right-wing crank, with his long, offensive,
quixotic obsession with President Obama's birth certificate. He'd flirted
with politics for decades, but it was hard to take him seriously. He reminded me of one of those old men ranting on about how the country
was going to hell in a handbasket unless people started listening to him.

It was impossible to ignore Trump—the media gave him free wall-
to-wall coverage. I thought it was important to call him out for his
bigotry, which I did early and often, starting when he called Mexican
immigrants rapists and drug dealers the day he announced his candidacy. But it wasn't until I saw him dominate a debate with a crowded
field of talented Republican candidates—not with brilliant ideas or
powerful arguments but with ugly attacks that drew gasps—that I realized he might be for real.

Now here he was, with his hand on the Bible, promising to preserve, protect, and defend the Constitution of the United States. The
joke, it turned out, was on us.

It started to rain, and people around us fumbled with the thin
plastic ponchos we'd been given. Backstage, I had urged Bill to wear
his trench coat. The day was unusually warm, and Bill didn't think he
needed it. Now he was glad he'd worn it—a small wifely victory on
a torturous day. As awkward as the ponchos looked, they could have
looked worse. I had heard that the first batch of white ponchos that
arrived could have looked something like KKK hoods from a certain
angle, and a sharp-eyed inaugural organizer quickly replaced them.

The new President's speech was dark and dystopian. I heard it as
a howl straight from the white nationalist gut. Its most memorable
line was about "American carnage," a startling phrase more suited to

a slasher film than an inaugural address. Trump painted a picture of a bitter, broken country I didn't recognize.

I knew we still had real challenges, ones I had talked about endlessly on the campaign trail: income inequality and the increasing concentration of corporate power, continuing threats from terrorism and climate change, the rising cost of health care, the need to create more and better jobs in the face of accelerating automation. The American middle class really had gotten screwed. The financial crash of 2008–2009 cost them jobs and ripped away their security. It seemed like no one was ever held accountable. Americans across a broad spectrum felt alienated, from culturally traditional white voters unsettled by the pace of social change, to black men and women who felt as if the country didn't value their lives, to Dreamers and patriotic Muslim citizens who were made to feel like intruders in their own land.

Trump was great at rubbing salt in their wounds. But he was wrong about so much. There had been seventy-five straight months of job growth under President Obama, and incomes for the bottom 80 percent were finally starting to go up. Twenty million more people had health insurance thanks to the Affordable Care Act, the greatest legislative achievement of the outgoing administration. Crime was still at historic lows. Our military remained by far the most powerful in the world. These are knowable, verifiable facts. Trump stood up there in front of the world and said the exact opposite—just as he had throughout the campaign. He didn't seem to see or value any of the energy and optimism I saw when I traveled around the country.

Listening to Trump, it almost felt like there was no such thing as truth anymore. It still feels that way.

My predecessor in the Senate, Daniel Patrick Moynihan, used to say, "Everyone is entitled to his own opinion, but not his own facts." We can disagree about policies and values, but claiming that 2 + 2 = 5 and having millions of Americans swallow it is very different. When the most powerful person in our country says, "Don't believe your eyes, don't believe the experts, don't believe the numbers, just believe me," that rips a big hole in a free democratic society like ours. As Yale history professor Timothy Snyder writes in his book *On Tyranny: Twenty Lessons from the Twentieth Century*, "To abandon facts is to abandon freedom. If nothing is true, then no one can criticize power, because there is no basis upon which to do so. If nothing is true, then all is spectacle."

Attempting to define reality is a core feature of authoritarianism. This is what the Soviets did when they erased political dissidents from historical photos. This is what happens in George Orwell's classic novel *Nineteen Eighty-Four*, when a torturer holds up four fingers and delivers electric shocks until his prisoner sees five fingers as ordered. The goal is to make you question logic and reason and to sow mistrust toward exactly the people we need to rely on: our leaders, the press, experts who seek to guide public policy based on evidence, ourselves. For Trump, as with so much he does, it's about simple dominance.

This trend didn't start with Trump. Al Gore wrote a book called *The Assault on Reason* in 2007. In 2005, Stephen Colbert coined the word "truthiness," inspired by how Fox News was turning politics into an evidence-free zone of seething resentments. And the Republican politicians whom Fox propelled to power had done their part, too. Republican strategist Karl Rove famously dismissed critics who lived in "the reality-based community"—words intended as a slight—saying they failed to grasp that "we're an empire now, and when we act, we create our own reality."

But Trump has taken the war on truth to a whole new level. If he stood up tomorrow and declared that the Earth is flat, his counselor Kellyanne Conway just might go on Fox News and defend it as an "alternative fact," and too many people would believe it. Just look at what happened several weeks into his presidency when Trump falsely accused President Obama of having wiretapped him, a claim that was widely and quickly debunked. A subsequent poll found that 74 percent of Republicans nevertheless thought it was at least somewhat likely to be true.

Trump's inaugural address was aimed squarely at millions of Americans who felt insecure and frustrated, even hopeless, in a changing economy and society. A lot of people were looking for someone to blame. Too many saw the world in zero-sum terms, believing that gains made by fellow Americans they viewed as "other"—people of color, immigrants, women, LGBT people, Muslims—were not earned and must be coming at someone's expense. The economic pain and dislocation were real, and so was the psychic pain. It made for a toxic, combustible mix.

I hadn't been blind to the power of this anger. During the campaign, Bill and I both went back and reread *The True Believer*, Eric Hoffer's 1951 exploration of the psychology behind fanaticism and mass movements, and I shared it with my senior staff. On the campaign trail, I offered ideas that I believed would address many of the underlying causes of discontent and help make life better for all Americans. But I couldn't—and wouldn't—compete to stoke people's rage and resentment. I think that's dangerous. It helps leaders who want to take advantage of that rage to hurt people rather than help them. Besides, it's just not how I'm wired.

Maybe that's why Trump was now delivering the inaugural address and I was sitting in the crowd.

What would I have said if it were me up there? It would have been daunting to find the words to match the moment. I probably would have gone through a million drafts. My poor speechwriters would have been sprinting only steps ahead of me carrying the thumb drive with the final draft to the teleprompter operator. But I would have relished the chance to move beyond the rancor of the campaign, reach out to all Americans regardless of who they voted for, and offer a vision of national reconciliation, shared opportunity, and inclusive prosperity. It would have been an extraordinary honor to be the first woman to take the oath. I won't pretend I hadn't dreamt of that moment—for me, for my mother, for my daughter, her daughter, everyone's daughters—and for our sons.

Instead, the world was listening to the new President's undimmed fury. I remembered the late Maya Angelou reading one of her poems at Bill's first inauguration. "Do not be wedded forever to fear, yoked eternally to brutishness," she urged us. What would she say if she could hear this speech?

Then it was done, and he was our President.

"That was some weird shit," George W. reportedly said with characteristic Texas bluntness. I couldn't have agreed more.

We headed up the stairs to leave the platform and go back inside the Capitol, shaking hands along the way. I saw a man off to the side who I thought was Reince Priebus, head of the Republican National Committee and incoming White House Chief of Staff. As I passed by, we shook hands and exchanged small talk. Later I realized it hadn't been Priebus at all. It was Jason Chaffetz, the then–Utah Congressman and wannabe Javert who made endless political hay out of my emails and the 2012 tragedy in Benghazi, Libya. Later, Chaffetz posted a picture of our handshake with the caption "So pleased she is not the President. I thanked her for her service and wished her luck. The investigation continues." What a class act! I came this close to tweeting back, "To be honest, thought you were Reince."

The rest of the day was a blur of greeting old friends and trying to avoid eye contact with those people who'd said terrible things about me during the campaign.

I ran into Supreme Court Justice Ruth Bader Ginsburg, walking slowly but with steely determination. If I had won, she might have enjoyed a nice retirement. Now I hoped she'd stay on the bench as long as humanly possible.

At lunch in the Capitol, I sat at our assigned table and commiserated with Congresswoman Nancy Pelosi, the Democratic leader in the House of Representatives, who I think is one of the shrewdest, most effective politicians in Washington. She deserves enormous credit for marshalling the votes for the 2010 Affordable Care Act under nearly impossible circumstances and for standing up for what's right whether she's in the majority or the minority. Republicans have demonized her for years because they know she gets things done.

Senator John McCain of Arizona came over and gave me a hug. He seemed nearly as distraught as I was.

The niece of a top official in the incoming Trump administration came over to introduce herself and whisper in my ear that she had voted for me but was keeping it a secret.

Congressman Ryan Zinke, soon to be Trump's Interior Secretary, brought his wife over to say hello. This was somewhat surprising, considering that in 2014 he had called me the "Antichrist." Maybe he'd forgotten, because he didn't come equipped with any garlic or wooden stakes, or whatever one uses to ward off the Antichrist. But I hadn't forgotten. "You know, Congressman," I said, "I'm not actually the Antichrist." He was taken aback and mumbled something about not having meant it. One thing I've learned over the years is how easy it is for some people to say horrible things about me when I'm not around, but how hard it is for them to look me in the eye and say it to my face.

I talked with Tiffany Trump about her plans to attend law school. I kidded with Republican Senator John Cornyn about how I performed much better than expected in his state of Texas. In the President's remarks at lunch, when he was away from the glare of his angry supporters, Trump thanked Bill and me for coming. Then, finally, we could leave.

Little did I know that the first controversy of the new administration had already begun over the size of the crowd at the inauguration. As is its practice, the U.S. National Park Service quickly published photos to mark the occasion. This time the new President disputed the photographic evidence showing only a modest crowd and demanded that the Park Service go with the lie that the crowds were "huge." This flew in the face of what we could all see with our own eyes. I had the same view Trump did up there on the platform. Unlike him, I could compare it to what I had seen at inaugurals since 1993. I understood why he became so defensive. There really was a difference.

The episode was silly, but also an early warning: we were in a "brave new world."

If the inauguration on Friday was the worst of times, Saturday turned out to be the best of times.

I decided to stay at home in Chappaqua, New York, rather than attend the Women's March protesting the new President. It was another tough call. I wanted badly to join the crowds and chant my heart out. But I believed it was important for new voices to take the stage, especially on this day. There are so many exciting young women leaders ready to play bigger roles in our politics. The last thing I wanted was to be a distraction from the genuine outpouring of grassroots energy. If I showed up, nasty politics would unavoidably follow.

So I sat on my couch and watched in delight as the networks reported huge crowds in dozens of cities across the United States and around the world. Friends sent me excited reports of packed subway cars and streets overflowing with women and men of all ages. I scrolled through Twitter and sent out gratitude and good vibes.

The Women's March was the biggest single protest in American history. Hundreds of thousands of people gathered in cities like New York, Los Angeles, and Chicago. Thousands also turned out in places like Wyoming and Alaska. In Washington, the march dwarfed the crowd that had gathered to see Trump's inauguration the day before. And it was completely peaceful. Maybe that's what happens when you put women in charge.

It was a far cry from what happened when women first marched on Washington, the day before Woodrow Wilson's inauguration in

1913. Thousands of suffragettes trooped down Pennsylvania Avenue demanding the right to vote, including Alice Paul, Helen Keller, and Nellie Bly. Men lined the way, gawking, jeering, and eventually turning into an angry mob. The police did nothing, and scores of marchers were injured. The violence drew the nation's attention to the suffragette cause. The superintendent of police was fired. Congress held hearings. And seven years later, the Nineteenth Amendment to the Constitution was ratified, granting women the right to vote.

Nearly a century later, we'd made a lot of progress, but our new President was a painful reminder of how far we still had to go. That's why millions of women (and many supportive men) were pouring into the streets.

I will confess that the day was bittersweet. For years all over the world, I had seen women driving grassroots movements, assuming power for themselves and their communities, forcing warring armies to the peace table, rewriting the destinies of nations. Were we now seeing the stirrings of something similar in the streets of our own country? It was awe-inspiring, as I said on Twitter at the end of the day.

Yet I couldn't help but ask where those feelings of solidarity, outrage, and passion had been during the election.

Since November, more than two dozen women—of all ages, but mostly in their twenties—had approached me in restaurants, theaters, and stores to apologize for not voting or not doing more to help my campaign. I responded with forced smiles and tight nods. On one occasion, an older woman dragged her adult daughter by the arm to come talk to me and ordered her to apologize for not voting—which she did, head bowed in contrition. I wanted to stare right in her eyes and say, "You didn't vote? How could you not vote?! You abdicated your responsibility as a citizen at the worst possible time! And now you want *me* to make *you* feel better?" Of course, I didn't say any of that.

These people were looking for absolution that I just couldn't give. We all have to live with the consequences of our decisions.

There had been a lot of days since the election when I wasn't in a very forgiving mood toward anyone, including myself. I was—and still am—worried about our country. Something is wrong. How could sixty-two million people vote for someone they heard on tape bragging about repeated sexual assault? How could he attack women, immigrants, Muslims, Mexican Americans, prisoners of war, and people with disabilities—and, as a businessman, be accused of scamming countless small businesses, contractors, students, and seniors—and still be elected to the most important and powerful job in the world? How can we as a nation allow untold thousands of Americans to be disenfranchised by voter suppression laws? Why did the media decide to present the controversy over my emails as one of the most important political stories since the end of World War II? How did I let that happen? How did we?

For all my concerns, though, watching the Women's March, I couldn't help but be swept up in the joy of the moment and feel like the unmistakable vitality of American democracy was reasserting itself before our eyes. My Twitter feed filled up with photos of marchers holding funny, poignant, indignant signs:

"So Bad, Even Introverts Are Here."

"Ninety, Nasty, and Not Giving Up!"

"Science Is Not a Liberal Conspiracy."

One adorable little boy had this message around his neck: "I ♥ Naps but I Stay Woke."

I also saw young girls holding up quotes from my speeches over the years: "Women's Rights Are Human Rights." "I Am Powerful and Valuable." On a tough weekend, seeing those words lifted my spirits.

The people in the streets were sending a message to me and all of us: "Don't give up. This country is worth fighting for."

For the first time since the election, I felt hopeful.

Just keep going.
No feeling is final.

—Rainer Maria Rilke

Grit and Gratitude

On November 9, it was cold and raining in New York City. Crowds on the sidewalks turned to face my car as we drove past. Some people were crying. Some raised their hands or fists in solidarity. There were little kids held aloft by their parents. This time, seeing them made my heart sink instead of soar.

My team had scrambled to find a hall for my concession speech. The soaring Jacob K. Javits Convention Center atrium where we had hoped to hold a victory party wasn't an option. At 3:30 A.M., after scouting a few locations, our advance staff walked into the lobby of the New Yorker Hotel in Midtown Manhattan, not far from where my family and I were staying. They asked the concierge to call and wake up the manager at home. At 4:30 A.M., they started to prepare one of the hotel's ballrooms for an event everyone had hoped would never happen. I learned later that the New Yorker was where Muhammad Ali recuperated after losing a bitterly fought fifteen-round heavyweight championship fight to rival Joe Frazier in 1971. "I never wanted to lose, never thought I would, but the thing that matters is how you lose," Ali said the following day. "I'm not crying. My friends should not cry." If we wrote it in a movie, no one would believe it.

That morning, Bill and I both wore purple. It was a nod to bipartisanship (blue plus red equals purple). The night before, I had hoped to thank the country wearing white—the color of the suffragettes—while standing on a stage cut into the shape of the United States under a vast glass ceiling. (We had really gone the distance on the symbolism.) Instead, the white suit stayed in the garment bag. Out came the gray and purple one I had intended to wear on my first trip to Washington as President Elect.

After I finished speaking, I hugged as many people in the ballroom as possible. There were lots of old friends and devoted campaign staffers, many of their faces wet with tears. I was dry-eyed and felt calm and clear. My job was to get through this morning, smile, be strong for everyone, and show America that life went on and our republic would endure. A life spent in the public eye has given me lots of practice at that. I wear my composure like a suit of armor, for better or worse. In some ways, it felt like I had been training for this latest feat of self-control for decades.

Still, every time I hugged another sobbing friend—or one stoically blinking back tears, which was almost worse—I had to fight back a wave of sadness that threatened to swallow me whole. At every step, I felt that I had let everyone down. Because I had.

Bill, Chelsea, and her husband, Marc, were by my side, as they had been throughout. So were Tim Kaine and his wife, Anne Holton, who were extraordinarily kind and strong under these wrenching circumstances. I chose Tim for my running mate out of a superb field of candidates because he had executive experience, a stellar record as mayor, governor, and senator, a well-deserved reputation for decency and good judgment, and he was fluent in Spanish from his time as a missionary.

He would have been an effective partner and truth teller as my vice president. Also, I liked him a lot.

After delivering hugs and smiling so long and hard that my face ached, I asked my senior team to go back to our headquarters in Brooklyn and make sure everyone was okay. One final wave to the crowd, a final thank-you to Tim and Anne, a quick hug and kiss for Chelsea and Marc—who both knew everything I felt without me having to say a word—and Bill and I got into the backseat of a Secret Service van and were driven away.

I could finally let my smile drain away. We were mostly quiet. Every few minutes, Bill would repeat what he had been saying all morning: "I'm so proud of you." To that he now added, "That was a great speech. History will remember it."

I loved him for saying it, but I didn't have much to say in return. I felt completely and totally depleted. And I knew things would feel worse before they started feeling better.

It takes about an hour to drive from Manhattan to our home in Chappaqua. We live at the end of a quiet street full of trees, and whatever stress I'm feeling usually vanishes whenever I turn up the cul-de-sac. I absolutely love our old house and am always happy to be home. It's cozy, colorful, full of art, and every surface is covered with photos of the people I love best in the world. That day, the sight of our front gate was pure relief to me. All I wanted to do was get inside, change into comfy clothes, and maybe not answer the phone ever again.

I'll confess that I don't remember much about the rest of that day. I put on yoga pants and a fleece almost immediately. Our two sweet dogs followed me from room to room, and at one point, I took them outside and just breathed the cold, rainy air. Every once in a while, I'd turn on the news but then turn it off almost immediately. The question blaring in my head was, "How did this happen?" Fortunately, I had the good sense to realize that diving into a campaign postmortem right then would be about the worst thing I could do to myself.

Losing is hard for everyone, but losing a race you thought you would win is devastating. I remember when Bill lost his reelection as Governor of Arkansas in 1980. He was so distraught at the outcome that I had to go to the hotel where the election night party was held to speak to his supporters on his behalf. For a good while afterward, he was so depressed that he practically couldn't get off the floor. That's not me. I keep going. I also stew and ruminate. I run through the tape over and over, identifying every mistake—especially those made by me. When I feel wronged, I get mad, and then I think about how to fight back.

On that first day, I just felt tired and empty. The reckoning was still to come.

At some point, we ate dinner. We FaceTimed with our grandchildren, two-year-old Charlotte and her baby brother, Aidan, born in June 2016. I was reassured to see their mom. I knew Chelsea was hurting for me, which in turn hurt to think about, but those kids are an instant mood boost for all of us. We quietly drank them in, that day and every day after.

Perhaps most importantly, after sleeping hardly at all the night before, I climbed into our bed midday for a nice, long nap. I also went to bed early that night and slept in the next morning. I could finally do that.

I avoided the phone and email that first day. I suspected, correctly, that I was receiving a virtual avalanche of messages, and I couldn't quite handle it—couldn't handle everyone's kindness and sorrow, their bewilderment and their theories for where and why we had fallen short. Eventually, I'd dive in. But for now, Bill and I kept the rest of the world out. I was grateful for the one-billionth time that I had a husband who was good company not just in happy times but sad ones as well.

I doubt that many people reading this will ever lose a presidential election. (Although maybe some have: hi Al, hi John, hi Mitt, hope you're well.) But we all face loss at some point. We all face profound disappointment. Here's what helped me during one of the lowest points in my life. Maybe it'll help you too.

After that first day of laying low, I started reaching out to people. I answered a ton of emails; I returned phone calls. It hurt. There's a reason people isolate themselves when they're suffering. It can be painful to talk about it, painful to hear the concern in our friends' voices. Plus, in my case, we were all suffering. Everyone was so upset—for me, for themselves, for America. Often, I ended up doing the comforting rather than being comforted. Still, it was good to connect. I knew isolation wasn't healthy and that I'd need my friends now more than ever. I knew that putting off those conversations would only make them harder to have later on. And I badly wanted to thank everyone who had helped my campaign and make sure they were holding up okay under these circumstances.

What helped most was when someone said, "This has made me even more committed to the fight." "I'm stepping up my donations." "I've already started volunteering." "I'm posting more on Facebook; I won't stay quiet anymore." And best of all: "I'm thinking about running for office myself."

A young woman named Hannah, one of my field organizers in Wisconsin, sent me this note a few days after my loss:

> *The past two days have been very difficult. But when I think about how I felt on Tuesday morning, when I cried for an hour because I thought we were about to elect our first woman President, I know we cannot give up. Even though these last days have been a different kind of crying, your poise and grace have inspired me to stay strong. I do know that even though we have all been knocked down by this, we will rise. And through the next few years, we will be stronger together and keep fighting for what is right. From one nasty woman to another, thank you.*

Since I spent a lot of time worrying that my loss would permanently discourage the young people who worked for my campaign, learning that my defeat hadn't defeated them was a huge relief. It also roused me. If they could keep going, so could I. And maybe if I showed that I wasn't giving up, other people would take heart and keep fighting, too.

It was especially important to me that all the people who worked on my campaign knew how grateful and proud I was of them. They'd sacrificed a lot over the past two years, in some cases putting personal lives on hold, moving across the country, and working long hours for not that much money. They never stopped believing in me, each other, and the vision of the country we were working so hard to advance. Now many of them didn't know where their next paycheck would come from.

I did two things right away. First, I decided to write and sign letters to all 4,400 members of my campaign staff. Thankfully, Rob Russo, who has been managing my correspondence for years, agreed to oversee the whole project. I also made sure we were able to pay everyone through November 22 and provide health insurance through the end of the year.

On the Friday after the election, we threw a party at a Brooklyn hotel near our headquarters. Under the circumstances, it was surprisingly great. There was a fantastic band—some of the same musicians who played at Chelsea and Marc's wedding in 2010—and the dance floor was packed. It felt a little like an Irish wake: celebration amid the sadness. Let it never be said that the Hillary for America staff didn't stick together when it counted. To help matters, there was an open bar.

After everyone worked up a sweat, I took the microphone to say thank you. Everyone screamed "Thank *you*!" right back at me. Really, I couldn't have asked for a more good-natured, hardworking team. I told them how important it was that they not let this defeat discourage them from public service or from throwing themselves into future campaigns with as much heart and commitment as they had given to mine. I reminded them about the losing campaigns I'd worked on in my twenties, including Gene McCarthy in the 1968 Democratic primaries and George McGovern in 1972—and the beatings Democrats took until everything changed in '92. We had stuck it out. I was counting on them to keep going too.

I also said that I had brought a small gift for them. A women's advocacy group called UltraViolet had sent 1,200 red roses to my house earlier that day, and I had them packed up and brought them to the party. They lay in heaps near the exits. "Please take a few as you head home tonight," I told everyone. "Think about the hope they represent and the love and gratitude that so many people around the country feel for all of you."

It was an echo of an earlier moment. My team had spent Wednesday and Thursday packing up our campaign offices in Brooklyn, fueled by pizzas sent by well-wishers from all over the country. Our neighbors in the building had taped signs on the elevator doors that read, "Thank You for What You Did." As staffers carried their last boxes out of headquarters, they were greeted by a crowd of children and their parents. The kids had covered the sidewalk in chalk messages: "Girl Power!" "Stronger Together!" "Love Trumps Hate!" "Please Don't Give Up!" When bedraggled members of our team filed out for the last time, the children handed them flowers. One last act of kindness from a borough that had been good to us again and again.

Over the next few weeks, I dropped any pretense of good cheer. I was so upset and worried for the country. I knew the proper and respectable thing to do was to keep quiet and take it all with grace, but inside I was fuming. The commentator Peter Daou, who worked on my 2008 campaign, captured my feelings when he tweeted, "If Trump had won by 3 million votes, lost electoral college by 80K, and Russia had hacked RNC, Republicans would have *shut down America*." Nonetheless, I didn't go public with my feelings. I let them out in private. When I heard that Donald Trump settled a fraud suit against his Trump University for $25 million, I yelled at the television. When I read the news that he filled his team with Wall Street bankers after relentlessly accusing me of being their stooge, I nearly threw the remote control at the wall. And when I heard he installed Steve Bannon, a leading promoter of the "Alt-Right," which many have described as including white nationalists, as his chief strategist in the White House, it felt like a new low in a long line of lows.

The White House is sacred ground. Franklin D. Roosevelt hung a plaque over the fireplace in the State Dining Room inscribed with a line from a letter that John Adams sent to his wife on his second night living in the newly built White House: "I pray heaven to bestow the best of blessings on this house and all that shall hereafter inhabit it. May none but honest and wise men ever rule under this roof." I hope Adams would have been okay with a wise woman. I can't imagine what he would say if he could see who was walking those halls.

Letters started pouring in from people across the country, many so poignant that after reading a few, I had to put them away and go for a walk. A third-year law student from Massachusetts named Rauvin wrote about how she imagined that she and her female friends and classmates would look back on this time:

> On Nov. 8, 2016, we felt a sense of devastation, powerlessness, and disappointment that we had never felt before. So we cried. And then we squared our shoulders, picked each other up, and got to work. We moved onward and onward, keeping in mind that we would never, ever allow ourselves to feel again as we did that day. And though our anger and disappointment fueled us, it did not consume us, make us cynical or cruel. It made us strong. And eventually, eventually one of us will crash through that highest, hardest glass ceiling. And it will be because of our hard work, determination, and resilience. But it will also be because of you. Just you wait.

In a postscript, she added: "If I may recommend some salves: time with friends and family, of course, but also the first season of *Friday*

Night Lights, the new season of *Gilmore Girls*, the *Hamilton* cast album, Martha Stewart's mac and cheese, a good book, a glass of red wine." Good advice!

A woman named Holly from Maryland wrote with additional sensible guidance:

> *I hope you will sleep as late as you like and wear your sneakers all day. Get a massage and stand in the sun. Sleep in your own bed and take long walks with your husband. Giggle with your granddaughter and play patty-cake with your grandson. . . . Breathe. Think only about whether you want strawberries or blueberries with your breakfast, about which Dr. Seuss book to read to your grandchildren. Listen to the wind or Chopin.*

My friend Debbie from Texas sent me a poem to cheer me up. Her father told her that a friend of his wrote it after they worked for Adlai Stevenson, a two-time presidential candidate, on one of his landslide defeats to Dwight Eisenhower in the 1950s. I have to admit, it made me chuckle:

> *The election is now over,*
> *The result is now known.*
> *The will of the people*
> *Has clearly been shown.*
> *Let's all get together;*
> *Let bitterness pass.*
> *I'll hug your Elephant;*
> *And you kiss my Ass.*

Pam from Colorado sent me a box of a thousand handmade origami cranes held together by strings. She explained that, in Japan, a thousand folded cranes are a powerful symbol of hope and that hanging them in your home is considered extremely lucky. I hung them on my porch. I'd take all the luck and hope I could get.

I tried hard to let go of the burden of putting on a happy face or reassuring everyone that I was totally fine. I knew I would be fine eventually, but for those early weeks and months, I wasn't fine at all. And while I didn't spill my guts to everyone who crossed my path, I did answer honestly when asked how I was doing. "It'll be okay," I'd say, "but right now it's really hard." If I was feeling defiant, I'd respond, "Bloody, but unbowed," a phrase from "Invictus," Nelson Mandela's favorite poem. If they wanted to commiserate over the latest reports from Washington, sometimes I'd confess about how mad it all made me. Other times I'd say, "I'm just not quite up for talking about this." Everyone understood.

I also let people do things for me. This doesn't come easily to me. But Chelsea pointed out, "Mom, people want to do something helpful— they want you to let them." So when a friend said she was sending a box full of her favorite books . . . and another said he was coming up for the weekend even if it was just to take a walk together . . . and another said she was taking me to see a play whether I wanted to go or not . . . I didn't protest or argue. For the first time in years, I didn't have to consult a complicated schedule. I could just say "Yes!" without a second thought.

I thought a lot about my mother. Part of me was glad she wasn't around to experience another bitter disappointment. My narrowly losing the Democratic nomination to Barack Obama in 2008 had been hard for her, although she tried never to let me see it. Mostly, I just missed her. I wanted to sit down with her, hold her hand, and share all my troubles.

Friends advised me on the power of Xanax and raved about their amazing therapists. Doctors told me they'd never prescribed so many antidepressants in their lives. But that wasn't for me. Never has been.

Instead, I did yoga with my instructor, Marianne Letizia, especially "breath work." If you've never done alternate nostril breathing, it's worth a try. Sit cross-legged with your left hand on your thigh and your right hand on your nose. Breathing deeply from your diaphragm, place your right thumb on your right nostril and your ring and little fingers on your left. Shut your eyes, and close off your right nostril, breathing slowly and deeply through your left. Now close both sides and hold your breath. Exhale through the right nostril. Then reverse it: inhale through the right, close it, and exhale through the left. The way it's been explained to me, this practice allows oxygen to activate both the right side of the brain, which is the source of your creativity and imagination, and the left side, which controls reason and logic. Breathe in and out, completing the cycle a few times. You will feel calmer and more focused. It may sound silly, but it works for me.

It wasn't all yoga and breathing: I also drank my share of chardonnay.

I spent time in nature. The day after my concession, Bill and I were in an arboretum near our home. It was the perfect time of year for traipsing—crisp but not freezing, with the smell of fall in the air. We were lost in thought when we met a young woman out hiking with her three-month-old daughter strapped to her back and her dog underfoot. She seemed a little embarrassed to stop and greet us, but she said she couldn't help herself—she needed to give me a hug. It turned out, I needed it too. Later that day, she posted a photo of us on Facebook, which quickly went viral. The "HRC in the Wild" meme was born.

Throughout November and December, Bill and I laced up our shoes and hit the trails again and again, slowly working through why I lost, what I could have done better, what in the world was going to happen to America now. We also spent a fair amount of time talking about what we'd have for dinner that night or what movie to watch next.

I took on projects. In August 2016, we had bought the house next door: a classic ranch we had always liked the looks of, with a backyard that connected to ours. The idea was to have plenty of room for Chelsea, Marc, their kids, our brothers and their families, and our friends. Plus, I was getting a little ahead of myself and thinking about how to accommodate the large team that travels with a President. Through September and October, we had been quietly remodeling, but with the campaign in high gear, there hadn't been much time to think about any of that. Now I had nothing but time on my hands. I spent hours going over plans with the contractor and my interior decorator and friend Rosemarie Howe: paint swatches, furniture, a swing set for the backyard. Over the fireplace, I hung a vintage suffragette banner that Marc had given me that declared "Votes for Women." In the family room, we put up a colorful painting of the balloon drop at the Democratic National Convention. Bill and I had both gotten a kick out of those balloons, Bill especially. A memory of happier times.

By Thanksgiving, the work on the house was done. That morning, I walked around making sure everything was perfect before our friends and family descended for dinner. At one point, I stood on the front porch and saw some people gathered down at the corner of our street around a bunch of colorful homemade "Thank You" signs stuck in the ground. Kids from the neighborhood had made them for me for Thanksgiving, covered in hearts and rainbows and American flags. It was one of many kind gestures—not just from friends and loved ones but also from complete strangers—that made that first month more bearable.

Every Thanksgiving, it's become our tradition since leaving the White House to host a bunch of Chelsea's friends who don't travel home for the holiday or who hail from other countries and want to experience an American Thanksgiving in all its glory. There are always twenty or thirty of us sitting around long folding tables decorated with leaves, pinecones, and votive candles—nothing too high blocking people's views, so conversation moves easily back and forth. We start our meal with grace by Bill and then go around the table so everyone can say what he or she is thankful for during the past year. When it was my turn, I said I was grateful for the honor of running for President and for my family and friends who supported me.

Back in our old house, I organized every closet in a blitz of focused energy that sent our dogs scurrying from every room I entered. I called friends and insisted they take a pair of shoes they'd once said they liked or a blouse I suspected would fit just right. I have often been that pushy friend, so most of them knew to expect it. I also organized jumbled heaps of photos into albums, threw out stacks of old magazines and disintegrating newspaper clippings, and sorted through probably a million business cards that people had handed me over the years. With every gleaming drawer and every object placed in its correct, appointed spot, I felt satisfied that I had made my world just a little more orderly.

Some of my friends pushed me to go on vacation, and we did get away with Chelsea, Marc, and the grandkids for a few days to the Mohonk Mountain House, a favorite spot of mine in upstate New York. But after twenty months of nonstop travel for the campaign—on top of four years of globe-trotting as Secretary of State—I just wanted to sit in my quiet house and be still.

I tried to lose myself in books. Our house is packed with them, and we keep adding more. Like my mother, I love mystery novels and can plow through one in a single sitting. Some of my recent favorites are by Louise Penny, Jacqueline Winspear, Donna Leon, and Charles Todd. I finished reading Elena Ferrante's four Neapolitan novels and relished the story they tell about friendship among women. Our shelves are weighed down with volumes about history and politics, especially biographies of Presidents, but in those first few months, they held no interest for me whatsoever. I went back to things that have given me joy or solace in the past, such as Maya Angelou's poetry:

You may write me down in history
With your bitter, twisted lies,
You may trod me in the very dirt
But still, like dust, I'll rise. . . .

You may shoot me with your words,
You may cut me with your eyes,
You may kill me with your hatefulness,
But still, like air, I'll rise.

On raw December days, with my heart still aching, those words helped. Saying them out loud made me feel strong. I thought of Maya and her rich, powerful voice. She wouldn't have been bowed by this, not one inch.

I went to Broadway shows. There's nothing like a play to make you forget your troubles for a few hours. In my experience, even a mediocre play can transport you. And show tunes are the best soundtrack for tough times. You think you're sad? Let's hear what Fantine from *Les Misérables* has to say about that!

By far my favorite New York City performance was way off Broadway: Charlotte's dance recital. It's enchanting to watch a bunch of squirming, giggling two-year-olds trying to dance in unison. Some are intensely focused (that would be my granddaughter), some are trying to talk to their parents in the audience, and one girl just sat down and took off her shoes in the middle of everything. It was lovely mayhem. As I watched Charlotte and her friends laugh and fall down and get up again, I felt a twinge of something I couldn't quite place. Then I realized what it was: relief. I had been ready to completely devote the next four or eight years to serving my country. But that would have come with a cost. I would have missed a lot of dance recitals and bedtime stories and trips to the playground. Now

I had those back. That's more than a silver lining. That's the mother lode.

Back at home, I caught up on TV shows Bill had been saving. We raced through old episodes of *The Good Wife*, *Madam Secretary*, *Blue Bloods*, and *NCIS: Los Angeles*, which Bill insists is the best of the franchise. I also finally saw the last season of *Downton Abbey*. That show always reminds me of the night I spent in Buckingham Palace in 2011 during President Obama's state visit, in a room just down the hall from the balcony where the Queen waves to the crowds. It was like stepping into a fairy tale.

On the Saturday after the election, I turned on *Saturday Night Live* and watched Kate McKinnon open the show with her impression of me one more time. She sat at a grand piano and played "Hallelujah," the hauntingly beautiful song by Leonard Cohen, who had died a few days before. As she sang, it seemed like she was fighting back tears. Listening, so was I.

> *I did my best, it wasn't much,*
> *I couldn't feel, so I tried to touch*
> *I've told the truth, I didn't come to fool you*
> *And even though it all went wrong*
> *I'll stand before the lord of song*
> *With nothing on my tongue but hallelujah.*

At the end, Kate-as-Hillary turned to the camera and said, "I'm not giving up and neither should you."

I prayed a lot. I can almost see the cynics rolling their eyes. But pray I did, as fervently as I can remember ever doing. Novelist Anne Lamott once wrote that the three essential prayers she knows are "Help,"

"Thanks," "Wow." You can guess which one I reached for last fall. I prayed for help to put the sadness and disappointment of my defeat behind me; to stay hopeful and openhearted rather than becoming cynical and bitter; and to find a new purpose and start a new chapter, so that the rest of my life wouldn't be spent like Miss Havisham from Charles Dickens's *Great Expectations*, rattling around my house obsessing over what might have been.

I prayed that my worst fears about Donald Trump wouldn't be realized, and that people's lives and America's future would be made better, not worse, during his presidency. I'm still praying on that one, and I can use all the backup you can muster.

I also prayed for wisdom. I had help from Bill Shillady, the United Methodist minister who co-officiated at Chelsea and Marc's marriage and led the memorial services for my mother. During the campaign, he sent me devotionals every day. On November 9, he sent me a commentary that originally appeared in a blog by Pastor Matt Deuel. I read it many times before the week was out. This passage in particular really moved me:

> *It is Friday, but Sunday is coming.*
>
>   *This is not the devotional I had hoped to write. This is not the devotional you wish to receive this day.*
>
>   *While Good Friday may be the starkest representation of a Friday that we have, life is filled with a lot of Fridays.*
>
>   *For the disciples and Christ's followers in the first century, Good Friday represented the day that everything fell apart. All was lost. And even though Jesus told his followers that three days later the temple would be restored . . . they betrayed, denied, mourned, fled, and hid. They did just about everything but feel good about Friday and their circumstances.*
>
>   *You are experiencing a Friday. But Sunday is coming!*

Death will be shattered. Hope will be restored. But first, we must live through the darkness and seeming hopelessness of Friday.

I called Reverend Bill, and we talked for a long time.

I reread one of my favorite books, *The Return of the Prodigal Son* by the Dutch priest Henri Nouwen. It's something I've gone back to repeatedly during difficult times in my life. You may know the parable about the younger of two sons who strays and sins but finally comes home. He's welcomed lovingly by his father but resented by his older brother, who had stayed behind and served his father honorably while the younger brother did whatever he wanted. Maybe it's because I'm the oldest in our family and something of a Girl Scout, but I've always identified with the older brother in the parable. How grating it must have been to see his wayward sibling welcomed back as if nothing had happened. It must have felt as if all his years of hard work and dutiful care meant nothing at all. But the father says to the older brother, "Have I not taken good care of you? Have you not been close to me? Have you not been at my side learning and working?" Those things are their own reward.

It's a story about unconditional love—the love of a father, and also *the* Father, who is always ready to love us, no matter how often we stumble and fall. It makes me think of my dad, a flinty, tight-lipped man who nevertheless always made sure I knew what I meant to him. "I won't always like what you do," he'd tell me, "but I will always love you." As a kid, I would come up with elaborate hypotheses to test him. "What if I robbed a store or murdered somebody? Would you still love me then?" He'd say, "Absolutely! I'd be disappointed and sad, but I will always love you." Once or twice last November, I thought to myself, "Well, Dad, what if I lose an election I should have won and let an unqualified bully become President of the United States?

Would you still love me then?" Unconditional love is the greatest gift he gave me, and I've tried to give it to Chelsea and now to Charlotte and Aidan.

Nouwen sees another lesson in the parable of the Prodigal Son: a lesson about gratitude. "I can choose to be grateful even when my emotions and feelings are still steeped in hurt and resentment," he writes. "I can choose to speak about goodness and beauty even when my inner eye still looks for someone to accuse or something to call ugly. I can choose to listen to the voices that forgive and to look at the faces that smile even while I still hear words of revenge and see grimaces of hatred."

It's up to us to make the choice to be grateful even when things aren't going well. Nouwen calls that the "discipline of gratitude." To me, it means not just being grateful for the good things, because that's easy, but also to be grateful for the hard things too. To be grateful even for our flaws, because in the end, they make us stronger by giving us a chance to reach beyond our grasp.

My task was to be grateful for the humbling experience of losing the presidential election. Humility can be such a painful virtue. In the Bible, Saint Paul reminds us that we all see through a glass darkly because of our humbling limitations. That's why faith—the assurance of things hoped for and the conviction of things unseen—requires a leap. It's because of our limitations and imperfections that we must reach out beyond ourselves, to God and to one another.

As the days went by, November turned into December, and that horrible, no good, very bad time came to a close, I began to rediscover my gratitude. I felt the good effects of all that walking and sleep; I was getting calmer and stronger. I found myself thinking of new projects I'd like to take on. I started accepting invitations to events that spoke to my heart: a Planned Parenthood dinner, the Women in the World

summit and the Vital Voices gala celebrating women leaders and activists from around the world, and gatherings with students at Harvard,
Wellesley, and Georgetown. Those rooms were full of purposeful energy. I soaked it all up and found myself thinking more about the future
than the past.

Do what you feel in your heart to be right—for you'll be criticized anyway. You'll be "damned if you do and damned if you don't."

—Eleanor Roosevelt

Competition

For us, there is only the trying. The rest is not our business.

—T. S. Eliot

Get Caught Trying

I ran for President because I thought I'd be good at the job. I thought that of all the people who might run, I had the most relevant experience, meaningful accomplishments, and ambitious but achievable proposals, as well as the temperament to get things done in Washington.

America was doing better than any other major country, but there was still too much inequality and too little economic growth. Our diversity was an advantage, spurring creativity and vitality, but rapid social and economic change alienated people who thought too much was happening too fast and felt left out. Our position in the world was strong, but we had to cope with a combustible mix of terrorism, globalization, and the advances in technology that fueled them both.

I believed that my experiences in the White House, Senate, and State Department equipped me to take on these challenges. I was as prepared as anyone could be. I had ideas that would make our country stronger and life better for millions of Americans.

In short, I thought I'd be a damn good President.

Still, I never stopped getting asked, "Why do you want to be President? Why? But, really—why?" The implication was that there must be something else going on, some dark ambition and craving for power. Nobody psychoanalyzed Marco Rubio, Ted Cruz, or Bernie Sanders about why they ran. It was just accepted as normal. But for me, it was regarded as inevitable—people assumed I'd run no matter what—yet somehow abnormal, demanding a profound explanation.

After the election, I thought a lot about this. Maybe it's because I'm a woman, and we're not used to women running for President. Maybe it's because my style of leadership didn't fit the times. Maybe it's because I never explained myself as bluntly as this.

So let me start from the beginning and tell you how and why I made the decision to run.

"You might lose," Bill told me. "I know," I said. "I might lose."

The problems started with history. It was exceedingly difficult for either party to hold on to the White House for more than eight years in a row. In the modern era, it had happened only once, when George H. W. Bush succeeded Ronald Reagan in 1989. No nonincumbent Democrat had run successfully to succeed another two-termer since Vice President Martin Van Buren won in 1836, succeeding Andrew Jackson.

There was still a lot of pent-up anger and resentment left over from the financial crash of 2008–2009, and while that had happened on the Republicans' watch, Democrats had presided over a recovery that had been too slow.

There also was "Clinton fatigue" to consider. Pundits were already complaining that the election would be an exhausting contest between two familiar dynasties: the Clintons and the Bushes.

Then there was the matter of my gender. No woman had ever won the nomination of a major party in the history of our country, let alone the presidency. It's easy to lose sight of how momentous that is, but when you stop to consider what it means and the possible reasons behind it, it's profoundly sobering.

It was a chilly day in autumn 2014, and Bill and I had been having the same conversation for months now. Should I run for President for a second time? Lots of talented people were ready to jump on board with my campaign if I ran. The press and most of the political class assumed I was already running. Some of them were so convinced by the caricature of me as a power-hungry woman that they couldn't imagine me doing anything else. I, on the other hand, could imagine lots of different paths for myself.

I already knew how it felt to lose. Until you experience it, it's hard to comprehend the ache in your gut when you see things going wrong and can't figure out how to fix them; the sharp blow when the results finally come in; the disappointment written on the faces of your friends and supporters. Political campaigns are massive enterprises with thousands of people working together toward a common goal, but in the end, it's intensely personal, even lonely. It's just your name on the ballot. You're embraced or repudiated all by yourself.

The race against Barack Obama in 2008 was close and hard-fought. By the end, he led in the all-important delegate count, but our popular vote totals were less than one-tenth of a percent apart. That made it all the more painful to accept defeat and muster up the good cheer to campaign vigorously for him. The saving grace was the respect I had for Barack and my belief that he would be a good President who would do everything he could to advance the values we both shared. That made it a lot easier.

Did I want to put myself through a grueling race all over again?

My life after leaving politics had turned out to be pretty great. I had joined Bill and Chelsea as a new board member of the Clinton Foundation, which Bill had turned into a major global philanthropy after leaving office. This allowed me to pursue my own passions and have an impact without all the bureaucracy and petty squabbles of Washington. I admired what Bill had built, and I loved that Chelsea had decided to bring her knowledge of public health and her private sector experience to the foundation to improve its management, transparency, and performance after a period of rapid growth.

At the 2002 International AIDS Conference in Barcelona, Bill had a conversation with Nelson Mandela about the urgent need to lower the price of HIV/AIDS drugs in Africa and across the world. Bill figured he was well positioned to help, so he began negotiating agreements with drugmakers and governments to lower medicine prices dramatically and to raise the money to pay for it. It worked. More than 11.5 million people in more than seventy countries now have access to cheaper HIV/AIDS treatment. Right now, out of everyone being kept alive by these drugs in developing countries around the world, more than half the adults and 75 percent of the children are benefiting from the Clinton Foundation's work.

After recovering from heart-bypass surgery in 2004, Bill joined with the American Heart Association to start the Alliance for a Healthier Generation, which has helped more than twenty million students in more than thirty-five thousand American schools enjoy healthier food and more physical activity. The Alliance made agreements with major beverage companies to reduce calories in drinks available in schools by 90 percent, and also partnered with Michelle Obama's Let's Move! initiative.

The foundation is also fighting the opioid epidemic in the United States; helping more than 150,000 small farmers in Africa increase their incomes; and bringing clean energy to island nations in the Caribbean and Pacific.

In 2005, Bill started the Clinton Global Initiative, a new model of philanthropy for the twenty-first century that brought together leaders from business, government, and the nonprofit sector to make concrete commitments for action on everything from distributing clean water, to improving energy efficiency, to providing hearing aids to deaf children. The annual conferences highlighted the most exciting commitments and their results. No one could just show up and talk; you had to actually do something. After twelve years, CGI members, and their affiliates in CGI America and CGI International, had made more than 3,600 commitments, which have improved the lives of more than 435 million people in more than 180 countries.

Among CGI's greatest hits were sending 500 tons of medical supplies and equipment to West Africa for those fighting the Ebola epidemic, and helping raise $500 million to support small businesses, farms, schools, and health care in Haiti. In the United States, at no expense to taxpayers, CGI helped launch an amazing partnership led by the Carnegie Corporation of New York to meet President Obama's goal of 100,000 new STEM (science, technology, engineering, and mathematics) teachers. And it supported the creation of America's largest private infrastructure fund—$16.5 billion invested by public employee pension funds, led by the American Federation of Teachers (AFT) and North America's Building Trades Unions (NABTU)—which has created 100,000 jobs and provided skills training to a quarter-million workers every year.

When I joined the foundation in 2013, I teamed up with Melinda Gates and the Gates Foundation to launch an initiative called No Ceilings: The Full Participation Project to advance rights and opportunities for women and girls around the world. I also created a program called Too Small to Fail to encourage reading, talking, and singing to infants and toddlers to help their brains develop and build vocabulary. And Chelsea and I started a network of leading wildlife conservation organizations to protect the endangered African elephants from poachers. None of these programs had to poll well or fit on a bumper sticker. They just had to make a positive, measurable difference in the world. After years in the political trenches, that was both refreshing and rewarding.

I knew from experience that if I ran for President again, every-thing Bill and I had ever touched would be subject to scrutiny and attack—including the foundation. That was a concern, but I never imagined that this widely respected global charity would be as savagely smeared and attacked as it was. For years, the foundation and CGI had been supported by Republicans and Democrats alike. Independent philanthropy watchdogs CharityWatch, GuideStar, and Charity Navi-gator gave the Clinton Foundation top marks for reducing overhead and having a measurable positive impact. CharityWatch gave it an A, Charity Navigator gave it four stars, and GuideStar rated it platinum. But none of that stopped brutal partisan attacks from raining down during the campaign.

I have written about the foundation at some length here because a recent analysis published in the *Columbia Journalism Review* showed that during the campaign there was twice as much written about the Clinton Foundation as there was on any of the Trump scandals, and nearly all of it was negative. That gets to me. As Daniel Borochoff, the founder of CharityWatch, put it, "If Hillary Clinton wasn't running for President, the Clinton Foundation would be seen as one of the great humanitarian charities of our generation." I believe that's exactly what it is and what it will continue to be, and I was proud to be a part of it.

Beyond my work with the foundation, I also spent time in 2013 and 2014 writing a book called *Hard Choices* about my experiences as Secretary of State. The book was long—more than six hundred pages about foreign policy!—but I still had more stories left on the cutting room floor and a lot more things I wanted to say. If I didn't run for President, there could be more books to write. Maybe I could teach and spend time with students.

What's more, like many former government officials, I found that organizations and companies wanted me to come talk to them about my experiences and share my thoughts on the world—and they'd pay me a pretty penny to do it. I continued giving many speeches without pay, but I liked that there was a way for me to earn a very good living without working for any one company or sitting on any boards. It was also a chance to meet interesting people.

I spoke to audiences from a wide range of fields: travel agents and auto dealers, doctors and tech entrepreneurs, grocers and summer camp counselors. I also spoke to bankers. Usually I told stories from my time as Secretary of State and answered questions about global hot spots. I must have recounted the behind-the-scenes story of the raid that brought Osama bin Laden to justice at least a hundred times. Sometimes I talked about the importance of creating more opportunities for women, both around the world and in corporate America. I rarely got partisan. What I had to say was interesting to my audiences, but it wasn't especially newsworthy. Many of the organizations wanted the speeches to be private, and I respected that: they were paying for a unique experience. That allowed me to be candid about my impressions of world leaders who might have been offended if they heard. (I'm talking about you, Vladimir.)

Later, my opponents spun wild tales about what terrible things I must have said behind closed doors and how as President I would be forever in the pocket of the shadowy bankers who had paid my speaking fees. I should have seen that coming. Given my record of independence in the Senate—especially my early warnings about the mortgage crisis, my votes against the Bush tax cuts, and my positions in favor of financial regulation, including closing the tax loophole for hedge funds known as carried interest—this didn't seem to be a credible attack. I didn't think many Americans would believe that I'd sell a lifetime of principle and advocacy for any price. When you know why you're doing something and you know there's nothing more to it and certainly nothing sinister, it's easy to assume that others will see it the same way. That was a mistake. Just because many former government officials have been paid large fees to give speeches, I shouldn't have assumed it would be okay for me to do it. Especially after the financial crisis of 2008–2009, I should have realized it would be bad "optics" and stayed away from anything having to do with Wall Street. I didn't. That's on me.

This is one of the mistakes I made that you'll read about in this book. I've tried to give an honest accounting of when I got it wrong, where I fell short, and what I wish I could go back and do differently. This isn't easy or fun. My mistakes burn me up inside. But as one of my favorite poets, Mary Oliver, says, while our mistakes make us want to cry, the world doesn't need more of that.

The truth is, everyone's flawed. That's the nature of human beings. But our mistakes alone shouldn't define us. We should be judged by the totality of our work and life. Many problems don't have either/or answers, and a good decision today may not look as good ten or twenty years later through the lens of new conditions. When you're in politics, this gets more complicated. We all want—and the political press demands—a "story line," which tends to cast people as either saints or sinners. You're either revered or reviled. And there's no juicier political story than the saint who gets unmasked as a sinner. A two-dimensional cartoon is easier to digest than a fully formed person.

For a candidate, a leader, or anyone, really, the question is not "Are you flawed?" It's "What do you do about your flaws?" Do you learn from your mistakes so you can do and be better in the future? Or do you reject the hard work of self-improvement and instead tear others down so you can assert they're as bad or worse than you are?

I've always tried to do the former. And, by and large, so has our country, with our long march toward a more perfect union.

But Donald Trump does the latter. Instead of admitting mistakes, he lashes out, demeans, and insults others—often projecting by accusing others of doing what he himself has done or is about to do. So if he knows that the Donald J. Trump Foundation is little more than a personal piggy bank, he'll turn around and accuse, with no evidence, the well-respected Clinton Foundation of being corrupt. There's a method to this madness. For Trump, if everyone's down in the mud with him, then he's no dirtier than anyone else. He doesn't have to do better if everyone else does worse. I think that's why he seems to relish humiliating people around him. And it's why he must have been delighted when Marco Rubio tried to match him in slinging crude personal insults during the primaries. Of course, it hurt Rubio much more than Trump. As Bill likes to say, never wrestle a pig in the mud. They have cloven hooves, which give them superior traction, and they love getting dirty. Sadly, Trump's strategy works. When people start believing that all politicians are liars and crooks, the truly corrupt escape scrutiny, and cynicism grows.

But I'm getting ahead of myself. Back to 2014, and deciding to run for President.

We've talked about my work at the foundation, my book, and my speeches, but by far the best part about my life after government—and probably the most compelling reason *not* to run—was being a grandmother. I loved it even more than I'd expected. Bill and I found ourselves looking for any excuse to drive down to Manhattan so we could drop by Chelsea and Marc's and see little Charlotte, who was born that September. We became the world's most enthusiastic babysitters, book readers, and playmates. We were doubly blessed when Aidan arrived in June 2016.

Running for President again would mean putting all this—my wonderful new life—on hold and climbing back on the high wire of national politics. I wasn't sure I was ready to do that.

My family was incredibly supportive. If I wanted to run, they would be there for me 100 percent. Chelsea had campaigned relentlessly in 2008, becoming a superb surrogate and sounding board for me. Bill knows more than almost anyone alive about what it takes to be President. He was convinced I was the best person for the job and strenuously denied that this was just a husband's love talking.

Still, the obstacles were daunting. Yes, I had left the State Department with some of the highest approval ratings of anyone in public life—one poll from the *Wall Street Journal* and NBC News in January 2013 put me at 69 percent. I was also the most admired woman in the world, according to the annual Gallup poll. Ah, the good old days.

But I knew that my high approval rating was partly because Republicans had been willing to work with me when I was Secretary and praised my service. They had trained their fire on President Obama and largely left me alone. Also, the press corps covering me in those years genuinely cared about the work of diplomacy and the issues I dealt with, which meant the news coverage of my work was substantive and, for the most part, accurate. I knew it would be different if I ran for President again. And as Bill said—and history supported—the country's perennial desire for change would make it hard for any Democrat to win, especially one like me who was closely tied to the current administration.

In 2014, President Obama's approval rating was stuck in the low 40s. Despite the administration's best efforts, the economic recovery was still anemic, with wages and real incomes stagnating for most Americans. The administration had botched the rollout of the new health care marketplaces, a centerpiece of the President's signature legislative accomplishment, the Affordable Care Act. A new terrorist group, ISIS, was seizing territory in Iraq and Syria and beheading civilians live on the internet. There was even a terrifying Ebola epidemic in Africa that many Americans worried would jump to the United States. Thankfully, the Obama administration reacted swiftly to shore up our public health defenses and support Ebola response efforts in West Africa. Despite the facts, conservative partisans warned breathlessly— and with zero evidence—that ISIS terrorists would sneak across our

southern border and bring Ebola with them. It was a right-wing conspiracy theory trifecta.

In the run-up to the 2014 midterms, Bill and I both campaigned
hard across the country for endangered Democratic incumbents and
competitive challengers. Late at night, we'd compare notes about the
anger, resentment, and cynicism we were seeing, and the vicious Republican attacks fueling it.

For years, GOP leaders had stoked the public's fears and disappointments. They were willing to sabotage the government in order to block
President Obama's agenda. For them, dysfunction wasn't a bug, it was a
feature. They knew that the worse Washington looked, the more voters
would reject the idea that government could ever be an effective force
for progress. They could stop most good things from happening and
then be rewarded because nothing good was happening. When something good did happen, such as expanding health care, they would focus
on tearing it down, rather than making it better. With many of their
voters getting their news from partisan sources, they had found a way to
be consistently rewarded for creating the gridlock voters say they hate.

The success of this strategy was becoming evident. In 2014, in
Georgia and North Carolina, I campaigned for two smart, talented,
independent-minded candidates who should have had a good chance
to win: Michelle Nunn and Senator Kay Hagan. Both races were
tight up until the end. But days before the election, a savvy Georgia
political observer confided to me that he'd seen private polling that
showed Nunn and other Democrats cratering. Republicans were using
fears about ISIS and Ebola to scare people and raise questions about
whether a Democrat, especially a woman, could really be tough enough
on national security.

In several states, Republicans ran an ad mixing images of Ebola
responders in hazmat suits with photos of President Obama playing
golf. It's ironic to remember that now, with Donald Trump spending
about 20 percent of his new presidency at his own luxury golf clubs.

I sometimes wonder: If you add together his time spent on golf, Twitter, and cable news, what's left?

Bill told me about a particularly troubling conversation he had with an old friend who lived up in the Ozarks of northern Arkansas. He had become an endangered species in Arkansas—a still-loyal, progressive Democrat. Bill called and asked our friend if he thought two-term Senator Mark Pryor could be reelected. Mark was a moderate Democrat with a golden name. (His father, David, was an Arkansas legend, having served as Congressman, Governor, and Senator.) Mark had voted for Obamacare because he believed everyone deserved the high-quality health care he received when he suffered from cancer as a young man. Our friend said he didn't know, and he and Bill agreed the best way to find out was to visit a certain country store deep in the Ozarks where a couple hundred people regularly came out of the woods to buy food and talk politics.

When our friend got back, he called Bill and told him what the store owner had said: "You know, I always supported Clinton, and I like Mark Pryor a lot. He's a good man and fair to everyone. But we're going to give Congress to the Republicans." The store owner was no fool. He knew the Republicans wouldn't do anything *for* him and his neighbors. But he thought the Democrats hadn't done anything, either. "And at least the Republicans won't do anything *to* us," he said. "The Democrats want to take away my gun and make me go to a gay wedding."

Sure enough, Mark lost big on Election Day to Tom Cotton, one of the most right-wing members of Congress. It wasn't that voters were turning away from the policies Mark and other Democrats had championed—in fact, in the same election, they passed an increase in the state's minimum wage. But the politics of cultural identity and resentment were overwhelming evidence, reason, and personal experience. It seemed like "Brexit" had come to America even before the vote in the United Kingdom, and it didn't bode well for 2016. Our party might have won the popular vote in five of the past six presidential elections, but the political landscape for the 2016 race was shaping up to be extremely challenging.

As if all this wasn't enough to worry about, there was also the simple, inescapable fact that I was turning sixty-eight years old. If I ran and won, I would be the oldest President since Reagan. I suspected there'd be waves of rumor-mongering about my health—and everything else in my life. It would be invasive, crass, and insidious. But contrary to persistent rumors made up and spread by the right-wing media, my health was excellent. I had recovered fully from the concussion I suffered in late 2012. And the whole world could see I had no trouble keeping up a punishing travel schedule. I admired the likes of Diana Nyad, who at the age of sixty-four became the first person to swim from Cuba to Florida without a shark cage. When she finally emerged back on dry land, she offered three pieces of advice: Never ever give up. You're never too old to chase your dreams. And even if something looks like a solitary sport, it's a team effort. Words to live by!

Still, is this how I wanted to spend my time? Did I really want to put myself back in front of the firing squad of national politics for years on end, first in the campaign and then, hopefully, in the White House? Some of my dearest friends—including my longtime advisors and former chiefs of staff in the White House and the State Department, Maggie Williams and Cheryl Mills—told me I would be crazy to do it. Plenty of other people in my position had passed up the chance to run: everyone from General Colin Powell, to Mike Bloomberg, to New York Governor Mario Cuomo, who came so close to running, he had an airplane waiting on the tarmac to take him to New Hampshire when he finally decided "no."

So why did I do it?

I did it because when you clear away all the petty and not-so-petty reasons not to run—all the headaches, all the obstacles—what was left was something too important to pass up. It was a chance to do the most good I would ever be able to do. In just one day at the White House, you can get more done for more people than in months anywhere else. We had to build an economy that worked for everyone and an inclusive society that respected everyone. We had to take on serious national security threats. These were issues already on my mind all the time, and they would all require a strong, qualified President. I knew I would make the most of every minute. Once I started thinking about it that way, I couldn't stop.

As it happened, the person who gave me the chance to serve as Secretary of State would once again play a decisive role.

A month after I left the State Department in 2013, Barack and Michelle invited Bill and me to join them for a private dinner in the White House residence. The four of us talked about our kids and the experience of raising them in the fishbowl of the White House. We discussed life after the Oval Office. Barack and Michelle mused about maybe one day moving to New York, just as we had done. That prospect still felt very far away. We all had high hopes for Barack's second term. There was a lot of unfinished business, both at home and around the world. We ended up staying for hours, talking late into the night. If (back in the heated days of 2008) any of us could have gotten a glimpse of that evening, we wouldn't have believed it.

Over the next year or so, the President and I kept in regular touch. He invited me back for lunch that summer, and the two of us sat out on the terrace outside the Oval Office eating jambalaya. I think he was just a tiny bit jealous of my newfound freedom, which was a good reminder of how all-consuming the job is. We had lunch again the following spring. Some of the time the President and I talked about work, especially the foreign policy challenges he was facing in the second term. But gradually, as 2013 turned into 2014, our conversations turned more frequently to politics.

President Obama knew the challenges facing Democrats. He never took his reelection for granted, and while it was a resounding win in 2012 (the legitimately resounding kind), he knew that his legacy depended to a large degree on a Democratic victory in 2016. He made it clear that he believed that I was our party's best chance to hold the White House and keep our progress going, and he wanted me to move quickly to prepare to run. I knew President Obama thought the world of his Vice President, Joe Biden, and was close to some other potential candidates, so his vote of confidence meant a great deal to me. We had our differences in both style and substance, but overwhelmingly we shared the same values and policy goals. We both saw ourselves as pragmatic progressives trying to move the country forward in the face of implacable opposition from a Republican Party that had been taken over by the radical-conservative Tea Party fringe and was in thrall to its billionaire backers. I shared the President's sense of urgency about how much was at stake in 2016, but I still wasn't entirely sold that running was the right decision for me.

As I had found when he insisted that I become Secretary of State and literally wouldn't take no for an answer, President Obama is a persuasive and persistent advocate. In the summer of 2013, David Plouffe, Obama's former campaign manager who engineered my defeat in 2008, offered to provide any help and advice he could as I planned my next steps after leaving the State Department. I invited him over to my house in Washington, and quickly saw why the President had leaned on him so much. He really knew his stuff. We met again in September 2014, when he visited my house once more to give me a presentation about what it would take to build a winning presidential campaign. He spoke in detail about strategy, data, personnel, and timing. I listened carefully, determined that if I did jump into the race, I would avoid the mistakes that had dogged me the last time. Plouffe emphasized that time was of the essence, as hard as that was to believe more than two years before the election. In fact, he said I was late already and urged me to get started. He was right.

For me, political campaigns have always been something to get through in order to be able to govern, which is the real prize. I'm not the most natural politician. I'm a lot better than I'm usually given credit for, but it's true that I've always been more comfortable talking about others rather than myself. That made me an effective political spouse, surrogate, and officeholder, but I had to adjust when I became a candidate myself. At the beginning, I had to actively try to use the word *I* more. Luckily, I love meeting people, listening, learning, building relationships, working on policy, and trying to help solve problems. I would have loved to meet all 320 million Americans one at a time. But that's not how campaigns work.

In the end, I came back to the part that's most important to me. We Methodists are taught to "do all the good you can." I knew that if I ran and won, I could do a world of good and help an awful lot of people.

Does that make me ambitious? I guess it does. But not in the sinister way that people often mean it. I did not want to be President because I want power for power's sake. I wanted power to do what I could to help solve problems and prepare the country for the future. It's audacious for anyone to believe he or she should be President, but I did.

I started calling policy experts, reading thick binders of memos, and making lists of problems that needed more thought. I got excited thinking about all the ways we could make the economy stronger and fairer, improve health care and expand coverage, make college more affordable and job training programs more effective, and tackle big challenges, such as climate change and terrorism. It was honestly a lot of fun.

I talked with John Podesta, a longtime friend who had been Bill's Chief of Staff in the White House and was also a top advisor to President Obama. If I was going to do this again, I would need John's help.

He promised that if I ran, he'd leave the White House and become chairman of my campaign. He thought we could put together a fantastic team very quickly. An energetic grassroots group called Ready for Hillary was already drumming up support. All of that was very reassuring.

I thought back to what made me run for Senate the first time. It was the late 1990s and Democrats in New York were urging me to run, but I kept turning them down. No First Lady had ever done anything like that before. And I hadn't run for office since I'd been student government president at Wellesley College.

One day I visited a school in New York with the tennis star Billie Jean King for an event promoting an HBO special about women in sports. Hanging above our heads was a big banner proclaiming the title of the film, *Dare to Compete*. Before my speech, the seventeen-year-old captain of the high school basketball team introduced me. Her name was Sofia Totti. As we shook hands, she bent down and whispered in my ear, "Dare to compete, Mrs. Clinton. Dare to compete." Something just clicked. For years, I had been telling young women to step up, participate, go for what you believe in. How could I not be willing to do the same? Fifteen years later, I was asking myself the same question.

There wasn't one dramatic moment where I declared, "I'm doing it!" Bill and I closed out 2014 with a trip to the beautiful home of our friends Oscar and Annette de la Renta in the Dominican Republic. We swam, ate good food, played cards, and thought about the future. By the time we got back, I was ready to run.

The most compelling argument is the hardest to say out loud: I was convinced that both Bill and Barack were right when they said I would be a better President than anyone else out there.

I also thought I'd win. I knew that Republicans had moved much further from the vital center of American politics than Democrats had, as nonpartisan political scientists have documented. But I still believed that the United States was a pretty sensible country. Previous generations faced much worse crises than anything we've seen, from the Civil War to the Great Depression, from World War II to the Cold War, and they responded by electing wise and talented leaders. Only rarely have Americans gotten carried away by extremes or enthralled by ideology, and never for long. Both major political parties, despite the madness of their respective nominating processes, nearly always managed to weed out the most extreme candidates. Before 2016, we'd never elected a President who flagrantly refused to abide by the basic standards of democracy and decency. If I was the best-qualified candidate, had good ideas about the future, held my own on the trail and in the debates, and demonstrated a capacity to get things done with both Republicans and Democrats, it was reasonable to believe I could get elected and be able to govern effectively.

That's why I ran.

There are things I regret about the 2016 campaign, but the decision to run isn't one of them.

I started this chapter with some lines from T. S. Eliot's poem "East Coker" that I've always loved:

> *There is only the fight to recover what has been lost*
> *And found and lost again and again: and now, under conditions*
> *That seem unpropitious. But perhaps neither gain nor loss.*
> *For us, there is only the trying. The rest is not our business.*

When I first read that, as a teenager in Park Ridge, Illinois, it struck a chord somewhere deep inside, maybe in that place where dim ancestral memories of indomitable Welsh and English coal miners hid alongside half-understood stories from my mother's childhood of privation and abandonment. "There is only the trying."

I went back to that poem a few years later, in 1969, when my classmates at Wellesley asked me to speak at our graduation. Many of us were feeling dismayed and disillusioned by the Vietnam War and the racial injustice in America, the assassinations of Dr. Martin Luther King Jr. and Robert F. Kennedy, and our seeming inability to change our country's course. My paraphrasing gave Eliot's elegant English verse a Midwestern makeover: "There's only the trying," I told my classmates, "again and again and again; to win again what we've lost before."

In the nearly fifty years since, it's become a mantra for me and our family that, win or lose, it's important to "get caught trying." Whether you're trying to win an election or pass a piece of legislation that will help millions of people, build a friendship or save a marriage, you're never guaranteed success. But you are bound to try. Again and again and again.

I want to be thoroughly used up when I die, for the harder I work, the more I live. Life is no "brief candle" to me. It is a sort of splendid torch which I have got hold of for the moment; and I want to make it burn as brightly as possible before handing it on to future generations.

—George Bernard Shaw

Getting Started

You could say my campaign for President began with a snappy internet video filmed in April 2015 outside my home in Chappaqua. Or you could point to my formal announcement speech that June on Roosevelt Island in New York. But I think it started with something a lot more ordinary: a Chipotle burrito bowl.

If you're wondering what I'm talking about, you probably don't spend much time in the carnival fun house of cable and internet news. It was April 13, 2015, in Maumee, Ohio. Chipotle was a pit stop on my road trip from New York to Iowa, home of the first-in-the-nation caucus. It was a purposefully low-key trip. No press, no crowds. Just me, a few staff, and Secret Service agents. We bundled into an over-sized black van I call "Scooby" because it reminds me of the *Scooby-Doo* Mystery Machine (our van has less shaggy psychedelic charm, but we love it just the same), and set out on our thousand-mile journey. I had a stack of memos to read and a long list of calls to make. I had also googled every NPR station from Westchester to Des Moines—all set for a long drive.

In Maumee, we pulled into the parking lot of a strip mall off the highway for lunch. I ordered a chicken burrito bowl with a side of guacamole. Nick Merrill, my traveling press secretary, made fun of me for eating it out of the little cup with a spoon, bypassing the chips. Nobody in the restaurant thought it was remarkable that I was there. In fact, nobody recognized me. Bliss!

But when members of the press found out, they reacted like a UFO had landed in Ohio and an extraterrestrial had wandered into a Chipotle. CNN ran grainy footage from the restaurant's security camera, which made it look a little like we were robbing a bank. The *New York Times* did an analysis that concluded my meal was healthier than the average Chipotle order, with fewer calories, saturated fat, and sodium. (Good "get" for the *Times*; they really ate CNN's lunch on that one.) The whole thing felt silly. To paraphrase an old saying, sometimes a burrito bowl is just a burrito bowl.

Soon I was back in Iowa, the state that handed me a humbling third-place finish in 2008. Like the road trip, I wanted this first visit to be no-frills. I would do more listening than talking, just as I had at the start of my first Senate campaign in New York. My new state director, Matt Paul, who knew Iowa inside and out after years of working for Governor Tom Vilsack and Senator Tom Harkin, agreed. Iowans wanted to get to know their candidates, not just listen to them give speeches. That's exactly what I wanted, too.

When Donald Trump started his campaign, he seemed confident that he already had all the answers. He had no ideological core apart from his towering self-regard, which blotted out all hope of learning or growing. As a result, he had no need to listen to anyone but himself.

I approached things differently. After four years traveling the world as Secretary of State, I wanted to reconnect with the problems that were keeping American families up at night and hear directly about their hopes for the future. I had a core set of ideas and principles but wanted to hear from voters to inform new plans to match what was really going on in their lives and in the country.

One of the first people I met in New Hampshire, another early contest state, provided a case in point. Pam was a grandmother in her fifties with gray hair and the air of someone who carries a lot of responsibility on her shoulders. She was an employee of a 111-year-old family-run furniture business I visited in Keene. We were talking about how to help small businesses grow, but Pam had a different challenge on her mind. Her daughter had gotten hooked on pain medication after giving birth to a baby boy, which led to a long struggle with drug addiction. Eventually Child and Family Services started calling Pam, warning that her grandson could end up in foster care. So she and her husband, John, took the child in, and Pam found herself back in the role of primary caretaker she thought she had finished years before.

Pam wasn't the complaining type. This was a labor of love, and she was glad to pick up the slack, especially now that her daughter was in treatment. But she was worried. A lot of families in town were facing similar struggles. In New Hampshire, more people were dying from drug overdoses than from car crashes. The number of people seeking treatment for heroin addiction had soared 90 percent over the past decade. For prescription drugs, the number was up 500 percent.

I knew a little about this. At the time, Bill and I were friends with three families who had lost young adult children to opioids. (Sadly, that number has now grown to five.) One was a charismatic young man who worked at the State Department while he was in law school. A friend of his offered some pills, he took them, went to sleep that night, and never woke up. Others took drugs after drinking, and their hearts stopped. After these tragedies, the Clinton Foundation partnered with Adapt Pharma to make available free doses of the opioid antidote naloxone (Narcan), which can save lives by helping prevent overdoses, to every high school and college in the United States.

On that first visit to New Hampshire, in a coffee shop in downtown Keene, a retired doctor leaned in and asked, "What can you do about the opioid and heroin epidemic?" It was chilling to hear that word, *epidemic*, but it was the right one. In 2015, more than thirty-three thousand people died from overdosing on opioids. If you add to that the number from 2014, it's more Americans than were killed in the entire Vietnam War. Resources for treatment couldn't come close to keeping up. Parents liquidated their savings to pay for their kids' treatment. Some called the police about their own children because they had tried everything else.

Yet despite all this, substance abuse wasn't getting much national attention, either in Washington or in the national media. I didn't think about it as a campaign issue until I started hearing stories like Pam's in Iowa and New Hampshire.

I called my policy team together and told them we had to get working right away on a strategy. My advisors fanned out. We held town hall meetings and heard more stories. In one session in New Hampshire, a substance abuse counselor asked anyone who had been impacted by the epidemic to raise his or her hand. Nearly every hand in the room went up. A woman in treatment told me, "We're not bad people trying to get good. We're sick people trying to get well."

To help her and millions of others do that, we came up with a plan to expand access to treatment, improve training for doctors and pharmacists prescribing prescription drugs, reform the criminal justice system so more nonviolent drug offenders end up in rehab instead of prison, and make sure every first responder in America carries naloxone, which is close to a miracle drug.

This became a model for how my campaign operated in those early months. People told me story after story about the challenges their families faced: student debt, the high cost of prescription drugs and insurance premiums, and wages too low to support a middle-class life. I'd use those conversations to guide the policies already being hammered out back in our Brooklyn headquarters. I wanted my policy shop to be bold, innovative, industrious, and, most importantly, responsive to people's real-life needs. Jake Sullivan, my director of policy planning at the State Department; Ann O'Leary, a longtime advisor of mine who shared my passion for children and health care policy; and Maya Harris, a veteran civil rights advocate, built and led a great team.

You can compare this to how Trump operated. When the opioid epidemic finally started getting news attention, he jumped on it as a way of making people believe that America was falling apart. But once he became President, he turned his back on everyone who needed help by seeking to cut money for treatment.

The press often seemed bored by the roundtables where these conversations happened. Critics dismissed them as staged or carefully controlled. But I wasn't bored. I wanted to talk with people, not at them. I also learned a lot. To me, this was a big part of what running for President was supposed to be.

Over the long months that I had weighed running a second time, I thought a lot about what kind of campaign I'd want. I certainly wanted one different from the one I ran during my 2008 primary loss to Barack Obama. I studied what he did right and I did wrong. There was more to learn after 2012, when the President put together another strong campaign that helped him win reelection over Mitt Romney by a healthy margin despite a lackluster economy. His operations were two of the best ever. I paid attention.

My low-profile first trip to Iowa reflected some of the lessons that I kept in mind as I started to put my own organization in place. In 2008, I had been criticized for arriving in Iowa like a queen, holding big rallies and acting like victory was inevitable. I never thought that

was a fair description of me or our campaign; we believed I could prevail in a crowded and talented field, but we certainly didn't take Iowa
for granted. In fact, we recognized that it wasn't an ideal first contest
for me and spent a fair amount of 2007 trying to figure out how to
make the best of it. Still, the criticism stuck, and I took it seriously. This
time I was determined to run like an underdog and avoid any whiff of
entitlement.

I also wanted to build on the best parts of my 2008 effort, especially the fighting spirit of our campaigns in Ohio and Pennsylvania,
where I succeeded in forming a bond with working-class voters who
felt invisible in George W. Bush's America. I had dedicated my victory
in the Ohio primary to everyone "who's ever been counted out but
refused to be knocked out, for everyone who has stumbled but stood
right back up, and for everyone who works hard and never gives up."
I wanted to bring that spirit to the 2016 campaign, along with the best
lessons of Obama's victories.

We sought to set the right tone with my announcement video. It
showed a series of Americans talking excitedly about new challenges
they were taking on: two brothers starting a small business, a mom
getting her daughter ready for the first day of kindergarten, a college
student applying for her first job, a couple getting married. Then I appeared briefly to say that I was running for President to help Americans get ahead and stay ahead, and that I was going to work hard to
earn every vote. This campaign wasn't going to be about me and my
ambitions. It would be about you and yours.

There were other lessons to put into action. In 2008, the Obama
campaign had been way ahead of us in using advanced data analytics to
model the electorate, target voters, and test messages. It focused relentlessly on grassroots organizing and winning the delegates who would
actually decide the nomination. It also built a "no drama" campaign
organization that largely avoided damaging infighting and leaks.

John Podesta and I talked with President Obama and David Plouffe about how to construct a team that could replicate these successes. Plouffe was a big fan of Robby Mook, whom I ultimately chose as campaign manager. Robby had impressed David by helping me win against the odds—and against him—in Nevada, Ohio, and Indiana in 2008. In all three states, he put together aggressive field programs and competed hard for every vote. Then he went on to manage my friend Terry McAuliffe's successful longshot campaign for Governor of Virginia. Robby was on a roll—young but, like Plouffe, highly disciplined and levelheaded, with a passion for data and a talent for organizing.

Huma Abedin, my trusted and valued advisor for years, would be campaign vice chair. President Obama praised his pollsters Joel Benenson and John Anzalone and focus group expert David Binder, so I hired all three, as well as a veteran of the Obama data analytics team, Elan Kriegel. Navin Nayak came on board to coordinate all these different elements of opinion research. Here's how to keep it all straight: pollsters call up a random sample of people and ask their opinions about candidates and issues; focus groups gather a handful of people together in a room for an in-depth discussion that can last several hours; and data analytics teams make a lot of survey calls, crunch huge amounts of additional demographic, consumer, and polling data, and feed it all into complex models that try to predict how people will vote. These are all staples of modern campaigns.

To help guide messaging and create ads, I hired Jim Margolis, a respected Obama veteran, and Mandy Grunwald, who had been with me and Bill since our first national campaign in 1992. They worked with Oren Shur, my director of paid media, and several talented and creative ad agencies. I thought Jim's and Mandy's partnership would represent the best of both worlds. That's what I was going for with all my hiring decisions: mix the best available talent from the Obama campaigns with top-notch pros I already knew. The latter category included Dennis Cheng, who had raised hundreds of millions of dollars for my 2006 Senate reelection campaign and 2008 presidential campaign, and later helped build up the Clinton Foundation endowment; Minyon Moore, one of the most experienced political operatives in Democratic politics and a veteran of my husband's White House; and Jose Villarreal, a business leader who had worked with me at State and came on board to serve as my campaign treasurer.

As I built my team, I was focused on two tricky areas: how to strike the right balance with President Obama and his White House, and—drumroll for emphasis—how to improve my relationship with the press.

The challenge of striking a balance with President Obama wasn't personal at all. After four years in his Cabinet, we liked and trusted each other. There aren't many people in the world who know what it's like to run for President or live in the White House, but we had that in common, and it gave us a special bond. When he finally passed health care reform, something I had fought for long and hard, I was overjoyed and gave him a big hug before a meeting in the White House Situation Room. After his rough first presidential debate with Mitt Romney in 2012, I tried to cheer him up with a photoshopped image of Big Bird strapped to Mitt's family car. (Romney had promised to slash funding for PBS, and also famously took road trips with his dog on the roof of his car.)

"Please take a look at the image below, smile, and then keep that smile near at hand," I told the President.

"We'll get this done," he replied. "Just hold the world together five more weeks for me."

Now that we had switched places, and I was the candidate and he was the cheerleader, the challenge for me was navigating the tension between continuity and change. On the one hand, I believed deeply in what he had accomplished as President and desperately wanted to make sure a Republican wouldn't be able to undo it all. We might have areas of disagreement, such as on Syria, trade, and how to deal with an aggressive Russia, but by and large, I would defend his record, try to build on his accomplishments, and listen to his advice. He would call from time to time and share his thoughts on the race. "Don't try to be hip, you're a grandma," he'd tease. "Just be yourself and keep doing what you're doing." I was proud to have Barack's support, and nearly every day told audiences around the country that he didn't get the credit he deserved for putting our country back together after the worst financial crisis since the Great Depression.

At the same time, there were big problems that still needed fixing in America, and part of my job as candidate was to make it clear that I saw them and was ready to take them on. Inevitably, that meant pointing out areas where the Obama administration's efforts had fallen short, even if the main culprit was Republican obstruction.

It was a fine line to walk, as it would have been for Vice President Biden or anyone who had served in the Obama administration. If I failed to strike the right balance, I ran the risk of either seeming disloyal or being cast as the candidate of the status quo, both of which would be damaging.

In one of the first meetings of our new team, in a conference room on the twenty-ninth floor of a Midtown Manhattan office building, Joel Benenson presented the results of his early opinion research. He said Americans had two main "pain points" that would likely shape their views of the election: economic pressure and political gridlock. The economy was definitely in better shape than it had been after the financial crisis, but incomes hadn't begun to rise for most families, so people still felt like their progress was fragile and could be ripped away at any moment. And they had come to view dysfunction in Washington as a big part of the problem. They were right. I had seen that dysfunction firsthand and knew how hard it would be to break through it—although I think it's fair to say I underestimated how my opponents would wrongly accuse me of being responsible for a broken system. I had a record of success working with Republicans over the years.

I had plans for aggressive campaign finance reform, which would re-
move some of the profit motive behind the gridlock. And I believed we
had a strong shot at making progress. The problem remained: how to
find a compelling way to talk about the pain Americans felt and their
dissatisfaction with how things were going in the country, without reinforcing Republican criticisms of the Obama administration, which
would be self-defeating and just plain wrong.

Joel said I was starting from a strong place. Fifty-five percent of
voters in the battleground states had a favorable view of me, compared
with just 41 percent with an unfavorable view. Voters liked that I had
worked for Obama after losing to him in 2008. They thought it showed
loyalty and patriotism. They also thought I had done a good job as Secretary of State, and most believed I was ready to be President. But even
though I'd been in the public eye for decades, they knew little about
what I had actually done, much less why I had done it. This presented
both a challenge and an opportunity. Despite having near-universal
name recognition, I would have to reintroduce myself—not as an ex-
tension of Bill Clinton or Barack Obama but as an independent leader
with my own story, values, and vision.

There were also some warning signs to worry about. While my
approval ratings were high, just 44 percent of voters said they trusted
me to be their voice in Washington. That told us that some people respected me but weren't sure I was in it for them. I was determined to
change that perception. The reason I had gotten into public service was
to make life better for children and families, and now it was my job to
make sure people understood that.

There was something else we needed to do: avoid repeating past
problems with the political press corps. Over the years, my relationship
with the political press had become a vicious cycle. The more they went
after me, the more guarded I became, which only made them criticize
me more. I knew that if I wanted 2016 to be different, I was going
to have to try to change the dynamic and establish a more open and

constructive give-and-take. There was some precedent. As a Senator, I got along surprisingly well with the rough-and-tumble journalists of New York. And I grew downright fond of the State Department press corps, which consisted largely of journalists who had written about foreign policy for years. We talked easily, went out together on the road, toured Angkor Wat in Cambodia, dined in a Bedouin tent in Saudi Arabia, danced in South Africa, and had adventures all over the globe. For the most part, they covered me fairly, and when I felt they didn't, they were open to my criticism. Now I would try to establish a similar rapport with the political reporters covering the campaign. I knew they were under constant pressure to write stories that would drive clicks and retweets, and that negative stories sell. So I was skeptical. But it was worth a shot.

To help me do it, I hired Jennifer Palmieri, a savvy professional with strong press relationships. Jennifer had worked for John Podesta in the Clinton White House and at the Democratic think tank the Center for American Progress. Most recently, she had been President Obama's Communications Director in the White House. The President loved Jennifer, and so did I. I asked Kristina Schake, a former top aide to Michelle Obama, and later Christina Reynolds, who had worked on the John Edwards and Obama campaigns, to be her deputies. They were joined by national press secretary Brian Fallon, a graduate of the acclaimed Chuck Schumer school of communications and a former spokesman for the Department of Justice, and Karen Finney, the former MSNBC host who had first worked for me in the White House. When Jennifer, Kristina, and I sat down together for the first time, I let two decades' worth of frustrations with the press pour out. Buckle up, I said, this is going to be a rough ride. But I was ready to try whatever they recommended to get off on a better foot this time.

With my senior team coming together, we got to work building an organization that could go the distance. Presidential campaigns are like start-ups on steroids. You have to raise an enormous amount of money very quickly, hire a huge staff, deploy them across the country, and build a sophisticated data operation largely from scratch. As a candidate, you have to manage all that while maintaining a grueling campaign schedule that keeps you hundreds or thousands of miles from headquarters nearly every day.

In 2008, I had a good, hardworking team. But I allowed internal rivalries to fester and didn't establish a clear chain of command until it was too late. Still, we came so close to winning. I vowed that this time we would do things differently.

I was determined to have the best data, the most field organizers, the biggest fund-raising network, and the deepest political relationships. I was thrilled that Beth Jones, a talented manager working at the White House, agreed to be campaign chief operating officer. To lead our organizing and outreach efforts, I turned to three political pros: Marlon Marshall, Brynne Craig, and Amanda Renteria. I also hired experienced organizers to run the key early states. In addition to Matt Paul in Iowa, there was Mike Vlacich, who helped reelect my friend Senator Jeanne Shaheen in New Hampshire and led my efforts to beat Trump there in November; Emmy Ruiz, who helped lead us to victory in the Nevada caucus before moving to Colorado for the general and helping us win there, too; and Clay Middleton, a longtime aide to Congressman Jim Clyburn, who helped us win a landslide victory in the South Carolina primary.

To infuse the campaign with a spirit of innovation, we got advice from Eric Schmidt, the former CEO of Google, and other top tech leaders, and hired engineers from Silicon Valley. Stephanie Hannon, an experienced engineer, became the first woman to serve as chief technology officer on a major presidential campaign. I hired one of President Obama's former aides, Teddy Goff, to handle all things digital, along with my longtime advisor Katie Dowd and Jenna Lowenstein from EMILY's List. They had a tough job on their hands with a less-than-tech-savvy candidate, but I promised to be a good sport about every Facebook chat, tweetstorm, and Snapchat interview they recommended.

To make sure we built the most diverse team ever assembled by a presidential campaign, I brought in Bernard Coleman as the first-ever chief diversity officer, made sure women were half the staff, and hired hundreds of people of color, including for senior leadership roles.

We put our headquarters in Brooklyn and the office soon teemed with idealistic, sleep-deprived twentysomethings. It felt like a cross between a tech start-up and a college dorm. I've been a part of a lot of campaigns going all the way back to 1968, and this was the most collegial and collaborative I've ever seen.

So how did it go?

Well, we didn't win.

But I can say with zero equivocation that my team made me enormously proud. They built a fantastic organization in the early states and helped me win the Iowa caucus, despite tough demographics, as well as the Nevada caucus and the South Carolina primary. In the general election, they recruited fifty thousand more volunteers than the 2012 Obama campaign did and contacted voters five million more times. My team absorbed one gut punch after another and never gave up, never turned on one another, and never stopped believing in our cause. That doesn't mean there weren't disagreements and debates over a wide range of questions. Of course there were—it was a campaign, for heaven's sake. But even on the night of our landslide defeat in the New Hampshire primary or during the worst days of the email controversy, nobody buckled.

And have I mentioned that we went on to win the national popular vote by nearly three million?

It was a terrific group of people. And I'm not just talking about the senior leadership. All the young men and women crowded around desks at headquarters in Brooklyn, working impossible hours . . . all the field organizers who were the heart and soul of the campaign . . . all the advance staff who lived out of suitcases for two years, organizing and staging events across the country . . . volunteers of every age and background—more Americans volunteered more time for the 2016 campaign than for any campaign in U.S. history. My team was full of dedicated people who left families and friends to move someplace new, knock on doors, make phone calls, recruit volunteers, and persuade voters. They worked intensely while juggling relationships, welcoming newborn babies, and handling other family obligations. Two of my young communications aides, Jesse Ferguson and Tyrone Gayle, kept working through difficult cancer treatments, never losing their devotion to the campaign or their senses of humor.

Some of my favorite moments out on the trail were when a volunteer would come up to me as I shook hands on a rope line after a rally. They'd whisper in my ear about what a great job our local organizer was doing or how welcoming our staff was to people who wanted to help and how their enthusiasm was infectious. That always made my day. The fact that so many of these young people have decided to stay in politics and keep up the fight despite our loss makes me very happy and proud.

Having said all that, *of course* the campaign didn't go as planned. I ended up falling into many of the pitfalls I had worried about and tried to avoid from the start. Some of that was my own doing, but a lot of it was due to forces beyond my control.

Despite my intention to run like a scrappy challenger, I became the inevitable front-runner before I shook my first hand or gave my first speech, just by virtue of sky-high expectations.

The controversy over my emails quickly cast a shadow over our efforts and threw us into a defensive crouch from which we never fully recovered. You can read plenty more about that later in this book, but suffice it to say that one boneheaded mistake turned into a campaign-defining and -destroying scandal, thanks to a toxic mix of partisan opportunism, interagency turf battles, a rash FBI director, my own inability to explain the whole mess in a way people could understand, and media coverage that by its very volume told the voters this was by far the most important issue of the campaign. Most people couldn't explain what it was really all about or how the allegations that I was a threat to national security squared with the support I had from respected military and civilian national security experts, including Republicans and Independents, but they understandably came away with the impression I had done a big, bad thing.

One result was that, right away, I was back in my usual adversarial relationship with the press, clamming up and trying to avoid "Gotcha!" interviews at a time when I needed to be reintroducing myself to the country. I watched my approval numbers drop and my disapproval and distrust numbers rise, as my message about all the things I wanted to do as President was blocked or overwhelmed.

There were other disappointments as well. In 2008, critics had slammed me for not being accessible to voters and avoiding traditional grip-and-grin campaigning. This time they went the other way and ridiculed my intimate listening sessions. "Where are the rallies? Why can't she draw a crowd?" they'd ask. That "enthusiasm" question never really went away, even when we drew large crowds.

Other than Iowa and Nevada, where we built extensive organizations, I struggled in caucuses just as I had the last time. By their structure and rules, caucuses favor the most committed activists who are willing to spend long hours waiting to be counted. That gave the advantage to the insurgent left-wing candidacy of Bernie Sanders. My advantage came in primaries, which have secret ballots and all-day voting, like a typical election, and much higher turnout. The difference was most clear in Washington State, which held both a caucus and a primary. Bernie won the caucus in March, and I won the primary in May, in which three times as many people voted. Unfortunately, most of the delegates were awarded based on the caucus.

Ultimately, none of this mattered much after I built up a large delegate lead in March. What did matter, and had a lasting impact, was that Bernie's presence in the race meant that I had less space and credibility to run the kind of feisty progressive campaign that had helped me win Ohio and Pennsylvania in 2008.

One piece of advice that President Obama gave me throughout the campaign was that we needed more message discipline, and he was right. In 1992, Bill relied on James Carville and Paul Begala to help him shape his winning message, and they made sure that everyone in the campaign—including the candidate—stuck to it day after day after day. In 2016, my campaign was blessed with many brilliant strategists, and they helped me develop a message, Stronger Together, that reflected my values and vision and a clear contrast with Trump. It may not have been catchy enough to break through the wall of negative coverage about emails—maybe nothing could—but it was the case I wanted to make. And when voters got a chance to hear from me directly, at the convention and in the debates, polls showed they liked what they heard.

It's true, though, that we struggled to stay on message. My advisors had to deal with a candidate—me—who often wanted something new to say, as opposed to just repeating the same stump speech over and over. In addition, more than in any race I can remember, we were constantly buffeted by events: from the email controversy, to WikiLeaks, to mass shootings and terrorist attacks. There was no such thing as a "normal day," and the press didn't cover "normal" campaign speeches. What they were interested in was a steady diet of conflict and scandal. As a result, when it came to driving a consistent message, we were fighting an uphill battle.

Add all this together, and I think you get a picture of a campaign that had both great strengths and real weaknesses—just like every campaign in history. There are important lessons to learn from what we got right and what we got wrong. But I totally reject the notion that it was an unusually flawed or dysfunctional campaign. That's just wrong. My team battled serious headwinds to win the popular vote, and if not for the dramatic intervention of the FBI director in the final days, I believe that in spite of everything, we would have won the White House. I've been criticized harshly by political pundits for saying that, and even some of my supporters have said they agree with me but I shouldn't say it. If you feel this way, I hope you'll keep going and give my response a fair reading.

Since the election, I've asked myself many times if I learned the wrong lessons from 2008. Was I fighting the previous war when I should have been focused on how much our politics had changed?

Much has been made about my campaign's supposed overreliance on Obama-style big data, at the expense of more traditional political gut instinct and trusting folks on the ground. This is another criticism I reject. It's true that some of our models were off—just like everyone else's, including the media, the Trump campaign, everyone—probably because some Trump supporters refused to talk to pollsters or weren't honest about their preferences or because people changed their minds. It's also true that, like any large organization, we could have done a better job listening to the anecdotal feedback we were getting from folks on the ground. It's not like we didn't try. My team was constantly in touch with local leaders, and I had trusted friends reporting back to me from all over the country, including a big group of Arkansans—the Arkansas Travelers—who fanned out in nearly every state. I believe they helped us win the razor-close Missouri primary, and they were a constant source of information and perspective for me. But every precinct leader and party chair in the country wants more attention and resources. Sometimes they're right, sometimes they're wrong. You can't make those decisions blind. You have to be guided by the best data available. This isn't an either/or choice. You need both data *and* good old-fashioned political instinct. I'm convinced that the answer for Democrats going forward is not to abandon data but to obtain *better* data, use it more effectively, question every assumption, and keep adapting. And we need to listen carefully to what people are telling you and try to assess that too.

Still, in terms of fighting the previous war, I think it's fair to say that I didn't realize how quickly the ground was shifting under all our feet. This was the first election where the Supreme Court's disastrous 2010 *Citizens United* decision allowing unlimited political donations was in full force but the Voting Rights Act of 1965 wasn't because of another terrible decision by the court in 2013. I was running a traditional presidential campaign with carefully thought-out policies and painstakingly built coalitions, while Trump was running a reality TV show that expertly and relentlessly stoked Americans' anger and resentment. I was giving speeches laying out how to solve the country's problems. He was ranting on Twitter. Democrats were playing by the rules and trying too hard not to offend the political press. Republicans were chucking the rule book out the window and working the refs as hard as they could. I may have won millions more votes, but he's the one sitting in the Oval Office.

Both the promise and the perils of my campaign came together on a warm and brilliantly sunny June day in 2015, when I formally announced my candidacy in a speech to thousands of supporters on Roosevelt Island in New York's East River. Now the event seems almost like a quaint throwback to an earlier era of politics—a time when policies and polish were assets, not liabilities. Nonetheless, that hopeful, joyous day on Roosevelt Island will always rank as one of my favorites.

For weeks before the speech, I went back and forth with my team about what to say and how to say it. I've never been very adept at summing up my entire life story, worldview, and agenda in pithy sound bites. I was also acutely aware that, as the first woman to be a credible candidate for President, I looked and sounded different than any presidential candidate in our country's history. I had no precedent to follow, and voters had no historical frame of reference to draw upon. It was exhilarating to enter uncharted territory. But *uncharted*, by definition, means uncertain. If I felt that way, I was sure that a lot of voters would feel even more wary about it.

I also knew that despite being the first woman to have a serious chance at the White House, I was unlikely to be seen as a transformative, revolutionary figure. I had been on the national stage too long for that, and my temperament was too even-keeled. Instead, I hoped that my candidacy—and if things worked out, my presidency—would be viewed as the next chapter in the long progressive struggle to make the country fairer, freer, and stronger, and to beat back a seriously scary right-wing agenda. This framing took me directly into the politically dangerous territory of seeking a so-called third term after Obama and being seen as the candidate of continuity instead of change, but it was honest. And I thought placing my candidacy in the grand tradition of my progressive forebears would help voters accept and embrace the unprecedented nature of my campaign.

So when Huma suggested launching the campaign on Roosevelt Island, named after Franklin Delano, I knew it was the right choice. I'm something of a Roosevelt buff. First on the list will always be Eleanor. She was a crusading First Lady and progressive activist who never stopped speaking her mind and didn't give a damn what people thought. I return to her aphorisms again and again: "If I feel depressed, I go to work." "A woman is like a teabag: you never know how strong she is until she's in hot water." There was a minor Washington tempest back in the 1990s when a newspaper claimed I was having séances in the White House to commune directly with Eleanor's spirit. (I wasn't, though it would have been nice to talk to her now and then.)

I'm also fascinated by Eleanor's husband, Franklin, and her uncle Teddy. I was riveted by Ken Burns's seven-part documentary about all three Roosevelts that aired on PBS in 2014. I was particularly struck by the parallels between what Teddy faced as President in the early years of the twentieth century, as the industrial revolution upended American society, and what we faced in the early years of the twenty-first century. In both eras, disruptive technological change, massive income inequality, and excessive corporate power created a social and political crisis. Teddy responded by breaking up powerful monopolies, passing laws to protect working people, and safeguarding the environment. He may have been a Republican, but he put the capital *P* in *Progressive*. He was also a shrewd politician who managed to fend off the demands of angry populists on his left, who wanted to go even further toward Socialism, and conservatives on his right, who would have let the robber barons amass even more wealth and power.

Teddy found the right balance and called it the "Square Deal." I loved that phrase, and the more I thought about the challenges facing America in the years following the financial crisis of 2008–2009, the more I felt that what we needed was another Square Deal. We needed to regain our balance, take on the forces that had crashed our economy, and protect hardworking families shortchanged by automation, globalization, and inequality. We needed the political skill to restrain unchecked greed while defusing the most destructive impulses of resurgent populism.

On tough days out on the road, when reading the news felt like getting your teeth kicked in, I'd remember what Teddy said about those of us who climb into the arena. "It is not the critic who counts," he said, but the competitor "who strives valiantly; who errs, who comes short again and again, because there is no effort without error and shortcoming; but who does actually strive to do the deeds . . . who at the best knows in the end the triumph of high achievement, and who at the worst, if he fails, at least fails while daring greatly."

I also was inspired by Franklin Roosevelt's New Deal program of the 1930s, which saved capitalism from itself following the Great Depression, and by his vision of a humane, progressive, internationalist

America. Four Freedoms Park, at the tree-lined tip of Roosevelt Island, commemorates the universal freedoms FDR proclaimed during World War II: freedom of speech and worship, freedom from want and fear. It's a picturesque spot with a striking view of the New York skyline. Announcing my candidacy there felt right.

The final few days were a flurry of marking up drafts and rewriting lines with Dan Schwerin, my longtime speechwriter, who had been with me since the Senate. As the campaign went on, he would be joined by Megan Rooney, a wonderful writer who spent four years traveling the world with me at State and then went to the White House to write for President Obama. Despite our best efforts, when the morning of June 13 dawned, I was still not quite satisfied. I turned to the bottom of page 4, the key moment in the speech, when I was supposed to say, "That's why I'm running for President." What followed, "to make our economy work for you and for every American," was true and important. It was the result of deliberation and debate with my senior advisors, culminating a few days before around the table in my dining room in Washington. I had put down a draft in frustration, declared myself finished with all the slogans and sound bites, and said that I was really running for President to make the economy work for everyone, and why didn't we just say that and be done with it?

But something was missing—emotional lift, a sense that we were setting out on a common mission to secure our shared destiny. I remembered a note that Dan and I had received a few days earlier from Jim Kennedy, a great friend who has a deft way with words. He reflected on a line from Roosevelt's "Four Freedoms" speech: "Our strength is our unity of purpose." America is a family, Jim noted, and we should have one another's backs. In that moment, I had no idea that the election would turn into a contest between the divisiveness of Donald Trump and my vision of an America that's "stronger together." But it felt right to call for shared purpose, to remind Americans that there is much more that unites us than divides us.

I picked up my ballpoint pen and, playing off Jim's language, wrote, "We Americans may differ, bicker, stumble, and fall; but we are at our best when we pick each other up, when we have each other's back. Like any family, our American family is strongest when we cherish what we have in common and fight back against those who would drive us apart."

A few hours later, I was standing at the podium in the blinding June sun, looking out at the excited faces of cheering supporters. I saw little kids perched on their parents' shoulders. Friends smiled up at me from the front row. Bill, Chelsea, and Marc were glowing with pride and love. The stage was shaped like our campaign logo: a big blue *H* with a red arrow cutting across the middle. All around it, a sea of people clapped, hollered, and waved American flags.

I allowed myself a moment to think, "This is really happening. I am going to run for President, and I am going to win." Then I started to speak. It was hard to read the teleprompter with the sun in my eyes, but I knew the words well by this point. It was a long speech, full of policies and insights developed over the previous months of listening to people such as Pam in New Hampshire. That's not everyone's cup of tea. But I thought it was the kind of speech a candidate for the most important job in the world ought to give: serious, substantive, honest about the challenges ahead, and hopeful about our ability to meet them.

I told a couple jokes. "I may not be the youngest candidate in this race," I said, "but I will be the youngest woman President in the history of the United States." Little did I know that, in fact, I *would* end up being the youngest candidate, running against septuagenarians Bernie Sanders and Donald Trump.

I was pleased with how the speech was received. The journalist Jon Allen, who has followed me over the years, declared, "Clinton pretty much nailed the vision thing." Jared Bernstein, Joe Biden's former top economic advisor, smartly described it as a "reconnection agenda"

(I loved that) that aimed to "reunite economic growth with the prosperity of middle- and low-income families."

But it was E. J. Dionne, one of my favorite political commentators, who had the most thought-provoking—and, in retrospect, haunting—reaction. "Hillary Clinton is making a bet and issuing a challenge. The bet is that voters will pay more attention to what she can do for them than to what her opponents will say about her," E. J. wrote. "The challenge is to her Republican adversaries: Can they go beyond low-tax, antigovernment bromides to make credible counteroffers to the nurses, truckers, factory workers, and food servers whom Clinton made the heroes of her Roosevelt Island narrative about grace under pressure?"

We know now that I lost that bet—not because a Republican came along and made a more credible counteroffer to middle-class voters but because Donald Trump did something else: appeal to the ugliest impulses of our national character. He also made false promises about being on the side of working people. As Michael Bloomberg later said at the Democratic National Convention, "I'm a New Yorker, and I know a con when I see one." Me too.

As I would often do in big moments over the course of the campaign, I closed the speech by talking about my mother, Dorothy, who had passed away in 2011. She lived to be ninety-two years old, and I often thought about all the progress she witnessed over the course of her long life—progress won because generations of Americans kept fighting for what they knew to be right. "I wish my mother could have been with us longer," I said. "I wish she could have seen Chelsea become a mother herself. I wish she could have met Charlotte. I wish she could have seen the America we're going to build together." I looked out at the crowd and up at the New York skyline across the water, smiled, and said, "An America where a father can tell his daughter, yes, you can be anything you want to be—even President of the United States."

Time is the coin of your life. You spend it.
Do not allow others to spend it for you.

—Carl Sandburg

A Day in the Life

A presidential campaign is a marathon run at the pace of a sprint. Every day, every hour, every moment counts. But there are so many days—nearly six hundred, in the case of the 2015–2016 campaign—that you have to be careful not to burn out before hitting the finish line.

President Obama drilled this point home when I was getting ready to run. He reminded me that when we faced off in 2008, we would often end up staying at the same hotel in Iowa or New Hampshire. He said his team would be finished with dinner and getting ready to call it a night when we finally got there, completely spent. By the time he woke up the next morning, we'd be long gone. In short, he thought we overdid it. "Hillary," he said, "you've got to pace yourself this time. Work smart, not just hard." Whenever we saw each other, he'd say it again, and he'd tell John and Huma to remind me.

I tried to follow his advice. After all, he won twice. My approach came down to two words: routine and joy. At the beginning, I put some routines in place to keep my traveling team and me as healthy and productive as possible through one of the hardest things any of us would ever do. And we all tried our best to savor every moment that came our way—to find joy and meaning in the daily grind of campaigning. Not a day went by when we didn't.

Since the election, my life and routine have changed greatly. But I still treasure many moments from that long and sometimes strange trip. Many mental snapshots that I took along the way are in this chapter. So are a lot of details about a typical day on the trail: what I ate, who did my hair and makeup, what my mornings were like.

It may seem strange, but I get asked about these things constantly. Philippe Reines, my longtime advisor, who played Trump in our debate prep sessions, has my favorite explanation why. He calls it the "Panda Principle." Pandas just live their lives. They eat bamboo. They play with their kids. But for some reason, people love watching pandas, hoping for something—anything—to happen. When that one baby panda sneezed, the video became a viral sensation.

Under Philippe's theory, I'm like a panda. A lot of people just want to see how I live. And I do love spending time with my family and getting some sun, just like a panda—and while I'm not into bamboo, I like to eat.

I get it. We want to know our leaders, and part of that is hearing about Ronald Reagan's jelly bean habit and Madeleine Albright's pin collection.

In that spirit, if you've ever wondered what a day in the life of a presidential candidate is like—or if you've ever asked yourself, "Does Hillary Clinton just . . . eat lunch, like a normal person?"—this is for you.

Six A.M.: I wake up, sometimes hitting the snooze button to steal a few more minutes. Snoozing leaves you more tired—there are studies on this—but in that moment, it seems like such a great idea.

As often as we can, we arrange my schedule so I can sleep in my own bed in Chappaqua. Many nights, that isn't possible, and I wake up in a hotel room somewhere. That's okay; I can sleep anywhere. It's not unusual for me to sleep through a bumpy plane landing. But waking up at home is the best.

Bill and I bought our home in 1999 because we loved the bedroom. It's one and a half stories high with a vaulted ceiling and windows on three sides. When we first saw it as prospective home buyers, Bill said that we would always wake up happy here, with the light streaming in and the view of the garden around us. He was right.

There's a colorful portrait of Chelsea in her late teens on one wall of our bedroom, and photos of family and friends scattered everywhere. We loved the wallpaper in our bedroom in the White House—yellow with pastel flowers—so I tracked it down for this bedroom too. There are stacks of books on our bedside tables that we are reading or hoping to read soon. For years, we've been keeping careful track of everything we read. Plus, Bill being Bill, he has a rating system. The best books get three stars.

After waking up, I check my email and read my morning devotional from Reverend Bill Shillady, which is usually waiting in my inbox. I spend a few minutes in contemplation, organizing my thoughts and setting my priorities for the day.

Then it's time for breakfast. When I'm home, I head downstairs. On the road, I order room service. It's hard to plan exactly what or when I'll be eating over the course of the day, since we're always on the go, so breakfast is key. Usually I opt for scrambled egg whites with vegetables. When they're around, I add fresh jalapeños. Otherwise, it's salsa and hot sauce. I'm a black coffee and strong black tea person, and I drink a huge glass of water in the morning and keep drinking water all day long, since I fly a lot, which can be dehydrating.

Over breakfast, I start reading the stack of press clips and briefing papers that have arrived overnight from my staff. If I'm home, Oscar Flores, a Navy veteran who had worked in the White House and is now our residence manager, prints it all out for me. I also take another look at the day's schedule, which is a logistical masterpiece. My team—Lona

Valmoro, my invaluable scheduler since my Senate days, who also worked with me at the State Department; Alex Hornbrook, director of scheduling, who previously did the same job for Vice President Biden; and Jason Chung, director of advance—are miracle workers. They juggle dates and places with grace and create flawless events out of thin air. It isn't unusual to call them from the plane as we are landing at night to say, "We need to completely redo tomorrow's schedule to add one more state and two more events." Their answer is always "No problem."

If Bill's in town, he's probably still asleep. He's a night owl; I'm an early bird. But sometimes he'll get up with me, and we'll read the papers (we get four: the *New York Times*, the *New York Daily News*, the *New York Post*, and the *Journal News*, our local paper) and drink our coffee and talk about what we have going on that day. It's probably a lot like what's happening at that moment in our neighbors' houses, except in our case, one of us is running for President and the other one used to be President.

I try to find time for yoga or a strength and cardio workout. At home, I work out in an old red barn out back that we've converted into a gym and an office for Bill, with space in the converted hayloft for the Secret Service. I'm no match for Ruth Bader Ginsburg, however, who pumps iron and does planks and push-ups two days a week. Her regimen is daunting; mine is more forgiving. But if she can find the time and energy to exercise regularly, so can I (and you!). When I'm on the road, I have a mini exercise routine I've now done in hotel rooms across America.

Then there's hair and makeup. Long ago in a galaxy far, far away, having my hair and makeup done was a special treat every now and again. But having to do it every single day takes the fun out of it.

Luckily, I have a glam squad that makes it easy. Two hairdressers have taken great care of me in New York for years: John Barrett, whose full-service salon is in Manhattan, and Santa Nikkels, whose cozy salon is just a few minutes from my house in Chappaqua. They're both terrific—though a lot of people were baffled to discover, after my emails were made public, that I had regular "appointments with Santa."

When I'm in New York and need help with my makeup, I see Melissa Silver (recommended to me by *Vogue*'s Anna Wintour after she saw me at an event and knew I needed help).

On the campaign trail, I have a traveling team: Isabelle Goetz and Barbara Lacy. Isabelle is French and full of positivity; she doesn't walk so much as bop. She's been doing my hair on and off since the mid-1990s, which means we've been together through a lot of hairstyles. Barbara, like Isabelle, is perpetually cheerful. In addition to doing my makeup on the campaign, she does makeup for movies and TV shows such as *Veep*. I, of course, don't want to be compared with Selina Meyer in any way, shape, or form, but there's no denying, Julia Louis-Dreyfus looks fantastic.

While they get me ready, I'm usually on the phone or reading my briefings for the day. That hour is valuable, so I occasionally schedule calls with staff to discuss electoral strategy or a new policy. They usually don't mind speaking over the blow dryer. Isabelle and Barbara do their best to work around me until they tell me they need me to be still, *s'il vous plaît*.

At the beginning of the campaign, Isabelle and Barbara got me ready for the day once a week or so, as well as for big events such as debates. I tried to take care of my own hair and makeup the rest of the time. But photos don't lie, and since I looked better when they were with me, it became an everyday thing. When they travel with me, Isabelle and Barbara are always nearby, ready to touch me up before interviews or debates. Every time our plane lands, Isabelle rushes forward with hairspray, and Barbara spritzes my face with a vaporizer full of mineral water. "The air on planes is so dry!" she laments. Then she spritzes everyone else in the vicinity, including, at times, the Secret Service.

I appreciate their talents and like how they make me look. But I've never gotten used to how much effort it takes just to be a woman in the public eye. I once calculated how many hours I spent having my hair and makeup done during the campaign. It came to about six hundred hours, or twenty-five days! I was so shocked, I checked the math twice.

I'm not jealous of my male colleagues often, but I am when it comes to how they can just shower, shave, put on a suit, and be ready to go. The few times I've gone out in public without makeup, it's made the news. So I sigh and keep getting back in that chair, and dream of a future in which women in the public eye don't need to wear makeup if they don't want to and no one cares either way.

After hair and makeup, it's time to get dressed. When I ran for Senate in 2000 and President in 2008, I basically had a uniform: a simple pantsuit, often black, with a colorful shell underneath. I did this because I like pantsuits. They make me feel professional and ready to go. Plus, they helped me avoid the peril of being photographed up my skirt while sitting on a stage or climbing stairs, both of which happened to me as First Lady. (After that, I took a cue from one of my childhood heroes, Nancy Drew, who would often do her detective work in sensible trousers. "I'm glad I wore pants!" she said in *The Clue of the Tapping Heels* after hoisting herself up on the rafters of a building in pursuit of a rare cat.) I also thought it would be good to do what male politicians do and wear more or less the same thing every day. As a woman running for President, I liked the visual cue that I was different from the men but also familiar. A uniform was also an antidistraction technique: since there wasn't much to say or report on what I wore, maybe people would focus on what I was saying instead.

In 2016, I wanted to dress the same as I did when I wasn't running for President and not overthink it. I was lucky to have something few others do: relationships with American designers who helped me find outfits I could wear from place to place, in all climates. Ralph Lauren's team made the white suit I wore to accept the nomination and the red, white, and blue suits I wore to debate Trump three times. More than a dozen American designers made T-shirts to support my campaign and even held an event during New York Fashion Week to show them off.

Some people like my clothes and some people don't. It goes with the territory. You can't please everybody, so you may as well wear what works for you. That's my theory, anyway.

When I leave for several days on the road, I try to be superorganized, but inevitably I overpack. I throw in more outfits than I need, just in case the weather changes or something spills on me or an eager fan leaves makeup on my shoulder after an exuberant hug. Huma, someone who knows a thing or two about being stylish while working twenty-hour days, tries to advise me. She's the one who will tell me I have on two different earrings, which happened a few times. I also overdo it on reading material; for a while, I filled an entire rolling suitcase with briefing memos and policy papers. Oscar helps me load everything into the cars. Sometimes Bill, marveling at all the stuff I'm bringing, asks, "Are you running away from home?"

When the cars are loaded, the husband is hugged, and the dogs are cuddled, we're off.

We fly in and out of the Westchester County Airport, just a short drive from our house. I make a policy of trying not to be "wheels up" before 8:30 A.M. on the nights I sleep at home. Everyone on my team has at least an hour's drive home after we land in Westchester, and we often land late. An 8:30 A.M. start time means everyone gets at least some sleep.

For the primaries and the beginning of the general election, my traveling team was small. It consisted of Huma; Nick Merrill; trip director Connolly Keigher; Sierra Kos, Julie Zuckerbrod, and Barbara Kinney, who videotaped and photographed life on the trail; and my Secret Service detail, which was usually two agents, sometimes three. A rotating cast of additional staff joined depending on what was happening that day: speechwriters, members of the policy team, state organizers. By the end of the campaign, the team was much bigger and so was the plane.

A note about the Secret Service. Bill and I have been under Secret

Service protection since 1992, as soon as he secured the Democratic nomination for President. It took some getting used to, but after twenty-five years, it feels normal—and to their great credit, the agents bend over backward to be as unobtrusive as possible. They are somehow both low-key and ferociously vigilant. The agents are with us at our home all day every day. When I leave the house to do something casual around town—like go to the market or take a walk—agents come with me. They hang back and give me space to do whatever I'm doing. Sometimes I forget that they're there, which is exactly what they want. I'm grateful for the relationships we've built with many of these dedicated men and women over the years. We've also gotten to spend time with their spouses and children at the holiday party Bill and I host for our agents and their families every year, and I've met some of their extended families out on the campaign trail, too.

When Bill and I travel, whether into Manhattan to see a play or all the way to Nevada for campaign events, the Secret Service kicks into higher gear. They coordinate ahead of time to make sure they know the details of every place we'll visit: all the entrances and exits, the fastest traffic routes, and, just in case, backup routes and the nearest hospitals. They organize the motorcade, run background checks, and work with local police at every stop. It's an enormous undertaking, and they do it seamlessly.

The only part of this I have a hard time with is the size of the motorcade. I understand why it's necessary, but it drives me crazy to see people sitting in traffic that I've caused. This feels especially problematic when I'm campaigning—shutting down highways seemed like the quickest way to make people resent me, which was the exact opposite of what I wanted to do. So I always ask the lead agent to avoid using lights and sirens whenever possible. I'm also embarrassed to admit that I do a fair amount of backseat driving. That's pretty rich coming from someone who hasn't driven a car regularly in twenty-five years. Luckily, the agents are too polite to tell me to put a sock in it.

On a typical day on the trail, after leaving the house, our motorcade of two or three cars pulls up right to the plane on the tarmac. Door-to-door service is both a security must and an extremely nice perk. For the primaries and the beginning of the general, we flew in planes with nine or ten seats. The traveling press had a plane of their own, which took extra coordination. Eventually we chartered a Boeing 737 for the general election—big enough for all of us, with "Stronger Together" painted on the side and *H* logos on the tip of each wing.

The plane was our home away from home for months. For the most part, it served us well. Of course, there were occasional hiccups. One day we were in Little Rock and had to get to Dallas. The plane had a mechanical issue, so they sent another one. While we were waiting on the tarmac, my staff got off the plane to stretch their legs. I decided to close my eyes after a grueling few days. I woke up a few hours later and asked, "Are we there already?" In fact, we hadn't moved. At a certain point in a long campaign, all sense of time and space disappears.

Over the course of the campaign, we were joined by a number of flight attendants. They were all excellent, but my favorite was Elizabeth Rivalsi. She's a trained nutritionist and made fresh, delicious food for us in her kitchen in Queens, which she then packed into containers and brought on the plane: salmon salad, chicken tenders made with almond flour, poblano pepper soup. Her surprise smash hit was brownies made out of chickpea flour. She also had a big basket full of snacks that she regularly replenished with different items. It was a little adventure every time we boarded and checked out the stash. I have a weakness for Pepperidge Farm Goldfish crackers and was delighted to find out that 55 goldfish were only 150 calories—not bad! One time, Liz brought something I hadn't tried before: Flavor Blasted Goldfish. We passed around the bag and discussed whether it was better than the original. Some of my staff thought yes, which was incorrect.

As you can tell, we took eating seriously. Someone once asked what we talked about on long flights. "Food!" we chorused. It's funny how much you look forward to the next meal when you're living out of a suitcase. In 2008, we often relied on junk food to see us through; I remember a lot of pizza with sliced jalapeños delivered right to the plane. This time I was determined that we would all be healthier. I asked friends for good on-the-go snack recommendations. A few days later, shipments of canned salmon, as well as Quest and Kind protein bars, arrived at my house, which we lugged onto the plane in canvas totes. When the Quest bars got cold, they were too hard to eat, so we sat on them for a few minutes to warm them up, with as much dignity as one can muster at such a moment.

I also splurge every now and again on burgers and fries and enjoy every bite.

Several of us put hot sauce on everything. I've been a fan since 1992, when I became convinced it boosted my immune system, as research now shows that it does. We were always on the lookout for new concoctions. One favorite is called Ninja Squirrel Sriracha. Julie the videographer came back from vacation in Belize with four little bottles of the best hot sauce any of us have ever had: Marie Sharp's. We immediately loved the red habanero pepper flavor the most. Everyone quietly jockeyed for that bottle, then handed it over sheepishly when confronted. Eventually we realized we could just order more, and peace returned.

Then there was the food we eat all over the country. We had a few favorite spots: a Middle Eastern takeout place in Detroit; a Cuban restaurant by the airport in Miami; lattes made with honey and lavender from a bakery in Des Moines. At the Iowa State Fair, in the 100-degree August heat, I drank about a gallon of lemonade. Nick handed me a pork chop on a stick, which I devoured. When we got back to the plane, I told him, "I want you to know that I did not eat that pork chop on a stick because it is politically necessary. I ate that pork chop on a stick because it was delicious." He nodded wordlessly and kept eating his own state fair discovery: red velvet funnel cake.

One hot night in Omaha, Nebraska, I was consumed with the

desire for an ice cream bar—the simple kind, just vanilla ice cream with a chocolate shell. Connolly called an advance staffer, who kindly picked some up from the drugstore and met us at the plane on our way out of town. We said thank you and devoured them before they could melt.

One of my favorite places to eat and drink is the Hotel at Kirkwood Center in Cedar Rapids, Iowa. It's run by hospitality and culinary students from Kirkwood Community College, and they do a great job. On one of our first visits, I ordered a vodka martini with olives, as cold as they could make it. Cecile Richards, the indomitable leader of Planned Parenthood and a Texan, was with me, and she insisted I try it with Tito's Handmade Vodka, the pride of Austin. It was a great drink. After that, whenever we stay at Kirkwood, the waiter sends over an ice-cold Tito's martini with olives, without me even having to order it.

We take birthdays and holidays seriously on the road. We put up decorations on board for Halloween and Christmas, and there's always a supply of birthday cakes on hand. We can't light candles—no fire allowed on the plane—so we tell the birthday boy or girl to pretend that they're lit and make a wish. We even found an iPhone app that simulates a lighter, to take the game further, which we also used to "light" the menorah we had on board during Hanukkah.

I am famously hard to surprise on my birthday, but for 2016, my team managed to sneak a cake into my hotel suite in Miami and gather silently in the living room while I was on the phone in the bedroom. When I walked out, they both startled and delighted me with an enthusiastic rendition of "Happy Birthday" and a chocolate cake with turquoise frosting. Since it was still early in the morning, we brought the cake with us on the plane to eat later. The night before, we had all celebrated together with an Adele concert. Perfect.

My team and I lived a lot of life together during our year and a half on the road. Families changed. Babies were born. Beloved friends and family passed away. Some people got engaged; some got separated. We raised a glass when Lorella Praeli, our director of Latino outreach, took the oath to become an American citizen. Several of us traveled to New Haven, Connecticut, a few weeks after the campaign began to hit the dance floor at Jake Sullivan's wedding to Maggie Goodlander. We were often away from home, under the gun, pushing ourselves as hard as we could to win. As a result, we relied on one another. We came to know one another's habits and preferences. We'd often gather in my room in the evenings to order room service and talk about that day's news coverage or go over the next day's schedule. We watched the Olympics together, and the Republican debates. Both inspired yelling, though of different kinds.

We could be impatient with one another—frustrated, exhausted, demoralized—but we also made one another laugh, broke hard news gently, kept our wits about us, and always stayed focused on the road ahead.

It was grueling. Sometimes it wasn't fun at all. But it was also wonderful.

Every day on the trail was packed with events: rallies, roundtables, interviews, fund-raisers, OTRs ("off-the-records," or unannounced visits to shops, parks, libraries, schools, hospitals—really anywhere).

When we landed in a city, we'd jump from event to event. Sometimes our "drive time" would stretch to an hour or more. To make the most of it, we would schedule radio interviews back to back. I'd also FaceTime with Charlotte, who was now old enough to kind of have a conversation with me. I'd cheer as she spun around in her tutu. We'd sing songs together. Then I'd blow kisses, hang up, and head off to another event.

Rallies are a whole other world. It's thrilling to hear a crowd cheer for you. It's thrilling to hear them cheer for your ideas. But I'll admit that no matter how many times I've stood before large crowds, it's always a little daunting. Our rallies were diverse, boisterous, and happy—the kind of place you could bring your hundred-year-old mother or your one-year-old son. I loved seeing all the homemade posters kids would wave while smiling ear to ear. One of the best things about our campaign logo (the *H* with the → arrow) was that anyone can draw it, even little kids. We wanted children to spread out poster boards on their kitchen tables, grab markers and glitter pens, and go to town. They sent a lot of homemade *H* art to our campaign headquarters. We covered the walls with it.

For the music at our rallies, we chose a lot of empowering women artists—Sara Bareilles, Andra Day, Jennifer Lopez, Katy Perry, and Rachel Platten—as well as songs from Marc Anthony, Stevie Wonder, Pharrell Williams, and John Legend and the Roots. We loved to see our crowds singing along to the music. To this day, I can't hear "Fight Song," "Roar," or "Rise Up" without getting emotional.

Some people came to our rallies again and again. I got to know a few of them. A woman named Janelle came with her husband and daughter to a rally in Iowa headlined by Katy Perry, the first of many she did for me. Janelle had a homemade sign: "Thirteenth Chemo Yesterday. Three More. Hear Me Roar!" She was in the process of fighting breast cancer. I was with Bill, and we walked over to introduce ourselves. We had a nice long talk. Over the next eleven months, I saw her many times. She'd visit me on the trail, update me on her health, and her daughter would tell me how second grade was going. Janelle kept promising me that she'd see me at my inauguration. I kept telling her I'd hold her to it and she'd better be there. For my second debate against Trump in Saint Louis, I invited her to come as my guest.

My staff would bring groups of people backstage to meet me before I spoke, and those brief conversations were often very meaningful. I met a lot of women in their eighties and nineties who said how excited they were to finally vote for a woman for President. Many dressed up in pantsuits and pearls for the occasion. I imagined myself in thirty years, putting on nice clothes and going to hear my candidate speak. One, Ruline Steininger, even caucused for me in Iowa when she was

102 years old. She made it very clear that she was going to be around to vote for me on Election Day, and she was.

At an event at a large arena in New Hampshire, I stepped into a side room before going out to speak and met a group of public school employees. One of them, a man named Keith, who worked in a school library, told me his story. Keith was his mother's caregiver. She had Alzheimer's disease. He couldn't afford adult day care or a home health aide, so he had to bring his mom with him to work every day. That stopped me in my tracks. He got a little choked up talking to me, and I got a little choked up hearing it. I thanked him for sharing his story. Later, I told my policy staff, who were already working on plans for Alzheimer's research and elder care, to think even bigger.

On the rope lines at rallies, I encountered a feature of modern campaigning that has become far more prevalent since 2008: the selfie. There is no stopping the selfie. This is now how we mark a moment together. And to be clear, if you see me in the world and want a selfie and I'm not on the phone or racing to get somewhere, I'll be glad to take one with you. But I think selfies come at a cost. Let's talk instead! Do you have something to share? I want to hear it (provided it's not deeply insulting—I have limits). I'd love to know your name and where you're from and how things are going with you. That feels real to me. A selfie is so impersonal—although it does give your wrist a break from autographs, now obsolete.

Roundtable events were special. As I mentioned earlier, they gave me a chance to hear directly from people in a setting in which they felt comfortable. Sometimes those conversations were searing. I met a ten-year-old girl in Las Vegas who took a deep breath and described in a trembling voice how terrified she was of her parents being deported because they were undocumented. Everyone in that room wanted to give her a hug, but I was the lucky one. She came over and sat on my lap as I said what I'd say to Chelsea whenever she was anxious as a little girl: Don't you worry. Let me do the worrying for you. And also, you are very brave.

We tried to make time for OTRs, seeing local sights and dropping by local businesses, whenever we could. If we were running late, these would be the first to fall off the schedule—all the more reason not to announce them, so no one would be disappointed if we couldn't make it. My personal preference for an OTR was anywhere that sold kids' toys, clothes, or books. I would load up on gear for my grandchildren and the new babies of friends and staffers. I also picked up little presents for Bill on the road: ties, shirts, cuff links, a watch. He loves nothing more than to get something neat from a craftsman somewhere in America. It's just about his favorite thing.

For me, fund-raisers were a little more complicated than other campaign events. Even after all these years, it's hard for me to ask for other people's money. It's hard to ask someone to host an event for you in their home or business. But until the day comes that campaign finance reform is signed into law and upheld by the Supreme Court, if you want to run a viable national campaign, there's no way around it: you're going to have to do some serious fund-raising, online, by phone, by mail, and in person. I reject the idea that it's impossible to do it while maintaining your integrity and independence. Bernie Sanders attacked me for raising money from people who worked in finance. But I reminded him that President Obama had raised more money from Wall Street than anyone in history, and that didn't stop him from imposing tough new rules to curb risk and prevent future financial crashes. I would have done the same, and my donors knew it.

I was grateful to everyone who gave money to our campaign or helped raise it. We tried hard to use every penny wisely. The campaign staff will attest that Robby Mook in particular was downright stingy about travel expenses and office supplies. Snack budget? Absolutely not. Buy your own chips. Your own hotel room? Not a chance. Find a roommate. And while you're at it, take the bus instead of the train. We were all in this together: our fund-raising team working around the clock; our national campaign staff living and working on a tight budget; me, flying around the country going to fund-raisers; and our donors, opening their wallets to show their solidarity and support. Our campaign had more than three million donors. The average donation was under $100. And ours was the first campaign in history for which the majority of donors were women. That meant a lot to all of us.

Sometimes we just needed to have some fun. One beautiful summer evening, Jimmy and Jane Buffett hosted a concert for us at their home in the Hamptons on Long Island. I was the first presidential candidate Jimmy ever endorsed, and he wanted to do something special for me. So he, Jon Bon Jovi, and Paul McCartney played a set in a tent full of twinkly lights, and everyone danced on the lawn under the stars. It was magical.

But my favorite events were with kids. They'd sit cross-legged in front of me on the floor, or join me on a couch or drape themselves over chairs, and I'd answer their questions. "What's your favorite part about running for President?" Meeting kids like you. "Who's your favorite President?" With lots of love to Bill and President Obama, it's Abraham Lincoln. "What are you going to do to protect the planet?" Reduce our carbon footprint, invest in clean energy, protect wildlife, and fight pollution. The children listened with great seriousness and asked follow-ups. They were my kind of crowd. They also sometimes told me what was worrying them: for instance, the death of a pet or a grandparent's illness. Many kids asked what I would do about bullying, which made me want to become President even more. I had an initiative called Better Than Bullying ready to go.

I had a lot of respect for the press corps who traveled with us. For the most part, it was comprised of "embeds"—journalists permanently "embedded" with us from the beginning of the campaign till the end. That meant they got to know us and we got to know them. A lot of the embeds were journalists in their late twenties and early thirties, which made this assignment a big opportunity for them. They worked as long and hard as we did. Some veteran reporters also joined us for stretches. Network anchors and big-time columnists would parachute in for interviews and a taste of the road, but they never stayed long.

The traveling press corps asked tough questions. They were hungry. I had to admire that. With rare exceptions, they were also very professional. I can't say we were completely comfortable with one another, though. As I write elsewhere in this book, I tend to treat journalists with caution, and I often feel like they focus too much on the wrong things. I understand that political coverage has to be about the horse race, but it's become almost entirely about that and not about the issues that matter most to our country and to people's lives. That's something that has gotten increasingly worse over the years. That's not entirely the press's fault: the way we consume news has changed, which makes getting clicks all important, which in turn encourages sensationalism. Still, they're responsible for their part.

Having said that, I respected them. Once in a while, we'd go out for drinks or dinner as a group and have a wide-ranging, off-the-record talk. I'd bring Halloween candy and birthday cake back to their cabin on the plane. They'd sometimes roll oranges with questions written in Sharpie up the aisle and try to reach my seat all the way in front. Sometimes on night flights, we'd put on music and open the wine and beer. When any of them were sick or dealing with family problems—that happens during a long campaign—I'd ask Nick to keep me updated. Some of the journalists also started dating one another—that also happens during a long campaign—and since nothing makes me happier than playing matchmaker, I was always eager for the scoop. I also was delighted that many of the journalists assigned to our campaign were women. During the 1972 presidential campaign, the reporters who traveled with the candidates were called the boys on the bus. By 2016, it was the girls on the plane.

A lot of days and nights on the trail can blur into one another. You'd be surprised how many times we had to ask each other, "Were we in Florida or North Carolina yesterday?" It wasn't out of the ordinary for two people to answer at once, but with different states. But some days stood out, for better or worse.

One of the best days ever was November 2, 2016: game seven of the World Series, the night the Chicago Cubs made history. We were in Arizona for one of our final rallies. It was a big one: more than twenty-five thousand people came out. Before I went onstage, I asked for an update on the game. It was the top of the sixth inning. The Cubs led the Cleveland Indians 5–3. Gulp.

Like everyone in Cubs Nation, I had been following the playoffs and the series with all my fingers crossed. I started watching Cubs games with my dad when I was a little girl, sitting on his lap or on the floor near his chair in the den. We'd cheer and groan, and at the end of the season, we'd say, "Next year, we'll win the Series!" (To assuage my disappointment, I also became a Yankees fan. It didn't feel disloyal, because they were in the other league.)

Some people on my staff were fans, too—no one more than Connolly, who, like me, grew up outside Chicago. She carried a huge *W* flag with her on the road, and every time the Cubs won, putting them one step closer to their first world championship in 108 years, she draped it on the bulkhead of the plane or wore it like a cape. Whenever we could, we watched the games together, holding our breath.

That night in Arizona, when the rally was over, the first thing I asked was "Who won?" No one yet. The score was 6–6 in the ninth inning. We had a fifteen-minute drive back to the hotel. But that meant maybe missing the end of the game. We couldn't risk it. Instead, Philippe, who was traveling with us for the final stretch, pulled it up on his iPad, and we all stood around him to watch, standing on a section of grass in the parking lot. Capricia Marshall, one of my close friends and the former Chief of Protocol at the State Department, was there too. She's from Cleveland and is a big Indians fan, so she did some trash-talking.

Following an anxiety-inducing rain delay, the game went into extra innings. We stayed put in the parking lot. When Chicago recorded the final out in the bottom of the tenth to edge the Indians 8–7, Connolly was the happiest I've ever seen her. I reached for that *W* flag, and we stretched it out between us and took a million photos. Then we drove back to the hotel, ordered a bunch of food to my hotel suite, and watched the highlight reel—especially reliever Mike Montgomery's game-winning save, which he pulled off with a giant smile on his face, like he had all the confidence in the world that he was about to make our dreams come true.

A much less fun day was September 11, 2016, the day I was sick at the National September 11 Memorial Museum. It means a lot to me to commemorate that solemn day, so missing this event wasn't an option. But I felt awful. I'd been fighting a cough from what I thought was allergies for at least a month and saw my internist, Dr. Lisa Bardack, on September 9. She told me the cough was actually pneumonia, and I should take a few days off. I said I couldn't. She gave me strong antibiotics, and I went on with my schedule, including filming *Between Two Ferns* with comic Zach Galifianakis that afternoon. The next day, I stuck to a scheduled debate prep session. On Sunday, when I got to the memorial, the sun was beaming down. My head ached. You know the rest.

In a funny twist, when I arrived, one of the first people I saw was Senator Chuck Schumer, my friend and former colleague. "Hillary!" he said. "How are you? I just had pneumonia!" At this point, the fact that I had pneumonia wasn't public, so this was totally out of the blue. The difference between us was that Chuck didn't have to go out in public as a candidate when he was under the weather. He told me he had followed his doctor's orders and stayed home for a week. Looking back, I should have done the same. Instead, I ended up having to parade in front of the cameras after leaving my daughter's apartment—where I had gone to rest—to reassure the world that I was fine.

Luckily, most of my memories of being in New York during the campaign were a lot better.

I raced all over the city for the New York primary, hitting all five boroughs. I played dominoes in Harlem, drank *boba* tea in Queens, spoke at historic Snug Harbor on Staten Island, ate cheesecake at Junior's in Brooklyn, rode the subway in the Bronx (struggling with the MetroCard reader like a typical commuter), and had ice cream at a shop called Mikey Likes It on the Lower East Side. As I tucked into my ice cream, an English reporter who was part of the traveling press corps that day shouted, "How many calories are in that?" All of us, including the rest of the press, booed in response, me louder than anyone. In the end, we won the New York primary by 16 points.

I went on *Saturday Night Live* and taped that episode of Funny or Die's *Between Two Ferns*, which was surely one of the more surreal experiences of my life. It's an odd thing to be a politician on a comedy show. Your job isn't to be funny—you're not, especially compared with the actual comedians, so don't even try. Your job is to be the straight guy. That's pretty easy, especially for me, whose life is basically taking whatever's thrown my way. The most important thing is to be game. Luckily, I'm game for a lot. *SNL* asked me to play a character named Val the Bartender, who would pour drinks for Kate McKinnon, who played me. "Would you sing 'Lean On Me' together?" they asked. I said yes, even though I have a terrible singing voice. (For a couple weeks after, people would shout, "Hey, Val!" at me on the trail.) On *Between Two Ferns*, when Zach Galifianakis asked me, "I'm going to sneak up on you in a gorilla mask, is that cool?" I said sure. Why not? You only live once.

I marched in the 2016 New York City Pride Parade. Back in the day, in 2000, I was the first First Lady in history to march in a Pride parade. This time we had a big contingent from Hillary for America marching together behind a "Love Trumps Hate" banner. The New York City crowds cheered for us with gusto.

Most importantly, Bill and I welcomed the arrival of our grandson, Aidan, on June 18, 2016, at Lenox Hill Hospital on the Upper East Side of Manhattan. It was a sunny day with hardly a cloud in the sky—a prediction, perhaps, of his personality. He is the happiest little boy.

It's hard to ask more of a city than that.

There's one more group of days I want to describe, because they're unlike any other: debate prep.

It's the debate prep team's job to put me through my paces so I'm not hearing anything for the first time during the actual debate. My team, led by Ron Klain, Karen Dunn, and Jake, helped me prepare for all twelve debates. Ron is a lawyer and veteran political strategist who served in the Clinton and Obama White Houses. Karen, also a lawyer, worked for me in the Senate and later for President Obama. And Jake, who knew every word of every one of our policies, was a champion debater in college and grad school. All three had helped prepare President Obama for his debates as well. They worked with two indefatigable campaign staffers, Sara Solow and Kristina Costa, to produce thick briefing binders for me, covering hundreds of topics. As a lifelong fan of school supplies, I fussed over the tabs and dividers and armed myself with a bouquet of highlighters in every color. I spent evenings studying in hotel rooms across America and at my kitchen table. By the end, I knew my opponents' positions inside and out—in some cases, better than they did.

We held most of our debate prep sessions at the Doral Arrowwood, a hotel near my home in Westchester County. We were joined by more people from my team: campaign consultants Joel Benenson, Mandy Grunwald, and Jim Margolis; Tony Carrk, our head of research and an Obama debate-prep veteran; and Bob Barnett, who had helped prepare Democratic candidates for debates since Walter Mondale. We would gather at noon and work late into the evening. We'd practice specific exchanges, fine-tune answers, and try to plan out dramatic "moments" that would help shape the coverage of the debate, although often the most important clashes are the hardest to predict. The hotel would supply us with a smorgasbord that they'd replenish throughout the day—sandwiches, salads, fruit, bagels, and chicken soup. They also had a freezer full of Oreo ice cream bars that we kept emptying and they kept refilling. Anytime you looked around the room, you'd see someone holding one or the stick and wrapper on the table in front of them.

Debate prep helped me get ready emotionally for some of the most consequential moments of the campaign. A presidential debate is theater. It's a boxing match. It's high-stakes surgery. Pick your metaphor. One wrong move—one roll of the eyes or slip of the tongue—can spell defeat. In debate prep, I practiced keeping my cool while my staff fired hard questions at me. They'd misrepresent my record. They'd impugn my character. Sometimes I'd snap back and feel better for getting it off my chest. I'd think to myself, "Now that I've done that here, I don't have to do it on live TV." It worked.

I remember becoming frustrated with my team's advice at one point. I couldn't quite understand how they were recommending I handle a potentially contentious exchange with Bernie. Finally, I said to Jake, who had been peppering me with questions and grimacing at my answers, "Just show me! You do it!" So he became me, and I took on the role of attack dog against myself. It was a truly surreal experience. Finally, he mock-pleaded for mercy: "You're right, you're right, do it your way."

Then there was Philippe-as-Trump. That was a sight to see. The first time I walked into the room for a prep session with him, he was already at the podium, staring at the distant wall and refusing to make eye contact with me. "Oh God, he's ready to be obnoxious," I said. None of us had any idea.

Philippe took his character study very seriously, including the physicality. Trump looms and lurks on a debate stage, so Philippe did too, always hanging out on the edge of my peripheral vision. He wore a suit like Trump's (a little baggy), a tie like Trump's (way too long), and actual Trump-brand cuff links and a Trump-brand watch he found on eBay. He wore three-and-a-half-inch shoe heighteners, flailed his arms like Trump, shrugged and mugged like Trump. I didn't know whether to applaud or fire him.

The weeks that Philippe spent studying tapes of Trump in the Republican debates paid off. He knew how Trump's mind worked: how a question about Social Security would take Trump on a twisted journey into government waste, undocumented immigrants, and terrorism, always terrorism. He would say the craziest things—which I know Philippe is capable of doing all on his own, but he made clear to us from that first day that 90 percent of what he'd say was straight from the horse's mouth, with the remaining 10 percent being his best guess as to what Trump would say. I never knew which was which. In the end, Trump hardly said a thing in any of the three debates that I was hearing for the first time.

It quickly became evident that normal debate prep wouldn't work this time. Trump wouldn't answer any question directly. He was rarely linear in his thinking or speaking. He digressed into nonsense and then digressed even more. There was no point in refuting his arguments like it was a normal debate—it was almost impossible to identify what his arguments even were, especially since they changed minute to minute. Winning, we realized, would mean hitting hard (since he couldn't bear it), staying cool (since he often resorted to viciousness when cornered), throwing his own words back at him (since he couldn't stand hearing them), and making my own arguments with clarity and precision (since he couldn't do the same for himself).

At our last practice before the first debate, I walked in to find Philippe-as-Trump and Ron-as-me practicing the opening handshake. They were half joking, but Philippe had raised the issue that, unlike two men debating who just meet in the middle and shake hands, there was a question of whether Trump would try to hug or—dare I say it—kiss me. Not out of affinity or chivalry, but rather to create a moment where he would tower over me, making it clear he was a guy and I was a girl. Fair enough, I said, let's practice. Philippe came at me with his arms outstretched. I tried to stiff-arm him and get away. It ended with him literally chasing me across the room, putting me in a bear hug, and kissing the back of my head. What can I say? We were committed. If you haven't seen it, it's worth pulling up on YouTube.

It stopped being funny when we saw the *Access Hollywood* tape. I was not going to shake that man's hand. When we came onstage in the actual debate, I think my body language made it pretty clear he should stay away. And he did. But throughout that debate, which was town-hall style—meaning we weren't confined to standing at podiums and could walk around the stage—Trump stalked and lurked. Philippe had done the same thing during prep.

Several times a session—and we had twenty-one of them in the general—just as he had warned, Philippe-as-Trump would say something so outlandish, none of us could quite believe it. Then he'd tell us it was almost verbatim from a Trump rally, interview, or primary debate. One day Philippe-as-Trump started complaining about how the "Mike guy" screwed up and the "Mike guy" shouldn't get paid. We were totally confused but kept going. When the ninety-minute session was over, I asked, "Who is Mike?" It turns out he was saying "mic guy." Philippe explained that, on two occasions, Trump had blamed the microphone for bad audio and said the contractor shouldn't get paid.

After his dismal performance in the first debate, Trump really did say it was because his mic had been sabotaged. Philippe had called it.

In the end, thanks to our practice sessions, I felt that deep sense of confidence that comes with rigorous preparation. Like accepting the nomination, these debates were a first for me. The pressure you feel when you're about to walk onstage is almost unbearable—almost, but not quite. You bear it by working hard to get ready. You bear it by having good people by your side. You bear it by not just hoping but *knowing* you can handle a lot, because you already have.

At least, that's what always worked for me.

No matter how I spent the day or where in the country I happened to be, I always called Bill before falling asleep. We'd catch each other up on the latest news about the election or what was happening with our family and friends. Sometimes we vented frustrations about how the campaign was going. Then we'd take a moment to figure out when we'd see each other next, and say good night. I'd fall asleep feeling calmer and wake up in the morning with new energy and a list of new ideas to pursue. Even on the hardest days, those conversations kept me grounded and at peace.

It is hard *to be a woman.*

You must think like a man,

Act like a lady,

Look like a young girl,

And work like a horse.

—A sign that hangs in my house

Sisterhood

Above all, be the heroine of your life, not the victim.

—Nora Ephron

On Being a
Woman in Politics

In these pages, I put to paper years' worth of frustration about the tightrope that I and other women have had to walk in order to participate in American politics. I have a lot to say—I could fill an entire book—and not all of it is upbeat or even-tempered. But there is joy and pride to be found in this chapter, too. My experiences as a woman in politics have been complex and disappointing at times, but ultimately rewarding beyond measure.

In politics, the personal narrative is vital.

My husband had a powerful story to tell: he lived for a while on a farm with no indoor plumbing, his father died before he was born, he stopped his stepfather from beating his mother, he became the first in his family to go to college.

Barack Obama had a powerful story to tell: he was raised by his teenage mom and grandparents, his father was Kenyan, he spent part of his childhood living in Indonesia and grew up to become a community organizer and law professor whose story could have been written only in America.

Few people would say that my story was quite so dazzling.

I grew up in a white middle-class family in Park Ridge, a suburb of Chicago. My dad served during World War II and left every morning for his small business in the city along with all the other fathers in our neighborhood heading to their jobs. My mom stayed at home to take care of my brothers, Hugh and Tony, and me, like all the mothers in our neighborhood. And my life looked like the lives of all the girls I knew. We attended excellent public or parochial schools, where first-rate teachers had high expectations for us. I went to our local Methodist church for Sunday services and youth activities all week long. I was a Brownie, then a Girl Scout. I got my first summer job when I was thirteen, working at a park three mornings a week. My hangouts were everyone's hangouts: the public library, the local movie theater, swimming pools, skating rinks. My family watched TV together at night. When the Beatles performed for the first time on *The Ed Sullivan Show* in 1964, my friends and I gathered together around the screen, alternately silently captivated and shrieking with glee.

It's a story that many would consider perfectly ordinary. Don't get me wrong: I loved my childhood, and every year that passes, I appreciate more how hard my parents worked to give it to me. But my story—or at least how I've always told it—was never the kind of narrative that made everyone sit up and take notice. We yearn for that showstopping tale—that one-sentence pitch that captures something magical about America; that hooks you and won't let go. Mine wasn't it.

Yet there is another story of my life; one that I believe is as inspiring as any other. I wish I had claimed it more publicly and told it more proudly. It's the story of a revolution.

I was born right when everything was changing for women.

Families were changing. Jobs were changing. Laws were changing. Views about women that had governed our lives for millennia were changing—finally! I came along at just the right moment, like a surfer catching the perfect wave. Everything I am, everything I've done, so much of what I stand for flows from that happy accident of fate.

The fact that the women's movement happened alongside the civil rights movement—indeed, was entwined with it in many ways, compelling America to reckon with entrenched notions of human value and opening doors of opportunity that had previously been sealed shut to millions—made it that much more thrilling and meaningful.

I know that for a lot of people, including a lot of women, the movement for women's equality exists largely in the past. They're wrong about that. It's still happening, still as urgent and vital as ever.

And it was and is the story of my life—mine and millions of other women's. We share it. We wrote it together. We're still writing it. And even though this sounds like bragging and bragging isn't something women are supposed to do, I haven't just been a participant in this revolution. I've helped lead it.

I was one of just 27 women out of 235 students in my class at Yale Law School. The first woman partner at the oldest law firm in Arkansas. The first woman to chair the national board of the Legal Services Corporation. The person who declared on the world stage that "human rights are women's rights and women's rights are human rights." The first First Lady to be elected to public office. The first woman Senator from New York. In fact, for a few weeks, I was both. By a quirk of the calendar, I was sworn in before Bill left office.

And I was the first woman to be nominated for President by a major political party and win the national popular vote.

I never figured out how to tell this story right. Partly that's because I'm not great at talking about myself. Also, I didn't want people to see me as the "woman candidate," which I find limiting, but rather as the best candidate whose experience as a woman in a male-dominated culture made her sharper, tougher, and more competent. That's a hard distinction to draw, and I wasn't confident that I had the dexterity to pull it off.

But the biggest reason I shied away from embracing this narrative is that storytelling requires a receptive audience, and I've never felt like the American electorate was receptive to this one. I wish so badly we were a country where a candidate who said, "My story is the story of a life shaped by and devoted to the movement for women's liberation" would be cheered, not jeered. But that's not who we are. Not yet.

Maybe it's because we take this story for granted—yeah, yeah, the women's movement happened, why are we still talking about it? Maybe it's too female. Maybe it's at once too big (a sweeping historical shift) and too small (just another middle-class Midwestern girl finding her way in the world).

But I do think it's special.

It's not a typical political narrative, but it's mine.

This has to be said: sexism and misogyny played a role in the 2016 presidential election. Exhibit A is that the flagrantly sexist candidate won. A whole lot of people listened to the tape of him bragging about sexually assaulting women, shrugged, and said, "He still gets my vote."

But Donald Trump didn't invent sexism, and its impact on our politics goes far beyond this one election. It's like a planet that astronomers haven't precisely located yet but know exists because they can see its impact on other planets' orbits and gravities. Sexism exerts its pull on our politics and our society every day, in ways both subtle and crystal clear.

A note here on terminology. Others might have a different view, but here's how I see the distinction between sexism and misogyny. When a husband tells his wife, "I can't quite explain why and I don't even like admitting this, but I don't want you to make more money than me, so please don't take that amazing job offer," that's sexism. He could still love her deeply and be a great partner in countless ways. But he holds tight to an idea that even he knows isn't fair about how successful a woman is allowed to be. Sexism is all the big and little ways that society draws a box around women and says, "You stay in there." Don't complain because nice girls don't do that. Don't try to be something women shouldn't be. Don't wear that, don't go there, don't think that, don't earn too much. It's not right somehow, we can't explain why, stop asking.

We can all buy into sexism from time to time, often without even noticing it. Most of us try to keep an eye out for those moments and avoid them or, when we do misstep, apologize and do better next time.

Misogyny is something darker. It's rage. Disgust. Hatred. It's what happens when a woman turns down a guy at a bar and he switches from charming to scary. Or when a woman gets a job that a man wanted and instead of shaking her hand and wishing her well, he calls her a bitch and vows to do everything he can to make sure she fails.

Both sexism and misogyny are endemic in America. If you need convincing, just look at the YouTube comments or Twitter replies when a woman dares to voice a political opinion or even just share an anecdote from her own lived experience. People hiding in the shadows step forward just far enough to rip her apart.

Sexism in particular can be so pervasive, we stop seeing it. It reminds me of the opening anecdote from author David Foster Wallace's 2005 commencement speech at Kenyon College. Two young fish are swimming along. They meet an older fish swimming the other way, who nods at them and says, "Morning, boys, how's the water?" The two young fish swim on for a bit, until one looks at the other and asks, "What's water?"

"In other words," Wallace said, "the most obvious realities are often the ones that are the hardest to see and talk about."

I'd say that sums up the problem of recognizing sexism—especially when it comes to politics—quite nicely.

It's not easy to be a woman in politics. That's an understatement. It can be excruciating, humiliating. The moment a woman steps forward and says, "I'm running for office," it begins: the analysis of her face, her body, her voice, her demeanor; the diminishment of her stature, her ideas, her accomplishments, her integrity. It can be unbelievably cruel.

I hesitate to write this, because I know that women who should run for office might read it and say "no thanks," and I passionately believe that the only way we're going to get sexism out of politics is by getting more women into politics.

Still, I can't think of a single woman in politics who doesn't have stories to tell. Not one.

For the record, it hurts to be torn apart. It may seem like it doesn't bother me to be called terrible names or have my looks mocked viciously, but it does. I'm used to it—I've grown what Eleanor Roosevelt said women in politics need: a skin as thick as a rhinoceros hide. Plus, I've always had a healthy self-esteem, thanks no doubt to my parents, who never once told me that I had to worry about being prettier or thinner. To them, I was great exactly how I was. I don't know what magic they performed to make that stick in my head all these years—I wish I did, so that parents everywhere could learn the trick. All I know is, I've been far less plagued by self-doubt than a lot of women I know.

And yet . . . it hurts to be torn apart.

It didn't start with running for office. When I got glasses in the fourth grade—way smaller than the Coke-bottle ones I wore later in life—I was dubbed "four-eyes." It wasn't the most original taunt, but it stung. In junior high, a few unkind schoolmates noticed the lack of ankles on my sturdy legs and did their best to embarrass me. I did talk to my mom about that one. She told me to ignore it, to rise above, to be better. That advice prepared me well for a barrage of insults later on.

At college, I was spared some of the hostility many young women face because I went to Wellesley. Being at a women's college offered me the freedom to take risks, make mistakes, and even fail without making me question my fundamental worth. It also gave me opportunities to lead that I wouldn't have had at a coed college at that time. But once I left Wellesley, things changed.

When my friend and I went to take the law school admissions test in 1968, we were among the only women in the room. We were waiting for the test to start when a group of young men started harassing us. "You don't need to be here." "Why don't you go home and get married?" One said, "If you take my spot at law school, I'll get drafted, and I'll go to Vietnam, and I'll die." It was intense and personal. I just kept my eyes down, hoping the proctor would come to start the test, trying hard not to let them rattle me.

There was a professor at Harvard Law School who looked at me— a bright and eager college senior, recently offered admission—and said, "We don't need any more women at Harvard." That's part of why I went to Yale.

When I started out as an attorney, I would take cases in small rural courthouses in Arkansas, and people would come to watch the "lady lawyer"—it was such a novelty. You could hear them commenting from the gallery on what I was wearing and how my hair looked. One time in the early 1980s, I was trying a case in Batesville, Arkansas, and in the middle of the trial, in walked six men in full camouflage. They came in and sat right behind the lawyers and just stared hard at me. As any woman who's experienced that kind of staring knows, it was truly unnerving. Afterward the bailiff explained that it was deer season and these hunters had come into town from their camp for supplies. When they heard that a woman was trying a case in court, they had to see it for themselves.

I thought of that a few years later, when a woman doctor came to Arkansas from California to be an expert witness in a trial for my firm. She had short, spiky hair. My boss, the lead attorney on the case, told her to go buy a wig. Otherwise, he said, the jurors wouldn't be able to hear what she had to say. They'd be too focused on how she didn't look like a "normal" woman. I remember how taken aback she was at this request. I would have been too, not so long before, but by then I wasn't. That saddened me. I'd become used to a narrower set of expectations.

Once Bill entered politics, the spotlight on me was glaring and often unkind. I've written about this before but it's worth saying again: one of the reasons he lost the Governor's race in 1980 was because I still went by my maiden name. Let that sink in for a moment and please imagine how it felt. I was naïve. I didn't think anyone would care. Maybe people would even respect what it said about our marriage: that I wanted to preserve my pre-Bill identity, that I was proud of my parents and wanted to honor them, that Bill supported my choices. When he lost, and I heard over and over that my name—my name!—had played a part, I was heartsick that I might have inadvertently hurt my husband and let down his team. And I questioned whether there was room in public life for women like me, who might appear slightly unconventional but still had so much to offer.

So I added "Clinton" to Hillary Rodham. I asked my friends for hair, makeup, and clothing advice. That's never come easily to me, and until then, I didn't care. But if wearing contact lenses or changing my wardrobe would make people feel more comfortable around me, I'd try it.

Later, when Bill was running for President for the first time, I stumbled again. I now had the right name, wore makeup, styled my hair. But I hadn't tamed my tongue. One of Bill's opponents in the primary attacked my job at a Little Rock law firm as a way of going after Bill. This really got under my skin. "I suppose I could have stayed home and baked cookies and had teas," I told the press in exasperation, "but what I decided to do was pursue my profession." That did it. Suddenly I was in the middle of a full-blown political firestorm, with self-righteous moralists saying I had insulted American mothers. As someone who believes in supporting mothers, fathers, and families of all kinds, this hurt. And once again, I feared that my pursuit of my individual dreams—in this case, my career, which meant so much to me—would end up hurting my husband.

None of these experiences made me retreat from my beliefs. But I've never really been naïve again. Not much surprises me anymore. Throughout the 2016 campaign, my staff would come to me wide-eyed. "You'll never believe what Trump said today. It was vile." I always believed it. Not just because of who Trump is but because of who we can be at our worst. We've seen it too many times to be surprised.

In my experience, the balancing act women in politics have to master is challenging at every level, but it gets worse the higher you rise. If we're too tough, we're unlikable. If we're too soft, we're not cut out for the big leagues. If we work too hard, we're neglecting our families. If we put family first, we're not serious about the work. If we have a career but no children, there's something wrong with us, and vice versa. If we want to compete for a higher office, we're too ambitious. Can't we just be happy with what we have? Can't we leave the higher rungs on the ladder for men?

Think how often you've heard these words used about women who lead: angry, strident, feisty, difficult, irritable, bossy, brassy, emotional, abrasive, high-maintenance, ambitious (a word that I think of as neutral, even admirable, but clearly isn't for a lot of people).

The linguist George Lakoff both identified this problem and embodied it when he said about Senator Elizabeth Warren, "Elizabeth has a problem. She is shrill, and there is a prejudice against shrill women." How about we stop criticizing *how* she speaks—which is just fine, by the way—and start paying attention to *what* she has to say about families and the economy?

We're also called divisive, untrustworthy, unlikable, and inauthentic. Those words ring powerfully for me. As the campaign went on, polls showed that a significant number of Americans questioned my authenticity and trustworthiness. A lot of people said they just didn't like me. I write that matter-of-factly, but believe me, it's devastating.

Some of this is a direct result of my actions: I've made mistakes, been defensive about them, stubbornly resisted apologizing. But so have most men in politics. (In fact, one of them just became President with a strategy of "never apologize when you're wrong, just attack harder.")

I've been called divisive more times than I can count, and for the life of me, I can't understand why. Politics is a divisive business, it's true, and our country has gotten more polarized with every passing year. But what specifically did I do that was so unacceptable? Run for office? Lots of men do. Work on health care, one of the most contentious issues in America? Same. Cast votes as a Senator? So did my ninety-nine colleagues. When it comes to some of my most controversial actions—like my vote giving President Bush the authority to go to war in Iraq—I was far from alone. That doesn't make it right, but it also doesn't explain the venom targeted at me specifically. Why am I seen as such a divisive figure and, say, Joe Biden and John Kerry aren't? They've run for President. They've served at high levels of government. They've cast votes of all kinds, including some they regret, just like me. What makes me such a lightning rod for fury?

I'm really asking. I'm at a loss.

I know some of the distrust people feel toward me is because they've watched as I've been sucked into partisan investigations over the years—Whitewater, Travelgate, emails—each one carried out at significant taxpayer expense, each amounting to exactly nothing, but all of them leaving a mark on my reputation nearly impossible to erase.

But I think there's another explanation for the skepticism I've faced in public life. I think it's partly because I'm a woman.

Hear me out.

Historically, women haven't been the ones writing the laws or leading the armies and navies. We're not the ones up there behind the
podium, rallying crowds, uniting the country. It's men who lead. It's
men who speak. It's men who represent us to the world and even to
ourselves.

That's been the case for so long that it has infiltrated our deepest
thoughts. I suspect that for many of us—more than we might think—
it feels somehow *off* to picture a woman President sitting in the Oval
Office or the Situation Room. It's discordant to tune into a political
rally and hear a woman's voice booming ("screaming," "screeching")
forth. Even the simple act of a woman standing up and speaking to a
crowd is relatively new. Think about it: we know of only a handful of
speeches by women before the latter half of the twentieth century, and
those tend to be by women in extreme and desperate situations. Joan of
Arc said a lot of interesting things before they burned her at the stake.

Meanwhile, when a woman lands a political punch—and not even
a particularly hard one—it's not read as the normal sparring that men
do all the time in politics. It makes her a "nasty woman." A lot of
women have had that spat in their faces (and worse) for saying not that
much at all. God forbid two women have a disagreement in public.
Then it's a catfight.

In short, it's not customary to have women lead or even to engage
in the rough-and-tumble of politics. It's not normal—not yet. So when
it happens, it often doesn't feel quite right. That may sound vague, but
it's potent. People cast their votes based on feelings like that all the
time.

I think this question of "rightness" is connected to another powerful but undefinable force in politics: authenticity. I've been asked
over and over again by reporters and skeptical voters, "Who are you
really?" It's kind of a funny question when you think about it. I'm . . .
Hillary. You've seen me in the papers and on your screens for more than

twenty-five years. I'll bet you know more about my private life than you do about some of your closest friends. You've read my emails, for heaven's sake. What more do you need? What could I do to be "more real"? Dance on a table? Swear a blue streak? Break down sobbing? That's not me. And if I *had* done any of those things, what would have happened? I'd have been ripped to pieces.

Again, I wonder what it is about me that mystifies people, when there are so many men in politics who are far less known, scrutinized, interviewed, photographed, and tested. Yet they're asked so much less frequently to open up, reveal themselves, prove that they're real.

Some of this has to do with my composure. People say I'm guarded, and they have a point. I think before I speak. I don't just blurt out whatever comes to mind. It's a combination of my natural inclination, plus my training as a lawyer, plus decades in the public eye where every word I say is scrutinized. But why is this a bad thing? Don't we want our Senators and Secretaries of State—and especially our Presidents— to speak thoughtfully, to respect the impact of our words?

President Obama is just as controlled as I am, maybe even more so. He speaks with a great deal of care; takes his time, weighs his words. This is generally and correctly taken as evidence of his intellectual heft and rigor. He's a serious person talking about serious things. So am I. And yet, for me, it's often experienced as a negative.

Even some fair-minded people who want to like me feel that there's something too controlled about how I speak. Often, it's just about finding the right words. And *impulsive* doesn't mean the same thing as *truthful*. Just look at Donald Trump.

Still, there's no denying that my cautiousness has had the effect of making some people feel like they weren't getting the unvarnished me, which in turn prompted the question "What is she hiding?" This frustrated me to no end, and I never figured out how to solve it. I'm not sure there was a solution.

It's another variant on the impossible balancing act. If we're too

composed, we're cold or fake. But if we say what we think without caution, we get slammed for it. Can you blame us for feeling like we can't
win, no matter what we do?

Consider another emotional act: crying. I can think of many male
politicians who have teared up from time to time. Some have been
mocked for it; Senator Ed Muskie's political career was all but scut-
tled by his tears in the 1972 New Hampshire primary, even though
it may have just been snow blowing in his eyes. But many men have
been treated with compassion and even admiration for their displays of
emotion. Ronald Reagan, George H. W. Bush, Bob Dole, my husband,
George W. Bush, Barack Obama—they've all welled up at moments
of high sentiment. That makes sense because they are humans, and
sometimes humans cry.

But when a woman cries, it can be viewed far less charitably. I remember what happened to Pat Schroeder, the talented and hilarious
Congresswoman from Colorado who considered running for President in 1987. She ultimately decided against it, and when she held a
press conference to announce that, she cried for about three seconds.
Today, when you type "Pat Schroeder" into Google, the very first sug-
gestion is "Pat Schroeder crying." Twenty years later, she was *still* receiving hate mail because of it—mostly from women who felt like she
let them down.

I had my own famed tearful moment, just before the New Hampshire primary in 2008. I didn't even cry, not really. I was talking about
how tough running for office can be (because it can be very tough),
and my eyes glistened for a moment and my voice quavered for about
one sentence. That was it. It became the biggest news story in America.
It will, no doubt, merit a line in my obituary someday: "Her eyes once
watered on camera."

Interestingly, many would say that my tears turned out to be a good
thing for me. Dozens if not hundreds of pundits have commented
about how that moment "humanized" me. Maybe that's true. If so, I'm

both fine with that and a little beleaguered at the reminder that, yet again, I—a human—required "humanizing" at all.

Still, some sought to capitalize on my perceived vulnerability in the press and on the campaign trail. When he was asked about my tears, former Democratic Senator John Edwards of North Carolina, who was still in the presidential race at the time, jumped at the chance to call me weak. "I think what we need in a Commander in Chief is strength and resolve," he said. "Presidential campaigns are a tough business, but being President of the United States is also a very tough business. And the President of the United States is faced with very, very difficult challenges every single day and difficult judgments every single day. What I know is that I'm prepared for that." Shortly after, he dropped out.

In any case, this whole topic of "being real" can feel very silly. I wish we could just dismiss it and go about our business, whoever we are, without worrying about whether we are satisfying some indefinable standard of realness. As the Nigerian author Chimamanda Ngozi Adichie writes, "It's not your job to be likable. It's your job to be yourself."

Yet the issues of authenticity and likability had an impact on the most consequential election of our lifetimes, and it will have an impact on future ones. So there's something extremely serious going on here, too—especially since crude, abusive, fact-free rhetoric was characterized as authentic in 2016.

I've tried to adjust. After hearing repeatedly that some people didn't like my voice, I enlisted the help of a linguistic expert. He said I needed to focus on my deep breathing and try to keep something happy and peaceful in mind when I went onstage. That way, when the crowd got energized and started shouting—as crowds at rallies tend to do—I could resist doing the normal thing, which is to shout back. Men get to shout back to their heart's content but not women. Okay, I told this expert, I'm game to try. But out of curiosity, can you give me an example of a woman in public life who has pulled this off successfully—who has met the energy of a crowd while keeping her voice soft and low? He could not.

I'm not sure how to solve all this. My gender is my gender. My voice is my voice. To quote Secretary of Labor Frances Perkins, the first woman to serve in the U.S. Cabinet, under FDR, "The accusation that I'm a woman is incontrovertible." Other women will run for President, and they will be women, and they will have women's voices. Maybe that will be less unusual by then. Maybe my campaign will have helped make it that way, and other women will have an easier time. I hope so.

Near the start of my campaign, I met with my friend Sheryl Sandberg, the chief operating officer of Facebook, who has thought about these issues a great deal. She told me that if there was one thing she wanted everyone to know from her book *Lean In: Women, Work, and the Will to Lead*, it's this: the data show that for men, likability and professional success are correlated. The more successful a man is, the more people like him. With women, it's the exact opposite. The more professionally successful we are, the less people like us. Hearing it put that simply, with data behind it, felt like a lightbulb turning on. Here was proof of something so many women have felt intuitively throughout our lives.

Sheryl shared another insight: that women are seen favorably when they advocate for others, but unfavorably when they advocate for themselves. For example, there's virtually no downside to asking for a raise if you're a man. You'll either get it or you won't, but either way, you won't be penalized for trying. A woman who does the same is more likely to pay a price. Even if she gets a salary bump, she'll lose a measure of goodwill. The exception is when a woman asks for a raise on someone else's behalf. Then she's seen as generous and a team player. This, too, resonated with me. People like me when I'm in a supporting role: campaigning for my husband, serving as a member of President

Obama's Cabinet. It's okay for me to be a fierce advocate in those ca-
pacities. But when I stand up and say, "Now I'd like a chance to lead,"
everything changes.

You have a steep mountain to climb, Sheryl warned that day. "They
will have no empathy for you."

It's not easy for any woman in politics, but I think it's safe to say that
I got a whole other level of vitriol flung my way. Crowds at Trump
rallies called for my imprisonment more times than I can count. They
shouted, "Guilty! Guilty!" like the religious zealots in *Game of Thrones*
chanting "Shame! Shame!" while Cersei Lannister walked back to the
Red Keep. As Susan Bordo, a Pulitzer Prize–nominated gender studies
professor, put it in her book *The Destruction of Hillary Clinton*, "It was
almost medieval." Mary Beard, the Classics professor at the University
of Cambridge, observed that this venom harkened back to an even
earlier time. One popular image among Trump supporters, found on
everything from T-shirts to coffee mugs, depicted Trump holding up
my severed head, like Perseus from ancient Greek mythology, lifting
high the head of Medusa.

What in the world was this? I've been in politics for a long time,
but I was taken aback by the flood of hatred that seemed only to grow
as we got closer to Election Day. I had left the State Department one
of the most admired public servants in America. Now people seemed
to think I was evil. Not just "not my cup of tea" but evil. It was flab-
bergasting and frightening.

Was this all because I'm a woman? No. But I believe it was motivation for some of those chanters and some of that bile.

Later I read an interview with Margaret Atwood, the prescient author
of *The Handmaid's Tale*, which put the campaign into yet another historical
light. "You can find websites that say Hillary was actually a Satanist with
demonic powers," she said. "It's so seventeenth century that you can hardly

believe it." The Puritan witch hunts may be long over, but something fa-
natical about unruly women still lurks in our national subconscious.

That doesn't just affect me and other candidates. It affects our
supporters. Nearly four million people joined a Facebook group supporting my campaign, fittingly called Pantsuit Nation. It was a secret
group. It had to be. Otherwise its members were exposing themselves
to vicious sexist online harassment, from both the right and the left.

You can hardly open a newspaper these days without reading another grim story: female engineers reporting blatant harassment in Silicon Valley; women entrepreneurs making pitches to investment firms
and being propositioned in response; a new study finding that women
are given a harder time than men in job interviews; another finding
that women are penalized when they decline to reveal their salary history, while men end up making more when they do the same.

That's why it's so maddening that the basic fact that sexism is alive
and well should still be up for debate. I can't count the number of times
that good-hearted men who should know better dismiss the notion
that sexism and outright misogyny are still potent forces in our national life. "But things have changed," they say, as Donald Trump brags
about groping women and a few weeks later wins the presidency, as his
rally-goers chant "Trump that bitch," as the White House proudly re-
leases photos of old white men gleefully deciding which health services
to take away from women.

And on that fundamental question of whether it would be good to
see a woman—any woman, not just me—become President, the electorate is deeply, depressingly divided. A 2014 Pew Research Center
poll found that 69 percent of Democratic women and 46 percent of
Democratic men (not terrible, but you can do better than that, Democratic men!) said they hoped to see a female President in their lifetime,
but only 20 percent of Republican women and only 16 percent of Republican men did. In 2008, researchers found that more than a quarter
of the population expressed anger or upset feelings at the mere thought

of a female President. And after the 2016 election, the Diane D. Blair
Center of Southern Politics and Society at the University of Arkansas put out a report on the impact of sexism on the race. Researchers
asked people to respond to five statements that reflect sexist thinking, including "Feminists are seeking for women to have more power
than men" and "Discrimination against women is no longer a problem
in the United States." In results that surprised no one, more than a
third of respondents gave answers that were sexist. Trump voters were
more sexist than Clinton voters. Republicans were far more sexist than
Democrats. And not just men; women were quite sexist, too.

On that note, beginning even before I ran, political commentators wondered whether I'd inspire an unbeatable wave of women to
come out and vote for me, in the same way President Obama inspired
record-breaking black turnout. I hoped I would, of course, but I had
my doubts. Gender hasn't proven to be the motivating force for women
voters that some hope it might be. If it were, we'd probably have had a
woman president or two by now, don't you think? In the end, I won an
overwhelming majority of the votes of black women (94 percent) and
Latino women (68 percent), and I won women overall by a safe margin
(54 percent). But I failed to win a majority of white women, although
I did better with them than Obama did in 2012.

So yes, things have changed. Some things are a lot better. But many
are still bad. And they are connected—the bad is the backlash to the
good. Women's advancement has set into motion vast changes that inspire intense feelings of all kinds. Some of us are exhilarated. Others
feel a whole lot of rage.

The good news—and there is good news—is that there's another side
to all of this. It can also be deeply rewarding to be a woman in politics.
You know that just by being in the room, you're making government
more representative of the people. You're bringing a vital perspective

that would otherwise go unheard. That always made me stand up a little straighter. It's why I love the song "The Room Where It Happens" from Lin-Manuel Miranda's brilliant musical *Hamilton*:

> *No one really knows how the game is played*
> *The art of the trade*
> *How the sausage gets made*
> *We just assume that it happens*
> *But no one else is in the room where it happens.*

It felt really good to be in rooms where things happen—the Oval Office, the Senate chamber—as an advocate for issues that mattered to me: education, equal pay, health care, women's rights. Maybe those issues would have been close to my heart even if I were a man, but maybe not. Life naturally pushed me in their direction. A young mom interested in policy often ends up working on kids' issues. A First Lady is often involved with women's issues. That was okay with me. Some might have found it limiting, but I consider these real-life issues that affect us all.

Later, I moved into different realms: working to rebuild New York after 9/11 as a hometown Senator, supporting our troops and caring for our wounded warriors and all our vets as a member of the Senate Armed Services Committee, keeping our country and world safe as U.S. Secretary of State. I moved into different rooms: the Situation Room, foreign ministries, the United Nations. And I found that the decades of work I had done on women and families served me well in all those places, because it meant that I understood the intricacies of people's lives. I knew how governments could help or hurt families. I knew how to marshal resources and support to the people who needed them most. It turned out that my work on so-called women's and children's issues prepared me well for nearly everything else I've ever done.

I also believe the fact that I'm a woman is one reason why so many people open up to me about the details of their lives and families. They tell me about their children's medical diagnoses, their caregiving of aging parents, troubles in their marriages and family's finances, painful experiences with sexual harassment and discrimination. Warmhearted male politicians also receive these confessionals, but from what I can see, women hear them more often. Maybe it's easier to cry in front of us. Maybe it feels like talking to a girlfriend. All I know is that a lot of people have grabbed my hand and told me their worries and dreams, and that's been a unique privilege.

There's another thing that women confide in me about, and that's stories of their reproductive health. No essay about women in politics could be complete without talking about this. It is such a central part of women's lives: whether we become mothers and at what age and under what circumstances. Reproductive health in all its complexity—pregnancy, fertility, birth control, miscarriage, abortion, labor, birth—can comprise some of the most joyful and terrifying moments we will ever experience. But a lot of the time, we process these moments in silence. These stories go unspoken, even among women. Then I meet women at rallies or dinners or fund-raisers, or just taking a walk, and they take a deep breath and let it all out.

At this moment in America, more than forty-four years since *Roe v. Wade*, women's access to birth control and abortion is still under constant threat. I saw the effect of this in the 2016 election. Reproductive health was rarely mentioned in any of the primary debates, and when it was mentioned, it was often because I brought it up. I was dismayed when Bernie Sanders dismissed Planned Parenthood as just another part of "the establishment" when they endorsed me over him. Few organizations are as intimately connected to the day-to-day lives of Americans from all classes and backgrounds as Planned Parenthood, and few are under more persistent attack. I'm not sure what's "establishment" about that, and I don't know why someone running to be the Democratic nominee for President would say so.

After the election, Bernie suggested that Democrats should be open to nominating and supporting candidates who are anti-choice. Other topics, such as economic justice, are sacrosanct, but apparently women's health is not. I don't mean to criticize only Bernie here—a lot of progressives join him in thinking that reproductive rights are negotiable. And to be clear, I believe there's room in our party for a wide range of personal views on abortion. I've been working for a quarter century with Democrats and Republicans alike to reduce the number of abortions, in part by expanding access to birth control and family planning, and we've made progress. And I picked as my running mate Tim Kaine, a Democrat personally opposed to abortion because of his Catholic faith but supportive of women's rights as a matter of law and policy.

But when personal views on abortion become public actions— votes on legislation or judges or funding that erode women's rights— that's a different matter. We have to remain a big tent, but a big tent is only as strong as the poles that hold it up. Reproductive rights is central to women's rights and women's health, and it's one of the most important tent poles we've got. And remember: it's a constitutional right as defined in *Roe v. Wade*.

There's overwhelming evidence about what happens when these rights are denied. Texas has defunded Planned Parenthood and refused to expand Medicaid, and maternal mortality doubled between 2010 and 2014. That's the worst in the nation, and it's higher than the rate in many developing countries. Six hundred women have died in Texas— not from abortions, but from trying to give birth. The number of Texas teenagers having abortions actually increased when support for family planning was cut. In one county, Gregg, it went up 191 percent between 2012 and 2014.

Ultimately, I'm pro-choice, pro-family, and pro-faith because

I believe that our ability to decide whether and when to become mothers is intrinsic to our liberty. When government gets involved in this intimate realm—whether in places like China, which forced women to have abortions, or in Communist Romania, which forced women to bear children—it is horrific. I've visited hospitals in countries where poor women have no access to safe and legal abortion. I've seen what happens when desperate women take matters into their own hands.

As I see it, this issue comes down to the question: Who decides? We can debate the morality of abortion forever—and I have spent many hours engaged in such debates and surely will spend many more—but at the end of the day, who decides whether a woman gets or stays pregnant? A Congressman who has never met her? A judge who has spoken with her for maybe a few minutes? Or should the woman be able to make this momentous decision about her life, her body, her future, for herself?

Someone's got to decide. I say let women decide.

I'm not sure what we call our current era of feminism—I've lost count of which wave we're in. But there's a lot that feels new. There are all these new words. *Mansplaining.* The second I heard it, I thought, "Yes! We needed a word for that!" *Intersectionality*: an academic term for that vital idea that feminism must engage race and class. *Revenge porn. Trolls.* Modern twists on ancient harms.

While we're defining things, let's take a moment for *feminism*: "the advocacy of women's rights on the basis of the political, economic, and social equality of the sexes." Not domination. Not oppression. Equality. Or as the English writer and philosopher Mary Wollstonecraft put it 225 years ago, "I do not wish women to have power over men, but over themselves."

Then there's *emotional labor*. Now, that's a good one. It describes all the unpaid, uncounted, often unseen work that people—overwhelmingly women—perform to keep their families and workplaces humming along. Organizing office birthday parties. Arranging the kids' summer camp. Coordinating visits with in-laws. Helping the new employee feel welcome and included. The list is endless: all the little details without which life would devolve into chaos and misery. Not all women take on these tasks, and that's fine, and some men do, and I salute them—but it's largely women's work. Finally, someone thought to name it.

In my marriage, I've definitely been the one to perform the bulk of the emotional labor. I'm the one who schedules family visits, vacations, and dinners with friends. Bill has many positive qualities, but managing the logistical details of a household is not one of them. Of course, our situation is unique. For years, he was a Governor, then the President. He wasn't going to be the parent keeping track of the SAT registration deadline, although he always knew exactly what Chelsea was studying in school. We've also been privileged, since moving into the Governor's mansion years ago, to have people helping ensure that we're well fed and taken care of. Neither of us has had to make an emergency run to the store to pick up milk in decades. Still, even our privileged lives require a lot of small but vital actions and decisions to keep rolling along, and I'm the one who tends to handle them.

That labor extends to my friendships. In March 2017, a few of my close girlfriends came to New York for the weekend. A new friend joined us and asked, "How do you all know each other?" That led to my friends going around the table explaining in great detail how I have lovingly interfered in their lives over the years. "When I got sick, Hillary hounded me until I went to her doctor and called me immediately after for a full report." "That's nothing! When my little girl cut her face, Hillary insisted I get a plastic surgeon and then called back ten minutes later with the best one in Washington on the phone." They knew me well.

It happens at work, too. I make sure everyone has eaten, that my staff is wearing sunscreen if we're at an event in the baking sun. When reporters who traveled abroad with us got sick or injured, I made sure they had ginger ale and crackers and would send the State Department doctor to their room with Cipro and antinausea drugs.

None of this is unusual. I've seen women CEOs serve coffee at meetings, women heads of state walk tissues over to a sneezing staffer. It's also not new. It was women like Dr. Dorothy Height who did a lot of the unglamorous work of the civil rights movement, recruiting volunteers and organizing workshops and coordinating sit-ins and freedom rides. It is women who do a lot of the daily knitting in Congress, identifying problems, bringing together stakeholders, building effective coalitions. It's often women who handle constituent outreach, answering phones and responding to letters and emails. And in my experience, a lot of women make those calls and write those letters to Congress. We're not just the designated worriers in our families; we're also the designated worriers for our country.

I think all this may help explain why women leaders around the world tend to rise higher in parliamentary systems, rather than presidential ones like ours. Prime ministers are chosen by their colleagues— people they've worked with day in and day out, who've seen firsthand their talents and competence. It's a system designed to reward women's skill at building relationships, which requires emotional labor.

Presidential systems aren't like that. They reward different talents: speaking to large crowds, looking commanding on camera, dominating in debates, galvanizing mass movements, and in America, raising a billion dollars. You've got to give it to Trump—he's hateful, but it's hard to look away from him. He uses his size to project power: he looms over the podium, gets in interviewers' faces, glowers, threatens to punch people. I watched a video of one of our debates with the sound off and discovered that, between his theatrical arm waving and face making and his sheer size and aggressiveness, I watched him a lot more than I watched me. I'm guessing a lot of voters did the same thing. I also suspect that if a woman was as aggressive or melodramatic as he is, she'd be laughed or booed off the stage. In the end, even though I was judged to have won all three of our debates, his supporters awarded him points for his hypermasculine, aggressive behavior.

As for me, when it comes to politics, my style can be viewed as female. I've always focused on listening over speaking. I like town hall meetings because I get to hear from people and ask follow-up questions to my heart's content. I prefer one-on-one or small group conversations to big speeches and finding common ground over battling it out.

When I was a Senator, I spent a lot of time getting to know my colleagues, including gruff Republicans who wanted nothing to do with me at first. In 2000, Trent Lott, the Republican Leader, wistfully wondered if lightning would strike and I wouldn't take the oath of office. By 2016, he was telling people I was a very capable lady who did a good job—and he told my husband that I had done more to help the victims of Hurricane Katrina than anyone outside the Gulf Coast. A number of other conservative Republicans also came to like me when I was their colleague in the Senate, helping them pass bills, refilling their coffee cups in the Senate Dining Room, or sitting beside them in the Senate's private prayer meeting. One ultraconservative Senator came to see me to apologize for having hated me and saying terrible things about me over the years. He asked, "Mrs. Clinton, will you forgive me?" I know that might sound incredible now, but it's true. I told him that of course I would.

Dramatic spiritual conversions aside, emotional labor isn't particularly thrilling as far as the political media or some of the electorate is concerned. I've been dinged for being too interested in the details of policy (boring!), too practical (not inspiring!), too willing to compromise (sellout!), too focused on smaller, achievable steps rather than sweeping changes that have little to no chance of ever coming true (establishment candidate!).

But just as a household falls apart without emotional labor, so does politics grind to a halt if no one is actually listening to one another or reading the briefings or making plans that have a chance of working. I guess that might be considered boring. I don't find it boring, but you might. But here's the thing: someone has to do it.

In my experience, a lot of the time, it's women. A lot of the time, it's dismissed as not that important. And I don't think that's a coincidence.

"This is not okay," I thought.

It was the second presidential debate, and Donald Trump was looming behind me. Two days before, the world heard him brag about groping women. Now we were on a small stage, and no matter where I walked, he followed me closely, staring at me, making faces. It was incredibly uncomfortable. He was literally breathing down my neck. My skin crawled.

It was one of those moments where you wish you could hit Pause and ask everyone watching, "Well? What would *you* do?"

Do you stay calm, keep smiling, and carry on as if he weren't repeatedly invading your space?

Or do you turn, look him in the eye, and say loudly and clearly, "Back up, you creep, get away from me, I know you love to intimidate women but you can't intimidate me, so *back up*."

I chose option A. I kept my cool, aided by a lifetime of dealing with difficult men trying to throw me off. I did, however, grip the microphone extra hard.

I wonder, though, whether I should have chosen option B. It certainly would have been better TV. Maybe I have overlearned the lesson of staying calm—biting my tongue, digging my fingernails into a clenched fist, smiling all the while, determined to present a composed face to the world.

Of course, had I told Trump off, he surely would have capitalized on it gleefully. A lot of people recoil from an angry woman, or even just a direct one. Look at what happened to Elizabeth Warren, silenced in the Senate chamber for reading a letter from Coretta Scott King because it was critical of Jeff Sessions, a male Senator, during his confirmation hearing for Attorney General. (Moments later, Jeff Merkley, a male Senator, was allowed to read the letter. Funny how that worked.) Senator Kamala Harris was derided as "hysterical" for her entirely coolheaded and professional questioning of Jeff Sessions (him again) during a Senate hearing. As one writer put it, she was being "Hillary'd." Arianna Huffington was recently interrupted in a meeting of the Uber board of directors when she was making a point about—of all things— how important it was to increase the number of women on the board! And the man who talked over her did so to say that increasing women would only mean more talking! You can't make this up.

In other words, this isn't something that only happens to me. Not even close.

It also doesn't just happen to women on the Democratic side of politics. Trump made fun of Carly Fiorina's face because she competed against him for President. He lashed out against Megyn Kelly and Mika Brzezinski in gross, physical terms because they challenged him. Maybe that's why Nicolle Wallace, White House Communications Director for George W. Bush, has warned that the Republican Party is in danger of being "permanently associated with misogyny" if leaders don't stand up to Trump's treatment of women.

This hearkens back to a powerful ad we ran during the campaign called "Mirrors." It shows adolescent girls looking tentatively at themselves in the mirror—tucking their hair behind their ears, evaluating their profile, trying to decide if they are okay-looking, like so many girls do when they see themselves. Over their images, we ran a tape of cruel things Trump has said on the record about women over the years: "She's a slob." "She ate like a pig." "I'd look her right in that fat, ugly face of hers." Was this the voice we wanted in our daughters' heads? Our granddaughters'? Our nieces'? Or our sons' or grandsons' or nephews' heads for that matter? They deserve better than the toxic masculinity Trump embodies.

Well, he's in their heads now. His voice resounds far and wide.

Now it's on all of us to make sure his ugly words don't damage our girls—and boys—forever.

Two days before the debate, my team and I had finished a grueling morning debate prep session. We had taken a break for lunch. The television was on in the room, with no volume. Then a commentator came on to warn viewers that they were about to hear something vulgar. Boy, was that true.

I don't have a lot to say about the *Access Hollywood* tape that hasn't been said. I will just note that Donald Trump is gleefully describing committing sexual assault. That got somewhat lost in the shock of it all. Too many people focused on his boorishness—such a crude man, so vulgar. True. But even if he were the height of elegance and graciousness, it wouldn't make it okay that he's describing sexual assault.

For many, hearing the Donald Trump tape was literally sickening. As for me, it made me sad—for women and girls, for men and boys, for all of us. It was . . . horrible, just horrible. It still is. And it always will be, because that tape is never going away. It's part of our history now.

To divert attention from his own ugliness, Trump brought to our second debate three women who had accused my husband of bad acts decades ago, plus a woman whose accused rapist I had been ordered by a judge to represent back in Arkansas. It was an awful stunt.

I don't know what the Trump campaign was hoping to accomplish

other than the obvious: dredge up old allegations that had been lit-
igated years before, divert attention from the *Access Hollywood* tape,
throw me off my game, and distract voters from the election's unbelievably high stakes. He wasn't trying to make a stand for these women. He
was just using them.

This was a presidential debate. That's a big deal. We were supposed
to talk about issues that mattered to people's lives. Instead, Trump used
this moment to get back in his comfort zone. He loves to humiliate
women, loves to talk about how disgusting we are. He was hoping to
rattle me. I was determined not to give him that satisfaction.

Before I stepped onstage, Ron Klain said to me, "He's trying to get
in your head." I said, "Ya think?" Then I went out there and won the
debate.

Something I wish every man across America understood is how much
fear accompanies women throughout our lives. So many of us have
been threatened or harmed. So many of us have helped friends recover
from a traumatic incident. It's difficult to convey what all this violence
does to us. It adds up in our hearts and our nervous systems.

A few years ago, the hashtag #yesallwomen was trending for a
while. It spoke to me, like it did to so many others. In college and law
school, we had a million defensive habits: hold your keys like a weapon
when you're out alone at night, walk one another home no matter what.
Many women I know have been groped, grabbed, or worse. It even
happens to members of Congress. Senator Kirsten Gillibrand has written frankly about how Congressmen have leered at her and grabbed
her waist in the congressional gym.

I'm very lucky that nothing too bad ever happened to me. One
time in college, I went on a blind date with a young man who wouldn't
take repeated nos for an answer, and I had to slap him to get him away

from me. But he did back off, and I went to bed that night shaken but not traumatized. And when I was twenty-nine, working for Jimmy Carter's presidential campaign in Indiana, I had dinner one night with a group of older men who were in charge of the Democratic Party's get-out-the-vote operation in the state. I had been pestering them for a while for information about their Election Day plans, and they were annoyed with me. I started explaining once again what I needed to know from them and why. Suddenly one of the men reached across the table, grabbed me by my turtleneck, and yanked me toward him. He hissed in my face, "Just shut up." I froze, then managed to pull his hand from my neck, tell him to never touch me again, and walk out of the room on shaking legs. The whole incident probably lasted thirty seconds. I'll never forget it.

Yet that's nothing compared to the violence that millions of women and girls across our country endure on a regular basis.

About four months before Donald Trump's *Access Hollywood* tape was released, a very different message went viral. An unnamed woman known as Emily Doe who had been sexually assaulted while unconscious wrote a letter about her ordeal and read it in court to her attacker, a Stanford athlete. A friend forwarded the letter to me. I read it once, then immediately went back to the beginning and read it again. I hope I can meet the author someday and tell her how brave I think she is.

"To girls everywhere," she wrote, "I am with you . . .

> *On nights when you feel alone, I am with you. When people doubt you or dismiss you, I am with you. I fought every day for you. So never stop fighting, I believe you. As the author Anne Lamott once wrote, "Lighthouses don't go running all over an island looking for boats to save; they just stand there shining." Although I can't save every boat, I hope that by speaking today, you absorbed a small*

amount of light, a small knowing that you can't be silenced, a small
satisfaction that justice was served, a small assurance that we are
getting somewhere, and a big, big knowing that you are important,
unquestionably, you are untouchable, you are beautiful, you are to
be valued, respected, undeniably, every minute of every day, you are
powerful, and nobody can take that away from you.

Early on the morning of November 9, when it came time to decide on what I'd say in my concession speech, I remembered those words. Inspired by them, I wrote these:

"To all the little girls who are watching this, never doubt that you are valuable and powerful and deserving of every chance and opportunity in the world to pursue and achieve your own dreams."

Wherever she is, I hope Emily Doe knows how much her words and her strength meant to so many.

There's yet another side to the matter of women in politics. It's not just that politics can be rewarding for those women who choose to enter it. In the long run, it also makes our politics better for everyone. I believe this as strongly as I believe anything. We need our politics to resemble our people. When the people who run our cities, states, and country overwhelmingly look a certain way (say, white and male) and overwhelmingly have a shared background (wealthy, privileged) we end up with laws and policies that don't come close to addressing the realities of Americans' lives. And since that's a basic requirement of government, it's a pretty big thing to get wrong.

In other words, representation matters.

Is representation everything? Of course not. Just because I'm a woman, it doesn't mean I'd be a good President for women. (I would have been, but not only because of my gender.)

But it does matter, and often in concrete ways. I remember when I was pregnant with Chelsea, working at the Rose Law Firm in Little Rock, and repeatedly went to my superiors to ask about their maternity leave policy. They avoided the question until there was no longer any way to avoid it, then stammered that they didn't have a policy. "No woman who's worked here has ever come back after having a baby." So I wrote my own. I was a new partner and had the power to do that. But what about more junior lawyers or support staff? Would they have been expected to come in a few days after giving birth, or not come back to work at all? It took a woman in the room to notice a huge hole in the firm's policies and care enough to fix it.

Representation matters in less visible but no less valuable ways, too. I remember being riveted as a little girl whenever a woman appeared in our history lessons: Abigail Adams, Sojourner Truth, Ida Tarbell, Amelia Earhart. Even if it just amounted to a sentence in a dusty book—and often that's all they got—it thrilled me. The great men in our history books thrilled me too, but it meant something different, something quietly momentous, to learn that a woman had done something important. It opened the world up a little more. It made me dream a little bigger. I remember coming home from school and opening *Life* magazine to read about Margaret Chase Smith, the gutsy Republican Senator from Maine who stood up to Joe McCarthy. Years later, when I became First Lady, I wrote her a fan letter.

As a young woman, I was moved and inspired watching Barbara Jordan speak out eloquently for the rule of law on the House Judiciary Committee during the Watergate hearings; Geraldine Ferraro stand onstage as the vice presidential candidate for my party; Barbara Mikulski shake up the U.S. Senate; Dianne Feinstein take on the NRA; and Shirley Chisholm run for President. What hadn't felt possible suddenly was.

When Chelsea was a little girl, I saw the power of representation through a new lens. I watched her leaf through the pages of her children's books, searching intently for the girl characters. Now little girls have a new group of fictional heroines to look up to, including Wonder Woman and General Leia (she got a promotion from Princess). Slowly but surely, Hollywood is moving in the right direction.

That's why it meant so much to me to see all the little girls and young women at my campaign rallies and all the moms and dads pointing and saying, "Look. You see? She's running for President. You're smart like she is. You're tough like she is. You can be President. You can be anything you want to be."

After the election, I received a letter from a medical student named Kristin in Dearborn, Michigan. She wrote,

> I saw you speak for the first time as a small girl. My mom took me, and helped me up to stand on a fence and held me by the back of my overalls because I kept trying to wave to you and cheer you on. I was so ecstatic to hear such a smart woman speak, and I've never looked back. You never let that version of me down. I read your history as I got older, and then I got to see more speeches and read your writings. You never let down the older versions of me either.

To this day, even knowing how things turned out, the memories of all those proud and excited girls—and the thought of the women they will become—means more to me than I can express.

I know that there are some reading this who will sneer. Representation! It's so soft, so wimpy, so *liberal*. Well, if you can't imagine why it would matter for many of us to see a woman elected President—and that it wouldn't matter only to women, just like the election of Barack Obama made people of all races, not just African Americans, feel proud and inspired—I'd simply urge you to accept that it matters to many of your fellow Americans, even if it doesn't to you.

I wish so badly that I had been able to take the oath of office and achieve that milestone for women. Still, there were many feminist moments in this election we shouldn't forget. I will always remember Bill's speech at the 2016 Democratic National Convention. At one point, he uttered the memorable words, "On February 27, 1980, fifteen minutes after I got home from the National Governors Association conference in Washington, Hillary's water broke." Watching from our home in New York, I had to laugh. That was the first time *that* had ever been said about a presidential nominee. I thought it was about time.

There's another moment I want to note that a lot of people missed when it happened but which I will never forget.

A few days before election night 2016, Beyoncé and Jay-Z performed at a rally for me in Cleveland. Beyoncé took the microphone. "I want my daughter to grow up seeing a woman lead our country and know that her possibilities are limitless," she said. "We have to think about the future of our daughters, our sons, and vote for someone who cares for them as much as we do. And that is why I'm with her."

And then, that infamous 1992 quote appeared in giant block letters on a huge screen behind her. "I suppose I could have stayed home and baked cookies and had teas, but what I decided to do was pursue my profession."

Something that had been controversial was being reclaimed as a message of independence and strength—just like I had meant it to be all those years ago!—right before my eyes.

Thanks, Beyoncé.

Will we ever have a woman President? We will.

I hope I'll be around to vote for her—assuming I agree with her agenda. She'll have to earn my vote based on her qualifications and ideas, just like anyone else.

When that day comes, I believe that my two presidential campaigns will have helped pave the way for her. We did not win, but we made the sight of a woman nominee more familiar. We brought the possibility of a woman president closer. We helped bring into the mainstream the idea of a woman leader for our country. That's a big deal, and everyone who played a role in making that happen should feel deeply proud. This was worth it. I will never think otherwise. This fight was worth it.

That's why I am heartened that a wave of women across America have expressed more willingness to run for office after this election, not less. I'll admit, I was worried that it would go the other way. And I will always do my part to encourage more women to run and to send the message to little girls, teenagers, and young women that their dreams and ambitions are worth chasing.

Over the years, I've hired and promoted a lot of young women and young men. Much of the time, this is how it went:

ME: I'd like you to take on a bigger role.

YOUNG MAN: I'm thrilled. I'll do a great job. I won't let you
    down.

YOUNG WOMAN: Are you sure I'm ready? I'm not sure. Maybe
    in a year?

These reactions aren't innate. Men aren't naturally more confident than women. We tell them to believe in themselves, and we tell women to doubt themselves. We tell them this in a million ways, starting when they're young.

We've got to do better. Every single one of us.

What would happen if one woman told the truth about her life?
The world would split open.

—Muriel Rukeyser

Motherhood, Wifehood, Daughterhood, Sisterhood

I don't know what it's like for other women, but growing up, I didn't think that much about my gender except when it was front and center. Like in eighth grade, when I wrote to NASA to say that I dreamt of becoming an astronaut, and someone there wrote back: Sorry, little girl, we don't accept women into the space program. Or when the boy who beat me in a student government race in high school told me I was really stupid if I thought a girl could be elected President of the school. Or when I heard from Wellesley College: I was in. On these occasions, I felt my gender powerfully. But most of the time, I was just a kid, a student, a reader, a fan, a friend. The fact that I was female was secondary; sometimes it practically slipped my mind. Other women may have had different experiences, but that's how it was for me.

My parents made that possible. They treated my brothers, Hugh and Tony, and me like three individual kids, with three individual personalities, instead of putting me in a box marked "female" and them in a box marked "male." They never admonished me for "not acting like a girl" when I played baseball with the boys. They stressed the importance of education, because they didn't want their daughter to feel constrained by tired ideas of what women should do with our lives. They wanted more for me than that.

Later in life, I started to see myself differently when I took on roles that felt deeply and powerfully womanly: wife, daughter to aging parents, girlfriend, and most of all, mother and grandmother. These identities transformed me yet somehow also felt like the truest expressions of myself. They felt both like pulling on a new garment and shedding my skin.

I don't talk a lot about these pieces of my life. They feel private. They *are* private. But they're also universal experiences, and I believe in the value of women sharing our stories with one another. It's how we support each other through our private struggles and how we find the strength to build the best possible lives for ourselves.

These roles haven't been easy or painless. Sometimes they've been very painful indeed. But they have been worth it. My goodness, have they been worth it.

Years rolled on again, and Wendy had a daughter. This ought not to be written in ink but in a golden splash.

—J. M. Barrie

On the final night of the Democratic National Convention in July, my daughter introduced me to the nation. I was backstage, ready to walk onstage the instant she was done. At least, I was supposed to be ready. But I couldn't pull myself away from the television, where her face filled the screen. Hearing her talk, I was grateful for waterproof mascara. The fact that my poised, beautiful daughter was also standing up there as Charlotte and Aidan's mother—she had given birth to her son only five weeks earlier—made this even more special.

During a burst of applause near the end of her remarks, Jim Margolis, who was keeping his eye on the clock, yelled to me, "We've gotta go!" But Chelsea wasn't done, and I didn't want to miss any of it. Finally, Jim yelled, "Now we've *really* gotta go!" I snapped to attention, and we raced down the hall and up the stairs in the dark. I stepped out onstage in the nick of time.

From the moment she was born, Chelsea has captivated me. I suspect a lot of parents know what I mean. My child has me hooked. That night was no different. She looked so happy recounting stories of growing up. It's always interesting to me to hear her perspective of her childhood. You try so many things as a parent. I remember how hours after she was born, Bill walked around the hospital room with tiny Chelsea in his arms, explaining everything to her. We didn't want to waste a moment.

Here's what Chelsea talked about at the DNC: Our weekly trips to the library and church. Lazy afternoons outside lying on the grass and spotting shapes in the clouds. Playing a game of her invention, Which Dinosaur Is the Friendliest? She says I warned her not to be fooled, that even seemingly friendly dinosaurs were still dinosaurs. That sounds like me: wasting no opportunity to impart some practical advice, even in absurd circumstances.

She talked about her favorite books that we read to her and those she later read by herself and told us all about, like the science fantasy *A Wrinkle in Time*.

Mostly Chelsea talked about me always being there and how she always knew how much we loved and valued her. I cannot express the happiness it brings to hear my daughter say that. This was my number one priority every day of her childhood: making sure she knew that nothing was more important than her. I worried about this, because

Bill and I were extremely busy people. We worked long hours, we traveled frequently, and the phone in our house rang constantly, often with urgent news. It wouldn't be unexpected for a little girl growing up surrounded by all that to feel overlooked. Over the years, I've met politicians' kids who say, "I was pretty lonely. I had to compete with the whole world for my parents' attention." That was the worry that kept me up at night when Chelsea was young. I couldn't bear the thought.

One way we handled that was by not excluding her from our work. We talked about issues and politics with her starting from a young age. In her speech at the Democratic National Convention, she described how hard it was to see me lose the fight for health care reform in 1994, when she was fourteen. She was there to comfort me and help provide diversions, like watching *Pride and Prejudice* together.

For me, becoming a mother was the fulfillment of a long-held dream. I love children—love just sitting with them and being silly, love bringing smiles to their sweet faces. If you're ever looking for me at a party, you're likely to find me wherever the kids are. Before I even met my husband and thought about starting a family, I was a lawyer and advocate for children. When Bill and I learned that we were going to be parents, we were ecstatic. We jumped around our kitchen like we were kids ourselves.

Getting pregnant was not easy for me, but pregnancy itself was blessedly uneventful. Chelsea arrived three weeks early. I was gigantic and more than ready to meet my little one. Neither Bill nor I cared a bit whether the baby was a boy or girl. But when the doctor said, "It's a girl!" I felt so happy, it was like a sunburst beaming out of my chest. A girl!

I hadn't realized how much I wanted a daughter until she arrived. She was a wish so secret, I didn't even know that I had wished it. Then she was here, and I knew: she was what I always wanted.

If we'd had a son, I'm sure I would have been just as over the moon.

I would have realized at once that I had always wanted a son—a sweet little boy to raise into a strong and caring man.

But that's not what happened. We had a daughter. And not just any daughter but someone who brought such joy and love into our lives. It felt like fate. It was the greatest thing that ever happened to me by a mile.

There's just something about daughters. From the very beginning, I felt a rush of wisdom that I wanted to impart to her about womanhood: how to be brave, how to build real confidence and fake it when you have to, how to respect yourself without taking yourself too seriously, how to love yourself or at least try to and never stop trying, how to love others generously and courageously, how to be strong but gentle, how to decide whose opinion to value and whose to disregard quietly, how to believe in yourself even when others don't. Some of these lessons were hard-won for me. I wanted badly to save my daughter the trouble. Maybe Chelsea could skip all that and arrive more quickly at a place of self-assurance.

My desire to be the best mother in the world didn't translate into knowledge about how to do it. At first, I was pretty inept. In those early days, she wouldn't stop crying. I was nearly frantic. Finally, I sat down and tried my best to make eye contact with this squirming infant. "Chelsea," I said firmly, "this is new for both of us. I've never been a mother before. You've never been a baby. We're just going to have to help each other do the best we can." Those weren't magic words that stopped her wailing, but they helped, if for no other reason than that they reminded me I was completely new at this and should be gentle with myself.

Over the years, I've met so many frazzled new mothers who can't figure out how to soothe their babies or get them to nurse or sleep, and I see in their eyes that same discombobulation I felt in those early days of Chelsea's life. It reminds me all over again how having a newborn is like every switch in your body being flicked on simultaneously. Your brain becomes a one-track mind—is the baby okay, is the baby hungry, is the baby sleeping, is the baby breathing—playing on an endless loop. If you're a new mother reading this, sleep-deprived and semicoherent, maybe wearing a tattered sweatshirt and dreaming of your next shower, please know that so many of us have been right where you are. You're doing great. It'll get easier, so just hang in there. And maybe ask your partner or mom or friend to take over for a few hours so you can have that shower and get some sleep.

Chelsea was born in 1980, a time when opportunities for women were greater than ever before in human history. She wouldn't face some of the closed doors I had. Bill and I were determined that our daughter was never going to hear "Girls can't do that." Not if we could help it.

What I couldn't know back then, holding this tiny baby in my arms, is how much she would teach me about courage, confidence, and grace. Chelsea has an inner strength that amazes me. She is smart, thoughtful, observant, and even under stress or attack, conducts herself with poise and self-possession. She is gifted at friendship, always eager to meet new people but also comfortable with solitude. She trusts her mind and feeds it constantly. She stands up for what she believes. She is one of the toughest people I know, but her toughness is quiet and deliberate, easy to underestimate. That makes her even more formidable. Her smile is full of real joy.

Bill and I had a hand in all of this, I'm sure. But Chelsea has been Chelsea from the very start. I think most parents find that their children are more formed when they arrive than we expect. It's like Kahlil Gibran wrote in *The Prophet*: "Your children are not your children. They come through you but not from you. You may give them your love but not your thoughts, for they have their own thoughts. You may strive to be like them, but seek not to make them like you, for life goes not backward, nor tarries with yesterday."

Like all moms, I wanted to protect Chelsea from illness and injury, bullies, disappointments, and a dangerous world. I also had a different set of threats in mind, which are particular to the daughters of public figures. She grew up on the front page of newspapers. She was attacked by right-wing personalities on the radio and mocked on television when she was just thirteen years old—it still makes my blood boil. There were plenty of nights when I wondered if we had made a terrible mistake by subjecting her to this life. I worried not just that she'd feel self-conscious but also that she'd become too practiced in the art of putting on a happy face for the cameras. I wanted her to have a rich interior life: to be sincere and spontaneous; to own her feelings, not stifle them. In short, I wanted her to be a real person with her own identity and interests.

The only way I knew how to do that was to make her life as normal as possible. Chelsea had chores at the White House. If she wanted a new book or game, she had to save her allowance to buy it. When she was bratty—to her credit, an extremely rare occurrence—she was chastised and sometimes punished. Our go-to was no TV or phone privileges for a week.

But there's a limit to how much you can make life normal for the President's daughter. So we also decided to embrace and celebrate the incredible opportunities that her unusual childhood and adolescence afforded. She went on visits overseas with us: touring the Forbidden City in China, riding an elephant in Nepal, having conversations with Nelson Mandela. She even found herself at fourteen discussing *One Hundred Years of Solitude* with Gabriel García Márquez. Since she had always been interested in science and health, Bill made a point of introducing her to just about every scientist and doctor who visited the White House. She relished these conversations and experiences. "This is so cool!" she said the first time we saw Camp David, on her first flight on Air Force One, when she came along as I led the U.S.

delegation to the 1994 Winter Olympics in Norway. I watched her—
the questions she asked, her excited reflections on everything we saw
and experienced—and was delighted. She never grew bored or acted
entitled. She knew how special it all was.

Perhaps most important to me, Chelsea never needed to be reminded to thank everyone who made our lives both extraordinary and
ordinary: the White House staff, her teachers, her Secret Service detail,
her friends' parents. She treated them all the exact same way—even
heads of state. Her gratitude toward the people in her life ran deep. It
led to many "proud mom" moments for me, as the kids would say.

Over the years, I worried about Chelsea less and less, as it became clear I didn't have to. I also learned from her more and more. In
stressful moments, she's the calmest person in the room. She also seizes
every chance to be silly with her friends and, now, her kids. These are
the actions of someone who understands that life will throw a lot of
challenges your way, and you should build up your inner resources of
peace and happiness whenever you can.

And as was particularly evident in the 2016 campaign, she's intrepid. Chelsea traveled far and wide campaigning for me, and she did
it with Aidan, whom she was still nursing. It's like that line from the
late Ann Richards, the Governor of Texas: "Ginger Rogers did everything Fred Astaire did, just backward and in high heels." Chelsea did
everything an energetic campaign surrogate would do, just with a tiny
baby attached to her and all the gear that he required.

She'd call me from the road to tell me everything that she was seeing and hearing. "I'm not sure we're breaking through," she said, both
during the primary and the general. "It feels really hard to get the facts
out." Her time on the 2016 campaign trail started with a bang. On her
very first day, when she politely raised questions about Bernie's health
care plan—she has a master's degree in public health and a doctorate in
international relations with a focus on public health institutions, so she
knows what she's talking about—she got absolutely hammered for it.

I remember our conversation on the phone that night. Chelsea was frustrated with herself that her words didn't match what she knew or felt. (I can empathize!) She left some people with the impression that she thought Bernie wanted to get rid of all health care—an absurd notion and of course not what she meant or said. She felt awful—awful that she had left a false impression about anything, with anyone, and especially because it was related to something that she understands and cares about deeply. I wished I could give her a big hug. Instead, we talked it out.

Our conversation might seem a little different from the average mother-daughter talk, but underneath, it's a lot like anyone's. We started in problem-solving mode. We reviewed the policy and how better to talk about the differences between Bernie's plan and mine. Chelsea had been right on the specifics that day: at that stage in the campaign, Bernie's health care plan called for starting over to get to single payer, which is what she said. But we both knew that wasn't going to matter at this point. We returned to the basics: why my plan to improve the Affordable Care Act and add a public option was the right one to get to universal coverage. As you can tell, Chelsea and I are thought partners on this topic in particular, and her approach to thinking through problems and solutions is a lot like mine. (We recently shared a smile and a sigh when we heard Bernie called for improving the Affordable Care Act immediately by embracing the approach that I proposed as a candidate: a public option in fifty states and lowering the Medicare age to fifty-five.)

We gave ourselves a few minutes to vent about all the hate that at times seemed visceral toward me, our family, and all women stepping out. Then we switched gears and put the frustrating day behind us. We laughed about a photo of Charlotte at ballet class that Marc had sent us. We talked about how glad we were that Chelsea's low-level nausea seemed to have passed. (She was a few months pregnant.) And we said our I-love-yous and hung up, knowing that tomorrow would be another opportunity to make our case and grateful that we had each other's backs.

Every day, I was humbled by her fierce support of me. As a candidate, I was glad to have her in my corner, working diligently to explain important issues and why she believed so deeply in my plans—and me. And as her mom, I was and am so proud that she continues to rise above the attacks hurled at her every single day.

More than anyone else, it was Chelsea who helped me to see that my stance on same-sex marriage was incompatible with my values and the work I had done in the Senate and at the State Department to protect the rights of LGBT people. She impressed upon me that I had to endorse marriage equality if I was truly committed to equal human dignity, and as soon as I left the State Department, I did. Later, when I received the endorsement of the Human Rights Campaign, I thought of her. And it was Chelsea who told me about the Zika virus long before it was in the newspapers. "This is going to be a huge problem," she said, and she was right. We're still not doing enough.

When Charlotte was born, I felt the joy that comes with seeing your child take the great reservoir of love she has and enlarge it to include her own children, along with a true partner of her own. Marc is a great dad, and together they are fantastic parents. Sometimes Chelsea and I do a dance that I expect is familiar to a lot of new moms and grandmothers out there: I'll go to put the baby down for a nap or feed the toddler a snack, and Chelsea will swoop in. "Mom, that's not the way I do that." She can recite the latest American Academy of Pediatrics guidelines on sleep, infant feeding, and screen time, and I get to enjoy the special pleasure that comes from being a grandparent and knowing you don't have to worry about the baby, because your child is handling the worrying. You can just focus on being the most loving and helpful grandparent you can be.

Chelsea has been by my side at every difficult moment since she arrived on this planet, and I've leaned on her more than I ever thought I would. Late on election night, when it was clear I had lost, she was sitting next to me, looking at me with a face full of love, sending all her considerable strength and grace toward me as hard as she could. As always, she helped see me through the darkness.

I was confident that Bill would be great at parenting. His father died before Bill was born; he knew how lucky he was to have this chance that his own father never had. Still, a lot of men are thrilled to be dads but not so thrilled about all the work that a child requires. The writer Katha Pollitt has observed how even the most egalitarian relationships can contort under the strain of child rearing, and all of a sudden the mom is expected to do everything, while the dad pitches in here and there. She calls it becoming "gender Republicans"—a nifty phrase, if perhaps a little unfair to all the feminist Republicans out there, who really do exist.

I knew that I had enough energy and devotion for two, if it turned out that Bill wasn't a co-equal in the child-raising department. But I really hoped that wouldn't happen. Our marriage had always been a true partnership. Though he was Governor and then President—jobs that would seem to "beat" a lot of others, if you were the kind of person who ranked jobs like that—my career was important to me, too. So was my time and, more broadly, my identity. I couldn't wait to become a mother, but I didn't want to lose everything else about myself in the becoming. I was counting on my husband not just to respect that but also to join me in guarding against it.

So it was a wonderful thing when Chelsea arrived, and Bill dove into parenting with characteristic gusto. We arrived at the hospital with Bill clutching the materials from the Lamaze classes we had attended together. When it turned out that Chelsea was breech, he fought to be in the operating room with me and hold my hand during the C-section. Being Governor came in handy when he asked to be the first father ever permitted by that hospital to do so. After we brought her home, he handled countless midnight feedings and diaper changes. We took turns making sure the parade of family and friends who wanted to spend time with Chelsea were looked after. As our daughter grew up, we both read her good-night stories. We both got to know her teachers and coaches. Even when Bill became President, he rearranged his schedule as much as he could to have dinner with us nearly every night that he was in Washington. And when he was somewhere else in the world, he'd call Chelsea to talk about her day and go over her homework with her.

Every year, our daughter adored her father more and more. As she entered adolescence, I wondered if that would change at all. I remembered how my own dad and I grew somewhat distant from each other once I became a teenager. I provoked him with a lot of fiery political arguments. He was at a loss to navigate the occasionally stormy seas of teenage girlhood. Would that happen with Chelsea and Bill? As it turned out, no. He lived for their debates; the fiercer the better. He didn't leave me to deal with the "girl stuff": heartache, self-esteem, safety. He was right there with us.

Did I handle more of the family responsibilities, especially while Bill was President? Of course. He was President. This was something we'd talked through before he ran, and I was more than up for it.

But I never felt like I was alone in the work of raising our wonderful daughter. And I know a lot of wives of busy men who would say otherwise. Bill wanted to be a great President, but that wouldn't have mattered to him if he wasn't also a great dad.

Every time I see my husband and daughter laugh over some private joke that only they know . . . every time I overhear a conversation between them, two lightning-quick minds testing each other . . . every time I see him look at her with total love and devotion . . . I'm reminded again that I chose exactly the right person to have a family with.

I don't want to be married just to be married. I can't think of anything lonelier than spending the rest of my life with someone I can't talk to, or worse, someone I can't be silent with.

—Mary Ann Shaffer and Annie Barrows

My marriage to Bill Clinton was the most consequential decision of my life. I said no the first two times he asked me. But the third time, I said yes. And I'd do it again.

I hesitated to say yes because I wasn't quite prepared for marriage. I hadn't figured out what I wanted my future to be yet. And I knew that by marrying Bill, I would be running straight into a future far more momentous than any other I'd likely know. He was the most intense, brilliant, charismatic person I had ever met. He dreamt big. I, on the other hand, was practical and cautious. I knew that marrying him would be like hitching a ride on a comet. It took me a little while to get brave enough to take the leap.

We've been married since 1975. We've had many, many more happy days than sad or angry ones. We met in the library at Yale Law School one evening and started chatting, and all these years later, that conversation is still going strong. There's no one I want to talk to more than him.

I know some people wonder why we're still together. I heard it again in the 2016 campaign: that "we must have an arrangement" (we do, it's called a marriage); that I helped him become President and then stayed so he could help me become President (no); that we lead completely separate lives, and it's just a marriage on paper now (he is reading this over my shoulder in our kitchen with our dogs underfoot, and in a minute he will reorganize our bookshelves for the millionth time, which means I will not be able to find any of my books, and once I learn the new system, he'll just redo it again, but I don't mind because he really loves to organize those bookshelves).

I don't believe our marriage is anyone's business. Public people should be allowed to have private lives, too.

But I know that a lot of people are genuinely interested. Maybe you're flat-out perplexed. Maybe you want to know how this works because you are married and would like it to last forty years or longer, and you're looking for perspective. I certainly can't fault you on that.

I don't want to delve into all the details, because I really do want to hold on to what's left of my privacy as much as I can.

But I will say this:

Bill has been an extraordinary father to our beloved daughter and an exuberant, hands-on grandfather to our two grandchildren. I look at Chelsea and Charlotte and Aidan and I think, "We did this." That's a big deal.

He has been my partner in life and my greatest champion since the moment we met. He never once asked me to put my career on hold for his. He never once suggested that maybe I shouldn't compete for anything—in work or politics—because it would interfere with his life or ambitions. There were stretches of time in which my husband's job was unquestionably more important than mine, and he still didn't play that card. I have never felt like anything but an equal.

His late mother, Virginia, deserves much of the credit. She worked hard as a nurse anesthetist, held strong opinions, and had an unmatched zest for life. As a result, Bill is completely unbothered by having an ambitious, opinionated, occasionally pushy wife. In fact, he loves me for it.

Long before I thought of running for public office, he was saying, "You should do it. You'd be great at it. I'd love to vote for you." He helped me believe in this bigger version of myself.

Bill was a devoted son-in-law and always made my parents feel welcome in our home. Toward the end of my mother's life, when I wanted her to move into our house in Washington, he said yes without hesitation. Though I expected nothing less, this meant the world to me.

I know so many women who are married to men who—though they have their good qualities—can be sullen, moody, irritated at small requests, and generally disappointed with everyone and everything. Bill Clinton is the opposite. He has a temper, but he's never mean. And he's funny, friendly, unflappable in the face of mishaps and inconveniences, and easily delighted by the world—remember those balloons at the convention? He is fabulous company.

We've certainly had dark days in our marriage. You know all about them—and please consider for a moment what it would be like for the whole world to know about the worst moments in your relationship. There were times that I was deeply unsure about whether our marriage could or should survive. But on those days, I asked myself the questions that mattered most to me: Do I still love him? And can I still be in this marriage without becoming unrecognizable to myself—twisted by anger, resentment, or remoteness? The answers were always yes. So I kept going.

On our first date, we went to the Yale University Art Gallery to see a Mark Rothko exhibit. The building was closed, but Bill talked our way in. We had the building entirely to ourselves. When I think about that afternoon—seeing the art, hearing the stillness all around us, giddy about this person whom I had just met but somehow knew would change my life—it still feels magical, and I feel happy and lucky all over again.

I still think he's one of the most handsome men I've ever known.

I'm proud of him: proud of his vast intellect, his big heart, the contributions he has made to the world.

I love him with my whole heart.

That's more than enough to build a life on.

I looked up at the blue sky, feeling, in fact, a burst of energy, but mostly feeling my mother's presence, remembering why it was that I'd thought I could hike this trail.

—Cheryl Strayed

I've met a lot of strong people in my life but no one stronger than my mother.

People say that about their mothers all the time. But consider the life of Dorothy Howell.

Starting when she was three or four, her parents would leave her alone all day in their fifth-floor walk-up in Chicago. When she got hungry, she had to bundle herself up, walk down all those stairs, go to a nearby restaurant, produce a meal voucher, eat, and then walk all the way home. Alone.

At age eight, she was put on a train headed to California. Her parents were getting divorced, so they sent her and her three-year-old sister to live with their paternal grandparents. The little girls made the journey by themselves—no adults. It took four days.

Her grandmother wore long black Victorian dresses. Her grandfather hardly said a word. Their rules were incredibly strict. When my mother dared to go trick-or-treating one Halloween, the punishment was confinement to her bedroom for a full year, coming out only to go to school.

By the time she was fourteen, my mother couldn't take it anymore. She found a job as a housekeeper for a local family. She looked after the children in exchange for a place to live. She had one blouse and skirt that she washed every night. But the family was kind to her—finally, a little kindness. They encouraged her to keep going to high school.

When Mom graduated from high school, she moved back to Chicago because her mother sent her a letter suggesting that maybe they could be a family again. Despite everything, she missed her mom and wanted badly to be reunited. But when she got there, her mother made it clear that what she really wanted was a housekeeper. Something broke in my mom's heart forever. Still, she was a good daughter, and we dutifully visited my grandmother a few times a year.

Mom moved into a small apartment, found an office job, and met my dad, Hugh Rodham. They married in 1942 and after World War II had me, followed by my two brothers. We lived in a house in the suburbs. Mom, a homemaker, was a blur of constant energy, cooking, cleaning, hanging laundry, doing dishes, helping us with our homework, and sewing clothes for me. When I was in high school, she made me a dress—white with a print of red roses—that I thought was the prettiest I'd ever seen. She loved us intensely and worked hard to make our childhoods meaningful and fun. We played lots of games, read lots of books, went on lots of meandering walks, and talked about everything under the sun.

Back in the day, kids and their parents didn't consider each other friends. That's not how it worked. They were the parents. We were the kids.

But when I look back, there was no question that she was my best friend.

Even as a little girl, I saw how strong she was. She was so competent. When Mom said something, you knew that she meant it. When she told me to stand up for myself with a neighborhood bully, I did. She was so determined that some of her determination rubbed off on me.

She was not a huge personality. She didn't pound her fists on the table or yell like my dad did—that's not how she made her presence known. But she knew what she believed. She lived her values. She would do anything for us, and we would do anything for her. All of that made her powerful.

When I got older, the full extent of her loveless, lonely childhood hit me. I wondered if I could have survived such an ordeal with my spirit and dignity intact. She knew that she was worthy of love and decent treatment, even though the world told her otherwise for a long time. How did she hold on to that self-respect in the face of all that disregard? The most important people in her life told her she was nothing. How did she know that wasn't true? I marveled at the mental strength it must have taken to keep believing that a better day was coming, that she would find her place, that hard work would see her through, that her life had meaning despite how unfair fate had been to her.

When I became a mother myself and discovered how much patience and resilience it requires, I saw my mother's strength in a new way. She was raised with such neglect, to the extent that she was raised at all. How did she learn how to give my brothers and me such a loving and secure childhood? We talked about this. She said she carefully observed every family she ever met, including that family she worked for as a fourteen-year-old all those years ago. She paid attention to how the parents spoke to each other and to their kids. She saw that gentle firmness was possible and that families could actually laugh together, and not just sit in stony silence. Mostly, she figured it out on her own. It wasn't hard for her, she said. She loved us and was so happy to be around us, it was easy to show it.

But I know other people whose parents had cruel childhoods and who internalized that cruelty and dished it out to their own kids later. That's how abuse gets passed on through the generations. That's probably what happened with my grandmother, in fact. My mom singlehandedly stopped that cycle dead in its tracks.

In my experience, as people get older, either they start looking after their parents or their parents keep looking after them. My parents kept looking after me. When they visited, they fussed over me: Did I need a sweater? Was I hungry? I'm generally the one who looks after everyone else, so it was very sweet and rather amusing to have the roles reversed.

We were close. After Bill became Governor of Arkansas in 1979, my parents moved to Little Rock. Dad was retired, and they were ready for a new chapter to unfold, preferably as near to their beloved baby granddaughter as possible.

Dad died just a few months after Bill became President. I begged Mom to come live with us in the White House, but it wasn't surprising that she said no thank you. She was too independent for that. She did come visit us for weeks at a time, staying in a bedroom on the third floor. She even traveled a few times with Bill, Chelsea, and me on foreign trips.

After I became a Senator and we left the White House, Mom moved close by, to an apartment building in Northwest Washington, D.C. She loved walking around town; going to museums and the zoo (they're free in Washington!); having dinner with Bill and me a few nights a week; and seeing a lot of my brother Tony, who lives in Virginia just outside Washington with his wife, Megan, and my nephews Zach and Simon and niece Fiona.

A few years later, I asked again, and she finally agreed to come live with Bill and me, because it was getting too hard for her to live on her own. Mom had some heart problems, which meant that unpacking groceries or folding laundry could leave her breathless. She who was always in ceaseless motion now moved gingerly, and she worried about injuring herself.

I was glad that Mom agreed to live with us without my having to fight her on it, but I *was* ready to fight her on it. Her independence was important, but so were her health and safety. When she still lived alone, there were times I'd be at work in the Senate and realize that I hadn't heard from her all day and panic a little. Had she fallen? Was she okay? At our house, there were always people around. If Mom moved in, we wouldn't have to worry as much anymore.

Except it wasn't as easy as that. We discovered something many parents and children find out late in life: that the balance between

them is different once the child is grown and the parent is aging. Mom
didn't want to be mothered; she still wanted to mother. I didn't want
to encroach on her independence and dignity—the thought horrified me—but I also wanted to be straightforward with her about what
I thought she could and couldn't do anymore. No more walking down
the basement steps alone; they were too steep, she could fall. She did it
anyway. She bristled at any restriction and largely ignored my suggestions. Any time I felt impatient, I reminded myself that I would be just
as stubborn as she was.

There was one major fact that kept the balance steady between us:
I still needed my mother. I needed her shoulder to lean on; I needed
her wisdom and advice. I used to come home from a long day in the
Senate—or, in 2007 and 2008, from a day on the campaign trail—and
slide in next to her at our kitchen table and let all my frustrations and
worries tumble out. Mostly, she just listened. When she gave advice, it
always came down to the same basic idea: you know the right thing to
do. Do what's right.

Mom lived with us for five years, and I treasured every day. The
whole family did. Our home was a busy place thanks to her. Grandson
Zach came by after school to see her all the time. Tony and Megan
brought Fiona and Simon over frequently or took Mom back to their
home for the weekend. She relished her time with them. She talked to
my brother Hugh, who lived in Florida, every single day. Same with
Chelsea—not a day went by without a phone call, and every week,
Chelsea and Marc came to see her. She enchanted all our friends. Several of Chelsea's male friends adopted Mom as their honorary grandmother and would stop in to check on her and stay for dinner, debating
the finer points of philosophy or *The Sopranos*. She was good company:
quick-witted and well read. The day she died at ninety-two, she was
halfway through *The Mind's Eye* by Oliver Sacks.

We were so lucky to have her with us for so long. Many of my friends had lost their mothers by then, but here was mine, greeting me every morning and night with a sweet smile and a pat on the hand. I never missed a chance to tell her that I loved her. On a lot of nights, I made the choice to put aside my briefing books for an hour or two so we could watch something on TV (she adored *Dancing with the Stars*) or have a late dinner together. Briefing books could wait. This time with Mom was precious. I would have given anything to have that kind of time with my dad; I wasn't going to let this opportunity pass me by.

I was grateful for her long, full life, grateful for every moment we shared, grateful that I had the means to care for her the way I did, and grateful for the deep love she shared with Chelsea and the wise advice she gave her. I can't count the number of people across the country I've met who would love nothing more than to have their aging parents living comfortably at home with them. But they can't afford it, or they don't have the room. We had the room. We could afford it. I feel extraordinarily lucky for that. We didn't leave anything unsaid between us. I feel lucky for that, too.

After Mom died, even though I was Secretary of State, I felt just like a little girl again, missing my mother.

Isn't it funny how that happens.

A British publication once offered a prize for the best definition of a friend. Among the thousands of answers received were: "One who multiplies joys, divides grief, and whose honesty is inviolable." And "One who understands our silence." The winning definition read: "A friend is the one who comes in when the whole world has gone out."

—*Bits and Pieces* magazine

Every single one of these experiences—the joys and struggles of marriage, motherhood, and daughterhood—I have shared with my friends.

My friends are everything to me. Some have been by my side since I was five; I'm still friends with Ernie, who walked with me to kindergarten the first day. They've seen me at my worst, and I've seen them at theirs. We've been through it all: divorces, remarriages, births of children, deaths of parents and spouses. Some of my closest friends have passed away, and I miss them every single day, which makes me value the friends who are still with me even more. We've sat at each other's hospital bedsides. We've danced at our children's weddings. We've drunk good wine and eaten good food, gossiped and hiked and read books together. We have, in short, been an indivisible team.

Some of these friends are men, and some are women. And I want to take a moment to celebrate my male friends, who have been in my corner over the years come hell or high water. There are some out there who say women and men can't really be friends. I can't understand that. I don't know what I'd do without the men who challenge me, encourage me, hold me to account, and make me laugh so hard I can't breathe.

But my girlfriends . . . my girlfriends are something else entirely.

In my experience, there's a special strength at the heart of friendships between women. We get real with each other. We talk about raw and painful things. We admit to each other insecurities and fears that we sometimes don't admit even to ourselves.

Here's an example: I loved motherhood passionately. But there were days when it felt—there's no other way to say this—very, very boring. I would read the same children's book twenty times in a row and feel myself become duller. My colleagues were doing interesting, challenging work, and I was at home singing "Itsy Bitsy Spider" for the millionth time. I wondered if I was a monster for feeling this way, so I asked my friends. Their verdict: nope, just a normal mom.

When I struggled to get pregnant, I talked to my girlfriends. When Bill and I had trouble in our marriage, I talked to my girlfriends. When I lost the 2016 election, I talked to my girlfriends in a particularly open way about how it felt to fail. I have never hesitated to be honest with them, even if what I had to say was gloomy or blunt. They know who I am deep inside, so I'm never scared of losing their good opinion. There are a lot of people for whom I put on a happy face, but not my friends.

It's bewildering to me when female friendships are depicted in movies or on TV as catty or undermining. I'm sure there are relationships like that, but in my experience, they're not the norm. Friendships between women provide solace and understanding in a world that can be really hard on us. The pressure to be a perfect wife, mother, and daughter can be unbearable. What a relief it is to find people you can share it all with and be reassured that you're doing just fine.

If you're unconvinced that friends are worth it, consider the data. (Here is where my friends would say, "Of course Hillary has data.") Studies show that when seniors interact on a regular basis with friends, they have fewer problems with memory and depression, greater physical mobility, and are more likely to get regular checkups. Now that I'm officially in the senior category, I'm holding on even more tightly to my friends. They're literally keeping me strong.

Making friends in adulthood can be hard for anybody. For Bill and me, there are added complications. Do we let people into our lives who we don't know very well? What if they just want to get to know us in order to have a good story to tell? We've been burned by people who've done that. It's not fun to feel used.

Then there's the risk that people face when they become our friends. If you go out to dinner with me, your picture might be in the paper. You might be hounded by trolls online. You might lose friends who detest me because of my politics. You might even need to hire a lawyer. I almost want to offer a disclaimer to new friends: these side effects may occur.

It's for reasons like these that a lot of well-known public figures don't really make new friends. They close the circle. It's understandable. And yet I try to keep making new friends. Just in the past year, I've become close to a few new people, including a mystery writer I've been reading for years who is now my pen pal. For me, it's worth the risk. I get so much from my friendships: I learn so much, I laugh so much. And it feels really good to build my community, to feel connected to an ever-larger web of people from different backgrounds and different chapters of my life. I don't want to spend time just with politicians. Who in the world wants that?

I have spent so much of my life in the public eye, keeping a tight hold on what I say and how I react to things, that it is such a relief to have friends with whom I can be vulnerable and unedited. I don't just enjoy that, I *need* it. It keeps me sane.

It comes down to this for me: I don't want to live a narrow life. I want to a live a big, expansive one. I think of the poet Mary Oliver's question about what each of us plans to do with our one wild, precious life. To me, that answer includes staying open to new friends—hearing their stories and sharing mine in turn.

There's a special group of women I've met over the years I want to mention: other First Ladies, women Senators, and Secretaries of State. I wouldn't say we're intimates, but we know and understand one another in a way few others do. We know what it's like to see our husbands attacked and our marriages questioned relentlessly and have to explain that to our children. We know what it's like to be outnumbered in a vastly male-dominated field and to stay dignified and cheerful despite being patronized or talked over on a daily basis. It doesn't matter what political party we belong to. We're connected in a deeper way.

It reminds me of what Sandra Day O'Connor, who for a long time was the only woman on the Supreme Court, said when Ruth Bader Ginsburg joined her there: "The minute Justice Ginsburg came to the court, we were nine justices. It wasn't seven and then the women. We became nine. And it was a great relief to me."

The women who have walked the paths I've walked have been a relief to me, too. And I hope I've been the same to them.

I don't believe any of us gets through life alone. Finding meaning and happiness takes a village. My friends have been my village. I wouldn't have it any other way.

To console does not mean to take away the pain but rather to be there and say, "You are not alone, I am with you. Together we can carry the burden. Don't be afraid. I am here." That is consolation. We all need to give it as well as to receive it.

—Henri Nouwen

Turning Mourning
into a Movement

They radiated strength. They were proud women who had seen a lot, cried a lot, and prayed a lot. I walked around the room, introducing myself one by one to the dozen mothers who had come from all over the country. I listened to their stories and took in their quiet, fierce dignity.

It was November 2015. We were in the homey Sweet Maple Cafe on Chicago's West Side. Each of the mothers around the table had lost children to gun violence or in encounters with police officers. They had come to talk about what happened to their kids and to see if I would do something about it—or if I was just another politician after their votes.

Later, some of these mothers would form a traveling sisterhood: the Mothers of the Movement. They told their stories in churches and community centers and onstage at the Democratic National Convention. Their courage, their generosity of spirit, their refusal to give up—all of it inspired and motivated me.

Thanks in part to the Mothers' example, I ended up speaking frequently and forcefully throughout the campaign about gun violence, racial justice, police reform, and mass incarceration. These are complicated issues, substantively and politically, but listening to the Mothers' stories and watching the steady drumbeat of mass shootings and deadly police incidents that continued throughout 2015 and 2016 convinced me that they were too important to ignore. So I made criminal justice reform a priority with my very first policy speech, stressing the need for communities to respect the police who protect them and for the police to respect the people they serve. I also criticized the powerful National Rifle Association for its extreme opposition to commonsense gun safety measures. Going after the NRA is dangerous for candidates, but I felt compelled to speak out on behalf of the dead and injured victims of gun homicides, accidents, and suicides. If I had won, we could have made progress toward keeping guns out of the hands of criminals and domestic abusers and making sure fewer parents have to bury their children the way the Mothers of the Movement did. My profound disappointment that I couldn't deliver that outcome will never go away.

The Mothers' stories, and the stories of others who lost loved ones to gun violence, deserve to be told and heard. We've got to keep saying their names. In that first meeting in Chicago, there was no press and no audience—just us. I was accompanied by my senior policy advisor Maya Harris and director of African American Outreach LaDavia Drane.

Sybrina Fulton, whose unarmed seventeen-year-old son Trayvon Martin was shot and killed outside a convenience store near Orlando, Florida, in 2012, kicked things off. "We're just regular moms," she said. "We don't want to be community activists, we don't want to be the mothers of senseless gun violence, we don't want to be in this position—we were forced into this position. None of us would have signed up for this."

Trayvon was killed while wearing a hooded sweatshirt and taking a walk to buy some Skittles candy at the corner store. Jordan Davis was shot in Jacksonville, Florida, while listening to music in a car that a white man thought was too loud and too "thug." Twelve-year-old Tamir Rice was playing in a Cleveland park with a toy gun when he was shot by a police officer. Eric Garner was choked to death by an officer after selling loose cigarettes on a Staten Island street. Some of the stories were about criminal gun violence; others, excessive force by police officers. These issues require different policy solutions and different political responses. But the common theme that ran through all the stories was race. And the anguish all these mothers felt was the same—anguish that no mother, no parent, should have to bear.

Jordan's mother, Lucia McBath, remembers comforting her son after they heard about Trayvon's murder on the news. Jordan didn't know Trayvon. They lived in different parts of Florida. But the news hit him hard. "Mom, how did this happen to Trayvon? He wasn't doing anything wrong," he asked. Lucia didn't have a good answer. Nine months later, Jordan was dead as well. Now Travyon's and Jordan's moms were sitting at the same table.

"We lay in bed, and on our bad nights, our dark nights, we stare at the ceiling and cry," Gwen Carr told me. She's the mother of Eric Garner. "We replay in our heads over and over what happened to our children."

Hadiya Pendleton was a fifteen-year-old honor student when she was randomly shot in a Chicago park. Just a week before, she had performed with her high school band at President Obama's second inauguration in Washington. "There are no words for what we go through every day just waking up," her mother, Cleo, told me. "I didn't have a voice after Hadiya passed. For like three or four days, the only thing I could do was open my eyes and scream, literally at the top of my lungs."

My throat tightened as I listened to the Mothers tell these stories, watching them remain composed despite the shattering pain behind their words. The writer Elizabeth Stone says that having a child is like deciding to have your heart go walking around outside your body. The thought of something happening to your kid is unimaginable to any parent. These mothers had lived that nightmare.

They also faced different, deeper fears that I never had to think about. My daughter and grandchildren are white. They won't know what it's like to be watched with suspicion when they play in the park or enter a store. People won't lock their car doors when they walk by. Police officers won't pull them over for driving in the "wrong" neighborhood. Gangs aren't likely to settle their feuds on the streets where they walk to school.

"As people of color, we feel the greatest impact of this injustice, of this inhumane treatment," Gwen Carr said. "Some people say that we're racist because we say 'Black lives matter.' We know that *all* lives matter, but we need people to understand that black lives matter *also*. So treat us as such. Don't just treat us like common animals. We're not. We're American citizens, and we deserve fair treatment."

Treating everyone with care and respect is especially important for the men and women charged with keeping us all safe. I feel strongly about this: the vast majority of police officers are honorable, brave public servants who put their lives on the line every day to protect others. As a Senator, I spent years fighting for first responders who served at Ground Zero and later suffered lasting health effects. They paid a terrible price for serving the rest of us. I also have the unique experience of being guarded around the clock for more than twenty-five years by highly trained men and women committed to take a bullet for me if a threat ever came. If that doesn't teach you to respect the courage and professionalism of law enforcement, nothing will. The officers I've known have been proud of their integrity, disgusted by the use of excessive force, and eager to find new and better ways to do their jobs. Every time a police officer falls in the line of duty—something that happens with sickening frequency—it's a reminder of how much we owe them and their families.

Throughout the campaign, I had many meetings and discussions with law enforcement members to hear their views about what we could do better. In August 2016 I met with a group of retired and current police chiefs from across the country, including Bill Bratton from New York, Charlie Beck from Los Angeles, and Chuck Ramsey from Philadelphia. They stressed the importance of building relationships between their officers and the communities they serve. They also stressed that part of what we owe our officers is honesty and a willingness to confront hard truths.

One hard truth we all have to face is that we all have implicit biases. I have them, you have them, and police officers have them: deeply ingrained thoughts that can lead us to think "Gun!" when a black man reaches for his wallet. Acknowledging this during the campaign may have cost me the support of some police officers and organizations, who seemed to think my concern for dead children and other victims showed a presumption of wrongdoing by police. That stung. But I was grateful for the support of other law enforcement officers who wanted to rebuild bonds of trust that would make them and all of us safe and who thought I was the best candidate to make that happen. Dallas Sheriff Lupe Valdez said at the Democratic National Convention, "We put on our badges every day to serve and protect, not to hate and discriminate." She and other officers believe, as I do, that we can work together to improve policing without vilifying the men and women who put their lives on the line to do it.

As a candidate, I worked with civil rights advocates and law enforcement leaders to develop solutions that would help, from body cameras to new training guidelines for de-escalating tense situations. I also spoke often about the importance of trying harder to walk in one another's shoes. That means police officers and all of us doing everything we can to understand the effects of systemic racism that young black and Latino men and women face every day, and how they are made to feel like their lives are disposable. It also means imagining what it's like to be a police officer, kissing his or her kids and spouse good-bye every day and heading off to do a dangerous but necessary job.

This kind of empathy is hard to come by. The divisions in our country run deep. As Maria Hamilton said to me, "It's been like that for five hundred years, Hillary. People just haven't been talking about it." Her unarmed son Dontre was killed in 2014, shot more than a dozen times by a police officer in Milwaukee after a scuffle in a public park, where he had fallen asleep on a bench. Her words were a reminder that for these mothers and generations of black parents before them, the killing and mistreatment of young black men and women was tragic but not shocking. This has been the reality of life in America for a long time. But we can't accept it as our inevitable future.

Maria's words pointed to the complex relationship between race and gun violence. It is not a coincidence that it is the leading cause of death for young black men, outstripping the next nine causes of death combined. That is the result of decades of policy choices, neglect, underinvestment, gangs and thugs, and adversarial policing in communities of color. That said, it's a mistake to think that gun violence is a problem just for black people or poor people or only in cities. Gun violence touches every class, color, and community, with thirty-three thousand people dying from guns each year—an average of ninety a day. That's a particularly devastating fact because gun violence is largely preventable. Other developed nations don't have this problem. They have commonsense laws to keep guns out of the hands of dangerous people. Those laws work. They save lives. The United States has made a cruel choice as a country not to take simple steps that would help prevent—or at least lessen—this epidemic.

The Mothers know this all too well. Consider the story of Annette Nance-Holt. She worked hard to rise through the ranks of the Chicago Fire Department, becoming a battalion chief. She and her ex-husband, Ron, a Chicago police commander, did everything they could to give their son, Blair, a safe, comfortable, middle-class life. They taught him to be generous and humble, and to feel grateful for all he had. By the time he was sixteen, Blair was a kind, hardworking, music-loving high school student on the honor roll. He was planning to go to college to study business, the first step to accomplishing his dream of being in the music industry.

Even though Annette and Ron devoted their lives to keeping their city safe, in the end, they couldn't protect their beloved child. One day in 2007, Blair was riding a public bus from school to his grandparents' store, where he sometimes helped out. A young gang member opened fire on a group of teenagers, aiming for someone in a rival gang. A friend sitting next to Blair jumped up to run to the back of the bus, but Blair pushed her back into the seat. He saved her life, but was killed himself.

All the mothers around the table with me that day in Chicago had stories like that. And they each had decided to do whatever she could to protect other children from suffering the fate of their own. They were focused intensely on curbing gun violence, reforming policing, and ensuring accountability for these deaths. Sybrina Fulton founded the Trayvon Martin Foundation to support families and to advocate for gun safety reforms. Geneva Reed-Veal, whose twenty-eight-year-old daughter, Sandra Bland, died after being jailed for a minor traffic violation, redoubled her community work through her church. All of the mothers were discovering that their stories and moral authority could make them powerful public advocates. As Cleo Pendleton put it, "When I found my voice, I couldn't shut up."

But progress was far too slow. They were understandably frustrated by how hard it was to even get a hearing from local authorities and the U.S. Justice Department, let alone action. Too many of them had been brushed off or insulted, and even attacked in the media. Sybrina and her ex-husband had to listen to their son's killer tell the press they "didn't raise their son right" and later make a small fortune auctioning off the gun that killed Trayvon.

"We need better laws," Gwen Carr told me. "If there's a crime, there should be accountability, whether you wear blue jeans, a blue business suit, or a blue uniform. We need accountability across the board, and we're not getting that."

The others agreed, and they clearly weren't sure I'd turn out to be any different from the other politicians who'd already let them down. Still, they had accepted my invitation to this meeting in Chicago and were generous with sharing their stories. Now they were waiting to see what I'd do.

Lezley McSpadden was direct with me. Her eighteen-year-old son, Michael Brown, was shot and killed in 2014 by a police officer in Ferguson, Missouri. "Are we going to see change?" Lezley asked. "Once again we're around a table, we're pouring our hearts out, we're getting emotional, we tell you what we feel—but are we going to see any change? Are we going to see some action?"

The politics of guns have been toxic for a long time. Despite the fact that, according to a June 2017 Quinnipiac University poll, 94 percent of Americans support comprehensive background checks for gun sales, including 92 percent of gun owners, many politicians have shied away from taking on the NRA. The vocal minority of voters against gun safety laws have historically been more organized, better funded, and more willing to be single-issue voters.

In the 1990s, my husband fought hard to pass both a ten-year ban on assault weapons and the Brady Bill, which, for the first time, required background checks on many gun purchases at federally licensed firearms dealers. In the years since, that law has blocked more than two million purchases by convicted felons, domestic abusers, and fugitives. The NRA funded an intense backlash to the new safety measures and helped defeat a lot of Democratic members of Congress in the disastrous 1994 midterm elections. Then, in 2000, the NRA helped beat Al Gore.

After these searing political experiences, it became conventional wisdom that it was safer for Democrats to say nothing at all about guns and hope the NRA stayed away.

I never agreed with this approach. I thought it was wrong on the policy and wrong on the politics. I've always hated gun violence on a gut level and was proud that Bill's administration had taken on the NRA and won. My commitment to stopping senseless gun violence deepened after going to Littleton, Colorado, in 1999. Bill and I visited with grieving family members of teenagers killed in the Columbine High School massacre. We huddled together over coffee cups and memorial books in a local Catholic church. I had thought about those kids every day since I'd heard the news a month earlier. I was especially moved by the story of seventeen-year-old Cassie Bernall. Press accounts at the time said that one of the student-killers asked her if she believed in God. After Cassie said yes, he shot her. When I met Cassie's mother, Misty, I gave her a big hug and asked her to tell me about her daughter. We sat down together and started looking at photos. Some of the Columbine families talked to Bill and me about what more could be done to keep other schools and families safe from gun violence. I believed we needed new measures that would go even further than what the Clinton administration had accomplished.

Later, as a Senator, I represented rural upstate New York as well as the cities. I understood and appreciated the perspective of law-abiding gun owners wary of any new regulations. I remembered my father teaching me to shoot in rural Pennsylvania, where we spent summers when I was growing up. I also lived in Arkansas for many years and went on a memorable December duck hunting expedition with some friends in the 1980s. I'll never forget standing hip deep in freezing water, waiting for the sun to rise, trying to stave off hypothermia. I did manage to shoot a duck, but when I got home, Chelsea, who had just watched *Bambi*, was outraged by the news that I'd shot "some poor little duck's mommy or daddy."

These experiences reinforced for me that, for many Americans, hunting and gun ownership are ingrained in the culture. Many see them as links to our frontier past and to the age-old American ethic of self-reliance. For a lot of people, being able to own a gun is a matter of fundamental freedom and self-defense. It's also a source of security and confidence in a chaotic world. I understand all that. It's why this issue is so emotionally charged. For people on both sides of the debate, it's intensely personal.

In all my political campaigns, I've done my best to strike a fair balance between standing up for commonsense gun safety measures and showing respect for responsible gun owners. I've always said that I recognize the Second Amendment and have never proposed banning all guns.

Yet, even before I got into the 2016 race, NRA chief Wayne La-Pierre promised his organization would "fight with everything we've got" to stop me from becoming President. He warned that if I won, it would mean "a permanent darkness of deceit and despair forced upon the American people." All he was missing was a tinfoil hat.

Wayne LaPierre helped make the NRA one of the most reactionary and dangerous organizations in America. Instead of being concerned with the interests of everyday gun owners, many of who *support* commonsense safety protections, the NRA has essentially become a wholly owned subsidiary of the powerful corporations that make and sell guns. Their bottom line and twisted ideology are all that matters to them, even if it costs thousands of American lives every year.

I had a healthy appreciation for the political damage the NRA could do. I'd seen it before and expected worse this time. But I also knew that a lot of swing voters, especially women, were as horrified by gun violence as I was, and were open to smart solutions that would keep their families and communities safer. So I shook off the threats and got to work.

My team and I collaborated with gun safety advocates such as the organization Moms Demand Action to develop new proposals for keeping guns out of the hands of domestic abusers and other violent criminals. I called for universal background checks, barring anyone on the terrorist no-fly list from buying a gun, and giving survivors and families the right to hold gun makers and sellers accountable. For example, I believed that families who lost children in the 2012 mass shooting at Sandy Hook Elementary School in Newtown, Connecticut, should be able to sue Remington Arms for marketing its AR-15 assault rifle to civilians. It infuriated me that a special law gave gun manufacturers immunity from such suits.

After the massacre of nine parishioners at Mother Emanuel Church in Charleston, South Carolina, in June 2015, my team focused on why the twenty-one-year-old white supremacist killer was able to buy a gun despite having an arrest record that should have been flagged by the required background check. We found that, under current law, if a background check is not completed after three days, a store is free to sell a gun with no questions asked. This is the result of an amendment the NRA designed and pushed through Congress during the debate over the Brady Bill in 1993. Experts say that more than fifty-five thousand gun sales that should have been blocked have been allowed to proceed because of what we started calling the "Charleston loophole." I made closing it and other gun loopholes a major part of my campaign.

Listening to the Mothers' stories in Chicago, I was more sure than ever that taking on the gun lobby was the right thing to do, whatever the cost. I told them about some of the reforms that my policy team had been working on, and asked them to stay in touch with us and not be shy about sending ideas and criticisms. I said how much hearing their stories meant to me and how determined I was to be their champion. I'm sure my words failed me, but it was hard to express how honored I felt by their willingness to open up so completely with me. "We're better than this, and we need to act like we are," I said.

As our meeting broke up, the Mothers started talking intensely among themselves. Soon they were taking photos and making plans. Many of them had never met before, but they were already bonding like sisters. I saw how powerful they were together. Later, when they decided to go on the road for my campaign, traveling around South Carolina and other early primary states to speak on my behalf, I was moved and grateful. The Mothers of the Movement were born.

Over the months that followed, I always looked forward to running into the Mothers out on the trail. On hard days, a hug or smile from them would give me an extra boost. And I made a point to be upbeat around them. I figured there was enough sadness in their lives, so the least I could do was to be cheerful with them.

But it wasn't easy. New tragedies kept unfolding. In July 2016 a black man named Philando Castile was shot seven times during a traffic stop in the Twin Cities, while his girlfriend Diamond Reynolds and her four-year-old daughter sat in the car. Later, video showed the little girl pleading with her mother to stay quiet so she wouldn't be killed as well. "I don't want you to get shooted," she said. "Okay, give me a kiss," Diamond responded. "I can keep you safe," her tiny daughter assured her, before starting to cry. Two weeks later, I met with the grieving family in Minnesota and heard about how beloved Castile was in the community, including at the magnet school in Saint Paul where he worked, and that he and Diamond had planned to get married.

That same month, five police officers were ambushed and killed by a sniper in Dallas while protecting a peaceful protest march. I was horrified by the news and quickly canceled an event I had been planning to do with Joe Biden in Scranton, Pennsylvania. It didn't feel right to go to a campaign rally on the day after such a tragedy. Instead, I went to a conference of ministers in Philadelphia and paid tribute to the fallen officers and offered prayers for their families. I called Mayor Mike Rawlings and offered my support. Dallas Police Chief David Brown urged Americans to stand with the brave men and women who risk their lives to keep the rest of us safe. "We don't feel much support most days. Let's not make today most days," he said. I agreed completely. Less than two weeks later, another three officers were ambushed and killed in Baton Rouge, Louisiana. And as I'm writing this, a New York City police officer, a mother of three, was gunned down in cold blood. This violence—against police, against young black men and women, against anyone—must stop.

Since the election, I've often thought about my time with the Mothers of the Movement. Whenever I've started to feel sorry for myself, I've tried to remember how these mothers persevered through infinitely harder circumstances. They're still doing everything they can to make our country a better place. If they can, so can I and so can we all.

I think about how I felt standing with them in a prayer circle, like we did at the Trayvon Martin Foundation's annual dinner in Florida. Eight of us leaning our heads together, clasping hands, looking downward in contemplation. One of the Mothers led us in prayer, her voice rising and falling as she thanked God for making all things possible.

I remember something Gwen Carr said on our visit to the Central Baptist Church in Columbia, South Carolina. In the first days after losing her son, Eric, she couldn't even get out of bed. But then, she said, "The Lord talked to me and told me, 'Are you going to lay here and die like your son, or are you going to get up and uplift his name?'" She realized in that moment that none of us can rest as long as there are others out there to be helped. She said, "I had to turn my sorrow into a strategy, my mourning into a movement."

Guns became a flash point in both the primaries and the general election. Bernie Sanders, who loved to talk about how "true progressives" never bow to political realities or powerful interests, had long bowed to the political reality of his rural state of Vermont and supported the

NRA's key priorities, including voting against the Brady Bill five times in the 1990s. In 2005, he voted for that special immunity law that protects gun makers and sellers from being sued when their weapons are used in deadly attacks. The NRA said the Protection of Lawful Commerce in Arms Act was the most important gun-related legislation in more than twenty years. Then-Senator Barack Obama and I had voted against it. I couldn't believe Bernie continued to support the law ten years later when he ran for President.

I hammered him on the issue every chance I got. We had a revealing exchange in a town hall debate in March 2016. A man stepped up to the microphone to ask a question. His fourteen-year-old daughter had been shot in the head during a shooting spree outside a Cracker Barrel restaurant. After a few scary days on life support, she pulled through and ended up being the lone survivor of the attack. The father asked what we were going to do to address the epidemic of gun violence stalking our country.

"I am looking at your daughter, and I'm very grateful that she is laughing and she is on a road to recovery," I said. "But it never should have happened." I told him about some of the steps I wanted to take to keep families safe, including repealing the immunity protection for gun manufacturers. The moderator then asked Bernie his thoughts about a new lawsuit challenging that corporate immunity. To my surprise, the Senator doubled down. He argued passionately that people like me who talked about suing gun makers were really talking about "ending gun manufacturing in America." To him, the idea that a manufacturer could be held liable for what happens with its guns was tantamount to saying that "there should not be any guns in America." I couldn't have disagreed more strongly. No other industry in our country has the kind of protection he supported for gun manufacturers. And in every other situation, he was the loudest voice in the room calling for corporations to be held accountable for their actions. Why was this one issue so different? As I told the crowd, it was like he was reading straight from the NRA's talking points. After months of pressure from activists and victims' families, Bernie finally said he would reconsider his vote.

Bernie and I disagreed on guns, but the Republicans were far more extreme. Just days after terrorists shot and killed fourteen people and seriously injured twenty-two others at an office holiday party in San Bernardino, California, Senate Republicans blocked a bill to stop individuals on the no-fly list from buying guns and explosives. I thought it was a no-brainer that if you're too dangerous to get on a plane, you're too dangerous to buy a gun! But the Republicans refused to defy the NRA.

Then there was Donald Trump. From the start of the campaign, he did everything he could to ingratiate himself with the gun lobby, which may have been wary that a New York billionaire with a history of being sympathetic to gun control wouldn't be a natural ally. So he overcompensated. He promised to force schools to allow guns in classrooms and to overturn efforts President Obama made to strengthen the background check system. After the rampage at Umpqua Community College in Roseburg, Oregon, in which eight students and one professor were killed, Trump called the attack horrible but didn't seem to think anything could be done about it. "You're going to have these things happen," he said flippantly. After the June attack at the Pulse nightclub in Orlando that killed forty-nine young people, many of them LGBT people of color, Trump said it was "too bad" that people at the club "didn't have guns attached to their hips"—even though all the research and a growing body count prove that more guns mean more deaths.

Republicans liked to rile up their base with tales about how I was going to shred the Constitution and take away their guns. It didn't matter that I said the opposite as clearly as I could, including in my acceptance speech at the Democratic National Convention: "I'm not here to repeal the Second Amendment. I'm not here to take away your guns. I just don't want you to be shot by someone who shouldn't have a gun in the first place." I was used to being the gun lobby's favorite villain. But as he so often did, Trump took it to another level. In August 2016,

he told a rally in North Carolina that if I were elected President, there'd
be no way to stop me from appointing liberal justices to the Supreme
Court. Well, he said, maybe the "Second Amendment people" might
find a way to stop me. Many of us took that to mean: maybe someone
would shoot me.

Trump's remark caused a stir in the press. I was particularly concerned that if a "Second Amendment person" came after me, he'd be
coming after my security detail of Secret Service agents. His campaign
tried to downplay the comment, but everyone heard the innuendo loud
and clear. Later, there were reports that the Secret Service told Trump's
team to get their candidate to knock it off.

As for the NRA, it kept its promise to do everything it could to
stop me. All told, the gun lobby spent more than $30 million sup-
porting Trump, more money than any other outside group and more
than double what it spent to support Mitt Romney in 2012. About
two-thirds of that money paid for more than ten thousand negative
ads attacking me in battleground states. The organization didn't have
the guts to take on my specific policy proposals—which were widely
popular, even with a lot of gun owners. Instead, it went for fearmonger-
ing and demonizing. In one ad, a woman is alone in bed when a robber
breaks into the house. "Don't let Hillary leave you protected with nothing but a phone," the narrator warns, suggesting falsely that I would
have stopped law-abiding Americans from having a gun.

I'm sure that some of my fellow Democrats will look at this high-
priced onslaught and conclude, as many have in the past, that standing
up to the NRA just isn't worth it. Some may put gun safety on the
chopping block alongside reproductive rights as "negotiable," so as not
to distract from populist economics. Who knows—the same might
happen to criminal justice reform and racial justice more broadly. That
would be a terrible mistake. Democrats should not respond to my defeat by retreating from our strong commitments on these life-or-death

issues. The vast majority of Americans agree that we need to do more on gun safety. This is a debate we can win if we keep at it.

As I met more survivors of gun violence and the families of victims, I was amazed at how many shared the Mothers of the Movement's conviction that they had to channel their private pain into public action.

One of the most powerful voices came from someone who had trouble speaking: former Arizona Congresswoman Gabby Giffords, who was shot in the head in 2011 while meeting with constituents in the parking lot of a Tucson supermarket. Before the shooting, Gabby was a rising political star: brilliant, magnetic, and effective. After the shooting, she had to persevere through intense physical therapy and relearn how to walk and talk. Nonetheless, she and her husband, the former astronaut and fighter pilot Captain Mark Kelly, became passionate advocates for gun safety. I loved campaigning with them and watching crowds fall in love with Gabby, just as I had. "Speaking is difficult for me," she would say, "but come January, I want to say these two words: Madam President."

Other advocates were less famous but no less courageous, including the families of Sandy Hook Elementary victims in Newtown, Connecticut. Every time I tried to talk about the massacre of little children that happened at that school in 2012, I started to choke up. I don't know how some of the grieving parents found the strength to share their experiences at campaign events, but I will always be grateful that they did.

Nicole Hockley joined me at a town hall meeting in New Hampshire. Her six-year-old son, Dylan, was shot to death despite a special education teacher's heroic efforts to shield him from the bullets. After the massacre, Nicole became the managing director of Sandy Hook

Promise, an organization that has trained nearly two million people across the country to identify potentially violent behavior and intervene before there's a dangerous attack.

One of Nicole's partners at Sandy Hook Promise is Mark Barden. His seven-year-old son, Daniel, was killed that day. Mark remembers how, on the morning of the shooting, Daniel woke up early so that he and Mark could watch the sunrise together. And when it came time for his older brother, Jake, to go to school, Daniel ran down the driveway to give him a hug and kiss good-bye.

After the shooting, Mark and his wife, Jackie, were the ones who sued Remington Arms, the company that makes the military-grade weapon the killer used in the attack. They argued that Remington should be held responsible for selling and marketing military weapons to civilians. (The case has been dismissed and is now on appeal.)

Then there's Nelba Márquez-Greene, who spoke with me at an event in Hartford, Connecticut. She lost her six-year-old daughter, Ana, at Sandy Hook. The night before the shooting, she and her husband took Ana and Isaiah, Ana's younger brother, out for a family dinner at the Cheesecake Factory. They splurged and ordered two rounds of dessert. Isaiah, also a Sandy Hook student, heard the shots that killed his sister from a nearby classroom. The family buried Ana two days before Christmas, her unopened gifts sitting under the tree.

Nelba, a therapist for troubled youth, now runs the Ana Grace Project, which trains teachers and schools how to reduce social isolation and create safe and welcoming communities for students. At the start of the school year following the shooting, Nelba wrote an open letter to the teachers in their district. "When you Google 'hero,' there should be a picture of a principal, a school lunch worker, a custodian, a reading specialist, a teacher, or a bus monitor," she wrote. "Real heroes don't wear capes. They work in America's schools."

One of those heroes was Dawn Hochsprung, the principal of

Sandy Hook Elementary. When Dawn heard the gun shots, she raced into the hallway. She saw the gunman and lunged at him to knock the weapon out of his hands. She died trying to protect her students.

During the campaign, I met Dawn's grown daughter, Erica Smegielski. When she died, Dawn had been helping Erica plan her summer wedding. Erica couldn't imagine walking down the aisle without her mom. But slowly she pieced her life back together and managed to have a joyous wedding celebration. Then Erica went to work at Everytown for Gun Safety, Mike Bloomberg's organization that advocates for commonsense gun laws. Erica threw herself into my campaign, speaking all over the country and telling her story in a powerful television ad. She once told me that I reminded her of Dawn. It's a compliment I'll never forget.

As hard as the politics of guns are, and as divided as the country feels, we've got to do better. The NRA can spend all it wants. Donald Trump can pal around with Alex Jones, the conspiracy theorist who has called the Sandy Hook massacre a hoax. What a despicable lie. They're on the wrong side of justice, history, basic human decency. And it's because of the Sandy Hook parents, the Mothers of the Movement, Gabby and Mark, and so many other incredibly brave survivors and family members that I know in my heart that one day we will stem the tide and save lives.

I think about something I heard Erica say during the campaign. She was explaining how she picked herself up after the loss of her mother and decided to devote her life to gun safety. "What if everyone who faced tough odds said, 'It's hard, so I'm going to walk away'?" she asked. "That's not the type of world I want to live in."

Me neither, Erica.

I love people who harness themselves, an ox to a heavy cart,

who pull like water buffalo, with massive patience,

who strain in the mud and the muck to move things forward,

who do what has to be done, again and again.

—Marge Piercy

Idealism
and Realism

Service is the rent we pay for living.

It is the very purpose of life, and not something you do in your spare time.

—Marian Wright Edelman

Change Makers

One of the most persistent challenges I faced as a candidate was being perceived as a defender of the status quo, while my opponents in the primaries and the general election seized the sought-after mantle of "change." The same thing happened to me in 2008. I never could figure out how to shake it.

Change might be the most powerful word in American politics. It's also one of the hardest to define. In 1992 and 2008, *change* meant electing dynamic young leaders who promised hope and renewal. In 2016, it meant handing a lit match to a pyromaniac.

The yearning for change springs from deep in the character of our restless, questing, constantly-reinventing-itself country. That's part of what makes America great. But we don't always spend enough time thinking about what it takes to actually make the change we seek. Change is hard. That's one reason we're sometimes taken in by leaders who make it sound easy but don't have any idea how to get anything done. Too often we fail to think big enough or act fast enough and let opportunities for change slip away. Or we don't have the patience to see things through.

I've been thinking about what it means to be a change maker for most of my life. My journey took me from student-activist to citizen-advocate to politician–policy maker. Along the way, I never stopped searching for the right balance of idealism and realism. Sometimes I had to make painful compromises. But I've also had the great privilege of meeting people whose lives were healthier, freer, and fuller because of my work. Today, despite losing in 2016, I am more convinced than ever that driving progress in a big, raucous democracy like ours requires a mix of principle and pragmatism—plus a whole lot of persistence.

Nobody did more to help me understand this than Marian Wright Edelman, the founder of the Children's Defense Fund and my first boss. When I met her in the spring of 1970, her accomplishments were already stunning. She was the first black woman to pass the bar exam in Mississippi, after having graduated from Yale Law School in 1963. She became a civil rights lawyer for the NAACP in Jackson and established a Head Start program for poor kids who desperately needed it. Marian worked with Dr. King and opened Bobby Kennedy's eyes to the reality of poverty in America by taking him to tiny shacks in the Mississippi Delta and introducing him to children so hungry they were nearly catatonic.

Marian showed me what it takes to make real and lasting change. She gave me my start as an activist, held me to account as I grew into a national leader, and was there for me when things fell apart as a candidate.

I was in my early twenties when I met Marian, but I'd already spent a lot of time trying to figure out how to be an effective activist.

My parents—especially my mother—raised me and my brothers in the Methodist tradition of "faith in action." At church, we were taught to be "doers of the word, not hearers only." That meant stepping outside the pews, rolling up our sleeves, and doing "all the good you can, for all the people you can, in all the ways you can, as long as ever you can." That credo, attributed to the founder of Methodism, John Wesley, inspired generations of Methodists to volunteer in hospitals, schools, and slums. For me, growing up in a comfortable middle-class suburb, it provided a sense of purpose and direction, pointing me toward a life of public service.

My activist faith was sharpened by the social upheavals of the 1960s and 1970s. In college and law school, my friends and I spent many long nights debating the morality and efficacy of civil disobedience, dodging the draft, and other forms of resistance. What would it take to end an unjust war in Vietnam, expand civil rights and women's rights, and combat poverty and injustice? Should our goal be reform or revolution? Consensus or conflict? Should we protest or participate?

The "Left," of which we considered ourselves a part, was divided. Radicals talked about revolution and believed conflict was the only way to drive change. Not surprisingly, I agreed more with the liberals who argued that the system had to be reformed from the inside. Partly it was a question of temperament—I'm a pragmatist by both nature and nurture—but I was also watching and learning as events swirled around me.

At Wellesley, I tried to find ways to push the college toward more progressive positions through negotiation rather than disruption. I ran for student government president in 1968 because I thought I could do a good job convincing college administrators to make changes that students wanted. My platform included adding students to faculty committees, recruiting more students and faculty of color, opening up the curriculum, and easing curfews and other social restrictions. I won and spent the next year trying to translate the demands of restive students into measurable change on campus.

That summer, I was in Chicago's Grant Park when antiwar protests outside the Democratic National Convention turned into a melee that shocked the nation. My longtime close friend Betsy Ebeling and I narrowly missed being hit by a rock thrown by someone in the crowd behind us. Mayor Richard Daley's police force was clearly more to blame for the violence than the kids in the park were. But the whole scene left me worried that the antiwar movement was causing a backlash that would help elect Richard Nixon and prolong the war. It was a terrifying, infuriating, exhilarating, and confusing time to be a young activist in America.

In May 1970, just a few days after four unarmed college student protesters were shot and killed by National Guardsmen on the campus of Kent State University in Ohio, I spoke to the fiftieth anniversary convention of the League of Women Voters in Washington. The civic organization had invited me after my Wellesley graduation speech made national news the previous year. I wore a black armband in memory of the students who had been killed at Kent State. In my remarks, I tried to explain the tension so many young activists were feeling, wavering "back and forth between thinking that talk at this point was useless, and believing somehow that we had to continue using words." This was a time when eighteen-year-old kids could be drafted to fight a war they believed was wrong but didn't yet have the right to vote. Many of my peers were beside themselves with anger and despair. They had given up hope that progress was possible, at least through traditional means.

I had read an article in the *Washington Post* about League of Women Voters members holding a vigil on the steps of the Capitol to protest Nixon's recent invasion of Cambodia. Nixon had promised to end the war and now seemed to be escalating it instead. I believed invading Cambodia was both immoral and illegal. But I knew not everyone in the audience wanted to hear this. That vigil at the Capitol was controversial, even internally. One member from Connecticut who had not participated was quoted by the *Post* as saying she didn't believe in protests and was afraid the vigil would tar the league's reputation. I thought that was absurd and said so. "Not to stand up and protest today against the forces of death is to be counted among them," I said, using the kind of hypercharged language that was common back then, at least for student activists. "People—living, breathing, caring human beings—who have never been involved before must be now. The luxury of long-range deliberation and verbiage-laden analysis must be forgone in favor of action."

Despite the hot (and verbiage-laden!) rhetoric, my idea of action wasn't terribly radical. I urged league members to use their economic power—"Do you know what kind of activities the corporations that you invest in are engaged in? How much longer can we let corporations run us?"—and to help antiwar activists use the political system more effectively. I felt passionately that nobody could sit on the sidelines in a time of such upheaval.

Considering everything that was going on, my friends and I sometimes wondered whether going to Yale Law School was a morally defensible choice or if we were selling out. A few of our classmates were indeed there just to open the door to a big paycheck and the chance to defend corporations that exploited workers and consumers. But for many of us, our legal education was arming us with a powerful new weapon as activists. The law could seem arid and abstract in our classrooms and textbooks, but we cheered for crusading lawyers across the country who were driving change by challenging injustices in court. When I started volunteering at the New Haven Legal Services Clinic, I saw firsthand how the law could improve or harm lives. I still believed there was a place for protests—and I moderated a mass meeting at Yale where students voted for a campus strike after the Kent State shootings, in part because the male students couldn't agree which of them should take charge—but more and more, I was coming to see how the system could be changed through hard work and reform.

All this crystalized for me when I went to work for Marian at the Children's Defense Fund. She sent me to her home state of South Carolina to gather evidence for a lawsuit seeking to end the practice of incarcerating teenagers in jails with adults. A civil rights lawyer lent me his car, and I drove all over the state going to courthouses, meeting with parents of thirteen-, fourteen-, or fifteen-year-old boys who were stuck in jail with grown men who had committed serious felonies. It was eye-opening and outrageous.

Next, I went undercover—really!—in Dothan, Alabama, to expose segregated schools that were trying to evade integration. Posing as the young wife of a businessman who had just been transferred to the area, I visited the all-white private school that had just opened in town and received tax-exempt status. When I started asking questions about the student body and curriculum, I was assured that no black students would be enrolled. Marian used the evidence that I and other activists gathered in the field to pressure the Nixon administration to crack down on these so-called segregated academies. It was thrilling work because it felt meaningful and real. After years spent studying social justice from a distance, I was finally doing something.

Another early job for Marian was going door-to-door in a work-ing-class Portuguese neighborhood in New Bedford, Massachusetts, to figure out why so many families were keeping their children out of school. One answer was that, in those days, most schools couldn't accommodate children with disabilities, so those kids had no choice but to stay home. I'll never forget meeting one young girl in a wheel-chair on the small back porch of her house. She told me how badly she wanted to go to school. But the wheelchair made it impossible. It seemed like it should be such a simple problem to solve.

This became a clarifying moment for me. I had been raised to be-lieve in the power of reason, evidence, argument, and in the centrality of fairness and equality. As a campus liberal in the foment of the six-ties, I took "consciousness raising" seriously. But talking about fairness alone wouldn't get a ramp built for this girl's wheelchair at the local public school. Raising public awareness would be necessary but not sufficient for changing school policies and hiring and training new staff to give students with disabilities an equal education. Instead of waiting for a revolution, the kind of change this girl needed was more likely to look like the sociologist Max Weber's description of politics: "a strong and slow boring of hard boards." I felt ready to do it.

Under Marian's leadership, we gathered data to document the scope of the problem. We wrote a report. We built a coalition of like-minded organizations. And we went to Washington to argue our case. It took until 1975, but the Children's Defense Fund's work eventually helped convince Congress to pass the Education for All Handicapped Children Act, requiring all public schools to make accommodations for students with disabilities.

This kind of work isn't glamorous. But my experience with CDF convinced me that *this* is how you make real change in America: step by step, year by year, sometimes even door by door. You need to stir up public opinion and put pressure on political leaders. You have to shift policies and resources. And you need to win elections. You need to change hearts *and* change laws.

Although I never imagined running for office myself, I came to see partisan politics as the most viable route in a democracy for achieving significant and lasting progress. Then, as now, plenty of progressive activists preferred to stand apart from party politics. Some saw both Democrats and Republicans as corrupt and compromised. Others were discouraged by repeated defeats. It was soul crushing to watch Democrats lose every single presidential election between 1968 and 1988 except one. But despite it all, I was attracted to politics. Even when I grew disillusioned, I knew that winning elections was the key that could unlock the change our country needed. So I stuffed envelopes for Gene McCarthy in New Hampshire, registered voters for George McGovern in Texas, set up field offices for Jimmy Carter in Indiana, and enthusiastically supported my husband's decision to run for office in Arkansas.

My identity as an advocate and activist remained important to me as I grew older. When I myself was lobbied and protested as a public official, it was a little like stepping through the looking glass. Whenever I grew frustrated, I'd remind myself how it felt to be on the other side of the table or out in the street with a sign and a megaphone. I'd been there. I knew that the activists giving me a hard time were doing their jobs, trying to drive progress and hold leaders accountable. That kind of pressure is not just important—it's mission-critical for a healthy democracy. As FDR supposedly told a group of civil rights leaders, "Okay, you've convinced me. Now make me do it."

Still, there was an inherent tension. Some activists and advocates saw their role as putting pressure on people in power, including allies, and they weren't interested in compromise. They didn't have to strike deals with Republicans or worry about winning elections. But I did. There are principles and values we should never compromise, but to be an effective leader in a democracy, you need flexible strategies and tactics, especially under difficult political conditions. I learned that the hard way during our battle for health care reform in the early nineties. Reluctance to compromise can bring about defeat. The forces opposed to change have it easier. They can just say no, again and again, and blame the other side when it doesn't happen. If you want to get something done, you have to find a way to get to yes.

So I've never had much respect for activists who are willing to sit out elections, waste their votes, or tear down well-meaning allies rather than engage constructively. Making the perfect the enemy of the good is shortsighted and counterproductive. And when someone on the left starts talking about how there's no difference between the two parties or that electing a right-wing Republican might somehow hasten "the revolution," it's just unfathomably wrong.

When I was Secretary of State, I met in Cairo with a group of young Egyptian activists who had helped organize the demonstrations in Tahrir Square that shocked the world by toppling President Hosni Mubarak in early 2011. They were intoxicated by the power of their protests but showed little interest in organizing political parties, drafting platforms, running candidates, or building coalitions. Politics wasn't for them, they said. I feared what that would mean for their future. I believed they were essentially handing the country over to the two most organized forces in Egypt: the Muslim Brotherhood and the military. In the years ahead, both fears proved correct.

I had similar conversations with some Black Lives Matter activists during the 2016 campaign. I respected how effectively their movement grabbed hold of the national debate. I welcomed it when activists such as Brittany Packnett and DeRay Mckesson pressed me on specific issues and engaged constructively with my team and me to make our platform better and stronger. And I was honored when they endorsed me for President. But I was concerned when other activists proved more interested in disruption and confrontation than in working together to change policies that perpetuate systemic racism.

This was on my mind during a memorable encounter with a few young activists in August 2015. They had driven up from Boston to attend one of my town hall meetings in Keene, New Hampshire. Well, *attend* is not quite the right word. *Disrupt* is more accurate. The town hall was focused on the growing problem of opioid abuse that was ravaging small towns across America, but the activists were determined to grab the spotlight for a different epidemic: the young black men and women being killed in encounters with police, as well as the broader systemic racism that devalued black lives and perpetuated inequities in education, housing, employment, and the justice system. In short: a cause worth fighting for.

They arrived too late to get into the town hall, but my staff suggested that we meet afterward so the activists could raise their concerns directly with me. Maybe we could even have a constructive back-and-forth. It started well enough. We were standing backstage in a small circle, which gave the discussion an intimate directness.

"What you're doing as activists and as people who are constantly raising these issues is really important," I said. "We can't get change unless there's constant pressure." Then I asked a question that I'd been wondering about for some time: how they planned to build on their early success. "We need a whole comprehensive plan. I am more than happy to work with you guys," I said.

But these activists didn't want to talk about developing a policy agenda. One was singularly focused on getting me to accept personal responsibility for having supported policies, especially the crime bill that my husband signed in 1994, which he claimed created a culture of mass incarceration. "You, Hillary Clinton, have been in no uncertain way, partially responsible for this. More than most," he declared.

I thought these activists were right that it was time for public officials—and all Americans, really—to stop tiptoeing around the brutal role that racism has played in our history and continues to play in our politics. But his view of the '94 crime bill was oversimplified beyond recognition.

The Violent Crime Control and Law Enforcement Act was passed during the crack epidemic that ravaged America's cities in the 1980s and early 1990s. It included important and positive provisions, such as the Violence Against Women Act and a ban on assault weapons. It set up special drug courts to keep first-time offenders out of prison, funded after-school and job opportunities for at-risk young people, and provided resources to hire and train more police officers. Unfortunately, the only way to pass the law was to also include measures that congressional Republicans demanded. They insisted on longer federal sentences for drug offenders. States that were already increasing penalties were emboldened. States that weren't doing so, started to. And all that led to higher rates of incarceration across the country. As chairman of the Senate Judiciary Committee, Joe Biden helped write the compromise legislation. Bernie Sanders voted for it. So did most congressional Democrats. It was also supported by many black leaders determined to stop the crime wave decimating their communities. As Yale Law School professor James Forman Jr. explains in his book *Locking Up Our Own: Crime and Punishment in Black America*, "African Americans have *always* viewed the protection of black lives as a civil rights issue, whether the threat comes from police officers or street criminals."

So, yes, the crime bill was flawed. It was a tough compromise. And it's fair to say, as Bill himself has done in the years since, that the negative consequences took a heavy toll, especially in poor and minority communities. "I signed a bill that made the problem worse," Bill said at a national conference of the NAACP in July 2015, referring to excessive incarceration. I agreed with him, which is why I was the first candidate to call for "an end to the era of mass incarceration" and proposed an aggressive agenda for criminal justice reform. It's painful now to think about how we're going backward on these issues under President Trump, with an Attorney General who favors longer sentences for drug offenders and less oversight of police departments, and who is hostile to civil rights and voting rights across the board.

So I understood the frustration of the Black Lives Matter activists, and I respected their conviction. I knew they spoke from a lifetime of being ignored and disrespected by authority figures. But I kept trying to steer the conversation back to the question of how to develop and advance a concrete agenda on racial justice.

"There has to be some positive vision and plan that you can move people toward," I said. "The consciousness raising, the advocacy, the passion, the youth of your movement is so critical. But now all I'm suggesting is—even for us sinners—find some common ground on agendas that can make a difference right here and now in people's lives."

We went round and round awhile longer on these questions, but it felt like we were talking past one another. I don't think any of us left the conversation very satisfied.

I took seriously the policies some of the Black Lives Matter activists later put forward to reform the criminal justice system and invest in communities of color. I asked Maya and our team to work closely with them. We incorporated the best of their ideas into our plans, along with input from civil rights organizations that had been in the trenches for decades. In October 2015, my friend Alexis Herman, the former Secretary of Labor, hosted a meeting in Washington for me with another group of activists. We had an engaging discussion about how to improve policing, build trust, and create a sense of security and opportunity in black neighborhoods. They spoke about feeling not only like outsiders in America but intruders—like someone no one wants, no one values. As one woman put it, "If you look like me, your life doesn't have worth." It was wrenching to hear a young American say that.

Finding the right balance between principle and pragmatism isn't easy. One example of how hard that was for me was the effort to reform welfare in the nineties—another tough compromise that remains controversial. Bill and I both believed that change was needed to help more people get the tools and support to transition from welfare to work, including assistance with health care and childcare. But Republicans in Congress were determined to rip up the social safety net. They wanted to slash funding and guarantees for welfare, Medicaid, school lunches, and food stamps; deny all benefits even to *documented* immigrants; and send children born out of wedlock to teen mothers to orphanages—all while offering little support to people who wanted to find work. It was cold-blooded. I encouraged Bill to veto the Republican plan, which he did. They passed it again with only minimal changes. So he vetoed it again. Then Congress passed a compromise plan. It was still flawed but on balance seemed like it would help more than it hurt.

It was a hard call. Bill and I lay awake at night talking it over. The new plan no longer block granted Medicaid and food stamps and instead put more money into them, along with childcare, housing, and transportation for people moving from welfare to work. We hoped Bill's administration would be able to fix some of the legislation's problems in a second term and keep pressing to do more to help Americans lift themselves out of poverty. Ultimately, he decided to accept the bad with the good and sign the legislation into law.

Two of the loudest voices opposing the compromise plan belonged to Marian Wright Edelman and her husband, Peter, who was an Assistant Secretary of Health and Human Services. Marian wrote an impassioned op-ed in the *Washington Post* calling this the "defining moral litmus test" of Bill's presidency. Peter resigned in protest. I respected Marian's and Peter's position—in fact, I expected no less from them—but it was painful to see one of the defining relationships of my life become strained.

There was never a full breach, and eventually we were drawn back together by the same shared passions that made us such close friends in the first place. Marian and I both threw ourselves into the fight to create the Children's Health Insurance Program, which emerged out of the ashes of the Clinton administration's failure to pass universal health care reform in 1993–1994. I learned a lot of lessons about what it takes to get things done in Congress, including how to work across the aisle and lean more effectively on outside allies like Marian. Those lessons paid off when CHIP became a bipartisan success story that continues to provide health care to millions of kids every year. Now Donald Trump proposes dismantling the program, which would be tragic.

In 1999, when I paid a visit to the Children's Defense Fund's farm in Tennessee for the dedication of a library in honor of the writer Langston Hughes, Marian and I went for a long walk around the grounds. It felt good to be back by her side. The next year, I watched with great pride as Bill awarded Marian the Presidential Medal of Freedom for her lifetime of advocacy.

Looking back, our disagreement over welfare reform was a testament to how deeply we both cared about policy—and to how different it is to be an advocate on the outside as opposed to a policy maker on the inside. What didn't change, though, and what ultimately brought us back together, was the passion we shared for children.

For me, it always comes back to children. The one core belief I've articulated more often and more fervently than any other in all my years in public life is that every child deserves the chance to live up to his or her God-given potential. I've said that line so many times, I've lost count. But the idea remains as powerful and motivating for me as ever. I continue to believe that a society should be judged by how we treat the most vulnerable among us, especially children, and that the measure of our success should be how many kids climb out of poverty, get a good education, and receive the love and support they deserve.

This has been a consistent through-line of my career, starting with my days with Marian at the Children's Defense Fund, and my work as a law student on early childhood development at the Yale Child Study Center and on child abuse at Yale–New Haven Hospital. Maybe it goes back even further, to the lessons I learned from my mother about her own painful childhood. She went out of her way to help girls in our town who were in trouble, in need, or just looking for a friend, because she believed that every child deserves a chance and a champion. I came to believe that too, and in every job I've ever held, I've tried to be that champion. It's a big part of why I ran for President and what I'd hoped to accomplish if I won.

I'm sure that in our hypercynical age, this sounds like just a lot of happy talk—the kind of thing politicians say when they're trying to show their softer side. After all, who doesn't love kids? Everybody professes to, even when their policies would actually hurt children. But I mean it. This is real for me.

Nothing makes me more furious than seeing kids get taken advantage of or mistreated—or not getting the opportunity, the support, the encouragement, and the security they need to succeed. You've already read about how hard it is for women in politics to express anger the way men do, and how I've struggled with the damned-if-you-do-damned-if-you-don't double bind that presents. But for me, there's always been an exception when it comes to children. I have zero patience for adults who hurt or neglect kids. My temper just boils over. That's what sparked many of the big battles I've taken on in my career.

For example, I fought so hard for health care reform in the nineties in part because of some children I met at a hospital in Cleveland. The kids all had preexisting conditions, so their families couldn't get insurance. One father of two little girls with cystic fibrosis told me the insurance company said, "Sorry, we don't insure burning houses." He pointed to his girls with tears in his eyes and said, "They called my little girls burning houses." His words nearly knocked the wind out of me. And the thought of those kids kept me going through every stumble and setback, until we finally convinced Congress to pass CHIP.

I had a similar experience early in 2016, when I read a story in the newspaper about the water crisis in Flint, Michigan. An alarming number of children were sick with lead poisoning, apparently because state authorities had failed to properly test or treat the water supply. I spent years as First Lady and as a Senator working to reduce the danger to kids from lead paint poisoning, which threatens the health of hundreds of thousands of young children across our country. But I'd never even heard of anything like what was happening in Flint.

The city used to be a thriving center for auto manufacturing, but, as vividly documented in Michael Moore's 1989 film *Roger & Me*, the city was slowly hollowed out by plant closings and job losses. By 2013, the median household income was less than $25,000, and more than 40 percent of residents, most of them black, lived in poverty. In 2013 and 2014, the city's emergency fiscal manager appointed by Michigan's Republican Governor came up with a plan to save a little money: instead of buying drinking water from Detroit's municipal system, as the city had long done, it would draw from the Flint River.

Almost immediately, families in town began to complain about the color, taste, and odor of the water, as well as rashes and other health concerns. Parents brought bottles of brown, smelly water to show officials. "This is what my baby is drinking," they said. "This is what she bathes in." They were ignored or given false assurances that the water was safe to drink. It was the cruelest kind of indifference. It turns out the Michigan Department of Environmental Quality never treated the river water with an anticorrosive agent that would have cost just $200 a day. That violation of federal law caused lead to leach from pipes into the city's water. Children under the age of five years old are the most vulnerable to lead poisoning, which can irreparably harm brain development and cause learning and behavioral problems. In Flint, thousands of kids may have been exposed, and the rate of lead poisoning diagnosed among children nearly doubled.

For two years or so, the state government hardly did anything about the problem. It wasn't until a group of outside doctors performed their own testing and exposed just how toxic the water was that the public health crisis became national news. When I heard about it in January 2016, I was appalled. I asked members of my team to go to Flint right away and see if they could learn more. I also called the Mayor, Karen Weaver, and asked, "What can I do to help?" She was eager for anything that would put a spotlight on Flint and pressure on the Governor to finally help fix things.

So that's exactly what I did. I raised a ruckus out on the campaign trail and on television, and called on the Governor to declare a state of emergency, which would trigger federal aid. Within a few hours, he did. That just made me more determined to keep banging the drum. At the end of the next Democratic primary debate, the moderator, Lester Holt, asked, "Is there anything that you really wanted to say tonight that you haven't gotten a chance to say?" I jumped at the opportunity to tell a national audience about what was happening in Flint.

"Every single American should be outraged," I said. "A city in the United States of America where the population which is poor in many ways and majority African American has been drinking and bathing in lead-contaminated water—and the Governor of that state acted as though he didn't really care." I was getting pretty worked up. "I'll tell you what," I continued, "if the kids in a rich suburb of Detroit had been drinking contaminated water and being bathed in it, there would've been action."

That comment may have made some people uncomfortable, but it's hard to deny that what happened in Flint never would have happened in an affluent community like Grosse Pointe. State authorities would have rushed to help, and resources would have poured in. By the same token, the schools in wealthy Bloomfield Hills are never going to look like the schools in Detroit, where children sit in classrooms infested with rodents and mold, with ceilings caving in and the heat barely functioning. All across the country, there are examples of poor communities and communities of color living with dangerous levels of toxic pollution—and it's always children who pay the biggest price.

After the debate, my campaign team was thrilled. Finally, they thought I was showing the kind of passion they believed voters wanted to see. For months, we had been losing the "outrage primary." Bernie was outraged about everything. He thundered on at every event about the sins of "the millionaires and billionaires." I was more focused on offering practical solutions that would address real problems and make life better for people. But now, in defense of those sick kids in Flint, I was the one full of righteous indignation.

A couple weeks later, I went to Flint to see what was happening for myself. It was even more heartbreaking than I imagined. Mayor Weaver and I sat down with a group of mothers in the pastor's office of the House of Prayer Missionary Baptist Church. I noticed that the church's water fountains were all marked "Out of Order," a small reminder of what this town had been living with for the past two years.

Then the mothers told me their stories. One shared that she'd been pregnant with twins when she had a reaction to the poisoned water. "It was so horrible," she said. First, she went to the emergency room with a rash. Then she had a miscarriage and needed a blood transfusion. It was emotionally devastating. What's more, it bothered her that every resident had to pay a hefty fee to use the water in the first place. Imagine, she said, "paying for poison."

"I have seizures now. That's something I didn't have before," another mom told me, fighting back tears. "Our lives have been just so damaged."

"Our conversations are not about birthdays anymore. They're not about swimming lessons," said a third mother. "They're about hospital visits and going to the ER."

One mom, Nakiya, introduced me to her adorable six-year-old son, Jaylon. He was scampering around us, taking pictures with a phone, smiling from ear to ear. Nakiya told me he'd been exposed to high levels of lead and was now having trouble in school. All I wanted to do was scoop Jaylon up in my arms, hold him tight, and promise that everything was going to be okay. Later, after speaking to the church congregation, I found Nakiya and Jaylon again. Barb Kinney, our campaign photographer, asked if he'd like to try out her fancy Nikon camera. Jaylon's eyes got big as flashbulbs, and he nodded his head. Soon he was snapping shots like a pro.

Before we left, I gave Jaylon a big hug. But I couldn't promise that everything would be okay or that the problems in Flint would go away anytime soon. In fact, I was worried that Republicans in Michigan and Washington still weren't taking the crisis seriously.

I wanted to do more to help. The people of Flint couldn't wait for the next election. They certainly couldn't wait for the Revolution. They needed change right away. "The Mayor said something that struck me," I told a few local leaders. "Rather than have people come in from the outside, let's hire people from the inside. Every church could be a dispensing station or an organizing hub." We made plans to keep in touch.

As soon as I got on the plane, I turned to Maya. I was burning with frustration over what I'd seen. "How could this have happened?" I fumed. "It's criminal! We've got to do something about it." Over the next several weeks, we worked with Mayor Weaver, local pastors, the community college, the NAACP, and others to line up support and funding for a new public-private partnership that hired unemployed young people to deliver clean water to families who needed it. Chelsea made two visits of her own and helped launch the Mayor's program. People from across the country also answered the call to help. Hundreds of union plumbers arrived to install water filters for free. Students at universities all over the Midwest raised funds for clean water deliveries. A kindergartner in New Hampshire, who lost his first tooth and received $5 from the tooth fairy, told his parents he wanted to donate it "so those little kids can have water." His mom was so proud, she sat down right away and wrote me a letter about it.

The situation in Flint is still dire. It's heartbreaking and outrageous. This is not something that should ever happen in America, period. It's lousy governance and shameful politics at their worst. It took until the end of 2016 for Congress to agree on a relief package. Most of the city's thirty thousand lead-based water pipes have yet to be replaced, forcing residents to continue to rely on bottled and boiled water. Five state officials, including the head of Michigan's health department, have been charged with involuntary manslaughter. Meanwhile, the schools are still inadequate, there aren't enough jobs, and too many children go to bed hungry.

This still infuriates me. But I do take some comfort in the compassion and generosity that many Americans showed when they learned about the crisis. One of the most rewarding parts of running for President was getting to see that spirit up close, in a million ways. For example, one day in September 2015, I held a town hall meeting in Exeter, New Hampshire. One of the residents who stood up to ask a question was a ninth-grade teacher, in the classroom for thirteen years, asking how we can help kids from low-income families find more opportunities for summer enrichment. Then a young woman stood up. She was just back from a year of working in a middle school in the Watts section of Los Angeles, through the AmeriCorps national service program. Next was someone who works with young survivors of commercial sexual exploitation and trafficking. Then a twenty-two-year veteran of the Navy with a son on active duty in the Marine Corps. One after another, these Americans asked me their questions, and each of them had his or her own extraordinary story of service and giving back to the community. That's part of what I love about America. Those people in Exeter, and everyone who lent a hand to help out in Flint, are examples of how real change happens. Progress comes from rolling up your sleeves and getting to work.

To me, Flint was so much more than something to rail about on the campaign trail, even if outrage is good politics. And in this case, it's possible that it wasn't good politics. I don't know if my advocacy for the heavily African American community of Flint alienated white voters in other parts of Michigan, but it certainly didn't seem to help, as I lost the state narrowly in both the primary and the general election. Either way, that's not what it was about for me. There were real live kids to help. Kids like Jaylon. And as I learned from Marian Wright Edelman nearly a half century ago, there's nothing more important than that.

Marian had one more lesson to teach me. In the dark days immediately following November 8, 2016, when all I wanted to do was curl up in bed and never leave the house again, Marian sent me a message. Come back to CDF, she said. The Children's Defense Fund was hosting a celebration in Washington for an inspiring group of kids who had beaten the odds, thriving despite poverty, violence, and abandonment. Before the election, Marian had asked me to deliver the keynote. Now she wanted me to know that it was even more important that I come.

It was hard to imagine giving a speech so soon after conceding the election. But if there was anyone who knew how to pick herself up, get back on her feet, and get back to work, it was Marian. She'd been doing it all her life and helping the rest of us do it too. For decades, I'd heard Marian say, "Service is the rent we pay for living." Well, I decided, you don't get to stop paying rent just because things don't go your way.

So there we were, on November 16, together again at the Children's Defense Fund. Marian stepped to the podium, and talked about our long partnership and all we'd done together to lift up children and families. Then she pointed to her two granddaughters sitting in the audience and said, "Because of all the paths she's paved for them, one day soon your daughter or my daughter or our granddaughters are going to sit in that Oval Office, and we can thank Hillary Rodham Clinton." I wanted to cry and curse and cheer all at the same time.

To leave the world a bit better, whether by a healthy child, a garden patch, or a redeemed social condition; to know even one life breathed easier because you lived. This is to have succeeded.

—attributed to Ralph Waldo Emerson

Sweating the Details

"The decisions a Commander in Chief makes can have a profound and lasting impact on all Americans, but none more so than the brave men and women who serve, fight, and die for our country." That was Matt Lauer introducing NBC's "Commander in Chief Forum" from the deck of the aircraft carrier U.S.S. *Intrepid* on September 7, 2016. I was standing just offstage listening to his introduction, nodding my head.

Lauer promised the forum would be an opportunity to "talk about national security and the complex global issues that face our nation." That's exactly what I wanted. With Election Day just two months away, it was time to have a serious discussion about each candidate's qualifications to be President and how he or she would lead the country. This wouldn't be a formal debate with me and Donald Trump onstage at the same time. Instead, we'd each do our own thirty-minute session answering questions from Lauer and the audience. I was confident that with a real focus on substance and a clear contrast of our records, Americans would see that I was ready to be Commander in Chief, and Donald Trump was dangerously unprepared.

Plus, I happen to love talking about foreign policy. As Secretary of State, I got to do that pretty much nonstop for four years in 112 countries. But as a candidate for President, I was rarely asked about anything beyond domestic issues. One exception was during a campaign stop in Iowa, when a voter asked a question about the dangers of unexploded bombs from the Vietnam War left behind in Laos. It was so surprising, I nearly dropped the microphone.

Lauer and NBC were promoting this forum as a chance to finally get serious about foreign policy and national security. I was slightly surprised that Trump had agreed to it. He had been tripped up on easy questions about nuclear weapons (he said that more countries could have them, including Saudi Arabia), NATO (he called it obsolete), torture (he was for it), and prisoners of war (he said he prefers soldiers who don't get captured). He kept lying about opposing the Iraq War even after a recording emerged of him saying he supported it. And he had a penchant for saying absurd things such as "I know more about ISIS than the Generals do, believe me." Nobody believed him. In fact, more than a hundred senior national security officials from Republican administrations publicly denounced him. Many signed a letter warning that Trump "lacks the character, values, and experience" to be Commander in Chief. They wrote that he would be "the most reckless President in American history," and would "put at risk our country's national security and well-being."

Trump's campaign signed up for this forum nonetheless. They won a coin toss and chose to go second. So there I was, waiting in the wings for Lauer to call me out to the stage.

He began with a broad question about the most important characteristic that a Commander in Chief can possess. I used my answer to talk about steadiness, a quality that nobody ever associates with

Donald Trump. Lauer cut in to say, "You're talking about judgment." That wasn't what I was talking about, exactly, but it was close enough. "Temperament and judgment, yes," I replied.

I've been around the block enough times to know that something bad was coming. Lauer had the look of someone proud of himself for having laid a clever trap.

"The word *judgment* has been used a lot around you, Secretary Clinton, over the last year and a half, and in particular concerning your use of your personal email and server to communicate while you were Secretary of State," Lauer said. "You've said it's a mistake. You said you made not the best choice. You were communicating on highly sensitive topics. Why wasn't it more than a mistake? Why wasn't it disqualifying, if you want to be Commander in Chief?"

It was disappointing but predictable that he had so quickly steered the supposedly high-minded "Commander in Chief Forum" to the subject of emails, months after the director of the FBI had announced there was no case and closed the investigation. I understood that every political reporter wanted his or her pound of flesh. But Lauer had already grilled me about emails in an interview back in April. I figured this must be about "balance." Many in the mainstream media bend over backward to avoid criticism from the right about being soft on Democrats. If Lauer intended to ask Trump tough questions, he had to make a show of grilling me, too.

Of course, that isn't balanced at all—because balanced doesn't mean strictly equal. It means reasonable. It means asking smart questions backed by solid reporting and making decisions about coverage that will help people get the information they need to make sound decisions. Picking the midpoint between two sides, no matter how extreme one of them is, isn't balanced—it's false equivalence. If Trump ripped the shirt off someone at a rally and a button fell off my jacket on the same day, the headline "Trump and Clinton Experience Wardrobe Malfunctions, Campaigns in Turmoil" might feel equal to some, but it

wouldn't be balanced, and it definitely wouldn't be fair. Most important, the voters wouldn't learn anything that would help them decide
who should be president.

The Lauer episode was a perfect example. I made a mistake with
my emails. I apologized, I explained, I explained, and apologized some
more. Yet here we were, after all these months, and after the FBI finished its work, at a forum supposed to be about the security of our
country, and to balance the fact that Trump was going to have a hard
time answering even the most straightforward questions, we were
spending our time on emails.

After the election, a report from Professor Thomas Patterson at
Harvard's Shorenstein Center on Media, Politics, and Public Policy
explained how damaging the pursuit of false equivalency can be. "If
everything and everyone are portrayed negatively, there's a leveling effect that opens the door to charlatans," it said. "The press historically
has helped citizens recognize the difference between the earnest politician and the pretender. Today's news coverage blurs the distinction."

Here I was, facing the blurring in real time, with a charlatan waiting in the wings. But what could I do? I launched into my standard
answer on the emails, the one I'd given a thousand times before: "It was
a mistake to have a personal account. I would certainly not do it again.
I make no excuses for it," and so forth. I also explained that, as the FBI
had confirmed, none of the emails I sent or received was marked as
classified.

Instead of moving on to any of a hundred urgent national security
issues, from the civil war in Syria, to the Iranian nuclear agreement, to
the threat from North Korea—the issues this forum was supposed to
be about—Lauer stayed on emails. He asked four follow-ups. Meanwhile, the clock was ticking, and my thirty minutes to discuss serious
foreign policy challenges were slipping away.

Finally, after learning absolutely nothing new or interesting, Lauer
turned to a question from one of the veterans NBC had picked to be

in the audience. He was a self-described Republican, a former Navy lieutenant who had served in the first Gulf War, and he promptly repeated the right-wing talking point about how my email use would have landed anyone else in prison. Then he asked how could he trust me as President "when you clearly corrupted our national security?"

Now I was ticked off. NBC knew exactly what it was doing here. The network was treating this like an episode of *The Apprentice*, in which Trump stars and ratings soar. Lauer had turned what should have been a serious discussion into a pointless ambush. What a waste of time.

When another veteran in the audience was finally allowed to ask about how to defeat ISIS, Lauer interrupted me before I began answering. "As briefly as you can," he admonished. Trump should have reported his performance as an in-kind contribution.

Later, there were rumors ginned up by fake news reports that I was so mad at him I stormed off stage, threw a tantrum, and shattered a water glass. While I didn't do any of that, I can't say I didn't fantasize about shaking some sense into Lauer while I was out there.

Now I wish I had pushed back hard on his question. I should have said, "You know, Matt, I was the one in the Situation Room advising the President to go after Osama bin Laden. I was with Leon Panetta and David Petraeus urging stronger action sooner in Syria. I worked to rebuild Lower Manhattan after 9/11 and provide health care to our first responders. I'm the one worried about Putin subverting our democracy. I started the negotiations with Iran to prevent a nuclear arms race in the Middle East. I'm the one national security experts trust with our country's future." And so much more. Here's another example where I remained polite, albeit exasperated, and played the political game as it used to be, not as it had become. That was a mistake.

Later, I watched Lauer soft-pedal Trump's interview. "What do you believe prepares you to make decisions that a Commander in Chief has to make?" he asked. Then he failed to call Trump out on his lies about Iraq. I was almost physically sick.

Thankfully, a lot of viewers reacted exactly the same way. The *Washington Post* published a stinging editorial:

> Judging by the amount of time NBC's Matt Lauer spent pressing Hillary Clinton on her emails during Wednesday's national security presidential forum, one would think that her home-brew server was one of the most important issues facing the country this election. It is not. There are a thousand other substantive issues—from China's aggressive moves in the South China Sea to National Security Agency intelligence-gathering to military spending—that would have revealed more about what the candidates know and how they would govern. Instead, these did not even get mentioned in the first of five and a half precious prime-time hours the two candidates will share before Election Day, while emails took up a third of Ms. Clinton's time.

Criticism of Lauer and NBC poured in. *New York Times* columnist Nicholas Kristof called the forum "an embarrassment to journalism." *Slate*'s Will Saletan described it as "one of the weakest, least incisive performances I've seen from a presidential forum moderator." And *The Daily Show*'s Trevor Noah had my favorite take: "During World War II, on multiple occasions, kamikaze planes crashed into the *Intrepid*, and last night Matt Lauer continued that tradition," he said. "I don't know what the f— he was doing, and neither did he."

Sadly, though, millions of people watched. And in my view, the "Commander in Chief Forum" was representative of how many in the press covered the campaign as a whole. According again to Harvard's Shorenstein Center, discussion of public policy accounted for just 10 percent of all campaign news coverage in the general election. Nearly all the rest was taken up by obsessive coverage of controversies such as email. Health care, taxes, trade, immigration, national security—all of it crammed into just 10 percent of the press coverage. The Shorenstein Center found that not a single one of my many detailed policy plans received more than a blip of press coverage. "If she had a policy agenda, it was not apparent in the news," it concluded. "Her lengthy record of public service also received scant attention." None of Trump's scandals, from scamming students at Trump University, to stiffing small businesses in Atlantic City, to exploiting his foundation, to refusing to release his taxes as every presidential candidate since 1976 has done— and on and on—generated the kind of sustained, campaign-defining coverage that my emails did.

The decline of serious reporting on policy has been going on for a while, but it got much worse in 2016. In 2008, the major networks' nightly newscasts spent a total of 220 minutes on policy. In 2012, it was 114 minutes. In 2016, it was just 32 minutes. (That stat is from two weeks before the election, but it didn't change much in the final stretch.) By contrast, 100 minutes were spent covering my emails. In other words, the political press was telling voters that my emails were three times more important than all the other issues combined.

Maybe this bothers me so much because I'm an unapologetic policy wonk. It's true that I sweat the details, whether it's the precise level of lead in the drinking water in Flint, the number of mental health facilities in Iowa, the cost of specific prescription drugs, or how exactly the nuclear triad works. Those aren't just details if it's your kid or your aging parent whose life depends on it—or, when it comes to nukes, if all life on earth depends on it. Those details ought to be important to anyone seeking to lead our country.

I've always thought about policy in a very practical way. It's how we solve problems and make life better for people. I try to learn as much as I can about the challenges people face and then work with the smartest experts I can find to come up with solutions that are achievable, affordable, and will actually make a measurable difference. For the campaign, I hired a policy team with deep experience in government and relied on an extensive network of outside advisors drawn from academia, think tanks, and the private sector. The crew in Brooklyn proudly hung a sign above their desks that read "Wonks for the Win." They produced reams of position papers. Many included budget scores, substantive footnotes—the whole nine yards. It felt like a White House-in-waiting, which is exactly what I had in mind. I wanted to be able to hit the ground running, ready to sign executive orders and work with Congress to pass as much legislation as possible in my first hundred days in office. I also wanted voters to know exactly what they could expect from me as President, how it would affect their lives, and be able to hold me accountable for delivering.

Over the course of the 2016 race, I also came to better appreciate other ways of thinking about policy: as a window to a candidate's character and a tool for mobilization.

Joe Biden likes to say, "Don't tell me what you value. Show me your budget, and I'll tell you what you value." This is something I've always believed as well: that the policies you propose say a lot about your principles and priorities. You can evaluate a candidate's childcare plan based on how much it will cost, who it will help, and whether it has a chance of passing Congress. But you can also see it as a window into the candidate's heart: this is a person who cares about children and believes society has a responsibility to help care for the most vulnerable among us. The piece that perhaps I undervalued is that, from this perspective, the details of the plan may matter less than how it's framed and sold to the public—in other words, the optics of it. I cared about the optics, but not nearly as much as I cared about the merits of the plans themselves, and it showed.

Policy can also be a source of inspiration. I don't know how many Trump supporters really believed that he'd build a giant wall across the entire southern border and get Mexico to pay for it. But hearing him say it got them excited. You don't have to like the idea to see that it gave them something to talk to their friends about, tweet, and post on Facebook. It was a rallying call more than it was a credible policy proposal, but that didn't make it any less powerful—especially if voters weren't hearing me talk about immigration or any of their economic concerns because of overwhelming coverage of emails.

These different ways of thinking about policy helped shape both the primaries and the general election in 2016.

From the beginning, I expected a strong primary challenge from the left. It happens almost every time, and it was clear this time that there was a lot of populist energy waiting to find a champion. Anger at the financial industry had been building for years. The Occupy Wall Street movement had helped shine a light on the problem of income inequality. And after years of biting their tongues about the Obama administration's compromises, left-wing Democrats were ready to let loose.

Senator Elizabeth Warren was the name most often mentioned as a potential candidate, but I wasn't convinced she was going to jump in. After all, she had joined all the other Democratic women Senators in signing a letter urging me to run. I've long admired Elizabeth's passion and tenacity, especially her farsighted efforts to create the Consumer Financial Protection Bureau in 2011, which has now returned nearly $12 billion to more than twenty-nine million Americans ripped off by predatory lenders, credit card companies, and other corporate miscreants. So before I announced my candidacy, I invited her to my house in Washington to take her temperature and see if we might be able to work together. I think we both were a little wary, but we approached each other with good faith, good intentions, and open minds. I came away convinced that if Elizabeth believed her views and priorities would be included and respected in my campaign, she might become my champion rather than my challenger. In our meeting, we talked about some of the issues she cares about most, including student debt and financial reform. Knowing that Elizabeth believes "personnel is policy," I asked her to recommend experts whose advice I could seek. She gave me a list, and my team methodically worked through it, making sure our agenda was informed by the perspectives of people she trusted. Two friends we share in common—the political consultant Mandy Grunwald, who also worked for Elizabeth, and the former financial regulator Gary Gensler, who served as my campaign's chief financial officer—helped us stay connected. Later, Elizabeth was on my list of potential choices for Vice President.

Elizabeth never joined the race, but Bernie Sanders, the Democratic Socialist Senator from Vermont, did. Even though I understood that a lot of Democratic primary voters were looking for a left-wing alternative, I admit I didn't expect Bernie to catch on as much as he did. Nothing in my experience in American politics suggested that a Socialist from Vermont could mount a credible campaign for the White House. But Bernie proved to be a disciplined and effective politician. He tapped into powerful emotional currents in the electorate. And he was aided by the fact that the primaries began with the white, liberal bastions of Iowa and New Hampshire, his neighboring state. When a *Des Moines Register* poll in January 2016 found that 43 percent of likely Iowa Democratic caucusgoers identified as Socialists, I knew there could be trouble ahead.

Bernie and I had a spirited contest of ideas, which was invigorating, but I nonetheless found campaigning against him to be profoundly frustrating. He didn't seem to mind if his math didn't add up or if his plans had no prayer of passing Congress and becoming law. For Bernie, policy was about inspiring a mass movement and forcing a conversation about the Democratic Party's values and priorities. By that standard, I would say he succeeded. But it worried me. I've always believed that it's dangerous to make big promises if you have no idea how you're going to keep them. When you don't deliver, it will make people even more cynical about government.

No matter how bold and progressive my policy proposals

were—and they were significantly bolder and more progressive than anything President Obama or I had proposed in 2008—Bernie would come out with something even bigger, loftier, and leftier, regardless of whether it was realistic or not. That left me to play the unenviable role of spoilsport schoolmarm, pointing out that there was no way Bernie could keep his promises or deliver real results.

Jake Sullivan, my top policy advisor, told me it reminded him of a scene from the 1998 movie *There's Something About Mary*. A deranged hitchhiker says he's come up with a brilliant plan. Instead of the famous "eight-minute abs" exercise routine, he's going to market "seven-minute abs." It's the same, just quicker. Then the driver, played by Ben Stiller, says, "Well, why not six-minute abs?" That's what it was like in policy debates with Bernie. We would propose a bold infrastructure investment plan or an ambitious new apprenticeship program for young people, and then Bernie would announce basically the same thing, but bigger. On issue after issue, it was like he kept proposing four-minute abs, or even no-minute abs. Magic abs!

Someone sent me a Facebook post that summed up the dynamic in which we were caught:

BERNIE: I think America should get a pony.

HILLARY: How will you pay for the pony? Where will the pony come from? How will you get Congress to agree to the pony?

BERNIE: Hillary thinks America doesn't deserve a pony.

BERNIE SUPPORTERS: Hillary hates ponies!

HILLARY: Actually, I love ponies.

BERNIE SUPPORTERS: She changed her position on ponies! #WhichHillary? #WitchHillary

HEADLINE: "Hillary Refuses to Give Every American a Pony"

DEBATE MODERATOR: Hillary, how do you feel when people say you lie about ponies?

WEBSITE HEADLINE: "Congressional Inquiry into Clinton's
  Pony Lies"
TWITTER TRENDING: #ponygate

Early in the race, in 2015, there was a day when Bernie and I both
happened to be in the Amtrak passenger lounge at New York's Penn
Station waiting for the train to D.C. We talked for a bit, and he said
he hoped we could avoid personal attacks, including on our families.
I know what that's like. I agreed and said I hoped we could keep our
debates focused on substance.

Yet despite this pledge, as time went on, Bernie routinely portrayed
me as a corrupt corporatist who couldn't be trusted. His clear implication
was that because I accepted campaign donations from people on Wall
Street—just as President Obama had done—I was "bought and paid for."

This attack was galling for many reasons, not least because Bernie
and I agreed on the issue of campaign finance reform; the need to get
dark money out of politics; and the urgency of preventing billionaires,
powerful corporations, and special interests from buying elections. We
both supported a constitutional amendment to overturn the disastrous
Supreme Court decision in *Citizens United* that opened the floodgates
to super PACs and secret money. I also proposed new measures to
boost disclosure and transparency and to match small donor contributions, based on New York City's successful system, which would help
level the playing field for everyday Americans.

Where Bernie and I differed was that he seemed to see the dysfunction of our politics almost solely as a problem of money, whereas
I thought ideology and tribalism also played significant roles. Bernie
talked as if 99 percent of Americans would back his agenda if only
the lobbyists and super PACs disappeared. But that wouldn't turn
small-government conservatives into Scandinavian Socialists or make
religious fundamentalists embrace marriage equality and reproductive rights. I also was—and am—concerned about the Republican-led

assault on voting rights, their efforts to gerrymander safe congressional districts, and the breakdown of comity in Congress. In addition to getting big money out of politics, I thought we had to wage and win the battle of ideas, while also reaching across the aisle more aggressively to hammer out compromises. That's how we can start to break down the gridlock and actually get things done again.

Because we agreed on so much, Bernie couldn't make an argument against me in this area on policy, so he had to resort to innuendo and impugning my character. Some of his supporters, the so-called Bernie Bros, took to harassing my supporters online. It got ugly and more than a little sexist. When I finally challenged Bernie during a debate to name a single time I changed a position or a vote because of a financial contribution, he couldn't come up with anything. Nonetheless, his attacks caused lasting damage, making it harder to unify progressives in the general election and paving the way for Trump's "Crooked Hillary" campaign.

I don't know if that bothered Bernie or not. He certainly shared my horror at the thought of Donald Trump becoming President, and I appreciated that he campaigned for me in the general election. But he isn't a Democrat—that's not a smear, that's what he says. He didn't get into the race to make sure a Democrat won the White House, he got in to disrupt the Democratic Party. He was right that Democrats needed to strengthen our focus on working families and that there's always a danger of spending too much time courting donors because of our insane campaign finance system. He also engaged a lot of young people in the political process for the first time, which is extremely important. But I think he was fundamentally wrong about the Democratic Party—the party that brought us Social Security under Roosevelt; Medicare and Medicaid under Johnson; peace between Israel and Egypt under Carter; broad-based prosperity and a balanced budget under Clinton; and rescued the auto industry, passed health care reform, and imposed tough new rules on Wall Street under Obama. I am proud to be a Democrat and I wish Bernie were, too.

Throughout the primaries, every time I wanted to hit back against Bernie's attacks, I was told to restrain myself. Noting that his plans didn't add up, that they would inevitably mean raising taxes on middle-class families, or that they were little more than a pipe dream—all of this could be used to reinforce his argument that I wasn't a true progressive. My team kept reminding me that we didn't want to alienate Bernie's supporters. President Obama urged me to grit my teeth and lay off Bernie as much as I could. I felt like I was in a straitjacket.

I eagerly looked forward to our first debate in October 2015. At last, that was a place where it would be appropriate to punch back. I held long prep sessions at my house to map out thrusts and parries with Jake, Ron Klain, Karen Dunn, and Bob Barnett, who played Bernie in our practice sessions.

I was determined to use this first debate with Bernie to go straight at the core differences between us. I wanted to debunk the false charge that I wasn't a true progressive and explain why I thought Socialism was wrong for America—and that those two propositions were in no way contradictory. It was beyond frustrating that Bernie acted as if he had a monopoly on political purity and that he had set himself up as the sole arbiter of what it meant to be progressive, despite giving short shrift to important issues such as immigration, reproductive rights, racial justice, and gun safety. I believed we could and should fight both for more equal economic opportunities *and* greater social justice. They go hand in hand, and it's wrong to sacrifice the latter in the name of the former.

As the date approached, the first debate took on added significance. Bernie was rising in the polls. Vice President Biden was considering jumping in the race. And I was set to testify before the Republican-created special congressional committee investigating the terrorist attacks in Benghazi. It seemed as if everything would come to a head during one week in October.

In the end, Biden bowed out. The Republicans swung at me and missed at the eleven-hour-long Benghazi hearing. And the debate went better than I could have hoped.

Beforehand, I was full of nerves but confident I had prepared as well as I possibly could and excited to finally stop biting my tongue and get in there and mix it up. I got my chance. Bernie and I clashed right out of the gate on Socialism and capitalism, whether Denmark should serve as a model for America, and what it means to be a progressive. "I love Denmark," I said (and I do), but we aren't Denmark. "We are the United States of America. It's our job to rein in the excesses of capitalism so that it doesn't run amok and doesn't cause the kind of inequities we're seeing in our economic system. But we would be making a grave mistake to turn our backs on what built the greatest middle class in the history of the world." My defense of the American system of free enterprise may not have helped me with those self-identified Socialists in Iowa, but what mattered to me in that moment was saying what I believed.

The moderator, CNN's Anderson Cooper, pressed me on whether I was really a progressive or just a squishy moderate or a shape-shifting opportunist. I explained that I had been consistent throughout my career in fighting for a set of core values and principles. "I'm a progressive," I said, "but I'm a progressive who likes to get things done." I thought that summed up my fundamental disagreement with Bernie fairly well.

Still, and this is important, Bernie deserves credit for understanding the political power of big, bold ideas. His call for single-payer health care, free college, and aggressive Wall Street reform inspired millions of Americans, especially young people. After I won the nomination, he and I collaborated on a plan to make college more affordable that combined the best elements of what we'd both proposed during the primaries. That kind of compromise is essential in politics if you want to get anything done. Then we worked together to write the most progressive Democratic platform in memory.

Bernie and I may have had different views about the role of policy—a road map for governing versus a tool for mobilization—but

Donald Trump didn't care about policy at all. He seemed proud of his ignorance and didn't even pretend to come up with plans for how he'd build his wall, fix health care, bring back all the lost jobs in manufacturing and coal mining, and defeat ISIS. It was like he'd just wave a magic wand. He ridiculed me for taking the job seriously. "She's got people that sit in cubicles writing policy all day," he told *Time* magazine. "It's just a waste of paper." I kept waiting for reporters and voters to challenge him on his empty, deceitful promises. In previous elections, there was always a moment of reckoning when candidates had to show they were serious and their plans were credible. Not this time. Most of the press was too busy chasing ratings and scandals, and Trump was too slippery to be pinned down. He understood the needs and impulses of the political press well enough that if he gave them a new rabbit every day, they'd never catch any of them. So his reckoning never came.

Trump also refused to prepare for our debates. It showed. When we went head-to-head for the first time on September 26, 2016, at Long Island's Hofstra University, he wilted under questioning and nearly had a full-on meltdown. He tried to turn it around by attacking me for not showing up fumbling and incoherent like he did. I wasn't having it. Yeah, I did prepare, I said. "You know what else I prepared for? I prepared to be President."

Later, Chuck Todd of NBC's *Meet the Press* actually criticized me for being too prepared. I'm not sure how that's possible—can you be too prepared for something so important? Does Chuck ever show up for *Meet the Press* and just wing it? The fact that I was up against Donald Trump—perhaps the least prepared man in history, both for the debates and for the presidency—made the comment even more puzzling. Were they so enthralled by his rabbit-a-day strategy that insults, false charges, and fact-free assertions were now the best evidence of authenticity?

I thought about that exchange often as I watched Trump's first hundred days in office. I even allowed myself a little chuckle when he fumed, "Nobody knew health care could be so complicated." He also discovered that foreign policy is harder than it looks. The President of China had to explain the complexity of the North Korea challenge to him. "After listening for ten minutes, I realized it's not so easy," Trump said. Can you hear my palm slapping my forehead? Sometimes it seems like Trump didn't even want to be President at all. "This is more work than in my previous life," he told a reporter. "I thought it would be easier."

I can't help but think about how different my first hundred days would have been. A haunting line from the nineteenth-century poet John Greenleaf Whittier comes to mind: "For all sad words of tongue and pen, the saddest are these: 'It might have been.'"

Trump's first major initiative was the Muslim ban, which immediately ran into trouble in court. Mine would have been a jobs and infrastructure package funded by raising taxes on the wealthiest Americans. He failed to start building his great, beautiful wall paid for by Mexico. I would have pushed for comprehensive immigration reform with a path to citizenship. He appointed an Attorney General whose record on civil rights was so problematic, Coretta Scott King once warned that making him a judge would "irreparably damage" the work of her husband, Dr. Martin Luther King Jr. I would have worked across the aisle on bipartisan criminal justice reform—there was a real opportunity there for progress. He tried to repeal Obamacare and strip health care away from tens of millions of Americans. I would have gone after the drug companies to bring down prices and fought for a public option to get us even closer to affordable, truly universal health care. He alienated allies like German Chancellor Angela Merkel, while embracing dictators like Russia's Vladimir Putin. What would I have done? There's nothing I was looking forward to more than showing Putin that his efforts to influence our election and install a friendly puppet

had failed. Our first face-to-face meeting would really have been something. I know he must be enjoying everything that's happened instead.
But he hasn't had the last laugh yet.

Since the election, I've been thinking a lot about how we can do a better job of pushing policy back into our politics.

I have a new appreciation for the galvanizing power of big, simple
ideas. I still think my health care and college plans were more achievable than Bernie's and that his were fraught with problems, but they
were easier to explain and understand, and that counts for a lot. It's
easy to ridicule ideas that "fit on a bumper sticker," but there's a reason
campaigns use bumper stickers: they work.

Bernie proved again that it's important to set lofty goals that
people can organize around and dream about, even if it takes generations to achieve them. That's what happened with universal health care.
For a hundred years, Democrats campaigned on giving all Americans
access to affordable, quality care. Bill and I tried to get it done in the
1990s, and we succeeded in creating CHIP, which provides coverage
to millions of kids. It wasn't until Obama was swept into office with
a supermajority in the Senate that we could finally pass the Affordable Care Act. Even then, the ACA was a hodgepodge of imperfect
compromises. But that historic achievement was possible only because
Democrats had kept universal health care as our North Star for decades.

There's a historical irony here: Bill's presidency is often associated
with small-bore initiatives such as midnight basketball and school
uniforms—the opposite of those big, transformative ideas that liberals dream about. But that view misses so much. I believe Bill's impact on our party and our country was profound and transformative.
He reinvented a moribund party that had lost five of the previous
six presidential elections, infusing it with new energy and ideas, and

proving that Democrats could be pro-growth *and* pro-environment, pro-business *and* pro-labor, pro–public safety *and* pro–civil rights. He reversed trickle-down economics, balanced the federal budget, challenged Americans to embrace a new ethic of national service with AmeriCorps, and presided over two terms of peace and broadly shared prosperity.

The new Democratic Party he built went on to win the popular vote in six of the next seven elections between 1992 and 2016. He also inspired a generation of modernizing progressives in other Western democracies, especially Tony Blair's New Labour Party in the United Kingdom. In short, there was nothing small bore about the Clinton presidency.

I believe my presidency also would have been transformative because of the big ideas I proposed to build an economy that works for everyone, not just those at the top. Here are a few of them:

First, we need the biggest investment in good jobs since World War II. This should include a massive infrastructure program that repairs and modernizes America's roads, bridges, tunnels, ports, airports, and broadband networks; new incentives to attract and support manufacturing jobs in hard-hit communities from Coal Country to Indian country; debt-free college and improved training and apprenticeship programs to help people without college degrees get higher-paying jobs; support for small business by expanding access to capital and new markets and cutting taxes and red tape; a big push to expand clean energy production, including deploying half-a-billion solar panels in four years; and major investments in scientific research to create the jobs and industries of tomorrow.

Second, to make the economy fairer, we need new rules and incentives to make it easier for companies to raise wages and share profits with employees and harder for them to ship jobs overseas and bust unions. We have to make sure Wall Street can't wreck Main Street again, and get smarter and tougher on trade so American workers aren't caught in an unwinnable race against subsidized or state-owned industries, substandard labor conditions, or currency manipulation.

Third, we have to modernize workforce protections with a higher minimum wage, equal pay for women, paid family and medical leave, and affordable childcare. We should defend and improve the Affordable Care Act to reduce prices and expand coverage, including with a public option.

Fourth, we can pay for all of this with higher taxes on the top 1 percent of Americans who have reaped the lion's share of income and wealth gains since 2000. This would also help reduce inequality.

I could go on, but that gives you a flavor of some of the things I would have tried to get done as President. Unfortunately, despite the fact that I talked about these ideas endlessly, they never got much media attention, and most people never heard about any of them. I failed to convince the press that economics was more important than emails. But it was. Just as frustrating is the fact that I never managed to convince some skeptics that I really was in it to help working families. I thought that based on my years fighting for health care reform, my record in helping create jobs as a Senator, my efforts to raise the alarm before the financial crisis, and my early commitment to address the opioid epidemic, people would see me as a proven change maker and a fighter for children and families. Instead, I never quite shook the false perception that I was a defender of the status quo.

In my more introspective moments, I do recognize that my campaign in 2016 lacked the sense of urgency and passion that I remember from '92. Back then, we were on a mission to revitalize the Democratic Party and bring our country back from twelve years of trickle-down economics that exploded the deficit, hurt the middle class, and increased poverty. In 2016, we were seeking to build on eight years of progress. For a change-hungry electorate, it was a harder sell. More hopeful voters bought it; more pessimistic voters didn't.

Another lesson from this election, and from the Trump phenomenon in particular, is that traditional Republican ideology is bankrupt. For decades, the big debates in American politics were about the size and role of government. Democrats argued for a more active federal government and a stronger social safety net, while Republicans argued for a smaller government, lower taxes, and fewer regulations. The country seemed fairly evenly divided, or perhaps tilted slightly to the center-right. Then Trump came along and pulled back the curtain on what was really going on. We learned that many Republican voters didn't have any problem with big government, so long as it was big government for them. Perhaps this has always been true—you may recall the infamous sign at Tea Party rallies that read, with no hint of irony, "Keep Your Government Hands off My Medicare"—but Trump brought it out into the open. He promised to protect Social Security, Medicare, and Medicaid, while abandoning free trade and getting tough on bankers, in direct contradiction of Republican orthodoxy. Instead of paying a price for it, he swept away all his more traditional GOP rivals. Once in office, Trump abandoned most of his populist promises and largely hewed to the party line. But that shouldn't obscure the fact that many of his voters wanted to chuck the orthodoxy and preserve entitlements. The reality is that doctrinaire trickle-downers who control Congress wield enormous power without having any real constituency for their policies outside the Republican donor class. When Republicans were opposing Obama or attacking me, they could unite against a common enemy, but now that they're in power and people actually expect them to deliver results, we're seeing that there's little holding the Republican Party together.

The implications of all this are potentially profound. If Trump can't deliver for working families, Democrats have to, and be able to explain it. It may be hard for us to match his grandiose promises, because we still believe in arithmetic, but we can offer real results. We still believe in trade, but we've got to be clearer about how we'd be tougher on countries trying to take advantage of American workers, and how we'd provide more funding up front for people hurt by foreign competition.

We still believe in immigration, but we have to make a better case that if done right it will help all working people.

Democrats should reevaluate a lot of our assumptions about which policies are politically viable. These trends make universal programs even more appealing than we previously thought. I mean programs like Social Security and Medicare, which benefit every American, as opposed to Medicaid, food stamps, and other initiatives targeted to the poor. Targeted programs may be more efficient and progressive, and that's why during the primaries I criticized Bernie's "free college for all" plan as providing wasteful taxpayer-funded giveaways to rich kids. But it's precisely because they don't benefit everyone that targeted programs are so easily stigmatized and demagogued. We've seen this with the Affordable Care Act. For years, it was attacked as a new subsidy for poor people of color. A lot of working-class whites didn't think it benefited them at all, especially if they lived in states where Republican leaders refused to expand Medicaid. In white-majority states where Medicaid was expanded, such as Arkansas and Kentucky, the beneficiaries were overwhelmingly white working families. But many voted for Trump anyway, betting he would take health care away from "others" and let them keep theirs. It was only when many Americans realized that repealing the ACA would take away universal protections they had come to enjoy, especially regarding preexisting conditions, that the law became popular. Medicaid's expansion has made it more popular, too.

The conclusion I reach from this is that Democrats should redouble our efforts to develop bold, creative ideas that offer broad-based benefits for the whole country.

Before I ran for President, I read a book called *With Liberty and Dividends for All: How to Save Our Middle Class When Jobs Don't Pay Enough,* by Peter Barnes, which explored the idea of creating a new fund that would use revenue from shared national resources to pay a dividend to every citizen, much like how the Alaska Permanent Fund distributes the state's oil royalties every year. Shared national resources include oil and gas extracted from public lands and the public airwaves used by broadcasters and mobile phone companies, but that gets you only so far. If you view the nation's financial system as a shared resource, then you can start raising real money from things like a financial transactions tax. Same with the air we breathe and carbon pricing. Once you capitalize the fund, you can provide every American with a modest basic income every year. Besides cash in people's pockets, it would also be a way of making every American feel more connected to our country and to one another—part of something bigger than ourselves.

I was fascinated by this idea, as was my husband, and we spent weeks working with our policy team to see if it could be viable enough to include in my campaign. We would call it "Alaska for America." Unfortunately, we couldn't make the numbers work. To provide a meaningful dividend each year to every citizen, you'd have to raise enormous sums of money, and that would either mean a lot of new taxes or cannibalizing other important programs. We decided it was exciting but not realistic, and left it on the shelf. That was the responsible decision. I wonder now whether we should have thrown caution to the wind and embraced "Alaska for America" as a long-term goal and figured out the details later.

Interestingly, some Republican elder statesmen such as former U.S. Treasury Secretaries James Baker and Hank Paulson recently proposed a nationwide carbon dividend program that would tax fossil fuel use and refund all the money directly to every American. They think it's a reasonable conservative response to the problems of climate change and income inequality, and a good alternative to government regulation. Under such a plan, working families with small carbon footprints could end up with a big boost in their incomes. We looked at this for the campaign as well, but couldn't make the math work without imposing new costs on upper-middle-class families, which I had pledged not to do. Still, it's tantalizing. A conservative government in Sweden created a similar program in 1991, and within a decade, it had reduced greenhouse gas emissions *and* expanded the economy by 50 percent, because so many Swedes used their tax rebates to increase energy efficiency, thus creating new jobs, increasing productivity, and lowering their electric bills.

We need to be thinking outside the box because the challenges we face are only getting bigger and more complex. Climate change is one example. Another is the long-term effects of automation and artificial intelligence, both on employment and national security. Bear with me here, because I have a lot to say about this. Over the past few years, I've had a series of alarming conversations with leading technologists in Silicon Valley who warn that this could be the first great technological revolution that ends up displacing more jobs than it creates. The impact of trade on our manufacturing industry received a lot more attention during the campaign, but many economists say that advances in technology actually have displaced far more jobs than trade in recent decades.

For instance, between 1962 and 2005, about four hundred thousand steelworker jobs disappeared. Competition from steel made in China and other countries was part of the problem. But technological innovation and automation were the bigger culprits. They allowed manufacturers to produce the same amount of steel with fewer and fewer workers, at lower costs.

The same story has been replicated across many industries, and it isn't slowing down anytime soon. The arrival of self-driving cars could displace millions of truckers and taxi drivers. Some economists estimate that automation could put a third of all American men aged twenty-five to fifty-four out of work by 2050. Even if we manage to create new industries and new categories of jobs to replace those we've lost, the speed and breadth of the changes we're facing will be destabilizing for millions of people.

I'm not suggesting that we should try to stop the march of technology. That would cause more problems than it solves. But we do need to make sure it's working more for us than against us. If we can figure that out, including how to talk about it in a way that Americans will understand and support, that will be both good policy and good politics.

There's another angle to consider as well. Technologists like Elon Musk, Sam Altman, and Bill Gates, and physicists like Stephen Hawking have warned that artificial intelligence could one day pose an existential security threat. Musk has called it "the greatest risk we face as a civilization." Think about it: Have you ever seen a movie where the machines start thinking for themselves that ends well? Every time I went out to Silicon Valley during the campaign, I came home more alarmed about this. My staff lived in fear that I'd start talking about "the rise of the robots" in some Iowa town hall. Maybe I should have. In any case, policy makers need to keep up with technology as it races ahead, instead of always playing catch-up.

Across the board, we should be unafraid to kick the tires on transformative ideas. Like taxing net worth instead of annual income, which would make our system fairer, reduce inequality, and provide the resources to make the major investments our country needs. Or a national service initiative much broader than anything we have now, perhaps even universal. We should totally reimagine our training and workforce development system so that employers and unions are true partners, and people who don't go to college can find a good job and enjoy a middle-class life. We need to completely rethink how Americans receive benefits such as retirement and health care so that they're universal, automatic, and portable. As you probably can tell by now, I love talking about this stuff. The point is, we have to think big and think different.

No matter what I do in the years ahead, I'll be chasing down new policy ideas that I think could make a difference. Not every election will be so filled with venom, misinformation, resentments, and outside interference as this one was. Solutions are going to matter again in politics. Democrats must be ready when that day comes.

Well-behaved women seldom make history.

—Laurel Thatcher Ulrich

Making History

"I just want to show you this," said David Muir, the young ABC News anchor, as he walked me to the window. "This is the crowd that's waiting for you."

It was late on Tuesday, June 7, 2016, the day of the final Democratic primaries. Muir and I were on the second floor of the Brooklyn Navy Yard, in a small room crowded with cameras, hot lights, and a TV crew making final arrangements for our interview. The window looked out onto a cavernous hangar that was packed with thousands of cheering people waving American flags and stomping their feet. In the middle stood an empty stage.

"Oh my gosh," I said, clasping my hands to my heart. "Look at that!"

"It's eight years ago to the day that you conceded. And tonight you will go out there for a very different reason," Muir said.

I thought back to that painful day in 2008 when I stood in front of a much more somber crowd in the National Building Museum in Washington, and thanked my supporters for putting eighteen million cracks in the highest, hardest glass ceiling. Now here I was, closer than ever to shattering that ceiling once and for all.

"Is it sinking in?" he asked.

"*This* is sinking it in, I can tell you that," I said, pointing to the crowd below. "It's an overwhelming feeling, David, really."

It had been a difficult week. Heck, it had been a difficult year. The primaries had gone on longer and been far more bruising than anyone expected. The delegate math hadn't been in question since March, but Bernie had hung on to the bitter end, drawing blood wherever he could along the way. I somewhat understood why he did it; after all, I stayed in the race for as long as I could in 2008. But that race was much closer, and I endorsed Barack right after the last primary. On this day in New York, Bernie was still more than a month away from endorsing me.

I spent the previous days campaigning like crazy in California. Even if I had the nomination locked up, I wanted to win California. I wanted to close out the primaries with a burst of enthusiasm and head toward our convention in Philadelphia with the wind at my back. The polls looked good, but I was anxious. Too many times in this campaign I had felt like Charlie Brown with the football. There had been the squeaker in Iowa and surprise losses in Michigan and Indiana. This time I wasn't going to leave anything to chance.

That Monday, I had raced all over Southern California, holding rallies, doing local TV and radio interviews, and trying to encourage as many of my supporters as possible to get out and vote. A little after 5:00 P.M., as we were driving to yet another rally at Long Beach City College, my phone started buzzing. The Associated Press had just sent out a breaking news alert. Its reporters had been canvassing superdelegates, the party leaders who join delegates selected in primaries and caucuses in choosing the nominee at the convention. According to the AP's latest count, I had just hit the magic number of delegates needed to win. "Hillary Clinton Becomes the Democratic Party's Presumptive Presidential Nominee," it declared. I had to read it twice to believe it.

You might think this was good news. I'd won! But that's not how I felt at all. I was focused entirely on the next day's California primary, along with the contests in Montana, New Mexico, North Dakota, New Jersey, and South Dakota. This news could very well depress turnout among my supporters. And I wanted to be able to walk out onstage Tuesday night and declare victory, not have it announced in an out-of-the-blue tweet from the Associated Press the day before. I told Huma and Greg Hale, an Arkansas farmer and event-production-and-visuals wizard whom I've known since he was four years old, that I imagined a sea of people waving small American flags as the backdrop, and they teased me about doing my own advance work. But I had been waiting for this moment for months, and I wanted it to be perfect.

We arrived at the college in Long Beach, and I went into a makeshift greenroom. It was part of a locker room and felt like a cage. I was annoyed and not sure what to say. What was the best way to acknowledge the news in my rally speech without making too big a deal of it? I wanted to just pretend it hadn't happened, but that didn't seem like a viable option. Nick, who with Huma was on the phone with the rest of the team in Brooklyn, suggested a formulation. "Why not say we're on the brink of a historic moment?" That would have to do, I grumbled.

I also was unsatisfied with the draft for the victory speech I was supposed to deliver on Tuesday night. It didn't feel right: too small, too political, not worthy of the moment. I felt the weight of expectations and history pressing down on me.

If the primaries were over, and I was the presumptive nominee, that meant I was now all that stood between Donald Trump and the White House. It would just be me and him, one-on-one, with stakes that couldn't possibly be higher. Everyone would be counting on me. We absolutely had to win.

On top of all that, I was about to become the first woman ever nominated by a major party for President of the United States. That goal has been so elusive for so long. Now it was about to be real.

I'd been thinking about all the women who had marched, rallied, picketed, went to jail, and endured ridicule, harassment, and violence so that one day someone like me could come along and run for President. I thought about the brave women and men who gathered in Seneca Falls, New York, in 1848 for the first great conference on women's rights. Frederick Douglass, the African American social reformer and abolitionist, was there. He described his fellow participants as "few in numbers, moderate in resources, and very little known in the world. The most we had to connect us was a firm commitment that we were in the right and a firm faith that the right must ultimately prevail."

Sixty-eight "ladies" and thirty-two "gentlemen" signed the Declaration of Sentiments, which asserted boldly, "We hold these truths to be self-evident that all men and women are created equal." All men *and* women. The backlash was fierce. The Seneca Falls 100 were called dangerous fanatics. They were also dismissed as batty old maids—I'm not sure how one can be both, but apparently these activists were. One newspaper declared, "These rights for women would bring a monstrous injury to all mankind." But those brave suffragettes never lost faith.

What could I say on Tuesday night that would be worthy of that legacy and the hope that millions were now investing in me?

For a long time, the campaign had been trying to figure out the best way to talk about the historic nature of my candidacy. There were brainstorming sessions in Brooklyn, as well as polls and focus groups. Many of our core supporters were very excited by the idea of finally breaking the glass ceiling. Celebrating that could help keep people energized and motivated in the general election. But some younger women didn't see what the big deal was. And many undecided women in battleground states didn't want to hear about it at all. Some were afraid that by leaning into the fact that I was a woman, my campaign would end up turning away men—a disheartening but all-too-real possibility. So that wasn't much help.

I was torn. I wanted to be judged on what I did, not on what I represented or what people projected onto me. But I understood how much this breakthrough would mean to the country, especially to girls and boys who would see that there are no limits on what women can achieve. I wanted to honor that significance. I just didn't know the best way to do it.

I carried all that uncertainty with me back from California, all the way to David Muir's interview room in the Brooklyn Navy Yard on Tuesday night. Results were starting to come in. I won the New Jersey primary. Bernie won the North Dakota caucus. The big prize, California, was still out there, but all signs pointed to another victory. Bill and I had worked hard on my speech, but I still felt unsettled. Maybe it was about not being ready to accept "yes" for an answer. I had worked so hard to get to this moment, and now that it had arrived, I wasn't quite sure what to do with myself.

Then Muir walked me over to the window, and I looked out at that crowd—at thousands of people who'd worked their hearts out, resisted the negativity of a divisive primary and relentlessly harsh press coverage, and poured their dreams into my campaign. We'd had big crowds before, but this felt different. It was something more than the enthusiasm I saw on the trail. It was a pulsing energy, an outpouring of love and hope and joy. For a moment, I was overwhelmed—and then calm. This was right. I was ready.

After the interview, I went downstairs to where my husband was sitting with the speechwriters going over final tweaks to the draft. I read it over one more time and felt good. Just as they were racing off to load the speech into the teleprompter, I said I had one more thing to add: "I'm going to talk about Seneca Falls. Just put a placeholder in brackets and I'll take care of it."

I took a deep breath. I didn't want the emotion of the moment to get to me in the middle of my speech. I said a little prayer and then headed for the stage. At the last moment, Huma grabbed my arm and whispered, "Don't forget to take a minute to savor this." It was good advice. The roar when I stepped out was deafening. I felt a surge of pride, gratitude, and pure happiness. I stood at the podium, my arms outstretched, taking it all in.

"Tonight's victory is not about one person," I said. "It belongs to generations of women and men who struggled and sacrificed and made this moment possible."

Like in my campaign launch speech on Roosevelt Island, I took the opportunity to talk about my mother. When I thought about the sweep of history, I thought about her. Her birthday had just passed a few days earlier. She was born on June 4, 1919—the exact same day that Congress passed the Nineteenth Amendment to the Constitution, finally granting women the right to vote.

"I really wish my mother could be here tonight," I told the crowd in Brooklyn. I had practiced this part several times, and each time, I teared up. "I wish she could see what a wonderful mother Chelsea has become, and could meet our beautiful granddaughter, Charlotte." I swallowed hard. "And, of course, I wish she could see her daughter become the Democratic Party's nominee for President of the United States."

A month and a half later, I was preparing to formally accept the nomination at the Democratic National Convention in Philadelphia. The

Republicans had just finished their convention in Cleveland. Trump had given a dark and megalomaniacal speech in which he described a badly broken American and then declared, "I alone can fix it." I wasn't sure how voters were going to react to that, but I thought it went against America's can-do spirit that says, "We'll fix it together." His speech, like his entire candidacy, was about stoking and manipulating people's ugliest emotions. He wanted Americans to fear one another and the future.

Other Republicans did their best Trump imitations at the GOP convention. New Jersey Governor Chris Christie, a former prosecutor, led the crowd through a mock indictment of me for various supposed crimes. The crowd shouted its verdict: "Guilty!" The irony, apparently lost on Christie but nobody else, was that the investigation into my emails was over, but the investigation into the closing of the George Washington Bridge as an act of political retribution was ongoing and would eventually cause two of Christie's allies to be sentenced to prison.

It was sad to watch the Republican Party go from Reagan's "Morning in America" to Trump's "Midnight in America." The dystopian, disorganized mess in Cleveland got panned by the press and offered us the chance to provide a clear contrast when Democrats gathered in Philadelphia on July 25.

Bill, Chelsea, my senior team, and nearly every Democratic leader in the country were there. I wasn't. The tradition is that the nominee does not arrive until the end. So I was home alone in Chappaqua, watching television and working on my acceptance speech. It was a little lonely, but I enjoyed the rare moment to myself after so many hectic months on the campaign trail.

Michelle Obama stole the show on the first night with her graceful, fiercely personal speech. Just as she had done for eight years, she represented our best selves as Americans and reminded us that "When they go low, we go high." Senator Cory Booker, whom I had also considered as a potential Vice President, gave a rousing and heartfelt speech. Riffing off one of the most powerful lines from the Declaration of Independence, he urged Americans to follow the example of our Founders and "pledge to each other our lives, our fortunes, and our sacred honor."

On the second day, the convention got down to business with formal nominations and then a roll call vote by state. Since the outcome is rarely in doubt, this can be a somewhat tedious affair. But when you're the one getting nominated, it feels like high drama.

In 2008, I had surprised the convention by appearing on the floor with the New York delegation in the middle of the roll call. I moved to suspend the vote and nominate Barack Obama by acclamation. Up at the podium, Nancy Pelosi asked if there was a second for my motion, and the whole arena roared its approval.

This time we expected a full roll call. When it was Illinois's turn, my best friend from growing up, Betsy Ebeling, stepped to the microphone and announced ninety-eight votes for me. "On this historic, wonderful day, in honor of Dorothy and Hugh's daughter and my sweet friend—I know you're watching—this one's for you, Hill." Back in Chappaqua, I couldn't stop smiling.

Slowly, state by state, the tallies grew, and I got closer and closer to a majority of delegates. Then, a little after 6:30 P.M., South Dakota put me over the top, and my supporters in the hall broke into sustained jubilation. There were still more states to go, so the roll call went on. Finally, we came to Vermont, which had asked to go last. Bernie came forward and, in an echo of eight years before, said, "I move that Hillary Clinton be selected as the nominee of the Democratic Party for President of the United States." The place erupted.

The long primary was over. The final delegate count was 2,842 for me and 1,865 for Bernie. I know it couldn't have been easy for him to make that statement on the floor, and I appreciated it.

That evening, the actor Elizabeth Banks emceed a joyful and

moving series of testimonials from people who had gotten to know me over the years—people who let me into their lives, and became a part of mine.

There was Anastasia Somoza, whom I met when she was just nine years old. Anastasia was born with cerebral palsy, and became a passionate advocate for people with disabilities. She worked on my first campaign for Senate, interned in my office, and became a lifelong friend.

Jelani Freeman, another former intern in my Senate office, lived in six different foster homes between the ages of eight and eighteen. Many kids in that situation never graduate from high school. Jelani got a master's degree and a law degree. He said that I encouraged him to persevere and rise as high as he could. The real story was that he was the one who encouraged me. His example inspired me to keep up my advocacy for children, especially kids in foster care.

Ryan Moore also spoke. When I first met him, Ryan was seven years old and wearing a full body brace that must have weighed forty pounds. He was born with a rare form of dwarfism that kept him in a wheelchair, but it didn't dim his unbeatable smile and sense of humor. I met Ryan's family at a health reform conference in 1994 and learned about their battles with the insurance company to pay for his costly surgeries and treatments. Their story—and Ryan's tenacity—kept me going through all the ups and downs of our battle for health care reform.

Then there was Lauren Manning, who was gravely injured on 9/11. More than 82 percent of her body was badly burned, giving her a less than 20 percent chance of survival. But she fought her way back and reclaimed her life. Lauren and her husband, Greg, became vocal advocates on behalf of other 9/11 families. I did everything I could as a Senator to be a champion for them, as well as for the first responders who got sick from their time at Ground Zero.

I found it very moving to listen to these friends tell their stories, just as it had been to see Betsy during the roll call. It was like an episode of that old television program *This Is Your Life*. I was flooded with memories and pride in everything we'd accomplished together.

But none of that prepared me for what Bill had to say when it was his turn to speak.

He looked great up there at the podium, with his distinguished shock of white hair and dignified bearing. "Back where he belongs," I thought. Four years before, he had masterfully laid out the case for reelecting Barack Obama. This time he left the economic statistics behind and spoke from the heart.

"In the spring of 1971, I met a girl," he began. I knew right away that this was going to be different. In fact, I don't think there's ever been a major political speech like it. Bill talked about how we met and fell in love. "We've been walking and talking and laughing together ever since," he said, "and we've done it in good times and bad, through joy and heartbreak." He took the American people by the hand and walked them down the path of our lives together, with love, humor, and wisdom. He shared private little moments, like the day we dropped Chelsea off at college for the first time. "There I was in a trance just staring out the window trying not to cry," Bill recalled, "and there was Hillary on her hands and knees desperately looking for one more drawer to put that liner paper in."

Sitting by myself in the home we'd made together, surrounded by the mementos of our life and love, I felt like my heart was bursting. "I married my best friend," Bill said. It was like hearing a love letter read out loud on national television.

As soon as the speech wrapped up, I jumped in our van and raced over to a country inn down the road, where a large group of friends and neighbors had gathered. I was positively beaming when I walked in. What a night!

A camera crew was waiting, ready to connect me directly to the arena in Philadelphia. An adorable six-year-old girl named Remie came over and gave me a hug. We were both wearing red, and I complemented her dress as she smiled bashfully. With Remie by my side, I was ready to speak to the convention and the country.

Onstage in Philadelphia, the giant video screen above the arena began flashing the pictures of every previous U.S. President, one white man after another, until finally Barack Obama. Then the screen appeared to shatter into a million pieces, and there I was, live from Crabtree's Kittle House Restaurant and Inn in Chappaqua. On the convention floor, people held up red and blue placard signs that said, "History."

I thanked the convention for the incredible honor they'd given me. "And if there are any little girls out there who stayed up late to watch," I said, as the camera pulled back to show little Remie and our other friends crowded behind me, "let me just say, I may become the first woman President, but one of you is next."

I hugged and thanked everyone I could find. I didn't want to leave, didn't want the night to end. Later, I heard that social media was buzzing with parents posting pictures of their daughters who had indeed stayed up late to watch, while others shared photos of mothers and grandmothers who hadn't lived to see this day. A writer named Charles Finch tweeted, "There are days when you believe the arc of history thing." That's exactly how it felt: like all of us together were bending the arc of history just a little bit further toward justice.

The next day, I sneaked into Philadelphia so I could make a surprise appearance with President Obama after his speech. He was masterful, of course, and incredibly generous. He talked about what it takes to sit behind the desk in the Oval Office and make life-and-death decisions that affect the whole world, and how I'd been there with him, helping make those hard choices. He looked up at where Bill was sitting and said with a smile, "There has never been a man or a woman—not me, not Bill, nobody—more qualified." Bill loved it and jumped to his feet and applauded. When Barack finished, I popped out from backstage and gave him a big hug.

Then, on the final day of the convention, it was time for me to give the most important speech of my life. In some ways, this was easier than that night at the Brooklyn Navy Yard. I was ready to be the party's standard-bearer in the battle to come, and I was confident in the vision I wanted to share with the country. I would argue that Americans are always "stronger together," and that if we worked together, we could rise together. We could live up to our country's motto, e pluribus unum: "out of many, we are one." Trump, by contrast, would tear us apart.

We had settled on Stronger Together as our theme for the general election after a lot of thought and discussion. Remarkably, three separate brainstorming processes all led to the same answer. My team in Brooklyn had started with three basic contrasts we wanted to draw with Trump. He was risky and unqualified, but I was steady and ready to deliver results on Day One. He was a fraud who was in it only for himself, but I was in it for children and families and would make our economy work for everyone, not just those at the top. He was divisive, while I would work to bring the country together. The challenge was to find a way to marry all three together in a memorable slogan that reflected my values and record. Stronger Together did that better than anything else we could think of.

While the team in Brooklyn worked on this, I asked Roy Spence to spend some time thinking outside the box about campaign themes and messages. Roy is an old friend from the McGovern campaign who started a large ad agency in Austin, Texas. When Jake Sullivan and Dan Schwerin, my director of speechwriting, got on the phone with

Roy to exchange notes, they were shocked to hear him propose exactly the same phrase the team in Brooklyn had come up with: Stronger Together. Our top political consultants, Joel Benenson, Mandy Grunwald, and Jim Margolis, also reached the same conclusion independently. Considering how rarely all these smart people agreed on anything, we took it as a sign. Stronger Together it would be.

By the time I got to our convention, I felt even better about this decision. Trump's "I Alone Can Fix It" speech in Cleveland had provided the perfect foil. The history surrounding us in Philadelphia offered further inspiration. Independence Hall was just a few blocks from our hotel. It was there, 240 years before, that representatives from thirteen unruly colonies transformed themselves into a single, unified nation. It wasn't easy. Some of the colonists wanted to stick with the King. Some wanted to stick it *to* the King and go their own way. They had different backgrounds, interests, and aspirations. Somehow they began listening to one another and compromising, and eventually found common purpose. They realized they'd be stronger together than they ever could be on their own.

On Thursday, the last day of the convention, Bill and I sat around the dining room table in our suite at the Logan Hotel, going over a draft of my speech, trying to get it just right. I tried not to think about how many millions of people would be watching and how enormous the stakes would be. Instead, I focused on trying to make my argument as clear and compelling as possible. If I did a good job, and the country saw me without all the usual nonsense getting in the way, the rest would take care of itself. Suddenly, with a squeal of delight, our granddaughter, Charlotte, burst into the room and ran over to us. I put down the draft and chased after her, finally scooping her up in my arms and giving her a kiss. Any tension I'd been feeling drained away in a flash. There was nowhere else in the world I wanted to be other than right there, holding my granddaughter.

After a few more hours of tweaking and practicing, I put on another suffragette-white pantsuit and got ready to head to the arena. The television was still on, and just before I walked out the door, I saw Khizr and Ghazala Khan come to the podium. I had first heard about the Khans the previous December, when an intern on my speechwriting team came across the story of their son, Humayun, a heroic captain in the U.S. military who was killed protecting his unit in Iraq. I talked about Captain Khan in a speech in Minneapolis about counterterrorism and the importance of working with American Muslims, not demonizing them. My team followed up with the family and invited them to share their experiences at the convention.

None of us were prepared for how powerful it would be. Mr. Khan solemnly offered to lend Donald Trump his copy of the Constitution that he kept in his pocket. It instantly became one of the most iconic moments of the whole election. Like millions of others, I was transfixed. Watching Mr. and Mrs. Khan up there, still grieving, incredibly dignified, patriotic to the core, filled me with a rush of pride and confidence in our party and our country.

Then I had to hurry to the arena. We had NPR on the whole way so I didn't miss a minute.

I watched backstage as Chelsea gave a perfect introduction that brought me to tears.

"My parents raised me to know how lucky I was that I never had to worry about food on the table," she said. "I never had to worry about a good school to go to. That I never had to worry about a safe neighborhood to play in. And they taught me to care about what happens in our world and to do whatever I could to change what frustrated me, what felt wrong. They taught me that's the responsibility that comes with being smiled on by fate."

"I know my kids are a little young," she continued, "but I'm already trying to instill those same values in them."

Chelsea finished her remarks and introduced a film about my life by Shonda Rhimes. I love how Shonda makes tough, smart female characters come alive on television, and I was hoping she could do the same for me. Boy, did she deliver. Her film was funny, poignant, just perfect. When it was over, Chelsea came back on and welcomed me—"my mother, my hero"—to the stage. There was a deafening roar.

Looking out into that arena full of cheers and banners and music, with thousands of excited people and millions more at home, was one of the proudest and most overwhelming moments of my life.

"Standing here as my mother's daughter, and my daughter's mother, I'm so happy this day has come," I said. "Happy for grandmothers and little girls and everyone in between. Happy for boys and men, too—because when any barrier falls in America, for anyone, it clears the way for everyone. When there are no ceilings, the sky's the limit."

Even after everything that's happened, I still believe that.

I still believe that, as I've said many times, advancing the rights and opportunities of women and girls is the unfinished business of the twenty-first century. That includes one day succeeding where I failed and electing a woman as President of the United States.

On November 8 and the days that followed, hundreds of women visited the grave of the great suffragette leader Susan B. Anthony in Rochester, New York. They covered her headstone with "I Voted" stickers. People did the same to the statue in Seneca Falls commemorating the spot by the river where Amelia Bloomer first introduced Anthony to Elizabeth Cady Stanton, sparking the partnership at the heart of the suffragette movement.

A lot of women shared stories like this one, which I received from a woman named Marcia in California:

My mother is 92, in hospice care, and quite frail. A couple weeks
ago, my sister and I helped her vote, completing her mail-in ballot.
For President? "Hillary, of course," she told us. We cheered! In a soft,
weak voice, she whispered, "I did it. I did. I did." This will be her
last vote. And, because I live some distance from her, it may be the
last time I see her in this life. I will always cherish the memory of
her voting for a woman for President for the first time in her life.

In my concession speech, I said, "We have still not shattered that highest and hardest glass ceiling, but some day someone will—and hopefully sooner than we might think right now." History is funny that way.
Things that seem far off and impossible have a way of turning out to be
nearer and more possible than we ever imagined.

Of the sixty-eight women who signed the Declaration of Sentiments in 1848, only one lived to see the Nineteenth Amendment ratified. Her name was Charlotte Woodward, and she thanked God for
the progress she had witnessed in her lifetime.

In 1848, Charlotte was a nineteen-year-old glove maker living in
the small town of Waterloo, New York. She would sit and sew for hours
every day, working for meager wages with no hope of ever getting an
education or owning property. Charlotte knew that if she married, she,
any children she might have, and all her worldly possessions would
belong to her husband. She would never be a full and equal citizen,
never vote, certainly never run for office. One hot summer day, Charlotte heard about a women's rights conference in a nearby town. She
ran from house to house, sharing the news. Some of her friends were as
excited as she was. Others were amused or dismissive. A few agreed to
go with her to see it for themselves. They left early on the morning of
July 19 in a wagon drawn by farm horses. At first, the road was empty,
and they wondered if no one else was coming. At the next crossroads,
there were wagons and carriages, and then more appeared, all headed

to Wesleyan Chapel in Seneca Falls. Charlotte and her friends joined the procession, heading toward a future they could only dream of.

Charlotte Woodward was more than ninety years old when she finally gained the right to vote, but she got there. My mother had just been born and lived long enough to vote for her daughter to be President.

I plan to live long enough to see a woman win.

To know oneself is, above all, to know what one lacks.
It is to measure oneself against Truth,
and not the other way around.

—Flannery O'Connor

Frustration

Too long a sacrifice can make a stone of the heart.

—William Butler Yeats

Country Roads

"We're going to put a lot of coal miners and coal companies out of business." Stripped of their context, my words sounded heartless. Republican operatives made sure the clip was replayed virtually nonstop on Facebook feeds, local radio and television coverage, and campaign ads across Appalachia for months.

I made this unfortunate comment about coal miners at a town hall in Columbus just two days before the Ohio primary. You say millions of words in a campaign and you do your best to be clear and accurate. Sometimes it just comes out wrong. It wasn't the first time that happened during the 2016 election, and it wouldn't be the last. But it is the one I regret most. The point I had wanted to make was the exact opposite of how it came out.

The context is important. The moderator asked how I would win support from working-class whites who normally vote Republican.

Good question! I had a lot to say about that. I was looking right at my friend, Congressman Tim Ryan, who represents communities in southeastern Ohio suffering from job losses in coal mines and steel plants. I wanted to speak to their concerns and share my ideas for bringing new opportunities to the region. Unfortunately, a few of my words came out in the worst possible way:

> Instead of dividing people the way Donald Trump does, let's reunite around policies that will bring jobs and opportunities to all these underserved poor communities. So, for example, I'm the only candidate who has a policy about how to bring economic opportunity using clean renewable energy as the key into Coal Country. Because we're going to put a lot of coal miners and coal companies out of business, right Tim? And we're going to make it clear that we don't want to forget those people. Those people labored in those mines for generations, losing their health, often losing their lives to turn on our lights and power our factories. Now we've got to move away from coal and all the other fossil fuels, but I don't want to move away from the people who did the best they could to produce the energy that we relied on.

If you listened to the full answer and not just that one garbled sentence pulled out of it, my meaning comes through reasonably well. Coal employment had been going down in Appalachia for decades, stemming from changes in mining technology, competition from lower-sulfur Wyoming coal, and cheaper and cleaner natural gas and renewable energy, and a drop in the global demand for coal. I was intensely concerned about the impact on families and communities that had depended on coal jobs for generations. That's why I had proposed a comprehensive $30 billion plan to help revitalize and diversify the region's economy. But most people never heard that. They heard a snippet that gave the impression that I was looking forward to hurting miners and their families.

If you were already primed to believe the worst about me, here was confirmation.

I felt absolutely sick about the whole thing. I clarified and apologized and pointed to my detailed plan to invest in coal communities. But the damage was done.

For many people, coal miners were symbols of something larger: a vision of a hardworking, God-fearing, flag-waving, blue-collar white America that felt like it was slipping away. If I didn't respect coal miners, the implication was that I didn't respect working-class people generally or at least not working-class white men in small towns and red states. And with the clip of my comments playing on a loop on Fox News, there was basically nothing I could say to make people think otherwise.

The backlash was infuriating for many reasons. For one, there was the double standard. Donald Trump hardly went a single day on the campaign trail without saying something offensive or garbling a thought. He received criticism, but it rarely stuck (with a couple of big exceptions). Many in the press and political chattering class marveled at how Teflon-coated Trump seemed to be, ignoring their own role in making him so. I got none of this leeway. Even the smallest slipup was turned into a major event. Yet at the same time, I was routinely criticized for being too cautious and careful with my words. It was an unwinnable dynamic.

But the coal-mining gaffe felt terrible in ways that went beyond my normal frustrations over double standards. This wasn't some dumb comment about an unimportant issue. I genuinely cared a lot about struggling working-class families in fading small towns. I cared a lot about coal communities in particular. Not for political reasons—I knew

I wasn't going to win a lot of votes in places like West Virginia—but for personal ones.

I lived in Arkansas for years and fell in love with Ozark mountain towns a lot like those across Appalachia. In fact, coal had been mined in Arkansas for decades, and Bill and I knew retired miners suffering from black lung disease. As an attorney, he had represented more than a hundred of them, trying to help them get the benefits they deserved. When I got to the Senate, I worked with Senator Robert Byrd of West Virginia to do what I could to support legislation to protect the safety and pensions of coal miners.

I also represented once-prosperous industrial cities in upstate New York where factories had closed and jobs dried up, just like in southeastern Ohio and western Pennsylvania. I respected the defiant pride that so many who lived there felt for their hometowns and understood the mistrust they felt toward outsiders swooping in with grand pronouncements about their lives and futures. I found that by listening, building coalitions, and helping people to help themselves, we could start turning things around and create new opportunities for businesses and jobs. I worked with eBay to help small businesses in rural upstate communities get online and reach new customers. My office connected chefs and restaurant owners from Manhattan with farmers and winemakers in the Hudson Valley and the Finger Lakes in an effort to expand sales. And we worked with upstate universities to bring in new research grants that could help them become hubs for job-creating industries such as biotech and clean energy. I loved that work because it produced results and made people's lives better.

Appearing to dismiss the men and women of Coal Country—or any Americans working hard against the odds to build better lives for themselves and their families—wasn't something I could just shrug off. This really bothered me, and I wanted badly to do something about it.

It's worth pausing for a moment to be clear about the bigger picture. Terms like "working class" and "blue collar" get thrown around a lot and can mean different things to different people. Generally, when academics and political analysts talk about the working class, they mean people without a college degree. But frequently people use the term in a broader way. How much money people make, the kinds of jobs they do, the communities they live in, and a basic sensibility or set of values all get wrapped up together in our image of what it means to be working class. And there's often a tendency to equate working class with white and rural. How we think and talk about this has big implications for our politics.

I came of age in an era when Republicans won election after election by peeling off formerly Democratic white working-class voters. Bill ran for President in 1992 determined to prove that Democrats could compete in blue-collar suburbs and rural small towns without giving up our values. By focusing on the economy, delivering results, and crafting compromises that defused hot-button issues such as crime and welfare, he became the first Democrat since World War II to win two full terms.

By 2016, the country was more diverse, more urban, and more college-educated, with working-class whites making up a shrinking portion of the electorate. Barack Obama had written a new playbook about how to win the Presidency by mobilizing younger, more diverse voters. My campaign strategy was built on that playbook. But I still wanted to help those small towns that Bill had won twenty-four years before and the Rust Belt communities like those I had represented in the Senate. Even before the campaign began, I was focused on the shocking numbers of poor white women and men who were dying younger than their parents because of smoking, substance abuse, and suicide—what's been called an epidemic of despair. This decline in life expectancy was unprecedented in the modern history of our country. It's the kind of thing that happened in Russia after the disintegration of the Soviet Union.

Back in 2013 and 2014, I started talking about McDowell County, West Virginia, where more than one-third of the residents lived in poverty and only half had a high school degree. Jobs were scarce, and drug use was rampant. McDowell County was one of the poorest communities in the country, but lots of other small towns and rural areas were also dealing with stagnant wages and disappearing jobs. Social networks that provided support and structure in previous generations were weaker than ever, with schools failing, labor unions shrinking, jobs leaving, church attendance declining, trust in government falling, and families becoming more fractured. People trying to build a future in these hard-hit communities didn't face just ceilings on their aspirations. It was as if the floor had collapsed beneath them, too.

What could be done to help? I pointed to an ambitious effort in McDowell County led by the American Federation of Teachers under president Randi Weingarten and nearly a hundred partners from the local community, government, business, labor, nonprofits, and foundations. They recognized that the problems McDowell faced with its schools, jobs, housing, infrastructure, and public health were all connected, so they had to work on all of them at the same time, with new investments, fresh thinking, and lots of hard work. Their public-private partnership, named Reconnecting McDowell, had no guarantee of success, but I thought the effort was exciting. After a few years, it showed real results: the high school graduation rate increased from about 72 percent to nearly 90 percent, while dropout rates and teen pregnancy declined. The schools were wired with broadband, homes were connected with fiber, and every middle school student received a laptop.

But even the best philanthropic effort was unlikely to turn the tide across Appalachia unless it was backed up by strong, effective policies at both the state and federal levels—something that Republicans in Congress and state legislatures never supported.

Appalachian coal mining jobs had been in a long decline, but between 2011 and 2016, the bottom fell out. Nationwide, coal production fell by 27 percent. Nearly sixty thousand coal miners and contractors lost their jobs, 40 percent of them in Kentucky and West Virginia alone. Big coal companies such as Peabody Energy, Arch Coal, and Alpha Natural Resources went bankrupt, threatening the pensions of thousands of retired miners.

This was a crisis that demanded a serious response. There was a tension between the urgent imperative to reduce America's dependence on fossil fuels, especially coal, that were the main cause of climate change and the need to help the communities whose livelihoods had long depended on producing those fuels. I believed it was possible and imperative to do both. As I would say later in that ill-fated town hall, we had to move away from coal, but we couldn't move away from the hardworking people who kept America's lights on and our factories churning for generations.

When I launched my campaign for President in June 2015, I specifically mentioned Coal Country and the need to help distressed communities make the transition to a more sustainable economic future. It was a call I'd repeat in nearly every speech I gave, all over the country.

I also got to work developing the detailed plan to invest $30 billion in revitalizing coal communities that I mentioned earlier. Consulting with national experts and local leaders, my team came up with great ideas for new incentives to attract jobs and industries to Appalachia, improving infrastructure and broadband internet, training programs that would lead to real jobs instead of worthless certificates, and more support for schools and students. We also worked with the United Mine Workers of America union on steps to hold the coal companies accountable and guarantee health care and a secure retirement for miners and their families. I spoke out publicly when the union said it would be helpful, and I exerted pressure behind the scenes when needed. In the end, Peabody Energy, one of the biggest coal companies, agreed to extend benefits for more than twelve thousand retired miners and their families. If I had won the election, I would have used the full power of the federal government to do even more.

No other candidate came close to this level of attention to the real challenges facing coal communities. On the left, Bernie Sanders advocated for leaving all fossil fuels in the ground, including coal. On the right, Donald Trump made promises about reopening mines but offered zero credible ideas for how he'd reverse decades of decline and job loss. So it was frustrating and painful that thanks in large part to my one unfortunate comment and opposition in West Virginia to President Obama's executive order mandating a reduction in carbon dioxide emissions, both of those candidates were far more popular in the state than I was.

A few weeks after my "gaffe," I went to Appalachia to apologize directly to people I had offended. I knew it was unlikely to change the outcome of the upcoming West Virginia primary or the general election in November, but I wanted to show my respect. I wanted to make it clear that I would be a President for all Americans, not just the ones who voted for me.

Prominent Democrats in West Virginia suggested I fly in and out of Charleston and make a speech in front of a friendly audience. My team on the ground liked that—it would take the least amount of time away from my packed campaign schedule and would mean a warmer reception than I was likely to receive in more rural parts of the state. But that wasn't what I had in mind. I wanted to go deep into the southern coalfields to communities facing the biggest challenges, where Trump was most popular and my coal-miner gaffe was getting the most attention. As one of my advisors put it, that would be like Trump holding a rally in downtown Berkeley, California. That's pretty much what I was going for.

We designed a trip that would take me from eastern Kentucky to southern West Virginia to southeastern Ohio, concluding with an economic policy speech in Athens, Ohio, with my friend Senator Sherrod Brown, who was also on my list of potential choices for Vice President.

We started in Ashland, Kentucky, where I met with a dozen steelworkers who'd lost their jobs when the factory where they'd worked for decades closed. I also talked with men who worked on the railroads and watched as the decline of coal and steel production led to reductions in rail service, which in turn cost more jobs and further isolated the region.

I had known going into the campaign that many communities still hadn't recovered from the Great Recession, and a lot of working-class Americans were hurting and frustrated. Unemployment was down and the economy was growing, but most people hadn't had a raise in fifteen years. The average family income was $4,000 less than when my husband left office in 2001. I knew this backward and forward.

When I got out there and heard the deep despair, those numbers became ever more real. I listened to people talk about how worried they were about their kids' futures. A lot of men were embarrassed that they depended on disability checks to pay the bills and that the jobs they could find didn't pay enough to support a real middle-class life. They were furious that after all they'd done to power our economy, fight our wars, and pay their taxes, no one in Washington seemed to care, much less be trying to do anything about it.

Usually when I meet people who are frustrated and angry, my instinctive response is to talk about how we can fix things. That's why

I spent so much time and energy coming up with new policies to create jobs and raise wages. But in 2016 a lot of people didn't really want to hear about plans and policies. They wanted a candidate to be as angry as they were, and they wanted someone to blame. For too many, it was primarily a resentment election. That didn't come naturally to me. I get angry about injustice and inequality, abuse of power, lying, and bullying. But I've always thought it's better for leaders to offer solutions instead of just more anger. That's certainly what I want from my leaders. Unfortunately, when the resentment level is through the roof your answers may never get a hearing from the people you want to help most.

We left Kentucky and crossed into West Virginia. Just as I remembered from 2008, there was very spotty cell phone coverage as we drove into the Mountain State. That drove the traveling team nuts, but I was thinking more about the bigger problem of how the lack of connectivity hamstrung businesses and schools and held back economic development. Nearly 40 percent of people in rural America don't have access to broadband, and research shows those communities have lower incomes and higher unemployment. That's a solvable problem, and one I was eager to take on.

I thought back to how much I loved campaigning in West Virginia during the 2008 primary, when I won the state by 40 points. My favorite memory was celebrating Mother's Day with my mom and daughter in the small town of Grafton, West Virginia, where the holiday was invented a hundred years earlier. It was one of the last Mother's Days I ever had with my mom, and it was a great one.

We drove into Mingo County, arguably Ground Zero for the coal crisis. In 2011 there had been more than 1,400 miners in the county. By 2016, there were just 438. Our destination was the town of Williamson, home to a promising public-private partnership similar to Reconnecting McDowell that was trying desperately to marshal the resources and the political will needed to expand and diversify the local economy, as well as improve public health.

After about three hours, we arrived at the Williamson Health and Wellness Center. It was drizzling, but outside on the street was a crowd of several hundred angry protestors chanting "We want Trump!" and "Go home Hillary!" Many held up signs about the so-called war on coal. One woman explained to a reporter why she was supporting Trump: "We're tired of all the darn handouts; nobody takes care of *us*." Another had painted her hands red to look like blood and kept yelling about Benghazi. Standing with them was Don Blankenship, the multimillionaire former CEO of a large coal company who was convicted for conspiring to violate mine safety regulations after the Upper Big Branch mine explosion killed twenty-nine workers in 2010. He was due to report to prison just days later, but he made time to come protest me first.

I knew I wouldn't get a warm welcome in West Virginia. That was the point of my visit, after all. But this level of anger took me aback. This wasn't just about my comments in one town hall. This was something deeper.

Since the election, I've spent a lot of time thinking about why I failed to connect with more working-class whites. Many commentators talk as if my poor showing with that group was a new problem that stemmed mostly from my own weaknesses and Trump's unique populist appeal. They point to the white voters who switched from Obama to Trump as evidence. West Virginia, a heavily white working-class state, tells a different story. From Franklin Roosevelt's election in 1932 to Bill's reelection in 1996, Democrats won fourteen out of seventeen presidential elections there. Since 2000, however, we've lost every time, by increasingly bigger margins. In 2012 Obama lost to Mitt Romney by nearly two to one. It's hard to look at that trend and conclude that it is all about me or about Trump.

The most prominent explanation, though an insufficient one on its own, is the so-called war on coal. Democrats' long-standing support for environmental regulations that protect clean air and water and seek to limit carbon emissions has been an easy scapegoat for the misfortunes of the coal industry and the communities that have depended on it. The backlash reached a fevered pitch during the Obama administration, despite strong evidence that government regulation is not the primary cause for the industry's decline.

The Obama administration was slow to take on this false narrative. When it was getting ready to announce the sweeping new Clean Power Plan, which was seen as the most anti-coal policy yet, I thought the President should consider making the announcement in Coal Country and couple it with a big effort to help miners and their families by attracting new investments and jobs. That might have softened the blow a little.

In the end, President Obama announced the new regulations in the White House alongside his administrator of the U.S. Environmental Protection Agency (EPA). That was seen by many folks in West Virginia as another signal that Democrats didn't care about them. Once that perception takes hold, it's hard to dislodge.

That said, Democrats' problems with white working-class voters started long before Obama and go far beyond coal.

After John Kerry lost to George W. Bush in 2004, the writer Thomas Frank popularized the theory that Republicans persuaded whites in places like West Virginia to vote against their economic interests by appealing to them on cultural issues—in other words, "gays, guns, and God." There's definitely merit in that explanation. Remember my earlier description of the man in Arkansas who said Democrats wanted to take his gun and force him to go to a gay wedding?

Then there's race. For decades, Republicans have used coded racial appeals on issues such as school busing, crime, and welfare. It was no accident that Ronald Reagan launched his general election campaign in 1980 with a speech about "states' rights" near Philadelphia,

Mississippi, where three civil rights workers had been murdered in 1964. In 2005 the chairman of the Republican National Committee formally apologized for what's been called the southern strategy. But in 2016 it was back with a vengeance. Politics was reduced to its most tribal, "us" versus "them," and "them" grew into a big list: blacks, Latinos, immigrants, liberals, city dwellers, you name it. Like so many demagogues before him, Trump encouraged a zero-sum view of life where if someone else is gaining, you must be losing. You can hear the resentment in the words of that protestor in Williamson: "We're tired of all the darn handouts; nobody takes care of *us*."

It's hard to compete against demagoguery when the answers you can offer are all unsatisfying. And years of economic pain provided fertile ground for Republicans' cultural and racial appeals. Union membership, once a bulwark for Democrats in states like West Virginia, declined. Being part of a union is an important part of someone's personal identity. It helps shape the way you view the world and think about politics. When that's gone, it means a lot of people stop identifying primarily as workers—and voting accordingly—and start identifying and voting more as white, male, rural, or all of the above.

Just look at Don Blankenship, the coal boss who joined the protest against me on his way to prison. In recent years, even as the coal industry has struggled and workers have been laid off, top executives like him have pocketed huge pay increases, with compensation rising 60 percent between 2004 and 2016. Blankenship endangered his workers, undermined their union, and polluted their rivers and streams, all while making big profits and contributing millions to Republican candidates. He should have been the least popular man in West Virginia even before he was convicted in the wake of the death of twenty-nine miners. Instead, he was welcomed by the pro-Trump protesters in Williamson. One of them told a reporter that he'd vote for Blankenship for President if he ran. Meanwhile, I pledged to strengthen the laws to protect workers and hold bosses like Blankenship accountable—the fact that he received a jail sentence of just one year was appalling—yet I was the one being protested.

Some on the left, including Bernie Sanders, argue that working-class whites have turned away from Democrats because the party became beholden to Wall Street donors and lost touch with its populist roots. It's hard to believe that voters who embrace Don Blankenship are looking for progressive economics. After all, by nearly every measure, the Democratic Party has moved to the left over the past fifteen years, not to the right. Mitt Romney was certainly not more populist than Barack Obama when he demolished him in West Virginia. And Republicans are unabashedly allied with powerful corporate interests, including the coal companies trying to take away health care and pensions from retired miners. Yet they keep winning elections. During my visit, the Republican Majority Leader in the U.S. Senate, Mitch McConnell from Kentucky, was blocking West Virginia Senator Joe Manchin's legislation to protect coal miners' pensions. Why? Senator Brown said it was "because he doesn't like the United Mine Workers Union," which endorsed his Democratic opponent in 2014. Yet there was virtually no anti-Republican backlash, and to date, no political consequences for one of the most callous displays of disregard for the needs of coal miners I can remember.

Now, I've met a lot of open-minded, big-hearted men and women who live and work in poor, rural communities. It's hard to fault them for wanting to shake things up politically after so many years of disappointment. But anger and resentment do run deep. As Appalachian natives such as author J. D. Vance have pointed out, a culture of grievance, victimhood, and scapegoating has taken root as traditional values of self-reliance and hard work have withered. There's a tendency toward seeing every problem as someone else's fault, whether it's Obama, liberal elites in the big cities, undocumented immigrants taking jobs, minorities soaking up government assistance—or me. It's no accident that this list sounds exactly like Trump's campaign rhetoric.

But just because a situation can be exploited for political gain doesn't mean there's not a problem. The pain—and panic—that many blue-collar whites feel is real. The old world they talk wistfully about, when men were men and jobs were jobs, really is gone.

Don't underestimate the role of gender in this. In an economy where most women don't have any choice but to work and few men earn enough to support a family on their own, traditional gender roles get redefined. Under the right circumstances, that can be liberating for women, good for kids, and even good for men, who now have a partner in shouldering the economic burden. But if the changes are caused by the inability of men to make a decent living when they want to work and can't find a job, the toll on their sense of self-worth can be devastating.

It all adds up to a complex dynamic. There's both too much change and not enough change, all at the same time.

When people feel left out, left behind, and left without options, the deep void will be filled by anger and resentment or depression and despair about those who supposedly took away their livelihoods or cut in line.

Trump brilliantly tapped into all these feelings, especially with his slogan: Make America Great Again. Along with that were two other powerful messages: "What have you got to lose?" and "She's been there for thirty years and never did anything." What he meant was: "You can have the old America back once I vanquish the immigrants, especially Mexicans and Muslims, send the Chinese products back, repeal Obamacare, demolish political correctness, ignore inconvenient facts, and pillory Hillary along with all the other liberal elites. I hate all the same people you do, and, unlike the other Republicans, I'll do something to make your life better."

When my husband was a little boy, his uncle Buddy in Hope, Arkansas, liked to say: "Anybody who tries to make you mad and stop you from thinking is not your friend. There's a lot to be said for thinking." Like so much wisdom I've heard in my life, it's easier to say than to live by. The far easier choice is to play the pin-the-tail-on-the-donkey blame game—which is what has happened to Democrats in too many places.

One of the most important but least recognized facts in American politics is that Republicans tend to win in places where more people are pessimistic or uncertain about the future, while Democrats tend to win where people are more optimistic. Those sentiments don't track neatly with the overhyped dichotomy between the coasts and the heartland. There are plenty of thriving communities in both blue and red states that have figured out how to educate their workforces, harness their talents, and participate in the twenty-first-century economy. And some of the most doom-and-gloom Americans are relatively affluent middle-aged and retired whites—the very viewers Fox News prizes— while many poor immigrants, people of color, and young people are burning with energy, ambition, and optimism.

As an example, in 2016 I got whacked in Arkansas as a whole, but I won Pulaski County, home of Little Rock, the state's vibrant capital city, by 18 points. I lost Pennsylvania, but I won Pittsburgh with 75 percent of the vote. Trump may think of that city as an emblem of the industrial past—he contrasted it with Paris when he pulled out of the global climate agreement in 2017—but the reality is that Pittsburgh has reinvented itself as a hub of clean energy, education, and biomedical research. As I saw when I campaigned there many times, people in Pittsburgh are determined and optimistic about the future.

So I can't say what was in the hearts and minds of those men and women standing in the rain in Williamson chanting "Go home Hillary!" Did they despise me because they'd heard on Fox that I wanted to put coal miners out of business? Did some think I turned my back on them after they'd voted for me in the Democratic primary in 2008? Did they turn against me because I served as Obama's Secretary of State and believed climate change was a real threat to our future? Or did their rage flow from deeper tribal politics? All I knew for certain was they were angry, they were loud, and they hated my guts. I gave them a big smile, waved, and went inside.

Dr. Dino Beckett, the director of the Williamson Health and Wellness Center, was waiting for me, along with about a dozen locals and Senator Joe Manchin. They were eager to tell me about how they were working to turn around their struggling community. They had started an incubator to help local entrepreneurs get new small businesses off the ground. The county was trying to turn abandoned mining properties into industrial parks that could attract new employers. They knew they needed better housing infrastructure, so they put people to work refurbishing homes and businesses. They realized that many of their neighbors were struggling with opiate addiction and other chronic health issues such as diabetes, so they opened a nonprofit health clinic. A recovering drug addict who had become a counselor told me how meaningful the work was, even if stemming the epidemic of substance abuse was a Sisyphean endeavor.

To make sure I heard a cross section of perspectives, Dr. Beckett had invited a laid-off coal worker he knew from their children's school soccer team, Bo Copley, along with his wife, Lauren. Bo was a Republican and a fervent Pentecostal, with a T-shirt that said "#JesusIsBetter." He lost his job as a maintenance planner at a local mining operation the year before. Now the family was getting by on what Lauren could earn through her small business as a photographer. When it was Bo's turn to speak, his voice was heavy with emotion.

"Let me say my apologies for what we've heard outside," Bo began, with the chants of the protesters still audible. "The reason you hear those people out there saying some of the things that they say is because when you make comments like 'We're going to put a lot of coal miners out of jobs,' these are the kind of people that you're affecting."

He passed me a picture of his three little children, a son and two daughters. "I want my family to know that they have a future here in this state, because this is a great state," he said. "I've lived my entire life here. West Virginians are proud people. We take pride in our faith in God. We take pride in our family. And we take pride in our jobs. We take pride in the fact that we're hard workers."

Then he got to the heart of the matter. "I just—I just want to know how you can say you're going to put a lot of coal miners out of jobs and then come in here and tell us how you're going to be our friend, because those people out there don't see you as a friend."

"I know that, Bo," I replied. "And I don't know how to explain it other than what I said was totally out of context from what I meant." I badly wanted him to understand. I didn't have a prayer of convincing the crowd outside, but maybe I could make him see that I wasn't the heartless caricature I had been made out to be. I said how sorry I was and that I understood why people were angry.

"I'm going to do everything I can to help," I told him. "Whether or not people in West Virginia support me, I'm going to support you."

Bo looked at me and pointed to the photograph of his children. "Those are the three faces I had to come home and explain to that I didn't have a job," he said. "Those are the three faces I had to come home to and explain that we're going to find a way; that God would provide for us, one way or another, that I was not worried, and I had to try to keep a brave face so they would understand."

He said that earlier in the day he had picked up his young son from school and suggested they stop to get something to eat. "No, Daddy," his son replied, "I don't want us to use up our money." It was hard to hear that.

After the meeting ended, I went off to the side with Bo and Lauren. I wanted to let them know I appreciated their candor. Bo told me how he leaned on his Christian faith in a difficult time. It was everything to him. I shared a little about my faith, and, for a minute, we were just three people bonding over the wisdom of the prophet Micah: "To act justly, to love mercy, and to walk humbly with your God."

Bo was a proud man, but he knew he and his community needed help. Why, he asked, weren't there more programs in place already to help people who were ready and willing to work to find good jobs to replace the ones that had disappeared? Why wasn't there anywhere for someone like him to turn? I told him about my plans to bring new employers to the area and to support small businesses like his wife's. They weren't going to solve the region's problems overnight, but they would help make life better. And if we could get some positive results, people might start believing again that progress was possible. But I knew that campaign promises would go only so far. As we drove off for Charleston, I called my husband. "Bill, we have to help these people."

How do we help give people in rural counties such as Mingo and Mc-Dowell a fighting chance?

The most urgent need right now is to stop the Trump administration from making things a whole lot worse.

I hope by the time you read this, Republicans will have failed to repeal Obamacare, but that's far from certain. Trump's health care plan would have devastating consequences in poor and rural areas, especially for older people and families who rely on Medicaid. And at a time when opiate addiction is ravaging communities across rural America, Trump and Republicans in Congress proposed scrapping the Affordable Care

Act's requirement that insurers cover mental health services and addiction treatment. It alarms me to think about what this would mean for the recovering addicts, family members, doctors, counselors, and police officers I met in West Virginia and across the country who were all struggling to deal with the consequences of this epidemic.

Beyond health care, Trump wants to eliminate nearly all federal support for economic diversification and development in Coal Country. He's proposed shutting down the Appalachian Regional Commission, which has invested more than $387 million in West Virginia alone, helped create thousands of jobs, and supported community efforts such as the Williamson Health and Wellness Center. Appalachia needs more investment, not less; more access to fast, affordable, and reliable broadband for businesses and homes; more high-quality training programs that do a better job of matching students to jobs that actually exist, not just providing certificates that look nice in a frame on the wall but don't lead anywhere; and incentives such as the New Markets Tax Credit that can attract new employers beyond the coal industry and build a more sustainable economy.

Trump's promises are ringing increasingly hollow. After the election, he took a lot of credit for persuading the air-conditioning maker Carrier to keep hundreds of manufacturing jobs in Indiana rather than moving them to Mexico. Since then, we've learned it was essentially a bait and switch: Carrier received millions in subsidies from taxpayers and is still shipping out 630 jobs anyway. That kind of bait and switch shouldn't surprise anyone who's followed Trump's career.

Trump also promised to reopen coal mines and revive the industry to its former glory. But despite what he says, and what a lot of people want to believe, the hard truth is that coal isn't coming back. As Trump's own director of the National Economic Council, Gary Cohn, admitted in a moment of candor in May 2017, "Coal doesn't even make that much sense anymore." Politicians owe it to communities that have relied on the industry for generations to be honest about the future.

The entire debate over coal unfolds in a kind of alternative reality. Watching the news and listening to political speeches, you'd think coal is the only industry in West Virginia. Yet the truth is that the number of coal miners has been shrinking since the end of World War II. During the 1960s, fewer than fifty thousand West Virginians worked in the mines. By the end of the eighties, it was fewer than twenty-eight thousand. The numbers have gone up and down as the price of coal fluctuates, but it's been twenty-five years since the industry accounted for even 5 percent of total employment in the state. Today far more West Virginians work in education and health care, which makes protecting the Affordable Care Act vital to protecting West Virginian jobs.

Across the country, Americans have more than twice as many jobs producing solar energy as they do mining coal. And think about this: since 2001, a half million jobs in department stores across the country have disappeared. That's many times more than were lost in coal mining. Just between October 2016 and April 2017, about eighty-nine thousand Americans lost jobs in retail—more than all the people who work in coal mining put together. Yet coal continues to loom much larger in our politics and national imagination.

More broadly, we remain locked into an outdated picture of the working class in America that distorts our policy priorities. A lot of the press coverage and political analysis since the election has taken as a given that the "real America" is full of middle-aged white men who wear hard hats and work on assembly lines—or did until Obama ruined everything. There are certainly people who fit that description, and they deserve respect and every chance to make a decent living. But fewer than 10 percent of Americans today work in factories and on farms, down from 36 percent in 1950. Most working-class Americans have service jobs. They're nurses and medical technicians, childcare providers and computer coders. Many of them are people of color and women. In fact, roughly two-thirds of all minimum-wage jobs in America are held by women.

Repealing Obamacare or starting a trade war with China won't do anything to make these Americans' lives better. But raising the minimum wage would. It would help a lot. So would a large program to build and repair our bridges, tunnels, roads, ports, and airports and expand high-speed internet access to neglected areas. Strengthening unions and making it easier for workers to organize and bargain for better pay and benefits would help rebuild the middle class. Supporting overstretched families with paid leave and more affordable childcare and elder care would make a huge difference. So would a "public option" for health care and allowing more people to buy into Medicare and Medicaid, which would help expand coverage and bring down costs.

The other thing we should be honest about is how hard it's going to be, no matter what we do, to create significant economic opportunity in every remote area of our vast nation. In some places, the old jobs aren't coming back, and the infrastructure and workforce needed to support big new industries aren't there. As hard as it is, people may have to leave their hometowns and look for work elsewhere in America.

We know this can have a transformative effect. In the 1990s, the Clinton administration experimented with a program called Moving to Opportunity for Fair Housing, which gave poor families in public housing vouchers to move to safer, middle-income neighborhoods where their children were surrounded every day by evidence that life can be better. Twenty years later, the children of those families have grown up to earn higher incomes and attend college at higher rates than their peers who stayed behind. And the younger the kids were when they moved, the bigger boost they received.

Previous generations of Americans actually moved around the

country much more than we do today. Millions of black families migrated from the rural South to the urban North. Large numbers of poor whites left Appalachia to take jobs in Midwestern factories. My own father hopped a freight train from Scranton, Pennsylvania, to Chicago in 1935, looking for work.

Yet today, despite all our advances, fewer Americans are moving than ever before. One of the laid-off steelworkers I met in Kentucky told me he found a good job in Columbus, Ohio, but he was doing the 120-mile commute every week because he didn't want to move. "People from Kentucky, they want to be in Kentucky," another said to me. "That's something that's just in our DNA." I understand that feeling. People's identities and their support systems—extended family, friends, church congregations, and so on—are rooted in where they come from. This is painful, gut-wrenching stuff. And no politician wants to be the one to say it.

I believe that after we do everything we can to help create new jobs in distressed small towns and rural areas, we also have to give people the skills and tools they need to seek opportunities beyond their hometowns—and provide a strong safety net both for those who leave and those who stay.

Whether it's updating policies to meet the changing conditions of America's workers, or encouraging greater mobility, the bottom line is the same: we can't spend all our time staving off decline. We need to create new opportunities, not just slow down the loss of old ones. Rather than keep trying to re-create the economy of the past, we should focus on making the jobs people actually have better and figure out how to create the good jobs of the future in fields such as clean energy, health care, construction, computer coding, and advanced manufacturing.

Republicans will always be better at defending yesterday. Democrats have to be in the future business. The good news is we have a lot of ideas to help make life better in our modern economy. As you saw earlier, I proposed a whole raft of them in my campaign. So even as Democrats play defense in Trump's Washington, we have to keep pushing new and better solutions.

On that trip to West Virginia, I spent some time with a group of retired miners who were concerned about losing the health care and pensions they had been promised for years of dangerous labor, often in exchange for lower wages.

One retiree told me a story that has stuck in my memory ever since.

Many years ago, when he first went into the mines, he told his wife, "You're not going to have to worry. We're union. We'll have our health care, we'll have our pensions, you won't have to worry about nothing." But quietly, he still worried about his neighbors who didn't have the same benefits.

In 1992, he decided to vote for the first time in his life. He wanted to vote for Bill. When his friends at the mine asked him why, he said the only reason was health care. "You've got health care; what are you worried about?" they asked. But he was adamant. "There are other people that don't have health care," he would say. And when Obamacare was finally passed, he thought it didn't go far enough.

Now some coal companies were trying to take away benefits that had been promised long ago. The security he had assured his wife was rock solid was now in jeopardy.

"People need to worry about one another," he told me. "We are our brother's keeper, and we need to worry about other people. Me, personally, I have faith; I know God is going to get us through it. But we need to be worrying about our brother."

Most of the folks I met in places like Ashland, Kentucky, and Williamson, West Virginia, were good people in a bad situation, desperate for change. I wish more than anything that I could have done a better job speaking to their fears and frustrations. Their distrust went too deep, and the weight of history was too heavy. But I wish I could have found the words or emotional connection to make them believe how passionately I wanted to help their communities, and their families.

Where there's a will to condemn, evidence will follow.

—Chinese proverb

Those Damn Emails

Imagine you're a kid sitting in history class thirty years from now learning about the 2016 presidential election, which brought to power the least experienced, least knowledgeable, least competent President our country has ever had. Something must have gone horribly wrong, you think. Then you hear that one issue dominated press coverage and public debate in that race more than any other. "Climate change?" you ask. "Health care?" "No," your teacher responds. "Emails."

Emails, she explains, were a primitive form of electronic communication that used to be all the rage. And the dumb decision by one presidential candidate to use a personal email account at the office—as many senior government officials had done in the past (and continued to do)—got more coverage than any other issue in the whole race. In fact, if you had turned on a network newscast in 2016, you were three times more likely to hear about those emails than about all the real issues combined.

"Was there a crime?" you ask. "Did it damage our national security?"

"No and no," the teacher replies with a shrug.

Sound ridiculous? I agree.

For those of you in the present, you've most likely already heard more than your fill about my emails. Probably the last thing you want to read right now is more about those "damn emails," as Bernie Sanders memorably put it. If so, skip to the next chapter—though I wish you'd read a few more pages to understand how it relates to what's happening now. But there's no doubt that a big part of me would also be very happy to never think about the whole mess ever again.

For months after the election, I tried to put it all out of my mind. It would do me no good to brood over my mistake. And it wasn't healthy or productive to dwell on the ways I felt I'd been shivved by then-FBI Director Jim Comey—three times over the final five months of the campaign.

Then, to my surprise, my emails were suddenly front-page news again. On May 9, 2017, Donald Trump fired Comey. The White House distributed a memo by Deputy Attorney General Rod Rosenstein that excoriated Comey for his unprofessional handling of the investigation into my emails. They said that was the reason for firing him. (You read that right. Donald Trump said he fired Comey because of how unfair the email investigation was to . . . me.) Rosenstein cited the "nearly universal judgment" that Comey had made serious mistakes, in particular his decisions to disparage me in a July press conference and to inform Congress that he was reopening the investigation just eleven days before the election. Testifying before Congress on May 19, 2017, Rosenstein described Comey's press conference as "profoundly wrong and unfair."

I read Rosenstein's memo in disbelief. Here was Trump's number two man at the Justice Department putting in writing all the things I'd been thinking for months. Rosenstein cited the opinions of former

Attorneys General and Deputy Attorneys General of both parties. It was as if, after more than two years of mass hysteria, the world had finally come to its senses.

But the story quickly fell apart. On national television, Trump told NBC's Lester Holt that the real reason he fired Comey was the FBI's investigation into possible coordination between the Trump campaign and Russian intelligence. Or, as Trump called it, "this Russia thing." I wasn't surprised. Trump knew that, for all of Comey's faults, he wouldn't lie about the law. He had insisted that there was no case against me, despite Republican (and internal FBI) pressure to say there was, so when he confirmed the FBI's Russia investigation to Congress in 2017, I figured he was on borrowed time.

Still, it was incredible to see Comey go from villain to martyr in five seconds flat.

To make sense of this, you have to be able to keep two different thoughts in your head at the same time: Rosenstein was right about the email investigation, and Comey was wrong. But Trump was wrong to fire Comey over Russia. Both of those statements are true. And both are frustrating.

As painful as it is to return to this maddening saga, it's now more important than ever to try to understand how this issue ballooned into an election-tipping controversy. A lot of people still don't understand what it was all about; they just know it was bad. And I can't blame them: they were told that over and over again for a year and a half. For most of the general election campaign, the word *email* dominated all others when people were asked to name the first word that came to mind about me.

Right off the bat, let me say again that, yes, the decision to use personal email instead of an official government account was mine and mine alone. I own that. I never meant to mislead anyone, never kept my email use secret, and always took classified information seriously.

During the campaign, I tried endlessly to explain that I'd acted in good faith. I tried to apologize, though I knew the attacks being lobbed at me were untrue or wildly overstated, and motivated by partisan politics. Sometimes I dove deep into the tedious details. Other times I tried to rise above it all. Once I even told a bad joke. No matter what, I never found the right words. So let me try again:

It was a dumb mistake.

But an even dumber "scandal."

It was like quicksand: the more you struggle, the deeper you sink. At times, I thought I must be going crazy. Other times, I was sure it was the world that had gone nuts. Sometimes I snapped at my staff. I was tempted to make voodoo dolls of certain members of the press and Congress and stick them full of pins. Mostly, I was furious at myself.

Given my inability to explain this mess, I decided to let other voices tell the story this time. I hope that it helps to better connect the dots and explain what did and, equally important, didn't happen.

Nothing can undo what's done, but it does help with my frustration—and that's clearly good for my mental health!

Our best information is that she set it up as a matter of convenience.
—FBI Director Jim Comey, in congressional testimony, July 7, 2016

Yes, it was supposed to be convenient. Some doubted that explanation. But that's what the FBI concluded after months of investigation. And it's the truth.

A lot of young people today are used to carrying around multiple devices and having both a personal phone and one provided by their work. But I'm not a digital native. (I couldn't even have told you what that term meant until fairly recently.) I didn't send a single email while

I was in the White House as First Lady or during most of my first term in the U.S. Senate. I've never used a computer at home or at work. It was not until about 2006 that I began sending and receiving emails on a BlackBerry phone. I had a plain old AT&T account like millions of other people, and used it both for work and personal email. That was my system, and it worked for me.

Adding another email account when I became Secretary of State would have meant juggling a second phone, since both accounts could not be on the same State Department device. I knew that former Secretary of State Colin Powell had used personal email exclusively. I also knew that email wasn't where the bulk of a Secretary's work was done. All this added up to me not giving this much thought when I took office—there was a lot else going on—although, of course, I now wish I had.

In early 2009, I moved my email account from AT&T's server to one that my husband's office had previously set up in our Chappaqua home, which is guarded by the Secret Service. People have asked, "Why did you set up that server?" But the answer is that I didn't; the system was already there. My husband had been using an office server for years and had recently upgraded it. It made sense to me to have my email account on that same system. So I just moved my account onto it. I could keep using my BlackBerry in exactly the same way as I always had.

I emailed regularly with Chelsea and with Bill's team—he does not personally use email, and we are still phone people—and with relatives and friends. But very little of my work was via email during the next four hectic years. I held lots of meetings, talked on the telephone (on both regular and secure lines), read stacks of briefing papers, and traveled nearly a million miles to 112 countries to see people face-to-face.

When we went back later on and collected all my work-related emails, we found a lot like this:

From: H
To: John Podesta
Sent: Sunday, September 20, 2009 10:28 PM
Subject: Re: When could we talk?

I'm on endless calls about the UN. Could I call you early tomorrow? Would btw
6:30 and 8:00 be too early? Please wear socks to bed to keep your feet warm.

Yes, that's me telling my friend John to wear warm socks. Or, there's
this one, where I struggle to use my fax machine:

From: H
To: Huma Abedin
Sent: Wednesday, December 23, 2009 2:50 PM
Subject: Re: can you hang up the fax line, they will call again and try fax

I did.

—Original Message—
From: Huma Abedin
To: H
Sent: Wed Dec 23 14:43:02 2009
Subject: Re: can you hang up the fax line, they will call again and try fax

Yes but hang up one more time. So they can reestablish the line.

—Original Message—
From: H
To: Huma Abedin
Sent: Wed Dec 23 14:39:39 2009
Subject: Re: can you hang up the fax line, they will call again and try fax

I thought it was supposed to be off hook to work?

Here's one more that still makes me chuckle:

From: H

To: Huma Abedin

Sent: Wednesday, February 10, 2010 3:19 PM

Subject: Re: Diane Watson to retire

I'd like to call her.

But right now I'm fighting w the WH operator who doesn't believe I am who I say and wants my direct office line even tho I'm not there and I just [gave] him my home # and the State Dept # and I told him I had no idea what my direct office # was since I didn't call myself and I just hung up and am calling thru Ops like a proper and properly dependent Secretary [of] State— no independent dialing allowed.

In the end, what was meant to be convenient turned out to be anything but. If I had known all that at the time, there's no question I would have chosen a different system. Just about anything would have been better. Carving messages in stone and lugging them around town would have been better.

Laws and regulations did not prohibit employees from using their personal email accounts for the conduct of official Department business.
    —Report by the State Department Inspector General, May 2016

Sounds definitive, right? Every department in the federal government has an internal Inspector General who oversees legal and regulatory compliance. The State Department Inspector General and his top aides, one of whom had formerly worked for Republican Senator

Chuck Grassley, were no friends of mine. They looked for every opportunity to be critical. Yet when they examined all the rules in place when I was Secretary of State, they came to the above conclusion. There was a lot of confusion and consternation in the press about this question—in part because some of the rules changed after I left office. But as the Inspector General of the State Department spokesman confirmed: there was no prohibition on using personal email.

Prior to Secretary Kerry, no Secretary of State used a state.gov email address.

> —Karin Lang, the career diplomat responsible for managing the staff supporting the Secretary of State, in a June 2016 deposition

The use of private email didn't start with me. It also didn't end with me. Colin Powell exclusively used an AOL account. Secretary Kerry, who was the first Secretary of State to use a government email address, has said that he continued using his preexisting personal email for official business well into 2015. None of this was particularly remarkable. Nor was it a secret. I corresponded with more than a hundred government officials from my personal email account, including the President and other White House officials. The IT staff at the State Department often assisted me in using my BlackBerry, particularly when they realized how technologically challenged I was.

As for record keeping, because the overwhelming number of people with whom I was exchanging work-related emails were government personnel on their ".gov" email addresses, I had every reason to think the messages I sent should have been captured by the government's servers, archived, and made available for Freedom of Information Act (FOIA) requests.

With respect to potential computer intrusion by hostile actors, we did not find direct evidence that Secretary Clinton's personal email domain, in its various configurations since 2009, was successfully hacked.

—FBI Director Jim Comey, in a press conference on July 5, 2016

A lot of people suggested that the server maintained by my husband's office might be vulnerable to hacking. As it turned out, the State Department network and many other highly sensitive government systems, including at the White House and the Pentagon, were all hacked. Colin Powell's emails were hacked. But, as Comey stated, there has never been any evidence that my system was ever compromised. Ironically, it turns out it may have been one of the safest possible places for my email.

Everybody thought Hillary Clinton was unbeatable, right? But we put together a Benghazi special committee, a select committee. What are her numbers today? Her numbers are dropping.

—Republican Majority Leader Representative Kevin McCarthy, on Fox News, September 29, 2015

Here's where the story takes a turn into the partisan swamp. Republicans spent years shamelessly trying to score political points off the terrorist attack in Benghazi, Libya, in September 2012. It was a tragedy, and I lay awake at night racking my brain about what more could have been done to stop it. After previous tragedies, including the bombings of our embassy and Marine barracks in Beirut in 1983 that killed 241 Americans, and the bombings of our embassies in Kenya and Tanzania in 1998 that killed 12 Americans and hundreds of Africans, there were good-faith bipartisan efforts to learn lessons and improve security. But after the attacks in Benghazi, Republicans turned the deaths of four brave Americans into

a partisan farce. They weren't satisfied that seven congressional investigations (five of them led by Republicans) and an independent review
board conducted thorough factual reviews and concluded that neither
President Obama nor I were personally to blame for the tragedy. The
Republican committee chairmen had done their jobs, but their leaders
weren't satisfied. They wanted to score more political points. So they set
up a "new" special committee to damage me as much as possible.

As Kevin McCarthy, the number two House Republican, explained
in his moment of rare and unintentional candor, something had to be
done to hurt me. He was also trying to become Speaker and needed to
impress the right wing.

It wasn't until October 2015 that the Republicans finally asked
me to testify. By then, the investigation into the terrorist attack had
long since been overshadowed by their obsession with my emails. The
Republicans running the committee had scrapped ten planned hearings about security and other issues, and instead focused solely on me.
I had already testified about the attack in both the House and the Senate in 2013, so there wasn't much new ground to cover. Nonetheless,
I answered questions for eleven hours. As overtly partisan as the whole
exercise was, I was happy to have the chance to set the record straight.

The Republicans had delivered a massive binder of emails and
memos to me just before the hearing began, warning that they planned
to ask about any or all of them. Some I'd never seen before. The ques-
tioners tried to outdo one another in search of a "Gotcha!" moment
that would play on the news. It was all a little ham-handed. One Congressman pointed portentously to a paragraph in one of my emails, insisting it contained some damning revelation of wrongdoing. I directed
his attention to the next paragraph, which proved the opposite. And
so it went.

Afterward, the Republican chairman Trey Gowdy sheepishly admitted the whole exercise had failed to achieve much of anything.
When asked what new information had emerged over eleven hours

of grilling, he paused for several seconds and then couldn't come up with anything. I was down the hall in a small conference room, where I hugged my staff, who had labored so hard to prepare me for the hearing. I invited them back to my house in Northwest Washington, where we ate takeout Indian food and decompressed.

The press agreed that the committee was a bust for the Republicans. But I was experienced enough in the ways of Washington scandals to know that some damage had already been done. Accusations repeated often enough have a way of sticking, or at least leaving behind a residue of slime you can never wipe off.

There is no question that former Secretary Clinton had authority to delete personal emails without agency supervision.
—Department of Justice court filing, September 2015

The Benghazi Committee sent the State Department a blizzard of requests for documents. In August 2014, among 15,000 pages of emails provided to the committee were eight emails to or from me. At the time, nobody raised any questions to me about why I was using a non-state.gov account.

A few months later, during the fall of 2014, the State Department, in an attempt to complete its record keeping, sent a letter to each of the four previous Secretaries of State—me, Condoleezza Rice, Colin Powell, and Madeleine Albright—for copies of all work emails we might still have in our possession. None of the other Secretaries produced anything. Nothing about weapons of mass destruction and the deliberations that led up to the Iraq War. Nothing about the fallout over the mistreatment of detainees at Abu Ghraib prison or the use of torture. Nothing at all. Madeleine said she never used email at the State Department. Neither did Condi, although senior aides of hers used personal email accounts. Powell said he didn't keep any of his emails.

I directed my attorneys to collect and provide to the department any messages I had that could conceivably be considered related to official business. That came to more than 30,000 emails. They were intentionally expansive in what they determined to be work related. The State Department and the National Archives and Records Administration later determined that 1,258 of them were, in fact, purely personal, and did not need to be provided to the department.

More than 30,000 emails sounds like a lot. But that's over four years, and a lot of those consisted of "Thx," or "Pls Print"—or no reply at all. One of my aides once calculated the average number of emails he sent and received every day. Over four years, it was hundreds of thousands. That helps put the numbers in context.

Another 31,000 of the emails I had were personal and not related in any way to my job as Secretary of State. I got a lot of grief for saying they were about yoga sessions and wedding planning. But these messages also included communications with lawyers and doctors, information about my mother's estate, reports from family and friends about things happening in their personal lives, both happy and sad—in short, clearly private personal content. Naturally I didn't want strangers reading them.

So we checked to make sure we were following the rules, providing every relevant email I had, and deleted the personal ones.

Critics later pounced on the fact that I deleted my personal emails and accused me of acting improperly. But as the Justice Department said, the rules were clear, and they would have applied to personal emails sent on a government account as well. And for good reason: nobody wants his or her personal emails made public.

Lock her up!

—Trump advisor Michael Flynn at the Republican
National Convention, July 18, 2016

This quote could have been pulled from nearly any Trump rally of the entire campaign, but there's a certain poetic justice now in remembering how enthusiastic Michael Flynn was about sending me to jail.

The endless chants of "Lock her up!" once again exposed the viciousness of the Republican smear merchants and their most devoted followers. It was all depressingly familiar. For decades, political adversaries have accused me of every crime under the sun—even murder—and promised that I'd end up in jail one day.

You'd think that this history might have prompted fair-minded journalists to hesitate before setting off on another scandal jamboree. Or that voters might look at a long pattern of false accusations and be skeptical of new claims. But you'd be wrong. The vaguely remembered history of past pseudoscandals ended up reinforcing the general perception that "something shady must be going on with her" and fueling the much-discussed phenomenon of "Clinton fatigue."

Throughout the 2016 campaign, I watched how lies insinuate themselves into people's brains if hammered often enough. Fact checking is powerless to stop it. Friends of mine who made calls or knocked on doors for me would talk to people who said they couldn't vote for me because I had killed someone, sold drugs, and committed any number of unreported crimes, including how I handled my emails. The attacks were repeated so frequently that many people took it as an article of faith that I must have done *something* wrong.

The hysteria over emails kicked off in earnest in March 2015. On a Saturday night, my attorney, David Kendall, received an email from the *New York Times* asking several questions about my email practices and asking for responses "by late Sunday or early Monday at the latest." We scrambled to answer as many of the *Times*'s questions as we could. Clearly something was up. The *Times* article appeared online late Monday, March 2, with the headline "Hillary Clinton Used Personal Email Account at State Dept., Possibly Breaking Rules."

As the Inspector General's report eventually made clear, this was baloney. The *Times* observed darkly: "The revelation about the private email account echoes long-standing criticisms directed at both the former Secretary and her husband, former President Bill Clinton, for a lack of transparency and inclination toward secrecy." It wasn't until the eighth paragraph that the story noted, "Mrs. Clinton is not the first government official—or first Secretary of State—to use a personal email account on which to conduct official business."

The *Times*'s argument was that using personal email reinforced the narrative that I had a penchant for secrecy, but I've always found that charge odd. People know more about me and Bill than anybody in public life. We've made public thirty-eight years of our tax returns (thirty-eight years more than a certain someone), all my State Department emails, the Clinton Foundation tax returns and donors, medical information—yet we were secretive? When we sometimes did draw a line after going further than anyone in public life to be transparent, we didn't do it to be secretive—we did it to keep ourselves sane. Not to mention that someone trying to keep her email secret would be pretty dumb to use @clintonemail.com!

The facts didn't stop the hamster wheel of Washington scandal from spinning into rapid motion, as other media outlets sought to follow a story that must be important, because the *New York Times* had put it on the front page.

In an effort to calm things down, two days after the *Times* article appeared, I called for the public release of all the emails I had provided the State Department. I knew that would be a level of transparency unheard of in public life. In fact, more of my emails are now publicly available than every other President, Vice President, and Cabinet Secretary in our country's history combined. I had nothing to hide, and I thought that if the public actually read all of these thousands of messages, many people would see that my use of a personal account was never an attempt to cover up anything nefarious. The vast majority of the emails weren't particularly newsworthy, which may be why the press focused on any gossipy nugget it could find and otherwise ignored the contents. There were no startling revelations, no dark secrets, no tales of wrongdoing or negligence. They did, however, reveal something I felt was worth seeing: the hard work and dedication of the men and women of the State Department.

Once people did start reading, I was amused by some of the reactions, as I always am when people discover that I am, in fact, a real person. "I was one of the most ardent Hillary haters on the planet . . . until I read her emails," one writer declared. "I discovered a Hillary Clinton I didn't even know existed," she continued, "a woman who cared about employees who lost loved ones . . . who, without exception, took time to write notes of condolence and notes of congratulations, no matter how busy she was . . . who could be a tough negotiator and firm in her expectations, but still had a moment to write a friend with encouragement in tough times." Unfortunately, most people didn't read the emails; they just knew what the press and the Republicans said about them, so they figured they must contain some dark, mysterious secrets.

On March 10 I held a press conference. It wasn't a pleasant experience. The press was ravenous, and I was rusty, having been out of partisan politics for several years. "Looking back, it would've been better if I'd simply used a second email account and carried a second phone," I said. "But at the time, this didn't seem like an issue." That was true. And it didn't satisfy anyone. Right then and there, I should have known there would never be some magical words to prove how silly it was and make it go away.

Losing the story to another news outlet would have been a far, far better outcome than publishing an unfair story and damaging the **Times's** *reputation for accuracy.*

—*New York Times* public editor Margaret Sullivan on July 27, 2015

Late on July 23, 2015, the *Times* delivered another bombshell. A front-page article headlined "Criminal Inquiry Is Sought in Clinton Email Use" reported that two Inspector Generals had asked the DOJ "to open a criminal investigation into whether sensitive government information was mishandled in connection with the personal email account Hillary Rodham Clinton used as Secretary of State." Now my campaign had to deal with questions about whether I was being measured for an orange jumpsuit.

The Justice Department, however, clarified quickly that it had "received a referral related to the potential compromise of classified information" but "not a criminal referral." The *Times* had to publish two corrections and an editor's note explaining why it had "left readers with a confused picture."

Representative Elijah Cummings, the ranking Democrat on the Benghazi Committee, helped explain what happened: "I spoke personally to the State Department Inspector General on Thursday, and he said he never asked the Justice Department to launch a criminal investigation of Secretary Clinton's email usage. Instead, he told me the Intelligence Community IG [Inspector General] notified the Justice Department and Congress that they identified classified information in a few emails that were part of the FOIA review, and that none of those emails had been previously marked as classified."

Looking back after the election, the *Times* described the mix-up as "a distinction without a difference," because we now know that there was an investigation under way. But we also now know that there was a disagreement between the Department of Justice and the FBI about how to describe it appropriately. The DOJ's approach, reflected in the clarification to the *Times* story issued by its spokesperson, was intended to adhere to the long-standing policy of not confirming or denying the existence of an investigation—a rule that Comey respected scrupulously when he refused to say anything at all about the investigation into possible ties between Russia and the Trump campaign. But when it came to my emails, he had plenty to say. Regardless, the *Times* got into trouble because it gave its readers only one side of the story. The paper's Margaret Sullivan published a scathing postmortem headlined, "A Clinton Story Fraught with Inaccuracies: How It Happened and What Next?" Sullivan took the *Times* to task for its shoddy reporting. "You can't put stories like this back in the bottle—they ripple through the entire news system," she wrote. "It was, to put it mildly, a mess."

If all these respected, senior foreign service officers and experienced ambassadors are sending these emails, then this issue is not about how Hillary Clinton managed her email, but how the State Department communicates in the 21st century.

— Phil Gordon, a former Assistant Secretary of State and
National Security Council official, who had some of his emails
to me classified retroactively, in the *Times*, May 10, 2016

The Department of Justice's investigation, and pretty much everything else that followed, turned on questions of classification. The issue was no longer using personal email on the job. The question now was what should be considered classified, and did I or anyone else intend to mishandle it?

Despite its science-y name, classification isn't a science. Five people asked to look at the same set of documents could easily come to five different decisions. We see this every day across the government as different agencies disagree about what information should be considered classified. When I was Secretary, it was not uncommon for one of our Foreign Service Officers talking to foreign diplomats and journalists to report back on political or military developments in a country and file this information in an unclassified form. But a CIA agent in the same country, using covert informants and techniques, might gather the very same facts yet classify the report as secret. The very same information: Is it classified or not? Experts and agencies frequently disagree.

That's what happened when the State Department and the intelligence agencies reviewed my emails for release. Remember, I had asked for *all* of them to be published so that the American people could read them and judge for themselves. There were also a number of Freedom of Information Act requests working their way through the courts. The easiest thing to do would have been to just dump every email onto a website and be done with it, but the government has rules it has to follow in FOIA cases. You don't want to accidentally publish someone's Social Security number or cell phone number.

When reviewing my thirty thousand emails, in a number of instances, representatives of various U.S. intelligence agencies sought to retroactively classify messages that had not previously been marked as classified. Many State Department diplomats with long experience conducting sensitive diplomacy disagreed with those decisions. It was like a town changing speed limits and retroactively fining drivers who had complied with the old limit but not the new one.

For example, an email from Dennis Ross, one of our country's most experienced diplomats, was declared classified retroactively. It described back-channel negotiations he'd conducted with Israelis and Palestinians as a private citizen back in 2011. Government officials had already cleared him to publish the same information in a book, which he had done, but now different officials were trying to classify it. "It shows the arbitrariness of what is now being classified," Dennis observed.

Something similar happened to Henry Kissinger around the same time. The State Department released the transcript of a 1974 conversation about Cyprus between then-Secretary of State Kissinger and the director of the CIA, but much of the text was blacked out because it was now considered classified. This puzzled historians because State had published the full, unredacted transcript eight years before in an official history book . . . and on the department's website!

Another veteran diplomat, Ambassador Princeton Lyman, was also surprised to find some of his run-of-the-mill emails to me retroactively designated as classified. "The day-to-day kind of reporting I did about what happened in negotiations did not include information I considered classified," he told the *Washington Post*.

That is an absurdity. We might as well shut the department down.
                    —Former Secretary of State Colin Powell in the *Times* on
                    February 4, 2016, after learning that two messages sent to his
                    personal email account were being classified retroactively

Like Colin, I thought it was ridiculous that some in the intelligence agencies were now trying to second-guess the judgment of veteran diplomats and national security professionals in the State Department about whether messages they sent should be classified. It was doubly ridiculous to suggest that I should have second-guessed them in the moment.

Given all this, it's no surprise that many experts say that overclassification has become a big problem across the government. Even FBI Director Comey admitted as much in a Senate hearing, agreeing that a great deal of material that gets classified is, in fact, widely known to the public and poses little or no risk to national security.

Comey also confirmed that none of my emails was properly marked as classified, and therefore I would reasonably conclude they were not. His full exchange with Congressman Matt Cartwright of Pennsylvania in a congressional hearing on July 7, 2016, is worth reading:

CARTWRIGHT: You were asked about markings on a few
        documents—I have the manual here—marking national
        classified security information. And I don't think you
        were given a full chance to talk about those three

documents with the little *c*'s on them. Were they properly
documented? Were they properly marked according to the
manual?

COMEY: No.

CARTWRIGHT: According to the manual, if you're going
to classify something, there has to be a header on the
document? Right?

COMEY: Correct.

CARTWRIGHT: Was there a header on the three documents
that we've discussed today that had the little *c* in the text
someplace?

COMEY: No. There were three emails. The *c* was in the body,
in the text, but there was no header on the email or in the
text.

CARTWRIGHT: So if Secretary Clinton really were an expert
about what's classified and what's not classified, and we're
following the manual, the absence of a header would tell her
immediately that those three documents were not classified.
Am I correct in that?

COMEY: That would be a reasonable inference.

This is not a situation in which America's national security was endangered.

　　　　　　　　　　—President Barack Obama, on *60 Minutes*, October 11, 2015

This wasn't just the view of the Commander in Chief. Many top foreign policy officials from both parties agreed, and endorsed me for
President—like Michael Chertoff, George W. Bush's Secretary of
Homeland Security. "She's going to do a good job protecting the country," Chertoff told NPR. "In a world at war, you've got to focus on the

top priority which is protecting the United States and protecting our friends and allies."

The American people are sick and tired of hearing about your damn emails! Enough of the emails. Let's talk about the real issues facing America.
—Senator Bernie Sanders, in the first Democratic debate, October 13, 2015

I couldn't have said it better myself. I remain grateful for Bernie's wise comment in our first debate. There was a reason the crowd cheered so heartily. He was right that the whole controversy was nonsense. If only the press had treated it that way. I wish I could end this story right here. Unfortunately, the saga continued.

Our judgment is that no reasonable prosecutor would bring such a case.
—FBI Director Jim Comey, in a press conference on July 5, 2016

The FBI's security inquiry was thorough, professional—and slow. My lawyer wrote to the Department of Justice way back in August 2015, repeating my public pledge to cooperate completely and offering for me to appear voluntarily to answer questions. I wanted my interview to take place as quickly as possible, since the first Democratic primaries were looming. But we were repeatedly told, "Not yet."

It became clear that I would likely be the last witness interviewed. I understood this was the logical sequence, but I chafed at being unable to dispel the cloud of uncertainty looming over me.

Finally, in June 2016, they were ready to talk to me. We agreed to an interview on July 2, a sleepy Saturday on a hot holiday weekend. To avoid press hoopla as much as possible, we set it for 8:00 A.M. at the FBI Head-quarters in the J. Edgar Hoover Building in downtown Washington.

An elevator whisked me and my team up from the basement parking lot to the eighth floor, where we were brought to a secure conference room. Eight DOJ and FBI lawyers and agents were waiting for us. One of my attorneys, Katherine Turner, was eight and a half months pregnant, so there was a lot of baby-related small talk to help break the ice.

The interview lasted three and a half hours and was conducted largely by two FBI agents, although all the government lawyers asked some questions. They wanted to know how I had decided to use my personal email at the State Department, who I'd talked to, what I'd been told, what I knew about maintenance of the system, how I'd had the emails sorted, and other things. The agents were professional, precise, and courteous. Their questions were phrased carefully and not argumentative, and when they obtained an answer, they didn't try to badger. I thought it was conducted efficiently. When they said they had no further questions and thanked me, I apologized to them all, saying that I was sorry they'd had to spend so much time on this matter.

Director Comey had not been present during my Saturday interview. But three days later, on Tuesday, July 5, he held a very unusual press conference. It came as a complete surprise to us. We had no warning and had heard no feedback at all after the Saturday session.

Comey made a double-barreled announcement. First, he said that no criminal charges would be brought against anyone, stating that "no reasonable prosecutor" would bring a criminal case of mishandling classified information in this situation. We had expected that. Nonetheless, it was good to hear those words.

The second shot was both completely unexpected and inappropriate. Comey said that although my State Department colleagues and I had not violated the law about handling classified information, we—all three hundred of us who had written emails later classified—were nevertheless "extremely careless." He said the FBI had found that "the security culture of the State Department in general, and with respect to use of unclassified email systems in particular, was generally lacking in the kind of care for classified information found elsewhere in the government." It was one thing to go after me, but disparaging the entire State Department was totally out-of-bounds and revealed how much age-old institutional rivalries between agencies colored this entire process.

Much of the public and press reaction to Comey's announcement rightly focused on the overall conclusion that after months of controversy, there was no case. Critics predicting my imminent indictment were bitterly disappointed. But I was angry and frustrated that Comey had used his public position to criticize me, my staff, and the State Department, with no opportunity for us to counter or disprove the charge.

I felt a little like Ray Donovan, President Reagan's Secretary of Labor, who, after being acquitted of fraud charges, asked, "Which office do I go to to get my reputation back?"

My first instinct was that my campaign should hit back hard and explain to the public that Comey had badly overstepped his bounds—the same argument Rod Rosenstein would make months after the election. That might have blunted the political damage and made Comey think twice before breaking protocol again a few months later. My team raised concerns with that kind of confrontational approach. In the end, we decided it would be better to just let it go and try to move on. Looking back, that was a mistake.

The Director laid out his version of the facts for the news media as if it were a closing argument, but without a trial. It is a textbook example of what federal prosecutors and agents are taught not to do.

—Deputy Attorney General Rod Rosenstein, in his
May 9, 2017, memo to Attorney General Jeff Sessions

Rosenstein's damning memo about Comey's handling of the email investigation may have been exploited by the Trump White House to justify
firing the FBI Director in a bid to shut down the Russia investigation,
but its conclusions should still be taken seriously. After all, Rosenstein
is a veteran prosecutor who once again proved his independence by appointing respected former FBI Director Bob Mueller as Special Counsel.

According to Rosenstein, at the July 5 press conference, Comey
"usurped" the Attorney General's authority, "violated deeply engrained
rules and traditions" at the Justice Department, and "ignored another long-
standing principle: we do not hold press conferences to release derogatory
information about the subject of a declined criminal investigation."

Comey's excuse for breaking protocol and denouncing me in public
was that this was "a case of intense public interest." But as Matt Miller,
the Justice Department's Public Affairs Officer from 2009 to 2011,
pointed out the day after the press conference, "The Department in-
vestigates cases involving extreme public interest all the time." He said
that Comey's "willingness to reprimand publicly a figure against whom
he believes there is no basis for criminal charges should trouble anyone
who believes in the rule of law and fundamental principles of fairness."

Comey decided to go ahead with the press conference because of
supposed concerns he had with his boss, Attorney General Loretta
Lynch. His decision was reportedly influenced by a forged Russian
document that sought to discredit Lynch. It was fake, but Comey was
still concerned (more on that in the next chapter). Comey has also
pointed to the fact that Lynch and my husband had a brief, unplanned
conversation on a tarmac in Phoenix in late June 2016, when their
planes happened to be next to each other. Nothing inappropriate was
said in any way, but both of them came to regret exchanging pleasant-
ries that day because of the firestorm that followed. There's no doubt
that the optics were bad, but that didn't give Comey carte blanche to
ignore Justice Department policies and overstep his bounds. The implication that Lynch, a distinguished career prosecutor, was suddenly

compromised and couldn't be trusted is outrageous and insulting. It's also insulting to the former Deputy Attorney General Sally Yates and all the other senior Justice Department officials who were in the chain of command.

Unfortunately, that wasn't Comey's last—or most damaging—mistake.

He violated every rule in the book governing the conduct of federal law enforcement officials and did so in a way that was partisan and that indubitably affected the outcome of the election.

—Elliott Jacobson, one of Comey's former colleagues in the
U.S. Attorney's Office for the Southern District of New York
who has served as a prosecutor for nearly thirty-seven years, in
a letter to the editor of the *New York Times*, April 26, 2017

On October 28 I was headed to Cedar Rapids, Iowa, for a rally with the leaders of several major women's advocacy groups. My friend Betsy was with me on the plane. Annie Leibovitz, the legendary photographer, was along as well to snap candid photos of life on the trail. The election was just eleven days away, and early voting was already in full swing in thirty-six states and the District of Columbia. I was taking nothing for granted, but I was feeling good about our momentum coming out of three successful debates, strong poll numbers, and early-vote projections.

When we landed in Cedar Rapids, Robby Mook, Nick Merrill, and communications director Jennifer Palmieri said they had some news to share. "We have something to tell you, and it's not good," Jennifer said. I had a sinking feeling. Things had been going too well for too long. We were due for trouble. "What now?" I asked. "Jim Comey . . ." Jennifer began, and I immediately knew it was bad.

We didn't have a lot of information, because the internet had been very spotty on the flight, but Jennifer said it seemed that Comey had sent a brief, vaguely worded letter to eight different congressional committees saying that in connection with an unrelated case, "the FBI has learned of the existence of emails that appear to be pertinent" to the previously closed investigation into my handling of classified information—although "the FBI cannot yet assess whether or not this material may be significant."

Jason Chaffetz, the then-Chairman of the House Oversight Committee, immediately tweeted with glee: "Case reopened."

Was this a bad joke? It had to be. The FBI wasn't the Federal Bureau of Ifs or Innuendoes. Its job was to find out the facts. What the hell was Comey doing?

I got off the plane and into the waiting motorcade, beckoning Betsy to join me in the car. What a relief to have my friend with me.

By the time we finished the rally and got back to the plane, the team had learned more. I sat back down in my seat, across from Huma and Betsy, and asked Jennifer to fill me in. How much crazier could this story get?

A lot.

The unrelated federal investigation turned out to be the one into Huma's estranged husband, Anthony Weiner. His lawyers had turned over a laptop of his to the U.S. Attorney's Office. FBI agents from the New York field office searched the computer and found emails between Huma and me.

When we heard this, Huma looked stricken. Anthony had already caused so much heartache. And now this.

"This man is going to be the death of me," she said, bursting into tears.

After more than twenty years working with Huma, I think the world of her, and seeing her in such distress broke my heart. I looked at Betsy, and we both got up to comfort her. I gave her a hug while Betsy patted her shoulder.

In the days that followed, some people thought I should fire Huma or "distance myself." Not a chance. She had done nothing wrong and was an invaluable member of my team. I stuck by her the same way she has always stuck by me.

The more we learned, the more infuriating the story became. The FBI didn't ask Huma or me for permission to read the emails it found, which we would have granted immediately. In fact, they didn't contact us at all. At the time, the FBI had no idea if the emails were new or duplicates of ones already reviewed, or if they were personal or work related, let alone whether they might be considered classified retroactively or not. They didn't know anything at all. And Comey didn't wait to learn more. He fired off his letter to Congress two days before the FBI received a warrant to look at those emails.

Why make a public statement like this, which was bound to be politically devastating, when the FBI itself couldn't say whether the new material was important in any way? At the very end of his July 5 press conference, Comey had declared sanctimoniously, "Only facts matter," but here the FBI didn't know the facts and didn't let that stop it from throwing the presidential election into chaos.

Comey's actions were condemned swiftly by former Justice Department officials of both parties, including Republican Attorneys General Alberto Gonzales and Michael Mukasey, the latter of whom said that Comey "stepped way outside his job."

The Department of Justice's Inspector General also opened an investigation into Comey's conduct.

Before Comey sent his letter, Justice Department officials reminded Comey's deputies of the long-standing policy to avoid any activity that could be viewed as influencing an election. According to reporting by the *New York Times*, they also said there was no need to inform Congress before the FBI determined if the emails were pertinent. A member of Comey's team at the FBI also raised concerns. If Comey had waited until after the FBI had reviewed the emails, he would have learned quickly that there was no new evidence. Comey sent his letter anyway.

The result, according to Deputy Attorney General Rosenstein, was so damaging that "the FBI is unlikely to regain public and congressional trust until it has a Director who understands the gravity of the mistakes and pledges never to repeat them."

So why did Comey do it?

In a Senate Judiciary Committee hearing on March 3, 2017, Comey testified that he saw only two choices: "speak" or "conceal." But as Rosenstein noted in his memo, " 'Conceal' is a loaded term that misstates the issue. When federal agents quietly open a criminal investigation, we are not concealing anything; we are simply following the long-standing policy that we refrain from publicizing nonpublic information. In that context, silence is not concealment."

I can't know what was in Comey's head. I don't know if he had anything against me personally, or if he thought I was going to win the election and worried that if he didn't speak out he'd later be attacked by Republicans or his own agents. What I do know, though, is that when you're the head of an agency as important as the FBI, you have to care a lot more about how things really are than how they look, and you have to be willing to take the heat that goes along with the big job.

Whatever Comey was feeling or fearing, there is reason to be concerned about what was going on inside the FBI.

There's a revolution going on inside the FBI, and it's now at a boiling point.
—Rudy Giuliani on Fox News, October 26, 2016

According to Rudy and others with close ties to the FBI, there was a vocal faction within the bureau that was livid that, in their view, Comey had "let me off the hook" in July. "The agents are furious," Jim Kallstrom, the former head of the FBI's New York office and a close ally of the ex–New York Mayor, told the press. Kallstrom also endorsed Trump and described me as a "pathological liar" and member of "a crime family." Kallstrom claimed to be in touch with hundreds of FBI agents, both retired and current. "The FBI is Trumpland," is how another agent put it. The agent said I was regarded by some as "the Antichrist personified." The *New York Post* reported that "FBI agents are ready to revolt."

There was a rash of leaks designed to damage my campaign, including the quickly debunked false claim that indictments were coming relating to the Clinton Foundation.

Then Rudy, one of Trump's top surrogates, went on Fox News on October 26 and promised "a surprise or two that you're going to hear about in the next two days." It was just two days later that Comey sent his letter.

On November 4 Rudy was back on Fox News and confirmed that he had advance warning. "Did I hear about it? You're darn right I heard about it," he said. At the same time, he tried to backpedal on his statement.

Several months later, Comey was questioned about this in that same Senate Judiciary Committee hearing.

"Did anybody in the FBI during this 2016 campaign have contact with Rudy Giuliani about the Clinton investigation?" asked Senator Pat Leahy of Vermont. Comey said it was "a matter the FBI is looking into" and that he was "very, very interested" to learn the truth. "I don't know yet, but if I find out that people were leaking information about our investigations whether to reporters or private parties, there will be severe consequences," Comey said. This is a crucial question that must be answered. Comey owes it to the American people to say whether anyone at the FBI inappropriately provided Giuliani, Kallstrom, or anyone else with information. The bureau's new leaders and the Justice Department Inspector General have a responsibility to investigate this matter fully and ensure accountability.

It's galling that Comey took pains during the same period to avoid saying anything at all about the investigation into possible connections between the Trump campaign and Russian intelligence. This double standard has still never been explained adequately and it leaves me astonished.

The final week of the 2016 campaign was dominated by swirling questions about my emails and talk that the prayers of Trump supporters might finally be answered, and I'd somehow wind up in prison.

After nine days of turmoil—nine days in which millions of Americans went to the polls to vote early—and just thirty-six hours before Election Day, Comey sent another letter announcing that the "new" batch of emails wasn't really new and contained nothing to cause him to alter his months-old decision not to seek charges.

Well, great. Too little, too late. The rest is history.

There is one more angle worth considering before I turn the page on this sordid chapter: the role of the press.

The ongoing normalization of Trump is the most disorienting development of the presidential campaign, but the most significant may be the abnormalization of Clinton.

—Jonathan Chait in *New York* magazine, September 22, 2016

"Abnormalization" is a pretty good description of how it felt to live through the maelstrom of the email controversy. According to Harvard's Shorenstein Center, over the entire election, negative reports about me swamped positive coverage by 62 percent to 38 percent. For Trump, however, it was a more balanced 56 percent negative to 44 percent positive.

Coverage of my emails crowded out virtually everything else my campaign said or did. The press acted like it was the only story that mattered. To take just one egregious example, by September 2015, the

then *Washington Post* political reporter Chris Cillizza had already written at least fifty pieces about my emails. A year later, the *Post* editorial board realized the story was out of control. "Imagine how history
would judge today's Americans if, looking back at this election, the
record showed that voters empowered a dangerous man because of . . .
a minor email scandal," they wrote in a September 2016 editorial.

No need to imagine. It happened.

The *Post* went on: "There is no equivalence between Ms. Clinton's
wrongs and Mr. Trump's manifest unfitness for office."

That was one of many editorials and endorsements that got it right.
I was glad to be endorsed by nearly every newspaper in the country,
including some that hadn't backed a Democrat in decades, if ever. Unfortunately, I don't think many undecided voters read editorials, and
they almost never influence broadcast or cable news. It's the political
stories on the front page that get read and picked up on TV. So even
though some journalists and editors came to regret losing perspective
and overdoing the coverage of my emails—and after the election, a few
even shared their remorse in confidence—the damage was irreparable.

*Considered alongside the real challenges that will occupy the next Presi-
dent, that email server, which has consumed so much of this campaign,
looks like a matter for the help desk.*
     —*New York Times* endorsement of me for President, September 2016

The *Times*, as usual, played an outsized role in shaping the coverage of
my emails throughout the election. To me, the paper's approach felt
schizophrenic. It spent nearly two years beating me up about emails,
but its glowing endorsement applied some sanity to the controversy.
Then, in the homestretch of the race, when it mattered most, the paper
went right back to its old ways.

First, it devoted the entire top half of its front page to Comey's

October 28 letter, even though there was zero evidence of any wrongdoing and very few facts of any kind, and continued to give it breathless coverage for the rest of the week. Then, on October 31, the *Times*
ran one of the single worst stories of the entire election, claiming the
FBI saw no link between the Trump campaign and Russia. The truth
was that a very serious counterintelligence investigation was picking
up steam. The paper must have been sold a bill of goods by sources trying to protect Trump. It should have known better than to publish it
days before the election. In both cases, it seemed as if speculation and
sensationalism trumped sound journalism.

The *Times* was taken to task by its ombudsman for downplaying
the seriousness of Russia's meddling. "This is an act of foreign interference in an American election on a scale we've never seen, yet on most
days, it has been the also-ran of media coverage," wrote Liz Spayd
on November 5, three days before Election Day. In stark contrast to
reporting on my emails, "what was missing is a sense that this coverage is actually important." In a follow-up column in January, Spayd
noted that the *Times* knew in September the FBI was investigating the
Trump organization's ties to Russia, possibly including secret warrants
from the Foreign Intelligence Surveillance Court, yet didn't tell the
public. "It's hard not to wonder what impact such information might
have had on voters still evaluating the candidates," she wrote. Good
question! It gives a whole new meaning to what Bill likes to call "ma-
joring in the minors."

Over the years, going all the way back to the baseless Whitewater
inquisition, it's seemed as if many of those in charge of political coverage at the *New York Times* have viewed me with hostility and skepticism. They've applied what's sometimes called the "Clinton Rules." As
Charles Pierce put it in *Esquire* magazine, "the Clinton Rules state
that any relatively commonplace political occurrence or activity takes
on mysterious dark energy when any Clinton is involved." As a result,

a lot of journalists see their job as exposing the devious machinations of the secretive Clinton Machine. The *Times* has by no means been the only—or even the worst—offender, but its treatment has stung the most.

I've read the *Times* for more than forty years and still look forward to it every day. I appreciate much of the paper's terrific non-Clinton reporting, the excellent op-ed page, and the generous endorsements I've received in every campaign I've ever run. I understand the pressure that even the best political journalists are now under. Negative stories drive more traffic and buzz than positive or evenhanded ones. But we're talking about one of the most important news sources in the world—the paper that often sets the tone for everyone else—which means, I think, that it should hold itself to the highest standard.

I suppose this mini-rant guarantees that my book will receive a rip-her-to-shreds review in the *Times*, but history will agree that this coverage affected the outcome of the election. Besides, I had to get this off my chest!

This may shock you: Hillary Clinton is fundamentally honest.
>   —former *New York Times* editor Jill Abramson
>   in the *Guardian*, March 28, 2016

Jill Abramson, who oversaw years of tough political coverage about me, came to this conclusion by looking at data from the fact-checking organization PolitiFact, which found I told the truth more than any other presidential candidate in 2016, including both Bernie Sanders and Donald Trump, who was the most dishonest candidate ever measured. The fact that this was seen as surprising says a lot about the corrosive effect of the never-ending email controversy, and all the decades of baseless attacks that preceded it.

But her emails!

—the internet, 2017

The further we've gotten from the election, the more outlandish our excessive national focus on emails has seemed. "But her emails!" became a rueful meme used in response to the latest Trump revelations, outrages, and embarrassments.

As hard as it is to believe or explain, my emails were *the* story of 2016. It didn't matter that the State Department Inspector General said there were no laws or regulations prohibiting the use of personal email for official business. It didn't matter that the FBI found no reasonable legal grounds to bring any kind of case.

The original decision to use personal email was on me. And I never figured out how to make people understand where I was coming from or convince them that I wasn't part of some devious plot. But it wasn't me who determined how Comey and the FBI handled this issue or how the press covered it. That's on them.

Since the election, we've learned that Vice President Mike Pence used private email for official business when he was Governor of Indiana, like so many other state and federal officials across our country (including, by the way, many staff in the Bush White House, who used a private RNC server for government business and then "lost" more than twenty million emails). We've learned that Trump's transition team copied highly sensitive documents and removed them from a secure facility. We've learned that members of Trump's White House staff use encrypted messaging apps that seem to evade federal records laws. And we know now that Trump associates are under federal investigation for far more serious things. Yet most of the fulminating critics have gone silent. It's almost as if they never really cared about the proper maintenance of government records or the finer points of retroactive classification, and the whole thing was just a convenient political piñata.

The further we get from the election, the stranger it seems that this controversy could swing a national election with such monumental consequences. I picture future historians scratching their heads, trying to understand what happened. I'm still scratching mine, too.

When reason fails, the devil helps.

—Fyodor Dostoevsky

Trolls, Bots, Fake News, and Real Russians

Some people are blessed with a strong immune system. Others aren't as lucky. Their defenses have been worn down by disease or injury, so they're susceptible to all kinds of infections that a healthy person would easily fight off. When that happens to someone you love, it's terrible to watch.

The "body politic" works in much the same way. Our democracy has built-in defenses that keep us strong and healthy, including the checks and balances written into our Constitution. Our Founding Fathers believed that one of the most important defenses would be an informed citizenry that could make sound judgments based on facts and reason. Losing that is like losing an immune system, leaving a democracy vulnerable to all manner of attack. And a democracy, like a body, cannot stay strong through repeated injuries.

In 2016 our democracy was assaulted by a foreign adversary determined to mislead our people, enflame our divisions, and throw an election to its preferred candidate. That attack succeeded because our immune system had been slowly eroded over years. Many Americans had lost faith in the institutions that previous generations relied on for objective information, including government, academia, and the press, leaving them vulnerable to a sophisticated misinformation campaign. There are many reasons why this happened, but one is that a small group of right-wing billionaires—people like the Mercer family and Charles and David Koch—recognized long ago that, as Stephen Colbert once joked, "reality has a well-known liberal bias." More generally, the right spent a lot of time and money building an alternative reality. Think of a partisan petri dish where science is denied, lies masquerade as truth, and paranoia flourishes. Their efforts were amplified in 2016 by a presidential candidate who trafficked in dark conspiracy theories drawn from the pages of supermarket tabloids and the far reaches of the internet; a candidate who deflected any criticism by attacking others with made-up facts and an uncanny gift for humiliating zingers. He helped to further blur news and entertainment, reality TV and reality.

As a result, by the time Vladimir Putin came along, our democracy was already far sicker than we realized.

Now that the Russians have infected us and seen how weak our defenses are, they'll keep at it. Maybe other foreign powers will join them. They'll also continue targeting our friends and allies. Their ultimate goal is to undermine—perhaps even destroy—Western democracy itself. As the former Director of National Intelligence, James Clapper, told Congress, "If there has ever been a clarion call for vigilance and action against a threat to the very foundation of our democratic political system, this episode is it."

This should concern all Americans—Republicans, Democrats, Independents, everyone. We need to get to the bottom of it. The 2016 election may be over, but we have new elections coming up soon. I'm going to lay out what is known in as much detail as I can, so we can try to understand what happened and what we can do to prevent it from happening again. There's a lot we still don't know, investigations are on-going, and the story changes daily with breaking news. Trump, his allies, and others have vigorously denied accusations of wrongdoing. You can look at the facts and decide for yourself. But what should be beyond doubt is that foreign interference in our elections is wrong, period. And the threat we face, from without and within, is bigger than one campaign, one party, or one election. The only way to heal our democracy and protect it for the future is to understand the threat and defeat it.

V for Vendetta (and Vladimir)

President Obama once compared Vladimir Putin to a "bored kid at the back of the classroom." "He's got that kind of slouch," Obama said. When I sat with Putin in meetings, he looked more like one of those guys on the subway who imperiously spread their legs wide, encroaching on everyone else's space, as if to say, "I take what I want," and "I have so little respect for you that I'm going to act as if I'm lounging at home in my bathrobe." They call it "manspreading." That was Putin.

I've dealt with a lot of male leaders in my life, but Putin is in a class by himself. A former KGB spy with a taste for over-the-top macho theatrics and baroque violence (a public inquiry in the United Kingdom concluded that he probably approved the killing of one of his enemies in London by poisoning his tea with polonium-210, a rare radioactive isotope), Putin has emerged in the popular imagination as an archvillain straight out of a James Bond movie. Yet he's also perennially misunderstood and underestimated. George W. Bush famously said that after looking Putin in the eye, he found him "very straightforward and trustworthy," and was "able to get a sense of his soul." My somewhat tongue-in-cheek response was: "He was a KGB agent—by definition, he doesn't have a soul." I don't think Vladimir appreciated that one.

Our relationship has been sour for a long time. Putin doesn't respect women and despises anyone who stands up to him, so I'm a double problem. After I criticized one of his policies, he told the press, "It's better not to argue with women," but went on to call me weak. "Maybe weakness is not the worst quality for a woman," he joked. Hilarious.

Putin still smolders over what he views as the humiliations of the 1990s, when Russia lost its old Soviet dominions, and the Clinton administration presided over NATO's expansion. And things got a lot worse between us during my time as Secretary of State.

When President Obama and I came into office in 2009, Putin and his prime minister, Dmitry Medvedev, had swapped jobs as a way of thwarting constitutionally required term limits. Surprisingly, Medvedev showed some independence and a willingness to pursue better relations with the United States. We knew Putin was still the real power in Russia but decided to see if we could find some areas of shared interest where progress might be possible. That was the origin of the much-maligned "reset." It led to several concrete successes, including a new nuclear arms control treaty, new sanctions on Iran and North Korea, a much-needed supply route to equip our troops in Afghanistan, increased trade and investment, and expanded counterterrorism cooperation. In the spring of 2011, President Medvedev agreed to abstain on the UN Security Council resolution authorizing the use of force to protect civilians in Libya from the dictator Colonel Muammar Gaddafi, a decision that angered Putin.

President Obama and I agreed that seeking pragmatic cooperation with Russia on certain issues was not inconsistent with also standing up for our values and showing support for the democratic aspirations of the Russian people. I felt a responsibility to speak out against the Kremlin's repression of human rights in Russia, especially the intimidation and murder of journalists and political opponents. In October 2009, I was in Moscow and did an interview with one of the last remaining independent radio stations in the country. I expressed support for human rights and civil society, and I said that I thought a lot of Russians wanted the thugs who attacked journalists brought to justice. I knew Putin wouldn't be happy with me saying these things on his own turf, but I felt that if the United States accepted a gag order on these issues, that decision would reverberate, not just in Russia but also around the world.

The KGB taught Putin to be suspicious of everyone. Russia's troubles in the 1990s and the "color revolutions" of the 2000s—the string of popular revolts that toppled authoritarian regimes in several former Soviet bloc countries—took him from suspicious to paranoid. He came to view popular dissent as an existential threat. When he heard me and other Western leaders voice support for civil society in Russia, he saw it as a plot to undermine him.

For Putin, a pivotal moment came in 2011. In September he announced he would run for President again. In December there were widespread reports of fraud in parliamentary elections, which sparked domestic protests and international condemnation. At a conference in Lithuania focused on promoting democracy and human rights in Europe, I expressed America's concerns. "The Russian people, like people everywhere, deserve the right to have their voices heard and their votes counted," I said, "and that means they deserve fair, free, transparent elections and leaders who are accountable to them." Tens of thousands of Russians took to the streets amid chants of "Putin is a thief," an unprecedented popular challenge to his iron grip on the country. Putin, more paranoid than ever, thought it was a conspiracy orchestrated from Washington. He blamed me in particular, saying I "gave them a signal."

Putin quashed the protests and once again became President, but he was now running scared and seething with anger. In the fall of 2011, Putin had published an essay promising to regain Russia's regional and global influence. I read it as a plan to "re-Sovietize" the lost empire and said so publicly. Once back in office, Putin moved to put his vision into action. He consolidated power and cracked down on any remaining domestic dissent. He also took a more combative tone toward the West and nursed his personal grudge against me. By the way, that's not just how I saw it; *grudge* is also the word the U.S. government used in its official assessment.

In a series of memos, I warned President Obama that things were changing in Russia, and America would have to take a harder line with Putin. Our relationship was likely to get worse before it got better, I told the President, and we needed to make it clear to Putin that aggressive actions would have consequences.

There's a Bear in the Woods

During Obama's second term, when I was out of office, things did indeed go from bad to worse. When popular protests in Ukraine forced the country's corrupt, pro-Moscow leader to flee, Putin swung into action. He launched an operation to subvert and seize Ukraine's Crimean Peninsula, a vacation destination for wealthy Russians. That was followed by further efforts to destabilize eastern Ukraine, home to many ethnic Russians, eventually leading to a protracted civil war.

Watching from the sidelines, I was struck by the sophistication of the operation. It was much more effective than Russia's 2008 invasion of Georgia. Nationalist propaganda on television, radio, and social media radicalized ethnic Russians, while cyberattacks muzzled opposing voices. Undercover Russian paramilitary special forces swept into Crimea to organize protests, seize buildings, and intimidate or co-opt Ukrainian officials. Meanwhile, the Kremlin denied it all, despite the fact that the whole world could see photos of Russian soldiers carrying Russian weapons, driving Russian vehicles, and speaking with Russian accents. Putin called them indigenous "self-defense groups." Ukrainians called them "little green men." Once the occupation was a fait accompli, the Russians staged a rigged referendum to give themselves a patina of popular sovereignty and then annexed the peninsula, formally making it part of Russia.

The Russians did one other thing, which didn't get enough attention at the time but in retrospect was a sign of things to come. In early 2014, they released on Twitter and YouTube what they claimed was an audio recording of a private conversation between two veteran American diplomats, our Ambassador to Ukraine, Geoff Pyatt, and my friend and former advisor Toria Nuland, who was then the top State Department official for Europe. On the Russian tape, Toria used colorful language to express her exasperation about European foot-dragging over Ukraine. Moscow clearly hoped her words would drive a wedge between America and our allies. The incident didn't have lasting diplomatic repercussions, but it did show that the Russians were not just stealing information for intelligence purposes, as all countries do; they were now using social media and strategic leaks to "weaponize" that information.

In the wake of Russia's Ukraine operations, I expressed my concerns to some of my former national security colleagues. Moscow had clearly developed new capabilities in psychological and information warfare and was willing to use them. I was worried the United States and our allies weren't prepared to keep up or respond. I knew that in 2013, one of Russia's top military officers, Valery Gerasimov, had written an article laying out a new strategy for hybrid warfare. In previous generations, the Soviet military had planned to fight large-scale conflicts with massive conventional and nuclear forces. In the twenty-first century, Gerasimov said, the line between war and peace would blur, and Russia should prepare for under-the-radar conflicts waged through propaganda, cyberattacks, paramilitary operations, financial and energy manipulation, and covert subversion. The operations in Crimea and eastern Ukraine (and, I would argue, the harboring of NSA leaker Edward Snowden) proved that Putin was putting Gerasimov's theory into practice.

Sometimes these tactics are called "active measures." Thomas Rid, a professor of security studies at King's College London, offered a good primer in testimony before the Senate Intelligence Committee in March 2017. "Active measures are semicovert or covert intelligence operations to shape an adversary's political decisions," he explained. "The

tried and tested way of active measures is to use an adversary's weaknesses against himself," and the rise of the internet and social media
has created many new opportunities. As Senator Sheldon White-
house put it, "The Russians have been at this for a long time," and
now "they've adapted old methods to new technologies—making use
of social media, malware, and complex financial transactions."

I was also alarmed to see Russian money, propaganda, or other support aiding right-wing nationalist parties across Europe, including Marine Le Pen's National Front in France, Alternative for Germany (AfD),
and Austria's Freedom Party. According to the *Washington Post*, the
Kremlin has also cultivated leaders of right-wing American organizations
such as the NRA, the National Organization for Marriage, and individuals like the evangelist Franklin Graham. Putin has positioned himself
as the leader of an authoritarian, xenophobic international movement
that wants to expel immigrants, break up the European Union, weaken
the Atlantic Alliance, and roll back much of the progress achieved since
World War II. People laugh when Putin has himself photographed riding horses shirtless, winning judo matches, and driving race cars. But
the macho stunts are part of a strategy. He has made himself an icon
to traditionalists everywhere who resent their increasingly open, diverse,
and liberal societies. That's why he formed a close alliance with the Russian Orthodox Church, passed vicious antigay laws, and decriminalized
domestic violence. It's all about projecting an image of traditional masculinity, Christian morality, and white nationalist purity and power.

During the campaign, I asked my team to start working on a more
aggressive strategic approach toward Russia. I didn't want to be dragged
into a new Cold War, but the best way to avoid conflict and keep the
door open for future cooperation would be to send Putin a message
of strength and resolve on Day One. It's been said that he subscribes
to Vladimir Lenin's old adage: "Probe with bayonets. If you encounter
mush, proceed; if you encounter steel, withdraw." I wanted to be sure
that when Putin looked to America, he saw steel, not mush.

I wanted to go further than the Obama administration, which re-sisted providing defensive arms to the Ukrainian government or es-tablishing a no-fly zone in Syria, where Putin had launched a military intervention to prop up the murderous dictator Bashar al-Assad. I also intended to increase our investment in cybersecurity and pursue an all-hands-on-deck effort to secure cooperation between the government and the private sector on protecting vital national and commercial infrastructure from attacks, including nuclear power plants, electrical grids, dams, and the financial system.

All of this is to say that I had my eyes open. I knew Putin was a growing threat. I knew he had a personal vendetta against me and deep resentment toward the United States.

Yet I never imagined that he would have the audacity to launch a massive covert attack against our own democracy, right under our noses—and that he'd get away with it.

Since the election, we've learned a lot about the scope and sophis-tication of the Russian plot, and more information comes to light every day. But even during the campaign, we knew enough to realize that we were facing, in the words of Senator Harry Reid, "one of the gravest threats to our democracy since the Cold War." And it just got worse from there. I won't try to provide you a definitive account of every twist and turn of this saga—there are plenty of other sources for that—but I will try to share what I experienced, how it felt, and what I think we need to do as a nation to protect ourselves for the future.

The Budding Bromance

It was strange from the start. Why did Donald Trump keep blowing kisses to Vladimir Putin? He said he would give Putin an A for leader-ship, and described the Russian President as "highly respected within his country and beyond." Trump reveled in reports that Putin had called him "brilliant," even though the more accurate translation was "colorful."

In a particularly telling exchange on MSNBC's *Morning Joe,* Trump defended Putin's alleged murder of journalists. "At least he's a leader, unlike what we have in this country," Trump said. As if that wasn't bad enough, he added, "I think our country does plenty of killing also." No previous American presidential candidate would ever have dreamt of trashing our country like that or suggesting moral equivalency between American democracy and Russian autocracy. No wonder Putin liked Trump.

What was going on here? I was genuinely puzzled. This was far outside the bounds of normal American politics, especially for a Republican. How was the Party of Reagan letting itself become the Party of Putin?

I thought there were three plausible explanations for the budding Trump-Putin "bromance."

First, Trump has a bizarre fascination with dictators and strongmen. He praised Kim Jong-un, the murderous young ruler of North Korea, for his skill at consolidating power and eliminating dissent— "You've gotta give him credit," Trump said. He also talked admiringly about the 1989 Chinese massacre of unarmed student protesters at Tiananmen Square; he said it showed strength. Strength is what it's all about. Trump doesn't think in terms of morality or human rights, he thinks only in terms of power and dominance. Might makes right. Putin thinks the same way, albeit much more strategically. And Trump appears to have fallen hard for Putin's macho "bare-chested autocrat" act. He doesn't just like Putin—he seems to want to *be* like Putin, a white authoritarian leader who could put down dissenters, repress minorities, disenfranchise voters, weaken the press, and amass untold billions for himself. He dreams of Moscow on the Potomac.

Second, despite his utter lack of interest in or knowledge of most foreign policy issues, Trump has a long-standing worldview that aligns well with Putin's agenda. He is suspicious of American allies, doesn't think values should play a role in foreign policy, and doesn't seem to believe the United States should continue carrying the mantle of global leadership. Way back in 1987, Trump spent nearly $100,000 on full-page ads in the *New York Times*, the *Washington Post*, and the *Boston Globe* criticizing Ronald Reagan's foreign policy and urging America to stop defending allies who should be taking care of themselves. Trump said the world was taking advantage of the United States and laughing at us. Nearly thirty years later, he was saying the same things. He referred to America's alliances as if they were protection rackets, where we could extort weaker countries to pay tribute in exchange for safety. He threatened to abandon NATO and bad-mouthed the European Union. He insulted the leaders of countries such as Britain and Germany. He even got into a Twitter fight with Pope Francis! Given all this, it's no surprise that, once he became President, Trump bickered with our allies and refused to commit to the bedrock principle of mutual defense at a NATO summit. America's lost prestige and newfound isolation were embodied in the sad image of the other leaders of Western democracies strolling together down a lovely Italian street while Trump followed in a golf cart, all by himself.

All this was music to Putin's ears. The Kremlin's top strategic goal is to weaken the Atlantic Alliance and reduce America's influence in Europe, leaving the continent ripe for Russian domination. Putin couldn't ask for a better friend than Donald Trump.

The third explanation was that Trump seems to have extensive financial ties to Russia. In 2008, Trump's son Don Jr. told investors in Moscow, "Russians make up a pretty disproportionate cross section of a lot of our assets" and "we see a lot of money pouring in from Russia," according to the Russian newspaper *Kommersant*. In 2013, Trump himself said in an interview with David Letterman that he did "a lot of business with the Russians." A respected golf journalist named James Dodson reported that Trump's other son, Eric, told him, "We don't rely on American banks" to fund Trump golf projects, "we have all the funding we need out of Russia."

Without seeing Trump's tax returns, it's impossible to determine the full extent of these financial ties. Based on what's already known, there is good reason to believe that despite repeated bankruptcies and even though most American banks refused to lend to him, Trump, his companies, or partners, according to *USA Today*, "turned to wealthy Russians and oligarchs from former Soviet republics—several allegedly connected to organized crime." This was based on a review of court cases and other legal documents. Additionally, in 2008, Trump raised eyebrows by selling a mansion in Palm Beach to a Russian oligarch at an inflated price—$54 million more than he paid for it just four years earlier. In 2013, his Miss Universe pageant in Moscow was partly financed by a billionaire ally of Putin. To build Trump SoHo New York hotel, he partnered with a company called the Bayrock Group and a Russian immigrant named Felix Sater, formerly linked to the mafia, who was previously convicted of money laundering. (*USA Today* has done great reporting on all of this, if you want to learn more.)

Trump's advisors also had financial ties to Russia. Paul Manafort, whom Trump hired in March 2016 and promoted to campaign chairman two months later, was a Republican lobbyist who had spent years serving autocrats overseas, most recently making millions working for pro-Putin forces in Ukraine. Then there was Michael Flynn, the former head of the Defense Intelligence Agency who had been fired for good cause by President Obama in 2014. Then Flynn accepted money from Putin's Western-facing propaganda network, Russia Today (RT), and in December 2015 attended RT's tenth-anniversary gala in Moscow, where he sat at Putin's table (along with Green Party presidential candidate Jill Stein). There was also Carter Page, a former advisor to the Russian gas giant Gazprom, who traveled back and forth to Moscow frequently—including in July 2016, in the middle of the campaign. He seemed to be reading from the Kremlin's anti-American talking points.

Learning all this over the course of 2015 and 2016 was surreal. It felt like we were peeling an onion, and there was always another layer.

If you add together all these factors—Trump's affection for tyrants and hostility toward allies, sympathy for Russia's strategic aims, and alleged financial ties to shady Russian actors—his pro-Putin rhetoric starts to make sense. And this was all out in the open and well known throughout the campaign. It came to a head in late April 2016, when Trump called for improved relations with Russia in a major foreign policy speech at the Mayflower Hotel in Washington. The Russian Ambassador to the United States, Sergey Kislyak, applauded from the front row. (He later attended the Republican National Convention, but avoided ours.)

Republican national security experts were appalled by Trump's embrace of Putin. So was I. At every opportunity, I warned that allowing Trump to be Commander in Chief would be profoundly dangerous and play directly into Russia's hands. "It'll be like Christmas in the Kremlin," I predicted.

Breach

Then things got stranger.

In late March 2016, FBI agents met with my campaign lawyer, Marc Elias, and other senior staffers at our Brooklyn headquarters to warn us that foreign hackers could be targeting our campaign with phishing emails that tried to trick people into clicking links or entering passwords that would open up access to our network. We were already aware of the threat, because scores if not hundreds of these phishing emails were pouring in. Most were easy to spot, and we had no reason at the time to believe any were successful.

Then, in early June, Marc got a disturbing message from the Democratic National Committee. The DNC's computer network had been penetrated by hackers thought to be working for the Russian government. According to the *New York Times*, the FBI had apparently discovered the breach months earlier, in September 2015, and had informed a tech support contractor at the DNC, but never visited the office or did much to follow up. As a former head of the FBI Cyber Division told the *Times* later, that was a bewildering oversight. "We are not talking about an office that is in the middle of the woods of Montana," he said. The offices were just a mile and a half apart. After the election, FBI Director Comey admitted, "I might have walked over there myself, knowing what I know now."

Word didn't reach the DNC's leadership until April. They then brought in a respected cybersecurity firm called CrowdStrike to figure out what was going on, kick out the hackers, and protect the network from further penetration. The CrowdStrike experts determined that the hackers had likely come from Russia and that they had gained access to a large trove of emails and documents. All of this would become public when the *Washington Post* broke the story on June 14.

The news was unsettling but not shocking. The Russian government had been attempting to hack sensitive American networks for years, as had other countries, such as China, Iran, and North Korea. In 2014, Russians had breached the State Department's unclassified system and then moved on to the White House and the Pentagon. They also hacked think tanks, journalists, and politicians.

The general view was that all of these hacks and attempted hacks were fairly run-of-the-mill intelligence gathering, albeit with twenty-first-century techniques. That turned out to be wrong. Something far more insidious was happening. On June 15, one day after the DNC attack became public, a hacker named Guccifer 2.0—thought to be a front for Russian intelligence—claimed credit for the breach and posted a cache of stolen documents. He said he had given thousands more to WikiLeaks, the organization supposedly devoted to radical transparency. Julian Assange, the founder of WikiLeaks, promised to release "emails related to Hillary Clinton," although it wasn't at all clear what that meant.

The publication of stolen files from the DNC was a dramatic turn of events for several reasons. For starters, it showed that Russia was interested in doing more than collecting intelligence on the American political scene—it was actively trying to influence the election. Just as it had done a year earlier with the audio recording of Toria Nuland, Russia was "weaponizing" stolen information. It did not occur to me at the time that anyone associated with Donald Trump might be coordinating with the Russians, but it seemed likely that Putin was trying to help his preferred candidate. After all, he disliked and feared me, and had an ally in Trump. This was underscored when the Trump campaign removed language from the Republican Party platform calling for the United States to provide Ukraine with "lethal defensive weapons"— a gift to Putin that might as well have come with a ribbon and a bow.

Careful analysis of the documents from Guccifer also revealed an alarming prospect: at least one of the files seemed like it could have come from our campaign, not the DNC. Further research suggested that the file might have been stolen from the personal Gmail account of John Podesta, my campaign chairman. We couldn't be sure, but we feared that more trouble was coming.

Shouting into the Wind

On July 22, WikiLeaks published about twenty thousand stolen DNC emails. It highlighted a handful of messages that included offensive comments about Bernie Sanders, which predictably set off a firestorm among Bernie's supporters, many of whom were still angry about having lost the primaries. But nothing in the stolen emails remotely backed up the charge that the primaries had been rigged. Nearly all of the offending messages were written in May, months after I had amassed an insurmountable vote and delegate lead.

More important, though, was the fact that the Russians or their proxies had the sophistication to find and exploit those handful of pro-vocative stolen emails in order to drive a wedge between Democrats. That suggests a deep knowledge and familiarity of our political scene and its players. Also, imagine how many inflammatory and embarrass-ing things they would have found if they'd hacked Republican targets. (Spoiler alert: they did, but never released anything.)

The timing of the WikiLeaks release was terrible—and it didn't seem like a coincidence. I had defeated Bernie and locked up the nomi-nation in early June, but he hadn't endorsed me until July 12, and now we were working hard to bring the party together before the Demo-cratic National Convention started in Philadelphia on July 25. Plus, the news hit on the same day I was introducing Tim Kaine as my run-ning mate, turning what should have been one of the best days of our campaign into a circus.

The document dump seemed designed to cause us maximum dam-age at a critical moment. It worked. DNC chair Debbie Wasserman Schultz resigned two days later, and the opening of the convention was marred by loud boos and catcalls from Sanders supporters. I was sick about the whole thing. After so many long, hard months of campaign-ing, I wanted the convention to be perfect. It was my best chance until the debates to present my vision for the country directly to the voters. I remembered what a boost Bill received from his convention in Madi-son Square Garden in 1992, and I hoped to gain similar momentum. Instead, we were now dealing with a divided party and distracted press corps. Democratic leaders, especially Congresswoman Marcia Fudge of Ohio, Reverend Leah Daughtry, and Donna Brazile, helped bring order to the chaos. And Michelle Obama's masterful, moving speech brought the hall together and quieted the dissenters. Then Bernie spoke, endorsed me again, and helped cement the détente.

On July 27, the day before I formally accepted the Democratic nomination, Trump held one of his wild, stream-of-consciousness press conferences. He said that as President he might accept Russia's annexation of Crimea, deflected blame from the Kremlin for the DNC hack, and then, remarkably, urged the Russians to try to hack my email account. "Russia, if you're listening, I hope you're able to find the thirty thousand emails that are missing," he said, referring to the personal, non-work-related emails that were deleted from my account after everything else had been provided to the State Department. "I think you will probably be rewarded mightily by our press." As the *New York Times* described it, Trump was "urging a power often hostile to the United States to violate American law by breaking into a private computer network."

Katy Tur of NBC News followed up to see if this was a joke or he really meant it. She asked if Trump had "any qualms" about asking a foreign government to break into Americans' emails. Instead of backing off, he doubled down. "If Russia or China or any other country has those emails, I mean, to be honest with you, I'd love to see them," he said. He also refused to tell Putin not to try to interfere in the election: "I'm not going to tell Putin what to do; why should I tell Putin what to do?" This was no joke.

Despite Trump's attempts to cover for Putin, cybersecurity experts and U.S. intelligence officials were confident that the Russians were behind the hack. There still wasn't official consensus about whether their goal was to undermine public confidence in America's democratic institutions or if Putin was actively trying to derail my candidacy and help elect Trump. But I didn't have any doubt. And the timing of the public disclosure, as well as the specific nature of the material (did Russian intelligence really understand the ins and outs of DNC politics and the decisions of Debbie Wasserman Schultz?), raised the strong possibility that the Russians had gotten help from someone with experience in American politics—a truly alarming prospect.

We were doing a million things at once that week. The convention was all-consuming. So it was hard to stop and focus on the gravity of what was happening. But I realized we had crossed a line. This wasn't the normal rough-and-tumble of politics. This was—there's no other word for it—war. I told my team I thought we were at a "break glass" moment. "We're under attack," I said. It was time to take a much more aggressive public posture. Robby Mook did a round of interviews in which he pointed the finger squarely at Russia. He said they weren't trying just to create chaos, they were actively trying to help Trump. That shouldn't have been particularly controversial, but Robby was treated like a kook. Jennifer Palmieri and Jake Sullivan held a series of background briefings for news networks to explain in more detail. After the election, Jennifer wrote an op-ed in the *Washington Post* titled "The Clinton Campaign Warned You About Russia. But Nobody Listened to Us." She recalled how journalists were generally more interested in the gossipy content of the stolen emails rather than the prospect that a foreign power was trying to manipulate our election. The press treated our warnings about Russia like it was spin we'd cooked up to distract from embarrassing revelations—a view actively encouraged by the Trump campaign. The media was accustomed to Trump peddling crazy conspiracy theories—like that Ted Cruz's dad helped kill John F. Kennedy—and it acted as if the Russian hacking was "our" conspiracy theory, a tidy false equivalency that let reporters and pundits sleep well at night. As Matt Yglesias of the news site *Vox* described it later, most journalists thought the argument that Moscow was trying to help Trump was "outlandish and borderline absurd," and our attempt to raise the alarm "was just too aggressive, self-serving, and a little far-fetched."

Maybe the press wouldn't listen to us, but I figured they would listen to respected intelligence officials. On August 5, Mike Morell, the former acting director of the CIA, wrote a highly unusual op-ed in the *New York Times*. Despite being a strictly nonpartisan career professional, he said that he had decided to endorse me for President because of my strong record on national security, including my role in bringing Osama bin Laden to justice. By contrast, he said Trump was "not only unqualified for the job, but he may well pose a threat to our national security." Coming from America's former top spy, that was a shocking statement. But it paled compared with what Morell said next. Putin, he noted, was a career intelligence officer "trained to identify vulnerabilities in an individual and to exploit them." And here's the shocking part: "In the intelligence business," Morell said, "we would say that Mr. Putin had recruited Mr. Trump as an unwitting agent of the Russian Federation."

Morell's argument was not that Trump or his campaign was conspiring illegally with the Russians to rig the election—although he certainly didn't rule it out. It was that Putin was manipulating Trump into taking policy positions that would help Russia and hurt America, including "endorsing Russian espionage against the United States, supporting Russia's annexation of Crimea, and giving a green light to a possible Russian invasion of the Baltic States." That's an important point to keep in mind, because it often gets lost amid the intense focus on potential criminal acts. Even without a secret conspiracy, there was plenty of troubling pro-Putin behavior right out in the open.

Morell's op-ed was the equivalent of pulling the fire alarm in a crowded building. And yet, somehow, most in the media—and many voters—continued to ignore the danger staring us in the face.

Snakes!

I was not shocked to see the connection between WikiLeaks and the Russian intelligence services. At least that helped further discredit its odious leader, Julian Assange. In my view, Assange is a hypocrite who deserves to be held accountable for his actions. He claims to be a champion of transparency, but for many years, he's been helpful to Putin, one of the most repressive and least transparent autocrats in the world. It's not just that WikiLeaks avoids publishing anything Putin won't like and instead targets Russia's adversaries—Assange actually hosted a television show on RT, Putin's propaganda network, and receives adoring coverage there. And if hypocrisy isn't bad enough, Assange was charged with rape in Sweden. To avoid facing those charges, he jumped bail and fled to the Ecuadorian embassy in London. After years of waiting, Sweden eventually said it would no longer try to extradite him, but promised that if Assange came back to the country, the investigation could be reopened.

Assange, like Putin, has held a grudge against me for a long time. The bad blood goes back to 2010, when WikiLeaks published more than 250,000 stolen State Department cables, including many sensitive observations from our diplomats in the field. As Secretary of State, I was responsible for the safety of our officers around the world, and I knew that releasing those confidential reports put not only them in danger but also their foreign contacts—including human rights activists and dissidents who could face reprisals from their own governments. We had to move fast to evacuate vulnerable people, and, thankfully, we don't believe anyone was killed or jailed as a result. I thought Assange was reckless and wrong, and said so publicly.

The fact that these two old adversaries from my time as Secretary of State—Assange and Putin—seemed to be working together to damage my campaign was maddening. It was bad enough to have to go up against a billionaire opponent and the entire Republican Party; now I also had to take on these nefarious outside forces. The journalist Rebecca Traister observed once that there was "an *Indiana Jones*–style, 'It had to be snakes' inevitability" about me facing Trump. "Of course Hillary Clinton is going to have to run against a man who seems both to embody and have attracted the support of everything male, white, and angry about the ascension of women and black people in America," she wrote. I was up for the challenge. And I might add: Of course I had to face not just one America-bashing misogynist but three. Of course I'd have to get by Putin and Assange as well.

By midsummer 2016, the whole world knew that Trump and his team were cheering on the Russian attack on our democracy, and doing everything they could to exploit it. Trump never even tried to hide the fact that he was making common cause with Putin. But what if they were doing more than that? What if they were actually conspiring with Russian intelligence and WikiLeaks? There wasn't any evidence of that yet, but the coincidences were piling up.

Then, on August 8, Trump's longtime consigliere Roger Stone, who cut his teeth as one of Richard Nixon's "dirty tricksters," bragged to a group of Florida Republicans that he was in communication with Assange and predicted that an "October surprise" was coming. This was a shocking admission, made in public, from Trump's longest-serving political advisor. Stone made similar statements on August 12, 14, 15, and 18. On August 21, he tweeted, "Trust me, it will soon be Podesta's time in the barrel. #CrookedHillary". This was particularly notable because, as I mentioned earlier, we had determined there was a good chance that John's email might have been hacked, but didn't know for sure. Stone kept at it over the next few weeks, even calling Assange his "hero."

I wasn't the only one who noticed. At the end of August, Harry Reid, one of the congressional "gang of eight" who are briefed on the most sensitive intelligence matters, wrote a letter to FBI Director Comey that cited Stone's claims and asked for a full and thorough investigation. "The evidence of a direct connection between the Russian government and Donald Trump's presidential campaign continues to mount," Reid wrote. He also raised the prospect that there might be an attempt to falsify official election results. This was a reference to public reports that Russian hackers had penetrated voter registration databases in both Arizona and Illinois, prompting the FBI to warn state election officials across the country to upgrade their security. Like Morell's op-ed, Reid's letter was an attempt to shake the country out of its complacency and get the press, the administration, and all Americans focused on an urgent threat. It didn't work.

Drip, Drip, Drip

As we headed into the fall, troubling reports and rumors continued to swirl. Paul Manafort resigned on August 19 amid growing questions about his financial ties to Russia. On September 5, the *Washington Post* reported that U.S. intelligence agencies now believed there was "a broad covert Russian operation in the United States to sow public distrust in the upcoming presidential election and in U.S. political institutions." That meant it was much bigger than the DNC hack.

We heard there was a federal interagency task force digging into the Trump team's financial ties, but no reporters could get it confirmed on the record. There was also talk that the FBI was looking into strange computer traffic between Trump Tower and a Russian bank. Reporters were chasing that one, too, and *Slate*'s Franklin Foer eventually broke the story on October 31. Then there were the whispers going around Washington that the Russians had compromising information on Trump, possibly a salacious videotape from a Moscow hotel. But nobody had any proof.

At my first debate with Trump, on September 26, I went after him hard on Russia, and he continued to defend Putin and contradict the conclusions of our intelligence agencies, which they had shared with him personally. "I don't think anybody knows it was Russia that broke into the DNC," Trump insisted. "I mean, it could be Russia, but it could also be China. It could also be lots of other people. It also could be somebody sitting on their bed that weighs four hundred pounds, okay?" What was he talking about? A four-hundred-pound guy in his basement? Was he thinking of a character out of *The Girl with the Dragon Tattoo*? I wondered who told Trump to say that.

Meanwhile, Roger Stone continued to tweet warnings that WikiLeaks was preparing to drop another bomb on us, one that would destroy my campaign and land me in prison. He was such a bizarre character it was hard to know how seriously to take anything he said. But given what had happened already, who knew what other dirty tricks were coming our way.

Then came October 7, one of the most significant days of the entire campaign. I was in a prep session for the upcoming second debate, trying hard to stay focused on the task at hand.

The first thing that happened was that Jim Clapper, the Director of National Intelligence, and Jeh Johnson, the Secretary of Homeland Security, issued a brief statement that for the first time formally accused "Russia's senior-most officials" of ordering the hacking of the DNC. We already knew this, but the formal statement gave it the full weight of the U.S. government. Strikingly, the FBI did not join in the statement, and we later learned that Comey refused to do so, claiming it was inappropriate so close to the election. (Hmm.)

Then, at 4:00 P.M., the *Washington Post* broke the news of Trump's *Access Hollywood* tape, in which he bragged about sexually assaulting women. It was a catastrophe for Trump's campaign. Less than one hour later, WikiLeaks announced it had obtained fifty thousand of John Podesta's emails and published a first batch of about two thousand. It looked like an orchestrated attempt to change the subject and distract voters—and provided further reason to believe that WikiLeaks and its Russian patrons were very much in sync with the Trump campaign.

It turns out, Russian hackers had gained access to John's personal email account back in March, thanks to a successful phishing attack. WikiLeaks continued to release stolen emails almost every single day for the rest of the campaign. For a while, it seemed like the WikiLeaks gambit was failing. The *Access Hollywood* story dominated the headlines, put Trump on the defensive, and sent his Republican backers scurrying for cover. The press eagerly covered every stolen email that emerged—even reprinting John's favorite risotto recipe—but none of the stories monopolized the news cycle like the Trump tape.

I commiserated with John about the outrageous invasion of privacy—I was one of the few who knew what it felt like—but he took it in stride. He felt bad about some of the language he used. He felt even worse for the friends and colleagues who had sent him private messages and now had to see their words printed for all to see. And WikiLeaks hadn't bothered to redact personal information such as phone numbers and Social Security numbers, which victimized good people who deserved better.

In the end, though, most of John's emails were . . . boring. They revealed the nuts and bolts of a campaign at work, with staffers debating policies, editing speeches, and kibitzing about the daily ups and downs of the election. In fact, Tom Friedman of the *New York Times* wrote a column about how well the behind-the-scenes correspondence reflected on me and my team. "When I read WikiHillary, I hear a smart, pragmatic, center-left politician," he wrote, and "I am more convinced than ever she can be the President America needs today."

What was harder to see at the time was that the steady stream of stories guaranteed that "Clinton" and "emails" remained in the headlines up until Election Day. None of this had anything at all to do with my use of personal email at the State Department—nothing at all— but for many voters, it would all blend together. And that was before Jim Comey sent his misguided letter to Congress, which made it all much worse. As a result, we faced a perfect storm. And Trump did his best to amplify our problems, citing WikiLeaks more than 160 times in the final month of the campaign. He could barely contain his excitement whenever a new batch of stolen emails appeared.

Comparing the effects of WikiLeaks and *Access Hollywood* may prove the old Washington cliché about how the "drip, drip" of scandal can be even more damaging over time than a single really bad story. Trump's tape was like a bomb going off, and the damage was immediate and severe. But no other tapes emerged, so there was nowhere else for the story to go. Eventually the press and the public moved on. It's amazing how quickly the media metabolism works these days. By contrast, the WikiLeaks email dumps kept coming and coming. It was like Chinese water torture. No single day was that bad, but it added up, and we could never get past it. WikiLeaks played into people's fascination with "pulling back the curtain." Anything said behind closed doors is automatically considered more interesting, important, and honest than things said in public. It's even better if you have to do a little legwork and google around for the information. We sometimes joked that if we wanted the press to pay attention to our jobs plan, which I talked about endlessly to little avail, we should leak a private email about it. Only then would it be news worth covering.

WikiLeaks also helped accelerate the phenomenon that eventually came to be known as fake news. False story lines started appearing on Facebook, Reddit, Breitbart, Drudge Report, and other sites often claiming to be based on stolen emails. For example, WikiLeaks tweeted on November 6 that the Clinton Foundation paid for Chelsea's wedding, a totally false accusation, as the *Washington Post*'s Glenn Kessler later verified in his Fact Checker column. Kessler, who's never been shy about criticizing me, heard from readers who said this lie helped convince them to vote for Trump. After the election, he investigated and found it to be "a claim lacking any evidence," and he urged readers "to be more careful consumers of the news." The lack of evidence didn't stop the *New York Post* and Fox News from repeating the lie and giving it mass circulation. That really got under my skin. Bill and I were proud to pay for Chelsea and Marc's wedding and we treasure every memory of it. Lies about me and Bill are one thing, but I can't stand to see lies about Chelsea. She doesn't deserve that.

Russia's propaganda networks, RT and Sputnik, were eager purveyors of fake news. For example, U.S. intelligence agencies later pointed to an August 2016 video produced by RT titled "How 100% of the Clintons' 'Charity' Went to . . . Themselves." It was another lie. Since Bill and I have released our tax returns going back decades, it's public record that since 2001 we've donated more than $23 million to charities such as the Elizabeth Glaser Pediatric AIDS Foundation, educational institutions, hospitals, churches, the Children's Defense Fund, and the Clinton Foundation. And none of us—not Bill, not Chelsea, not me—has ever taken any money from the foundation.

At the time, I was barely aware that such silly Russian smears were circulating on American social media. And yet, according to a U.S. Intelligence assessment, that one RT video alone was viewed more than nine million times, mostly on Facebook.

Even if I had known that, it would have been hard to believe that many voters would take any of it seriously. Still, reporting from BuzzFeed and others was finding that the reach of fake news on Facebook and other outlets was far wider than anyone expected, and that much of it was being generated in faraway countries such as Macedonia. The whole thing was bizarre. And Trump did all he could to help fake news spread and take root, repeating fake headlines from Russian propaganda outlets like Sputnik at his rallies and retweeting extremist memes.

The day before the election, President Obama was campaigning for me in Michigan (yes, we campaigned in Michigan!), and expressed the frustration we all felt: "As long as it's on Facebook and people can see it, as long as it's on social media, people start believing it," he said, "and it creates this dust cloud of nonsense." Nonsense was right.

On October 30, Harry Reid wrote another letter to Jim Comey, trying one last time to focus the nation's attention back on the unprecedented foreign intervention in our election. The former boxer from Searchlight, Nevada, knew we were in the fight of our lives, and he couldn't believe no one was paying attention. Harry had been briefed by intelligence officials and was frustrated they weren't informing the American people about what was really going on. "It has become clear that you possess explosive information about close ties and coordination between Donald Trump, his top advisors, and the Russian government," he wrote to Comey. "The public has a right to know this information." And yet Comey—who was only too eager to speak publicly about the investigation into my emails—continued to refuse to say a word about Trump and Russia.

I was worried that we'd see even more direct tampering on Election Day. But what more could we do? My campaign and I had spent months shouting into the wind. All that was left was to make our strongest case to voters and hope for the best.

Dragnet

After the election, I tried to unplug, avoid the news, and not think too much about all this. But the universe didn't cooperate.

Just four days after the election, the Russian Deputy Foreign Minister bragged in an interview that his government had "contacts" with Trump's "immediate entourage" during the campaign. Both the Kremlin and Trump's people tried to walk back this remarkable admission, but the bell couldn't be unrung. A few days after that, President Obama ordered the Intelligence Community—the collection of the government's seventeen different intelligence agencies—to conduct a full review into Russian interference into the election.

Then, in early December, a twenty-eight-year-old man from North Carolina drove to Washington, D.C., with a Colt AR-15 assault rifle, a .38-caliber Colt revolver, and a knife. He had read on the internet that a popular local Washington pizzeria was secretly hosting a child sex abuse ring run by John Podesta and me. This particularly disgusting fake news got its start with an innocuous email released by WikiLeaks about John going out for pizza. It was quickly refracted through the dark corners of the internet and emerged as a blood-curdling conspiracy theory. Alex Jones, the right-wing talk show host effusively praised by Trump who claims that 9/11 was an inside job and the Sandy Hook massacre was a hoax, recorded a YouTube video about "all the children Hillary Clinton has personally murdered and chopped up and raped." Soon that young man from North Carolina was in his car on his way to Washington. When he got to the pizzeria, he searched everywhere for the children supposedly being held captive. There weren't any. He fired off one shot before being apprehended by police and eventually sentenced to four years in prison. Thankfully, no one was harmed. I was horrified. I immediately contacted a friend of mine who runs a bookstore on the same street. She told me that her employees also had been harassed and threatened by conspiracy nuts.

In early January, the Intelligence Community reported back to President Obama and published an unclassified version of its findings for the public. The headline was that Putin himself had ordered a covert operation with the goal of denigrating and defeating me, electing Trump, and undermining the American people's faith in the democratic process. That was no surprise to me or anyone else who had been paying attention, although it was notable that it was now the official view of the U.S. government. The real news, however, was that the Russian intervention had gone far beyond hacking email accounts and releasing files. Moscow had waged sophisticated information warfare on a massive scale, manipulating social media and flooding it with propaganda and fake news.

Soon it felt like every day there was a new revelation about the scope of the Russian operation, secret contacts with the Trump campaign, and an ongoing federal investigation digging into all of it. Congressional hearings began. The *New York Times* and the *Washington Post* competed to break scoop after scoop. I know I give the press a lot of grief, especially the *Times*, but this really was journalism at its finest.

wasn't just a former candidate trying to figure out why she lost.
I was also a former Secretary of State worried about our nation's national security. I couldn't resist following every twist and turn of the story as closely as possible. I read everything I could get my hands on. I called friends in Washington and Silicon Valley and consulted with national security experts and seasoned Russia hands. I learned more than I ever imagined about algorithms, "content farms," and search engine optimization. The voluminous file of clippings on my desk grew thicker and thicker. To keep it all straight, I started making lists of everything we knew about the unfolding scandal. At times, I felt like CIA agent Carrie Mathison on the TV show *Homeland*, desperately trying to get her arms around a sinister conspiracy and appearing more than a little frantic in the process.

That's not a good look for anyone, let alone a former Secretary of State. So instead, let me channel a TV show that I grew up watching as a kid in Park Ridge: *Dragnet*. "Just the facts, ma'am."

We've learned a lot about what the Russians did, what the Trump campaign did, and how the U.S. government responded. Let's go through it step-by-step.

What the Feds Did

First, we've learned that the federal investigation started much earlier than was publicly known.

In late 2015, European intelligence agencies picked up contacts between Trump associates and Russian intelligence operatives. Communications intercepts by U.S. and allied intelligence seem to have continued throughout 2016. We know now that by July 2016, the FBI's elite National Security Division in Washington had started investigating whether the Trump campaign and the Russians were coordinating to influence the election. They have also been looking into Paul Manafort's financial ties to pro-Putin oligarchs.

In the summer of 2016, according to the *Washington Post*, the FBI convinced a special Foreign Intelligence Surveillance Court that there was probable cause to believe that Trump advisor Carter Page was acting as a Russian agent, and they received a warrant to monitor his communications. The FBI also began investigating a dossier prepared by a well-respected former British spy that contained explosive and salacious allegations about compromising information the Russians had on Trump. The Intelligence Community took the dossier seriously enough that it briefed both President Obama and President Elect Trump on its contents before the inauguration. By the spring of 2017, a federal grand jury was issuing subpoenas to business associates of Michael Flynn, who resigned as Trump's national security advisor after lying about his Russian contacts.

We've also learned a lot about how various parts of the U.S. government reacted differently to the intelligence coming in over the course of 2016 about ties between the Trump campaign and Russia. The CIA seems to have been most alarmed and was also convinced that the Russian goal was to help Trump and hurt me. As early as August 2016, CIA Director John Brennan called his counterpart in Moscow and warned him to stop interfering in the election. Brennan also individually briefed the "gang of eight" congressional leaders and shared his concerns. This explains why Harry Reid sought to galvanize public attention on the threat in his August letter.

We've learned that the FBI took a different approach. They launched an investigation in July 2016, but Director Comey didn't inform congressional leaders, was slower than Brennan to come to the conclusion that Russia's goal was electing Trump, and refused to join other intelligence agencies in issuing a joint statement on October 7 because he didn't want to interfere close to an election—something that certainly didn't stop him when it came to trumpeting news about the investigation into my emails. Sources within the FBI also convinced the *New York Times* to run a story saying they saw "no clear link to Russia," countering Franklin Foer's scoop in *Slate* about unusual computer traffic between Trump Tower and a Russian bank. This is one of the stories the *Times*'s ombudsman later criticized.

It wasn't until after the election that the FBI finally came around and joined the rest of the Intelligence Community in putting out the January 2017 assessment that Russia had, in fact, been actively helping Trump. And in March 2017, Comey finally confirmed the existence of a federal investigation into possible coordination. Tyrone Gayle, one of my former communications aides, summed up how most of us felt hearing that news: "That sound you just heard was every ex-Clinton staffer banging their heads on the wall from California to D.C." Part of the frustration was knowing that the FBI's silence had helped Putin succeed and that more exposure could have given the American people the information they needed.

While Brennan and Reid had their hair on fire and Comey was dragging his feet, Republican Senate leader Mitch McConnell was actively playing defense for Trump and the Russians. We know now that even after he was fully briefed by the CIA, McConnell rejected the intelligence and warned the Obama administration that if it made any attempt to inform the public, he would attack it for playing politics. I can't think of a more shameful example of a national leader so blatantly putting partisanship over national security. McConnell knew better, but he did it anyway.

I know some former Obama administration officials have regrets about how this all unfolded. Former Homeland Security Secretary Jeh Johnson told the House Intelligence Committee in June 2017 that the administration didn't take a more aggressive public stance because it was concerned about reinforcing Trump's complaints that the election was "rigged" and being "perceived as taking sides in the election." Former Deputy National Security Advisor Ben Rhodes, whom I'd come to trust and value when we worked together in President Obama's first term, told the *Washington Post* that the Obama administration was

focused on a traditional cyber threat, while "the Russians were playing this much bigger game" of multifaceted information warfare. "We
weren't able to put all of those pieces together in real time," Ben said.

Mike McFaul, Obama's former Ambassador to Russia, summed it
up in a concise tweet:

> FACT: Russia violated our sovereignty during the 2016
>   election.
> FACT: Obama exposed that attack.
> OPINION: We should have focused on it more.

I understand the predicament the Obama administration faced, with
McConnell threatening them and everyone assuming I was going to
win regardless. Richard Clarke, President George W. Bush's top counterterrorism advisor on 9/11, has written about how hard it can be to
heed warnings about threats that have never been seen before, and certainly it was hard to imagine the Russians would dare to conduct such
a massive and unprecedented covert operation. And President Obama
did privately warn Putin directly to back off.

I do wonder sometimes about what would have happened if President Obama had made a televised address to the nation in the fall
of 2016 warning that our democracy was under attack. Maybe more
Americans would have woken up to the threat in time. We'll never
know. But what we do know for sure is that McConnell and other Republican leaders did everything they could to leave Americans in the
dark and vulnerable to attack.

What the Trump Team Did

Let's look at what we've learned since the election about the actions of
the Trump team.

We know now there were many contacts during the campaign and the transition between Trump associates and Russians—in person, on the phone, and via text and email. Many of these interactions were with Ambassador Kislyak, who was thought to help oversee Russian intelligence operations in the United States, but they included other Russian officials and agents as well.

For example, Roger Stone, the longtime Trump political advisor who claimed that he was in touch with Julian Assange, suggested in August 2016 that information about John Podesta was going to come out. In October, Stone hinted Assange and WikiLeaks were going to release material that would be damaging to my campaign, and later admitted to also exchanging direct messages over Twitter with Guccifer 2.0, the front for Russian intelligence, after some of those messages were published by the website The Smoking Gun.

We also know now that in December 2016, Trump's son-in-law and senior advisor, Jared Kushner, met with Sergey Gorkov, the head of a Kremlin-controlled bank that is under U.S. sanctions and tied closely to Russian intelligence. The *Washington Post* caused a sensation with its report that Russian officials were discussing a proposal by Kushner to use Russian diplomatic facilities in America to communicate secretly with Moscow.

The *New York Times* reported that Russian intelligence attempted to recruit Carter Page, the Trump foreign policy advisor, as a spy back in 2013 (according to the report, the FBI believed Page did not know that the man who approached him was a spy). And according to Yahoo News, U.S. officials received intelligence reports that Carter Page met with a top Putin aide involved with intelligence.

Some Trump advisors failed to disclose or lied about their contacts with the Russians, including on applications for security clearances, which could be a federal crime. Attorney General Jeff Sessions lied to Congress about his contacts and later recused himself from the investigation. Michael Flynn lied about being in contact with Kislyak and then changed his story about whether they discussed dropping U.S. sanctions.

Reporting since the election has made clear that Trump and his top advisors have little or no interest in learning about the Russian covert operation against American democracy. Trump himself repeatedly called the whole thing a hoax—and at the same time, blamed Obama for not doing anything about it. As recently as July 2017, he continued to denigrate the Intelligence Community and claimed that countries other than Russia might be responsible for the DNC hack. Former Deputy Attorney General Sally Yates tweeted in response that Trump's "inexplicable refusal to confirm Russian election interference insults career intel pros & hinders our ability to prevent in future."

But there is one area where Trump's team seems to have been intently interested: rolling back U.S. sanctions against Russia. That's what Flynn was discussing with the Russian Ambassador. The Reuters news service reported that Senate investigators want to know whether Kushner discussed it in his meetings as well, including whether Russian banks would offer financial support to Trump associates and organizations in return. And as soon as the Trump team took control of the State Department, it started working on a plan to lift sanctions and return to Russia two compounds in Maryland and New York that the Obama administration had confiscated because they were bases for espionage. Career diplomats at State were so concerned that they alerted Congress. As of this writing, the Trump administration is exploring returning the compounds without any preconditions. All of this is significant because it makes it a lot easier to see how a quid pro quo with Russia might have worked.

We'll surely continue to learn more. But based on what's already in the public domain, we know that Trump and his team publicly cheered on the Russian operation and took maximum advantage of it. In so doing, they not only encouraged but actually helped along this attack on our democracy by a hostile foreign power.

What the Russians Did

That brings us to what we've learned since the election about what the Russians did. We know already about the hacking and release of stolen messages via WikiLeaks, but that's just one part of a much larger effort. It turns out they also hacked the Democratic Congressional Campaign Committee and fed damaging information to local bloggers and reporters in various congressional districts across the country, which required sophistication. And that's just the beginning.

The official Intelligence Community report explained that the Russian propaganda strategy "blends covert intelligence operations—such as cyber activity—with overt efforts by Russian Government agencies, state-funded media, third-party intermediaries, and paid social media users, or 'trolls.'" Let's try to break down what it all means.

The simplest part is traditional state-run media; in this case, Russian networks such as RT and Sputnik. They use their global reach to push Kremlin talking points over the airwaves and social media, including malicious headlines like "Clinton and ISIS Funded by Same Money." Sputnik frequently used the same Twitter hashtag as Trump: #CrookedHillary. It's hard to know exactly how wide of a reach RT has. A *Daily Beast* article reported on claims that it had exaggerated its stats. It's probably more than you'd think (maybe hundreds of thousands) but not enough that it would have a big impact on an election by itself. But when RT propaganda gets picked up and repeated by American media outlets such as Fox News, Breitbart, and Alex Jones's Infowars, and posted on Facebook, its reach expands dramatically. That happened frequently during the campaign. Trump and his team also helped amplify Russian stories, giving them an even bigger megaphone.

The Russians also generated propaganda in less traditional ways, including thousands of fake news sites and individual internet "trolls" who posted attacks on Facebook and Twitter. As the Intelligence

Community reported, "Russia used trolls as well as RT as part of its influence efforts to denigrate Secretary Clinton . . . some social media accounts that appear to be tied to Russia's professional trolls—because they previously were devoted to supporting Russian actions in Ukraine—started to advocate for President Elect Trump as early as December 2015." Some of the stories created by trolls were blatantly false, like the one about the pope endorsing Trump, but others were simply misleading attacks on me or puff pieces about Trump. Much of this content was then fed into the same amplification process, pushed along by RT and then picked up by American outlets such as Fox.

The Russians wanted to be sure that impressionable voters in key swing states actually saw their propaganda. So they set out to game the internet.

Much of what we see online is governed by a series of algorithms that determine what content appears in our Facebook and Twitter feeds, Google search results, and so on. One factor for these algorithms is popularity. If lots of users share the same post or click on the same link—and if key "influencers" with large personal networks do as well—then it's more likely to pop up on your screen. To manipulate this process, the Russians "flooded the zone" with a vast network of fake Twitter and Facebook accounts, some carefully designed to appear like American swing voters. Some of these accounts were run by trolls (real live people), and others were automated, but the goal was the same: to artificially boost the volume and popularity of Russian and right-wing propaganda. The automated accounts are called "bots," short for robots. The Russians were not the only ones using them, but they took it to a whole other level. Researchers at the University of Southern California have found that nearly 20 percent of all political tweets sent between September 16 and October 21, 2016, were generated by bots. Many of them probably were Russian. These tactics, according to Senator Mark Warner, vice chair of the Intelligence Committee, could "overwhelm" search engines so that the voters' newsfeeds started showing headlines like "Hillary Clinton's Sick" or "Hillary Clinton's Stealing Money from the State Department."

According to Facebook, another key tactic is the creation of fake affinity groups or community pages that could drive conversations online and draw in unwitting users. Imagine, for example, a fake Black Lives Matter group created to push malicious attacks linking Democrats to the KKK and slavery, with the goal of driving down African American turnout. The Russians did things like that. The similarity of their attacks to organic right-wing memes helped. For example, a prominent Trump supporter and evangelical bishop, Aubrey Shines, produced an online video attacking me because Democrats "gave this country slavery, the KKK, Jim Crow laws." This charge was hugely amplified by the conservative media company Sinclair Broadcast Group, which distributed it to all of its 173 local television stations across the country, along with other right-wing propaganda. Sinclair is now poised to grow to 223 stations. It would reach an estimated 72 percent of American households.

When I learned about these fake groups spreading across Facebook and poisoning our country's political dialogue, I couldn't help but think about the millions of my supporters who felt so bullied and harassed on the internet that they made sure their online communities, such as Pantsuit Nation, were private. They deserved better, and so did our country.

Put all this together, and you've got multifaceted information warfare. Senator Mark Warner summed it up well: "The Russians employed thousands of paid internet trolls and botnets to push out disinformation and fake news at a high volume, focusing this material onto your Twitter and Facebook feeds and flooding our social media with misinformation," he said. "This fake news and disinformation was then hyped by the American media echo chamber and our own social media networks to reach and potentially influence millions of Americans."

It gets worse. According to *Time* magazine, the Russians targeted propaganda to undecided voters and to "soft" Clinton supporters who might be persuaded to stay home or support a third-party candidate— including by purchasing ads on Facebook. It's against the law to use foreign money to support a candidate, as well as for campaigns to coordinate with foreign entities, so a commissioner on the Federal Election Commission has called for a full investigation of this charge.

We know that swing voters were inundated. According to Senator Warner, "Women and African Americans were targeted in places like Wisconsin and Michigan." One study found that in Michigan alone, nearly half of all political news on Twitter in the final days before the election was false or misleading propaganda. Senator Warner has rightly asked: "How did they know to go to that level of detail in those kinds of jurisdictions?"

Interestingly, the Russians made a particular effort to target voters who had supported Bernie Sanders in the primaries, including by planting fake news on pro-Sanders message boards and Facebook groups and amplifying attacks by so-called Bernie Bros. Russian trolls posted stories about how I was a murderer, money launderer, and secretly had Parkinson's disease. I don't know why anyone would believe such things, even if you read it on Facebook—although it's often hard to tell on there what's a legitimate news article and what's not—but maybe if you're angry enough, you'll accept anything that reinforces your point of view. As the former head of the NSA, retired General Keith Alexander, explained to Congress, the Russian goal was clear: "What they were trying to do is drive a wedge within the Democratic Party between the Clinton group and the Sanders group and then within our nation between Republicans and Democrats." Perhaps this is one reason why third-party candidates received more than five million more votes in 2016 than they had in 2012. That was an aim of both the Russians and the Republicans, and it worked.

According to CNN, *Time*, and McClatchy, the Justice Department and Congress are examining whether the Trump campaign data analytics operation—led by Kushner—coordinated with the Russians to pull all this off. Congressman Adam Schiff, the top Democrat on the House Intelligence Committee, has said he wants to know whether they "coordinated in any way in terms of targeting or in terms of timing or in terms of any other measure." If they did, that also would be illegal.

Think this is bad? There's more. We knew during the campaign that Russian hackers had breached election systems in two states. Now we know that this effort was far more extensive than previously thought. In June 2017, officials from the Department of Homeland Security testified before Congress that election systems in as many as twenty-one states were targeted. Bloomberg News reported that the number could be as high as thirty-nine. According to a leaked NSA report, the accounts of more than a hundred local election officials across the country were also penetrated. In addition, hackers gained access to the software used by poll workers on Election Day. The goal of these intrusions seems to have been accessing voter registration information. Hackers attempted to delete or alter records of particular voters. They could also have used the data to better target their propaganda efforts. According to *Time*, investigators want to find out if any stolen voter information ended up with the Trump campaign.

I know that the slow unfolding of this news has inured many people to how shocking all this is. It feels a little like the frog in the pot that doesn't realize it's boiling because it happens so gradually. But step back and think about it: the Russians hacked our election systems. They got inside. They tried to delete or alter voter information. This should send a shiver down the spine of every American.

And why stop there? According to the *Washington Post*, the Russians used old-fashioned forgery to influence the election as well. The *Post* says Moscow surreptitiously got a fake document to the FBI that described a fabricated discussion between the chair of the

Democratic National Committee and an aide to financier and liberal donor George Soros about how Attorney General Lynch had promised to go easy on me in the email investigation. It was a bizarre fantasy straight out of the fever swamp. Jim Comey may well have known the document was a forgery, but the *Post* says he was concerned that if it became public, it would still cause an outcry. Its existence, however fraudulent, provided him with a new justification to disregard long-standing protocol and hold his infamous July press conference disparaging me. I don't know what Comey was thinking, but the idea that the Russians could have manipulated him into such a damaging misstep is mind-boggling.

Finally, to add one more bit of cloak-and-dagger mystery to this whole story, a lot of Russian officials seem to have had unfortunate accidents since the election. On Election Day itself, an officer in the New York consulate was found dead. The first explanation was that he fell off a roof. Then the Russians said he had a heart attack. On December 26, a former KGB agent thought to have helped compile the salacious Trump dossier was found dead in his car in Moscow. On February 20, the Russian Ambassador to the United Nations died suddenly, also from a heart attack. Russian authorities have also arrested a cybersecurity expert and two intelligence officials who worked on cyber operations and accused them of spying for the United States. All I can say is that working for Putin must be a stressful job.

If all this sounds unbelievable, I know how you feel. It's like something out of one of the spy novels my husband stays up all night reading. Even knowing what the Russians did in Ukraine, I was still shocked that they would wage large-scale covert warfare against the United States. But the evidence is overwhelming, and the Intelligence Community assessment is definitive.

What's more, we know now that the Russians have mounted similar operations in other Western democracies. After the U.S. election, Facebook found and removed tens of thousands of fake accounts in

France and the United Kingdom. In Germany, members of Parliament have been hacked. Denmark and Norway say the Russians breached key ministries. The Netherlands turned off election computers and decided to count every vote by hand. And most notably, in France, Emmanuel Macron's campaign was hit by a massive cyberattack just before the presidential election that sparked immediately comparisons with the operation against me. But because the French had watched what happened in America, they were better prepared. Macron's team responded to Russian phishing attacks with false passwords, and they seeded fake documents in with their other files, all in an attempt to confuse and slow down the hackers. When a trove of stolen Macron emails did appear online, the French media refused to provide the kind of sensationalized coverage we saw here, in part because of a law in France that guards against that happening close to an election. French voters also seem to have learned from our mistakes, and they soundly rejected Le Pen, the right-wing pro-Moscow candidate. I take some comfort knowing that our misfortune helped protect France and other democracies. That's something, at least.

The War on Truth

As I noted at the beginning of this chapter, one reason the Russian misinformation campaign was successful was that our country's natural defenses had been worn down over several years by powerful interests that sought to make it harder for Americans to distinguish between truth and lies. If you feel like it's gotten tougher to separate out fringe voices from credible journalists, especially online, or you find yourself arguing more and more with people over what should be knowable facts, you're not going crazy. There has been a concerted effort to discredit mainstream sources of information, create an echo chamber to amplify fringe conspiracy theories, and undermine Americans' grasp of objective truth. The McClatchy news service says federal investigators are looking into whether there were direct links between the Russian propaganda war and right-wing organizations such as Breitbart and InfoWars. But even if no direct ties ever come to light, we need to understand how the right-wing war on truth opened the door to the Russian attack.

After the election, a former conservative talk radio host in Wisconsin named Charlie Sykes came forward to explain how this worked. For years, he said, right-wing media and politicians conditioned their supporters to distrust anything they heard from the mainstream media, while pushing paranoid conspiracy theories from people such as Alex Jones and Trump himself—the chief promoter of the racist "birther" lie. "The price turned out to be far higher than I imagined," Sykes said. "The cumulative effect of the attacks was to delegitimize" the mainstream media and "essentially destroy much of the right's immunity to false information." This was useful for Trump when he became a candidate, because it helped him both deflect negative stories from mainstream sources and find a receptive audience for false attacks against me. It did the same for the Russians. And Trump has kept at it in the White House. "All administrations lie, but what we are seeing here is an attack on credibility itself," Sykes said. He quoted Garry Kasparov, the Russian chess grandmaster and Putin opponent who said, "The point of modern propaganda isn't only to misinform or push an agenda. It is to exhaust your critical thinking, to annihilate truth."

Rupert Murdoch and the late Roger Ailes probably did more than anyone else to make all this possible. For years, Fox News has been the most powerful and prominent platform for the right-wing war on truth. Ailes, a former advisor to Richard Nixon, built Fox by demonizing and delegitimizing mainstream media that tried to adhere to traditional standards of objectivity and accuracy. Fox gave a giant megaphone to voices claiming climate change was fake science, the falling unemployment rate was phony math, and you couldn't trust

Barack Obama's birth certificate. Ailes and Fox were so successful in polarizing the audience that by 2016, most liberals and conservatives got their news from distinctly different sources and no longer shared a common set of facts.

During the Obama years, the Breitbart News Network, backed by Robert and Rebekah Mercer and led by their advisor Steve Bannon, who is now Trump's top strategist, emerged to give Fox a run for its money. According to the Southern Poverty Law Center, Breitbart embraces "ideas on the extremist fringe of the conservative right." To give you a flavor, here are a few memorable Breitbart headlines:

BIRTH CONTROL MAKES WOMEN UNATTRACTIVE AND CRAZY

THERE'S NO HIRING BIAS AGAINST WOMEN IN TECH, THEY JUST SUCK AT INTERVIEWS

GLOBAL TEMPERATURES PLUNGE. ICY SILENCE FROM CLIMATE ALARMISTS

NAACP JOINS SOROS ARMY PLOTTING DC DISRUPTIONS, CIVIL DISOBEDIENCE, MASS ARRESTS

HOIST IT HIGH AND PROUD: THE CONFEDERATE FLAG PROCLAIMS A GLORIOUS HERITAGE

FACT CHECK: WERE OBAMA AND HILLARY FOUNDERS OF ISIS? YOU BET

This would be funny if it wasn't so scary. This kind of garbage "conditioned" Americans, to use Charlie Sykes's word, to accept the Russian propaganda that flooded our country in 2016.

Robert Mercer is a key figure to understand. A computer scientist, Mercer made billions of dollars by applying complex algorithms and data analysis to the financial markets. The hedge fund he helps run,

Renaissance Technologies, is wildly successful. By all accounts, Mercer is an extreme antigovernment right-winger. A profile in the *New Yorker* quoted one former Renaissance colleague as saying Mercer is "happy if people don't trust the government. And if the President's a bozo? He's fine with that. He wants it to all fall down." The *New Yorker* also reported that another former high-level Renaissance Technologies employee said Mercer hates Bill and me and once accused us of being part of a secret CIA drug-running scheme and of murdering our opponents. If you think these accusations sound batty, you're right. And this man is now one of the most powerful people in America.

Breitbart is only one of the organizations Mercer and his family control. Another is Cambridge Analytica, which has gained notoriety for using Facebook data to target voters for clients such as Trump. It's hard to separate reality from hype when it comes to Cambridge Analytica's track record, but it seems like a mistake to underestimate Mercer. As the *New Yorker* put it, "Having revolutionized the use of data on Wall Street," he "was eager to accomplish the same feat in the political realm." There's nothing inherently wrong with using big data and microtargeting—every campaign does it, including mine. The problem would come if the data were obtained or used improperly. After reports were published raising questions about whether Cambridge Analytica played a role in Brexit, British authorities are now investigating the company's alleged role with Leave.eu and whether Cambridge's techniques violated British and European privacy laws (which Cambridge denies).

Mercer is not alone. The Koch brothers, who run the second-largest privately held company in America, with extensive oil and gas holdings, have also invested huge sums of money, which has eroded the public's grasp on reality and advanced their ideological agenda. For example, they've spent tens of millions of dollars to fund a network of think tanks, foundations, and advocacy organizations to promote the false science of climate change denial and their agenda. We can expect more of that as the Kochs prepare to spend whatever it takes to consolidate their hold on state governments and expand their power in Washington.

And let's not forget Donald Trump himself. It took a little while for Mercer, the Kochs, and Fox News to realize that Trump could help take their war on truth to the next level, but their eventual support for his candidacy was invaluable. In many ways, Trump is the embodiment of everything they had been working toward, and the perfect Trojan horse for Putin. The journalist Masha Gessen, who covers Putin extensively, has observed: "It's not just that both Putin and Trump lie, it is that they lie in the same way and for the same purpose: blatantly, to assert power over truth itself."

What Now?

In a Senate hearing in June 2017, Senator Angus King of Maine asked Jim Comey, "Was the Russian activity in the 2016 election a one-off proposition? Or is this part of a long-term strategy? Will they be back?"

"They'll be back," Comey replied emphatically. "It's not a Republican thing or Democratic thing. It really is an American thing."

He returned to the point a few minutes later. "We're talking about a foreign government that, using technical intrusion, lots of other methods, tried to shape the way we think, we vote, we act. That is a big deal. And people need to recognize it," Comey said. "It's not about Republicans or Democrats. They're coming after America."

Comey is absolutely right about this. The January 2017 Intelligence Community report called the Russian influence campaign a "new normal," and predicted Moscow would continue attacking the United States and our allies. Given the success Putin has had, we should expect interference in future elections and even more aggressive cyber and propaganda efforts. Sure enough, since the election, there are new reports that Russia has launched cyberattacks against the U.S. military, including targeting the social media accounts of thousands of

American soldiers; that hackers have penetrated companies that run American nuclear power plants; and that Russia is expanding its spy networks inside the United States.

We should also expect the right-wing war on truth to continue. As Trump faces growing political and legal challenges, he and his allies will likely intensify their efforts to delegitimize the mainstream press, the judiciary, and anyone else who threatens his preferred version of reality.

Can anything be done to meet these twin threats and protect our democracy? The answer is yes, if we take this seriously. In 1940, a time of much greater danger for our country, the writer John Buchan wrote, "We have been shaken out of our smugness and warned of a great peril, and in that warning lies our salvation. The dictators have done us a marvelous service to remind us of the true values of life." Americans today need to be similarly alert and determined.

Here are four steps that would help.

First, we need to get to the bottom of what really happened in 2016. Investigators and the press should keep digging. Based on how things are going, it's possible that, as often happens in Washington scandals, the alleged cover-up will become the most serious legal and political problem facing Trump. But no matter what happens, the American people will still need to know the truth about what the Russians did. Therefore, I believe the Special Counsel investigation should be complemented by an independent commission with subpoena power, like the one that investigated 9/11. It should provide a full public accounting of the attack against our country and make recommendations to improve security going forward. It's hard to understand how Republicans, so eager to set up a special committee to go after me over Benghazi, could block such a step.

Second, we need to get serious about cyber warfare. Government and the private sector need to work together more closely to improve our defenses. It will require significant investments to protect our networks and national infrastructure, and Corporate America needs to see this as an urgent imperative, because government can't do it alone. At the same time, our military and intelligence agencies should accelerate development of our own offensive cyber and information warfare capabilities, so that we are prepared to respond to aggression in kind, if need be.

Right now we do not have an effective deterrent to prevent cyber and information warfare the way we do with conventional and nuclear conflicts. Russia, China, and others believe they can operate in a so-called gray zone between peace and war, stealing our secrets, disrupting our elections, manipulating our politics, and harassing our citizens and businesses without facing serious repercussions. To change that calculus, I believe the United States should declare a new doctrine that states that a cyberattack on our vital national infrastructure will be treated as an act of war and met with a proportionate response.

Third, we need to get tough with Putin. He responds only to strength, so that's what we must demonstrate. It was gratifying to see Emmanuel Macron, the new French President, condemn Russian interference and propaganda while standing next to Putin at a press conference in Paris. If the French can do it, surely our own leaders can. Congress recently passed legislation over Trump's objections to ratchet up sanctions on Russia, and he reluctantly signed it. We should keep doing everything we can to isolate Putin. As former Secretary of State Condoleezza Rice said in May, "I'm appalled by what the Russians did, and we ought to find a way, ultimately, to punish it." The Obama administration proved with crippling sanctions against Iran that this kind of pressure can force our adversaries to change course. Russia is a much bigger and more powerful nation, but we have a lot of tools at our disposal, and even Putin is vulnerable to pressure. We also should strengthen NATO; help our allies reduce their dependence on Russian energy supplies, a key source of leverage for Putin; and arm the Ukrainian government so it can resist Moscow's aggression.

Fourth, we need to beat back the assault on truth and reason here at home and rebuild trust in our institutions. Tim Cook, CEO of Apple, has called for "a massive campaign" against fake news. "All of us technology companies need to create some tools that help diminish the volume of fake news," he said.

Companies such as Facebook, Twitter, and Google have already begun taking steps—adjusting algorithms, deactivating bot networks, and partnering with fact-checkers—but they must do more. Facebook is now the largest news platform in the world. With that awesome power comes great responsibility, which it must accept.

The mainstream media also has a responsibility to do more to debunk the lies infecting our public life and more directly hold the liars accountable. American journalists who eagerly and uncritically repeated whatever WikiLeaks dished out during the campaign could learn from the more responsible way the French press handled the hack of Macron. It will also be important to remain vigilant against misinformation like the fake leak that MSNBC's Rachel Maddow exposed in July 2017. "One way to stab in the heart aggressive American reporting on that subject is to lay traps for American journalists," she warned. And while there has been a lot of terrific reporting on the Russia scandal, we need to see the same rigor brought to the blizzard of deception from the administration and Republicans in Congress on everything from the budget to health care to climate change. (I love it when CNN does real-time fact-checking in its on-screen chyron. More of that, please.)

Speaking of Republicans, ultimately it's on them to stop enabling Trump and genuflecting to billionaires such as the Mercers and the Kochs. Aggressive campaign finance reform and a reinvigorated Federal Election Commission would help a lot. But unless principled Republicans step up, our democracy will continue to pay the price.

We all have to do our part if we're going to rebuild trust in one another and our government. As Clint Watts, a former FBI agent and senior fellow at the George Washington University Center for Cyber and Homeland Security, put it in his testimony before the Senate Intelligence Committee: "Until we get a firm basis on fact and fiction in our own country . . . we're going to have a big problem." It's up to each one of us to stay informed and make good decisions with rigorous reasoning and real deliberation. This is especially important when it comes to voting. Choose wisely and don't fall for scams. The same way you try to be careful about where you put your money or the car you buy, be careful and informed with your vote. And we all have the ability to break out of our echo chambers and engage with people who don't agree with us politically. We can keep an open mind and be willing to change our minds from time to time. Even if our outreach is rebuffed, it's worth it to keep trying. We're all going to share our American future together— better to do so with open hearts and outstretched hands than closed minds and clenched fists.

Worse Than Watergate

As this story continues to unfold, there's a moment from the campaign that I keep replaying in my head over and over again. It was my third debate against Trump. He had just attacked me by quoting out of context a line from an email stolen by the Russians and released by WikiLeaks. The moderator, Chris Wallace of Fox News, was piling on as well. I thought the American people deserved to know what was really going on.

"The most important question of this evening, Chris, is finally, will Donald Trump admit and condemn that the Russians are doing this, and make it clear that he will not have the help of Putin in this election," I said. Trump retreated to his usual pro-Putin talking points: "He said nice things about me. If we got along well, that would be good."

Then, turning to me, he added, "Putin, from everything I see, has no respect for this person."

"Well," I fired back, "that's because he would rather have a puppet as President of the United States." Trump seemed befuddled. "No puppet. No puppet. You're the puppet," he stammered.

I think about that line every time I see him on TV now. When he's yucking it up in the Oval Office with the Russian foreign minister and divulging classified information. When he's giving the cold shoulder to the German Chancellor, Angela Merkel, and other European allies. When he's lying through his teeth about Russia or anything else. "No puppet. No puppet. You're the puppet." This man is President of the United States. And no one is happier than Vladimir Putin.

In mid-July 2017, as I was putting the finishing touches on this book, Trump met with Putin in Germany. He not only didn't challenge him publicly on interfering in our election—he actually floated the idea of a joint cybersecurity unit, which is a classic example of asking the fox to guard the henhouse. Then, the news broke that Donald Trump Jr., Paul Manafort, and Jared Kushner met in June 2016 with a Russian lawyer connected to the Kremlin who promised to provide damaging information about me and wanted to discuss easing the sanctions on Russia included in the Magnitsky Act. Donald Trump Jr. admitted all this! He was disappointed the dirt didn't pan out the way he'd hoped. You can't make this stuff up. I'm sure there's more to come, so stay tuned.

I know some will dismiss everything in this chapter as me trying to shift blame for my loss in 2016. That's wrong. This is about the future. In the nineteenth century, nations fought two kinds of wars: on land and at sea. In the twentieth century, that expanded to the skies. In the twenty-first century, wars will increasingly be fought in cyberspace. Yet our President is too proud, too weak, or too shortsighted to face this threat head-on. No foreign power in modern history has attacked us with so few consequences, and that puts us all at risk.

I'm not saying this as a Democrat or as a former candidate. I'm saying this as someone who loves our country and will always be grateful for the blessings America has given to me and to the world. I'm worried. I'm worried about our democracy at home, with lies and corruption threatening our bedrock values, institutions, and the rule of law. And I'm worried about the future of democracy around the world. Generations of farsighted leaders on both sides of the Atlantic came together to build a new liberal order out of the ashes of World War II. They defended universal human rights, defied totalitarianism, and delivered unprecedented peace, prosperity, and freedom. As Americans, that is our inheritance. We should be proud of it and we should protect it. But now, between Trump and Putin, all that is at risk.

In June 2017, Jim Clapper was asked how the Russia scandal compared with Watergate. "I lived through Watergate. I was on active duty then in the Air Force. I was a young officer. It was a scary time," he replied. "I have to say, though, I think when you compare the two, Watergate pales, really, in my view, compared to what we're confronting now."

I also lived through Watergate. I was a young attorney working for the House Judiciary Committee's impeachment inquiry into Richard Nixon. I listened to the tapes. I dug into all the evidence of Nixon's crimes. And I agree with Jim Clapper. What we are facing now—an attack on our democracy by our principal foreign adversary, potentially aided and abetted by the President's own team—is much more serious.

In three words I can sum up everything
I've learned about life: it goes on.
—Robert Frost

Election Night

The night of November 8, 2016, started with me chasing my grand-daughter and pretending to just miss catching her. Charlotte would squeal with glee and shout, "*Again!*" and I did it again. This went on for a while. It was almost enough to distract me from the television.

My family and senior staff had gathered at the Peninsula Hotel in New York to watch the returns. I've always dreaded election nights. There's nothing left to do but wait.

Hours earlier, in the predawn darkness, we finished a final whirl-wind campaign swing that took me from Pittsburgh to Grand Rap-ids, Michigan, to a massive rally in Philadelphia with the Obamas and Bruce Springsteen; *then* to another rally in Raleigh, North Carolina, capped by a raucous late-night duet between Jon Bon Jovi and Lady Gaga; and finally back to Westchester, where a crowd of fired-up sup-porters met us on the tarmac even though it was close to 4:00 A.M.

I was exhausted but happy and enormously proud of my team. Standing with Bill, Chelsea, Barack, and Michelle in front of tens of thousands of people at Philadelphia's Independence Hall was one of the high points of the entire campaign. The President hugged me and whispered in my ear, "You've got this. I'm so proud of you."

After a quick stop at home to shower and change, Bill and I voted at an elementary school in Chappaqua. People pulled out their cell phones to text friends or discreetly shoot photos of me getting ready to vote. I walked over to the table staffed by diligent volunteers and signed my name in the book of eligible voters. We joked about whether I had identification to prove I was really me. (They didn't make me produce a photo ID, but many Americans would have to do so, and too many would be turned away that day.)

Campaigns are full of minor annoyances and major frustrations, but at the end of the day, it's inspiring to watch our democracy whir into action. When all the arguments are made and rallies are finished and TV ads have aired, it comes down to regular people lining up and having their say. I've always loved that quip from Winston Churchill about how democracy is the worst form of government—except for all the others. I still believe that, even when our system feels totally nuts. (Electoral College, I'm looking at you!)

It's quite something to see your name on a ballot. After twenty months, twelve debates, and more speeches and town halls than I could count, it all came down to this. All over the country, 136 million people were going to look at my name and Donald Trump's name and make a decision that would shape the future of the country and the world.

Before I could mark my ballot, a woman walked up and asked if I would take a selfie with her. (There really are no boundaries for the selfie obsession—not even the sanctity of voting is off limits!) I told her I would be delighted to, as soon as I was finished voting. I filled in the bubbles by my name and the down-ballot candidates, walked the ballot over to the scanner, slid it in, and watched it disappear.

I felt pride, humility, and nerves. Pride because I knew we had given everything we had. Humility because I knew the campaign would be the easy part; governing in this contentious time would be hard. And nerves because elections are always unpredictable. Most of the polling and analysis looked positive. The day before, my chief pollster, Joel Benenson sent me an encouraging report. He said I was leading Trump by 5 points in a direct head-to-head, and by 4 points when third parties were factored in. "You're going to bring this home," Joel told me. Still, I knew our campaign faced hurricane-force headwinds, thanks to Comey and the Russians. Anything was possible.

Voting turned out to be the highlight of the day.

When we arrived at the Peninsula Hotel in the late afternoon, the word was, "Things are looking good." The streets were clogged with police officers and Secret Service agents. Our hotel was just a block away from Trump Tower. Both candidates would be within a stone's throw from each other as the results came in.

I tried to keep my head clear. Unlike my husband, who devours every exit poll and stray anecdote on Election Days, I didn't want to hear it. I'm not convinced the breathless reporting during the day is reliable. And why stress about something you can no longer do anything about? In a few hours, we would all know the outcome.

For weeks, I had been carrying around heavy binders full of memos relating to the transition and the first decisions I would have to make as President Elect. There were Cabinet Secretaries to pick, a White House staff to hire, and a legislative agenda to begin working on with Congress. I loved diving into the details of governing, but in the homestretch of the campaign, it was hard to focus on anything past Election

Day. Late at night, I would set aside time before bed to read a transition memo or review a few résumés. Sometimes I'd fall asleep halfway through. Other times I'd get fired up and call my team with some idea or plan I wanted us to get ready to pursue on Day One.

On Election Day, with the campaign all but finished, I had a chance to think in earnest about the work ahead. It was exciting. The hundreds of detailed policies we had proposed over the past twenty months hadn't gotten the press attention they deserved, but they provided a solid foundation for getting right to work tackling the nation's problems. I decided that first out of the gate would be an ambitious infrastructure program to create jobs while improving our roads, rails, airports, ports, mass transit systems, and broadband networks. There was a good chance the Democrats would retake the Senate, but I expected to face a hostile Republican majority in the House. In theory, infrastructure should have bipartisan appeal, but we'd learned that partisanship could overwhelm everything. So outreach would have to start right away.

The challenge went well beyond rounding up enough Republican votes to pass an infrastructure package. The election had further divided our country in troubling ways. Trust in government and in our fellow Americans was at historic lows. We were yelling at one another across deep fault lines of class, race, gender, region, and party. It would be my job to try to help bridge those divides and bring the country together. No President could do it alone, but it was important to set the right tone from the beginning. And I knew the press was poised to judge my transition and first hundred days on the basis of how well I reached out to disaffected Trump voters.

My first test—and opportunity—would be the speech on election night, which would be watched by tens of millions of Americans. It would be my final act as a candidate and my first act as President Elect. The advance staff, led by Greg Hale, had built an amazing set in the Javits Center in Midtown Manhattan. I would walk out beneath an actual glass ceiling and stand on a stage the shape of America. The podium would be right over Texas. When the votes were counted, we hoped the symbolic glass ceiling would be shattered forever. I had been thinking about what I wanted to say for a few weeks. My speechwriters Dan Schwerin and Megan Rooney had been working with Jake Sullivan and Jennifer Palmieri on a draft. I knew they also had a draft concession speech under way as well, but I preferred not to think much about that.

Once I got settled in our suite on the top floor of the Peninsula, I asked Dan and Megan to come up. Bill and Jake joined us, and we sat in a small office going over the latest draft. One challenge was how to balance the need to reach out to Trump voters and sound a note of reconciliation, while also giving my supporters the triumphant victory celebration they deserved. There was also history to consider. If everything went as we hoped, I would be giving this speech as the first woman elected President. We had to find a way to mark the significance of the moment without letting it overwhelm everything else.

Most of all, I wanted to reassure Americans about the strength of our democracy. The election had tested our faith in many ways. Trump had violated every norm in the book, including warning that he might not accept the results of the vote if it went against him. The Russians had interfered. So had the Director of the FBI, against long-standing Justice Department policy. And the news media had turned the whole thing into an absurd circus. A lot of Americans wondered what it all meant for our future. I wanted to answer those fears with a strong victory, a smooth transition, and an effective presidency that delivered real results. Winning with a broad coalition would help counter the idea that the country was hopelessly divided. I would argue that despite our differences, a strong majority of Americans had come together in defense of our core values.

We worked on an opening for the speech that would convey that confidence. The election, I would say, showed that "we will not be defined only by our differences. We will not be an 'us versus them' country. The American dream is big enough for everyone." I would promise to be a President for *all* Americans, not just those who voted for me, and

I'd talk about how much I had learned over the course of the campaign by listening to people share their frustrations. I would be candid
about how hard it had been to respond to the anger many felt and how
painful it was to see our country so divided. But, I'd say, the outcome
showed that "if you dig deep enough, through all the mud of politics,
eventually you hit something hard and true: a foundation of fundamental values that unite us as Americans."

I wanted to end the speech on a personal note. Throughout the
campaign, my mother's story had been an emotional touchstone. Her
perseverance spoke to the perseverance our country needed to over-
come its own adversity, as well as the long struggle for women's rights
and opportunities. With help from the poet Jorie Graham, we had
written a closing riff for the speech that made me tear up every time
I read it. I want to share it here because, as you know, I never got a
chance to deliver it that night:

> This summer, a writer asked me: If I could go back in time and
> tell anyone in history about this milestone, who would it be?
> And the answer was easy: my mother Dorothy. You may have
> heard me talk about her difficult childhood. She was aban-
> doned by her parents when she was just eight years old. They
> put her on a train to California, where she was mistreated by
> her grandparents and ended up out on her own, working as a
> housemaid. Yet she still found a way to offer me the boundless
> love and support she never received herself . . .
>
> I think about my mother every day. Sometimes I think
> about her on that train. I wish I could walk down the aisle
> and find the little wooden seats where she sat, holding tight to
> her even younger sister, alone, terrified. She doesn't yet know
> how much she will suffer. She doesn't yet know she will find
> the strength to escape that suffering—that is still a long way
> off. The whole future is still unknown as she stares out at the

vast country moving past her. I dream of going up to her, and sitting down next to her, taking her in my arms, and saying, "Look at me. Listen to me. You will survive. You will have a good family of your own, and three children. And as hard as it might be to imagine, your daughter will grow up and become the President of the United States."

I am as sure of this as anything I have ever known: America is the greatest country in the world. And, from tonight, going forward, together we will make America even greater than it has ever been—for each and every one of us.

The speechwriters went off to make final revisions, and I went back to the waiting game. The polls were starting to close on the East Coast, and results were coming in.

The first warning sign was North Carolina. President Obama had won it in 2008 but lost narrowly in 2012. We had campaigned aggressively there. Now things weren't looking good. It was early still, but black and Latino turnout wasn't as high as we'd hoped, and working-class white precincts likely to go for Trump seemed energized. The same was happening in Florida, the battleground state that in 2000 had decided the entire election. We had been hopeful that this time Florida would be the state that broke the Republicans' back and put our goal of 270 electoral votes within reach. The state's changing demographics, especially its growing Puerto Rican population around Orlando, as well as the pre–Election Day early vote numbers, seemed favorable to us. But when my campaign manager, Robby Mook, came into our suite with the latest numbers, I could tell he was nervous. Robby is as positive a person as you'll ever meet, so I figured the news must be bleak.

Soon the same story was replicated in other key states. In Ohio, the state that decided the 2004 election, things were downright bad. But we had expected that. I reminded myself we didn't have to win everywhere. We just needed to get to 270. Robby and John Podesta kept me and Bill up to date, but there wasn't much to say. All we could do was watch and wait.

Bill was full of nervous energy, chomping on an unlit cigar, calling our longtime friend Governor Terry McAuliffe in Virginia every ten minutes, and eagerly soaking up any information Robby could share. Chelsea and Marc were a calming presence, but they too were on edge. How could you not be? The waiting was excruciating. I decided to do the least likely thing in the world and take a nap. Hopefully, when I woke up, the picture would have improved. I was so bone-tired that even with all the stress, I was able to close my eyes and fall right asleep.

When I got up, the mood in the hotel had darkened considerably. Robby and John looked shaken. Old friends had gathered. Maggie Williams, Cheryl Mills, and Capricia Marshall were there. My brothers and their families were around. Someone sent out for whiskey. Someone else found ice cream—every flavor in the hotel kitchen.

I had won Virginia and Colorado, but Florida, North Carolina, Ohio, and Iowa were all long gone. Now all eyes were on Michigan, Pennsylvania, and Wisconsin, states that we'd counted on and that Democrats had won in every presidential election since 1992. We were getting killed in heavily white, working-class rural and exurban areas. To compensate, we had to run up big margins in the cities, especially Philadelphia, Pittsburgh, Detroit, and Milwaukee, and then everything would be decided in the suburbs. As the hours slipped by, the numbers got worse. Some of the urban precincts were slow to report, but it was getting harder and harder to see how we could find enough votes.

How had this happened? Certainly we'd faced an avalanche of challenges throughout the campaign. Jim Comey's letter eleven days before had knocked the wind out of us. But I thought we had clawed our way back. Things had felt good out on the road. The energy and enthusiasm had been electric. And all our models—as well as all the public polls and predictions—gave us an excellent chance at victory. Now it was slipping away. I felt shell-shocked. I hadn't prepared mentally for this at all. There had been no doomsday scenarios playing out in my head in the final days, no imagining what I might say if I lost. I just didn't think about it. But now it was as real as could be, and I was struggling to get my head around it. It was like all the air in the room had been sucked away, and I could barely breathe.

Not long after midnight, the Associated Press reported that I had won Nevada, which was a relief, and I had a good chance to prevail in New Hampshire, but it wouldn't be enough without Michigan, Wisconsin, and Pennsylvania. The experts were telling us that it might be so close that we'd need a recount or at least another day to sort everything out. After 1:00 A.M., I asked John Podesta to go over to the Javits Center to ask our supporters to go home and get some rest. Win, lose, or draw, I'd wait until Wednesday morning to speak.

Around the same time, John and I both got messages from the White House. President Obama was concerned that drawing out the process would be bad for the country. After so much hand-wringing about Trump undermining our democracy by not pledging to accept the results, the pressure was on us to do it right. If I was going to lose, the President wanted me to concede quickly and gracefully. It was hard to think straight, but I agreed with him. Certainly that's what I would have wanted had the shoe been on the other foot.

At 1:35 A.M., the AP called Pennsylvania for Trump. That was pretty much the ball game. Even with Wisconsin and Michigan outstanding, it was getting impossible to see a path to victory.

Soon there were reports that Trump was preparing to go to his own victory party at the nearby Hilton Hotel. It was time. I decided to make the call.

"Donald, it's Hillary." It was without a doubt one of the strangest moments of my life. I congratulated Trump and offered to do anything

I could to make sure the transition was smooth. He said nice things about my family and our campaign. He may have said something about how hard it must have been to make the call, but it's all a blur now, so I can't say for certain. It was all perfectly nice and weirdly ordinary, like calling a neighbor to say you can't make it to his barbecue. It was mercifully brief.

Then I called President Obama. "I'm sorry for letting you down," I told him. My throat tightened. The President said everything right. He told me I'd run a strong campaign, that I had done a great deal for our country, that he was proud of me. He told me there was life after losing and that he and Michelle would be there for me. I hung up and sat quietly for a few moments. I was numb. It was all so shocking.

At 2:29 A.M., the AP called Wisconsin and the election for Trump. He went on TV not long afterward to declare victory.

I sat in the dining room of my hotel suite, surrounded by people I loved and trusted. They were all in as much pain and shock as I was. Just like that, everything we had worked for was gone.

It looked like I was going to win the popular vote, maybe by a significant margin. There was some comfort in that fact. It meant that a majority of Americans hadn't embraced Trump's "us versus them" campaign, and that despite all our troubles, more people chose our platform and vision for the future. I had been rejected—but also affirmed. It was surreal.

I blamed myself. My worst fears about my limitations as a candidate had come true. I had tried to learn the lessons of 2008, and in many ways ran a better, smarter campaign this time. But I had been unable to connect with the deep anger so many Americans felt or shake the perception that I was the candidate of the status quo. And look what they'd thrown at me. I wasn't just running against Donald Trump. I was up against the Russian intelligence apparatus, a misguided FBI director, and now the godforsaken Electoral College. Yes, we knew the rules going in. We knew the states we had to win. Yet, it was infuriating that for the second time in five elections, a Democrat would win more votes but be robbed by this archaic fluke of our constitutional system. I'd been saying since 2000 that the Electoral College gave disproportionate power to less populated states and therefore was profoundly undemocratic. It made a mockery of the principle of "One person, one vote." In a cruel twist of fate, the Founders had also created it as a bulwark against foreign interference in our democracy—Alexander Hamilton cited protecting against foreign influence as a justification for the Electoral College in Federalist Paper No. 68—and now it was handing victory to Vladimir Putin's preferred candidate.

In my head, I heard the vicious "Lock her up!" chants that had echoed through Trump's rallies. In our second debate, Trump had said that if he won, he'd send me to prison. Now he *had* won. I had no idea what to expect.

The speechwriters gingerly approached with a draft of a concession speech. I honestly wondered why anyone would want to hear from me ever again.

The draft was too combative. It spoke to the fears of millions of Americans about a new President who had campaigned on bigotry and resentment. It said that they weren't alone, that I would keep fighting for them even now that the election was over. Did people even want me to fight for them? Was there any point in making an argument now? Maybe I should just be gracious, concede, and walk away.

Jake pushed back. Yes, he said, being gracious is important. But if we believe what we've said for the past six months about the dangers this guy poses to our country, then you can't act like that's not true anymore. People are scared and worried about what he'll do to their families. They want to hear from you.

A spirited discussion ensued. Eventually I asked the speechwriters to take another crack at a draft that was shorter and more gracious but not sugarcoated.

Bill was watching Trump's speech on television. He couldn't believe it. Neither could I. Eventually everyone left, and it was just us.

I hadn't cried yet, wasn't sure if I would. But I felt deeply and thoroughly exhausted, like I hadn't slept in ten years. We lay down on the bed and stared at the ceiling. Bill took my hand, and we just lay there.

In the morning, it was real. November 9 dawned raw and rainy. I tried to drink some orange juice, but I didn't have any appetite. I had a job to do. That's what I focused on. By the light of day, I saw more clearly what I needed to say.

The speechwriters came back with a new draft, and I told them I wanted to talk more about what it means to be a democracy. Yes, the peaceful transfer of power was one of our most important traditions—and the mere fact of my conceding honored that. But there's also the rule of law, equality, and freedom. We respect and cherish these things too, and we had to defend them. "Donald Trump is going to be our President," I would say. "We owe him an open mind and the chance to lead." But I would also challenge my supporters and all Americans to keep working for our vision of a better, stronger, fairer America. I was determined that my young staff and supporters not become discouraged. "This loss hurts," I would tell them. "But please, please never stop believing that fighting for what's right is worth it. It is always worth it."

Finally, I wanted to speak directly to the women and girls who had put their faith in me and my campaign. It pained me to think of how they must be feeling. Instead of making history and electing the first woman President, they now had to face a stinging rebuke and come to terms with the fact that the country had just elected someone who objectified women and bragged about sexual assault. A lot of women—and men—were waking up that morning asking whether America was still the country we had thought it was. Would there be a place for them in Trump's America? Would they be safe? Would they be valued and respected?

I couldn't answer those questions. I was asking them myself. But I could use this one last moment on the national stage to tell them how proud I had been to be their champion. I could say that while we didn't break that highest glass ceiling this time, "someday someone will—hopefully sooner than we might think right now." And I could say to all the little girls out there, with every ounce of conviction in my body: "Never doubt that you are valuable and powerful and deserving of every chance and opportunity in the world."

I got dressed and gathered my things. "One day you're going to have to show me pictures of what the stage looked like last night," I told Huma.

"It looked amazing," she replied, "built for a President."

It was time to go. The country was waiting, and this wasn't going to get any easier.

I thought about my mother. There was a time when I was very little, and a neighborhood bully started pushing me around. I ran home to hide, but my mother met me at the door. "There's no room for cowards in this house," she said. "Go back out there." The walk from my front door back to the street was one of the longest of my life. But I went. Mom was right, as usual.

I gathered my family, took a deep breath, and walked out the door.

Victory has a hundred fathers, but defeat is an orphan.

—John F. Kennedy

Why

I've spent part of nearly every day since November 8, 2016, wrestling with a single question: Why did I lose? Sometimes it's hard to focus on anything else.

I go back over my own shortcomings and the mistakes we made. I take responsibility for all of them. You can blame the data, blame the message, blame anything you want—but I was the candidate. It was my campaign. Those were my decisions.

I also think about the strong headwinds we faced, including the rise of tribal politics in America and across the globe, the restlessness of a country looking for change, excessive coverage of my emails, the unprecedented late intervention by the director of the FBI, the sophisticated misinformation campaign directed from the Kremlin, and the avalanche of fake news. Those aren't excuses—they're things that happened, whether we like it or not.

I think about all that, and about our deeply divided country and our ability to live, work, and reason together.

And that's all before I finish my morning cup of coffee. Then it starts over again.

In the spring of 2017, I was asked by thoughtful journalists such as Nicholas Kristof, Christiane Amanpour, Rebecca Traister, and Kara Swisher to reflect on what happened in 2016 and what lessons all Americans—and Democrats in particular—can learn from my defeat.

This is an important discussion to have. It's not only about the past—not by a long shot. After successfully interfering in one presidential election, Russia will certainly try to do it again. And Democrats are engaged in a vital debate right now about the future of our party, which turns in no small part on the question of what went wrong in 2016 and how to fix it.

Here's an example of the sort of questions I was getting:

"Could the campaign have been better?" Christiane Amanpour asked me. "Where was your message? Do you take any personal responsibility?"

"I take absolute personal responsibility," I replied. "I was the candidate. I was the person who was on the ballot." Then I explained that while we didn't run a perfect campaign, Nate Silver, the widely respected statistician who correctly predicted the winner in 49 states in 2008 and all 50 in 2012, has said that we were on our way to winning until Jim Comey's October 28 letter derailed us. You can agree or disagree with that analysis, but it's what Silver's data said.

The reaction to my interviews was negative, to put it mildly.

"Dear Hillary Clinton, please stop talking about 2016," wrote one columnist in *USA Today*. CNN, still stuck in false equivalency mode, declared, "Clinton, Trump can't stop airing their 2016 grievances." And one *New York Daily News* columnist decided the appropriate response was: "Hey, Hillary Clinton, shut the f— up and go away already." Seriously, they printed that in the newspaper.

I understand why some people don't want to hear anything that sounds remotely like "relitigating" the election. People are tired. Some are traumatized. Others are focused on keeping the discussion about Russia in the national security realm and away from politics. I get all that. But it's important that we understand what really happened. Because that's the only way we can stop it from happening again.

I also understand why there's an insatiable demand in many quarters for me to take all the blame for losing the election on my own shoulders and quit talking about Comey, the Russians, fake news, sexism, or anything else. Many in the political media don't want to hear about how these things tipped the election in the final days. They say their beef is that I'm not taking responsibility for my mistakes—but I have, and I do again throughout this book. Their real problem is they can't bear to face their own role in helping elect Trump, from providing him free airtime to giving my emails three times more coverage than all the issues affecting people's lives combined.

Other candidates who have lost the presidency have been allowed—even encouraged—to discuss what went wrong and why. After John Kerry lost the election in 2004, he quite reasonably said that the release of a tape from Osama bin Laden a day before the election had a significant effect on the outcome of the race. The press was interested in what he had to say. They want me to stop talking.

If it's all my fault, then the media doesn't need to do any soul searching. Republicans can say Putin's meddling had no consequences. Democrats don't need to question their own assumptions and prescriptions. Everyone can just move on.

I wish it were that easy. But it's not. So I'm going to try to explain how I understand what happened, both the unexpected interventions that swung the race at the end, and the structural challenges that made it close to begin with. You don't have to agree with my take. But counter with evidence, with a real argument. Because we have to get this right.

Here goes.

Common Critiques

The election was decided by 77,744 votes out of a total 136 million cast. If just 40,000 people across Wisconsin, Michigan, and Pennsylvania had changed their minds, I would have won. With a margin like that, everyone can have a pet theory about why I lost. It's difficult to rule anything out. But every theory needs to be tested against the evidence that I was winning until October 28, when Jim Comey injected emails back into the election.

For example, some critics have said that everything hinged on me not campaigning enough in the Midwest. And I suppose it is possible that a few more trips to Saginaw or a few more ads on the air in Waukesha could have tipped a couple thousand votes here and there.

But let's set the record straight. We always knew that the industrial Midwest was crucial to our success, just as it had been for Democrats for decades, and contrary to the popular narrative, we didn't ignore those states. In Pennsylvania, where public and private polls showed a competitive race similar to 2012, we had nearly 500 staff on the ground, 120 more than the Obama campaign deployed four years before. We spent 211 percent more on television ads in the state. And I held more than twenty-five campaign events there during the general election. We also blanketed Pennsylvania with high-profile surrogates like President Obama and Vice President Biden. In Michigan, where the polls showed us ahead but not by as much as we'd like, we had nearly 140 more staff on the ground than Obama did in 2012, and spent 166 percent more on television. I visited seven times during the general election. We lost both states, but no one can say we weren't doing everything possible to compete and win.

If there's one place where we were caught by surprise, it was Wisconsin. Polls showed us comfortably ahead, right up until the end. They also looked good for the Democrat running for Senate, Russ Feingold.

We had 133 staff on the ground and spent nearly $3 million on TV, but if our data (or anyone else's) had shown we were in danger, of course we would have invested even more. I would have torn up my schedule, which was designed based on the best information we had, and camped out there. As it is, while I didn't visit Wisconsin in the fall, Tim Kaine, Joe Biden, Bernie Sanders, and other high-profile surrogates did. So what went wrong? We'll get to that. But bear in mind that Trump received roughly the same number of votes in Wisconsin that Mitt Romney did. There was no surge in Republican turnout. Instead, enough voters switched, stayed home, or went for third parties in the final days to cost me the state.

Here's the bottom line: I campaigned heavily across Pennsylvania, had an aggressive ground game and lots of advertising, and still lost by 44,000 votes, more than the margin in Wisconsin and Michigan combined. So it's just not credible that the best explanation for the outcome in those states—and therefore the election—was where I held rallies.

Another easy explanation that doesn't stand up to scrutiny is that I lost because I didn't have an economic message. Joe Biden said the Democratic Party in 2016 "did not talk about what it always stood for—and that was how to maintain a burgeoning middle class." He said, "You didn't hear a single solitary sentence in the last campaign about that guy working on the assembly line making sixty thousand bucks a year and a wife making $32,000 as a hostess in a restaurant." I find this fairly remarkable, considering that Joe himself campaigned for me all over the Midwest and talked plenty about the middle class.

Also, it's just not true. Not even close. *Vox* did an analysis of all my campaign events and found that I talked about jobs, workers, and the economy far more than anything else. As the *Atlantic* put it in a piece titled, "The Dangerous Myth That Hillary Clinton Ignored the Working Class," I ran on "the most comprehensively progressive economic platform of any presidential candidate in history" and talked more about jobs in my convention speech than Trump did in his, as well as in our first debate, which was watched by eighty-four million people.

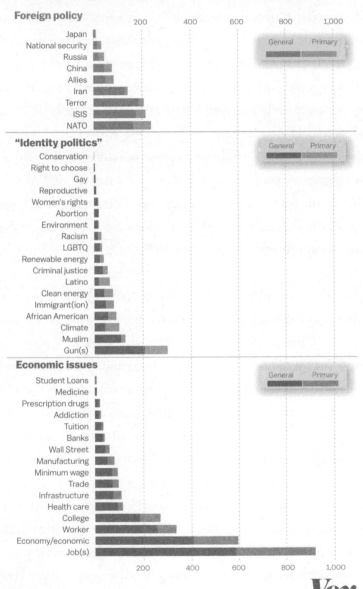

Word frequency of Clinton's speeches

Throughout the campaign we always tried to have a positive track of advertising on the air, laying out what I was for and where we needed to go economically. We did that even when we were also running spots highlighting Trump's unfitness for office. We actually filmed one ad outside the Milwaukee offices of a company called Johnson Controls, which was trying to get out of paying taxes in America by moving its headquarters overseas—what's known as a "corporate inversion." It was so cold that day I could barely feel my feet, but I insisted on doing it because I was furious about the shell game the company was playing at the expense of its workers and the American people. I talked about Johnson Controls' tax scheme virtually every day on the trail for months. So we can debate whether my economic message was effective, but you can't claim I didn't have one.

Here's one story that helps explain why this is so frustrating. The day after I accepted the nomination in Philadelphia, Bill and I hit the road with Tim Kaine and his wife, Anne, for a bus tour through factory towns across Pennsylvania and Ohio. It reminded me of our exhilarating bus trip in 1992 with Al and Tipper Gore. That was one of my favorite weeks of the entire '92 campaign. We met hardworking people, saw gorgeous country, and everywhere we went we felt the energy of a country ready for change. Twenty-four years later, I wanted to recapture that. We loaded onto our big blue bus, with "Stronger Together" emblazoned on the sides, and set out on a 635-mile journey. At every stop, Tim and I talked about plans to create jobs, raise wages, and support working families. In Johnstown, Pennsylvania, in rural Cambria County, we shared our ideas with steelworkers in a factory manufacturing wire for heavy industry. Afterward, one of the workers, a crane operator, told a reporter for the *Philadelphia Inquirer* that he didn't usually vote in presidential elections but might turn out this time because he liked what he heard. "I liked the idea of trying to get better wages for working-class people," he said. "We need them." It was music to my ears.

But you probably don't remember hearing anything about this bus tour. In fact, you may well have heard that I didn't campaign like this at all; that I ignored the Rust Belt, didn't have an economic message, and couldn't connect with working-class voters. Why the disconnect? The very same week that Tim and I were driving around Pennsylvania and Ohio, Donald Trump was picking a high-profile fight with the Khans, the grieving Gold Star parents of a fallen Muslim American war hero. That sucked up all the oxygen in the media. It was a short-term disaster for Trump, and his poll numbers tumbled. But it was also part of a pattern that over the long-term ensured that my economic message never got out and let Trump control the tempo of the race.

Was I Doomed from the Start?

Some pundits have also said my campaign was doomed from the start, either because of my weaknesses as a candidate or because America was caught up in a historic wave of angry, tribal populism sweeping the world. Maybe. But don't forget that I won the popular vote by nearly three million, roughly the same margin by which George W. Bush defeated John Kerry in 2004. It's hard to see how that happens if I'm hopelessly out of step with the American people.

Still, as I've discussed throughout this book, I do think it's fair to say there was a fundamental mismatch between how I approach politics and what a lot of the country wanted to hear in 2016. I've learned that even the best plans and proposals can land on deaf ears when people are disillusioned by a broken political system and disgusted with politicians. When people are angry and looking for someone to blame, they don't want to hear your ten-point plan to create jobs and raise wages. They want you to be angry, too.

You can see the same dynamic in a lot of personal relationships. I have friends who often get frustrated with their spouses who, instead of listening to them vent about a problem and commiserating, jump straight into trying to solve it. That was my problem with many voters: I skipped the venting and went straight to the solving.

Moreover, I have come to terms with the fact that a lot of people—millions and millions of people—decided they just didn't like me. Imagine what that feels like. It hurts. And it's a hard thing to accept. But there's no getting around it.

Whenever I do a job, such as Senator or Secretary of State, people give me high ratings. But when I compete for a job—by running for office—everything changes. People remember years of partisan attacks that have painted me as dishonest and untrustworthy. Even when they're disproven, those attacks leave a residue. I've always tried to keep my head down and do good work and hope to be judged by the results. That's usually worked, but not this time.

It seems as if many Trump voters were actually voting *against* me, more than they were voting *for* him (53 percent to 44 percent, in a September Pew Research Center poll). In exit polls, a significant number of people said they thought Trump was unqualified or lacked the temperament to be President . . . yet voted for him anyway. Of the 61 percent of all voters who said he was unqualified, 17 percent still voted for him. Of the 63 percent who said he didn't have the right temperament, 19 percent voted for him. The exit polls found that 18 percent of all voters viewed both me and Trump negatively, but they went for him 47 percent to 30 percent. Their antipathy toward me must have been even stronger than their concerns about his qualifications and temperament.

I'm not surprised by these findings. Gallup compiled a word cloud depicting everything Americans read, saw, or heard about me during several months of the campaign. It was dominated by a single giant word: *email.* Much smaller, but also visible were the words *lie* and *scandal.* Interestingly, in Trump's word cloud, immigration and Mexico stand out much more than jobs or trade. More on that shortly.

I don't believe all the negative feelings about me were inevitable. After all, I had high approval ratings when I left the State Department. This was the result of a relentless barrage of political attacks and negative coverage. But I also know that it was my job to try to break through all that noise and convince the American people to vote for me. I wasn't able to do it.

What Americans Have Heard or Read About Donald Trump

What specifically do you recall reading, hearing or seeing about Donald Trump in the last day or two?

GALLUP DAILY TRACKING
JULY 17–SEPT 18, 2016

What Americans Have Heard or Read About Hillary Clinton

What specifically do you recall reading, hearing or seeing about Hillary Clinton in the last day or two?

GALLUP DAILY TRACKING
JULY 17–SEPT 18, 2016

So yes, I had my shortcomings as a candidate. And yes, there was indeed a global populist wave and an anti–third term tradition in America. But—and this is important for determining what tilted the outcome of the election—those structural factors didn't pop up as a big surprise at the end. They were in play throughout the campaign. They probably kept the race closer than was justified based on our contrasting policy proposals and conduct, my record in public office, and the achievements of the Obama administration. If these factors were decisive, however, I should have been behind the whole way. And yet, despite consistent headwinds, nearly every public and private poll over two years showed me ahead, often way ahead.

By the homestretch, after two conventions and three debates watched by record numbers of Americans, I had emerged with clear momentum and a solid lead. *Vox*'s Ezra Klein called it "the most effective series of debate performances in modern political history." I was in a stronger position than President Obama had been four years before. So either all those surveys over all those months were wrong, or something changed in the final days of the race to shift enough voters in key states to make a difference.

Were all the polls wrong? We know now that some surveys were off, especially in Wisconsin, especially at the end. It's likely that some Trump voters refused to participate in surveys and so their feedback was missed, and that some people weren't truthful about their preferences. But overall, national polls in 2016 were slightly more accurate than they were in 2012. That year, the final polling average understated President Obama's actual victory by 3.1 points. In 2016, according to the website RealClearPolitics, the final average was off by just 1.2 points. In a race this close, that's not nothing. But it's hardly a massive error.

So no, all the polls weren't wrong. It's possible that my lead throughout the race was slightly overstated—but not significantly. It's reasonable to conclude, therefore, that something important and ultimately decisive happened at the very end.

The Bottom Falls Out

The evidence backs up the idea that there was a late shift away from me and toward Trump and third-party candidates. My support was strong in early voting across the country, and early-vote turnout roughly matched what our models predicted. But things collapsed in the final days and on Election Day itself.

In real time, it was hard to appreciate how fragile our position was. As I mentioned earlier, Joel Benenson's polling showed a solid lead in the final week. Our data analytics team was also surveying thousands of people each night. "We have seen our margins tighten across the battleground states," Elan Kriegel reported on November 3. But, he continued, "our national toplines have been +3 each of the last four nights." We were up by the same 3-point margin in Michigan, Wisconsin, and Pennsylvania, he said. Democratic Senate campaigns and party committees were seeing similar numbers, and some were even more optimistic.

Exit polls would later find that voters who were still making up their minds in those final days broke strongly for Trump. In Pennsylvania, a state with no early voting allowed at all, the margin among late-deciders was 54 to 37. In Wisconsin, where 72 percent of people voted on Election Day, it was 59 to 30. In Michigan, where 73 percent of people voted on Election Day, it was 50 to 39. And the pattern extended beyond the Midwest. In Florida, late-deciders went for Trump 55 to 38. That late surge was enough to put all these states in Trump's column.

Normally, campaigns have a decent sense of how undecided voters are likely to break, based on their past vote history and demographics. And history shows that most people who tell pollsters they're considering a third-party candidate will "come home" in the end. In the final days of the 2016 campaign, the voters you would expect to return to the Republican Party did so. But that didn't happen on our side. Many Democratic-leaning voters flirting with third-party candidates ended up actually pulling the lever for them. And some undecided voters we expected to ultimately choose us went to Trump instead or stayed home.

That included suburban moderates who might have voted for Republicans in the past but didn't like Trump and had been looking for an acceptable alternative right up until the end. On Election Day, a lot of them held their noses and voted for him anyway. It's revealing to compare the results in the suburbs of Denver and Las Vegas, where the vast majority vote early and I did well enough to carry both Colorado and Nevada, with the results in the Philadelphia suburbs, where nearly everyone voted on Election Day. The final Franklin & Marshall Poll in Pennsylvania, based on interviews nearly all conducted before October 28, found I had a 36-point margin over Trump in the four counties of the Philadelphia suburbs, leading 64 percent to 28 percent. By Election Day, I only beat Trump there by about 13 points. That loss of suburban support in the final week meant I couldn't match Trump's strength in rural areas and ended up narrowly losing the state.

Working-class white women also moved en masse in the final days. Trump led among this group nearly the whole campaign, but according to the NBC–*Wall Street Journal* poll, I had closed to within just 4 points during the October debates. Then, in the final week, Trump's margin grew to 24 points.

The Comey Effect

What happened in the homestretch that caused so many voters to turn away from me?

First, and most importantly, there was the unprecedented intervention by then FBI Director Jim Comey.

His October 28 letter about the investigation into my emails led to a week of wall-to-wall negative coverage. A look at five of the nation's top newspapers found that together they published 100 stories mentioning the email controversy in the days after Comey's letter, nearly half of them on the front page. In six out of seven mornings from October 29 to November 4, it was the lead story in the nation's news cycle. Trump understood that Comey's apparent imprimatur gave his "Crooked Hillary" attacks new credibility, and Republicans dumped at least $17 million in Comey-related ads into the battleground states. It worked.

On November 1 and 2, my campaign conducted focus groups with independent, swing voters in Philadelphia and Tampa, Florida. The undecideds weren't ready to jump to Trump yet, but in retrospect, the warning signs were blinking red. "I have concerns about this whole Weiner thing. I find it unsettling. I had been leaning toward Hillary, but now I just don't know," said one Florida voter. "I was never a fan of either one, but this email thing with Clinton has me concerned the past few days. Will they elect her and then impeach her? Was she giving away secret information?" said another.

Outside focus groups were hearing similar things. Researchers who track what consumers are talking about, essentially a word-of-mouth index, found "a sudden change," with a 17-point drop in net sentiment for me, and an 11-point rise for Trump. According to Brad Fay of Engagement Labs, which applies well-established consumer research techniques to study elections, "The change in word-of-mouth favorability metric was stunning, and much greater than the traditional opinion polling revealed."

Those concerns we heard in the focus groups help explain why Comey's letter was so devastating. From the beginning of the general election, we had understood the race to be a contest between voters' fear of risk and desire for change. Convincing Americans that electing Trump was just too big a risk was our best shot at overpowering the widespread desire for a change after eight years of Democratic control. In demographic terms, our strategy depended on compensating for expected weakness with working-class white voters (a trend that had been getting worse for Democrats for a long time) by doing better among college-educated suburban moderates—precisely the people most likely to be concerned about risk.

Before October 28, there was every reason to believe this strategy would work. Voters thought Trump was unqualified and temperamentally unfit. They worried he might blunder into a war. And they thought I was steady, qualified, and safe. Comey's letter turned that picture upside down. Now voters were worried my presidency would be dogged by more investigations, maybe even impeachment. It was "unsettling," as that Florida voter put it. When both candidates seemed risky, then the desire for change reasserted itself and undecideds shifted to Trump or a third party.

In the week that followed Comey's letter, Nate Silver found that my lead in national polling dropped by about 3 points, and my chances of winning the election shrunk from 81 percent to 65 percent. In the average battleground state, my lead was down to just 1.7 points—and the fact that there were few if any polls still in the field that late in the game in places such as Wisconsin meant that the damage could easily have been worse.

Then, on the Sunday afternoon before Election Day, Comey sent another letter explaining that, in fact, there was no new evidence to change his conclusion from July. By then it was too late. If anything, that second letter may have energized Trump supporters even more and made them more likely to turn out and vote against me. It also guaranteed that undecided voters saw two more days of headlines about emails and investigations.

Hours after Comey's second letter hit the news, Trump whipped up the outrage in a rally in Michigan: "Hillary Clinton is guilty. She knows it. The FBI knows it. The people know it," he said. "Now it's up to the American people to deliver justice at the ballot box on November 8." The crowd responded with loud chants of "Lock her up!"

Corey Lewandowski, Trump's former campaign manager, credited Comey's letter with reversing his candidate's fortunes. "With eleven days to go in this election cycle something amazing happened," he said. In his new book, *Devil's Bargain: Steve Bannon, Donald Trump, and the Storming of the Presidency*, Bloomberg News reporter Joshua Green reveals that the Trump campaign's data scientists thought the effect of Comey's letter was "pivotal." In an internal memo written five days before Election Day, they reported seeing "declining support for Clinton, shifting in favor of Mr. Trump" and predicted, "This may have a fundamental impact on the results." Sadly, they were right.

Silver, whose model had been more conservative than most throughout the race, concluded, "Clinton would almost certainly be President-Elect if the election had been held on Oct. 27 (the day before the Comey letter)." Professor Sam Wang, who runs the Princeton Election Consortium, called Comey's letter "a critical factor in the home stretch" and found a 4-point swing.

Here's a particularly stark way of understanding the impact: Even if Comey caused just 0.6 percent of Election Day voters to change their votes, and even if that swing only occurred in the Rust Belt, it would have been enough to shift the Electoral College from me to Trump.

This is why Paul Krugman, the Nobel Prize–winning economist and *New York Times* columnist, has started ironically tweeting "Thanks, Comey," every time he sees some new outrage from the Trump White House. Comey made a choice to excoriate me in public in July and then dramatically reopen the investigation on October 28, all while refusing to say a word about Trump and Russia. If not for those decisions, everything would have been different. Comey himself later said that he was "mildly nauseous" at the idea that he influenced the outcome of the election. Hearing that made me sick.

From Russia with No Love

The second big factor that caused the bottom to fall out at the end of the race was the Russian plot to sabotage my campaign and help elect Trump. Michael Morell, the former acting director of the CIA, has described it as "the political equivalent of 9/11."

The emails Russia stole from John Podesta and provided to WikiLeaks ensured that the words *Clinton* and *emails* were in the headlines even before Comey's letter. The subterranean torrent of fake news added to the problem. For voters, the stories merged to create an overpowering fog of scandal and mistrust. Even if there was no fire, there was enough smoke to choke our campaign.

Because no evidence has emerged yet of direct vote tampering, some critics insist that Russian interference had no impact on the outcome at all. This is absurd. The Kremlin's information warfare was roughly equivalent to a hostile super PAC unleashing a major ad campaign, if not worse. Of course it had an impact. (And for those obsessed with actual tampering, since we keep learning more about Russian intrusions into our election systems, maybe this is what the administration and Secretaries of State across the country should be investigating instead of a nonexistent epidemic of voter fraud.)

Nate Silver's website FiveThirtyEight.com looked at Google searches as a measure of how much the WikiLeaks story broke through with actual voters. He found that—except for immediately after Comey sent his letter on October 28—there were more searches about WikiLeaks than the FBI during the final weeks of the race. That did make some sense. The mainstream media provided blanket coverage of Comey, so there was no need to search for more information about that. The WikiLeaks stories, however, could send searchers down deep internet rabbit holes.

Google searches about WikiLeaks were particularly high in swing areas with large numbers of undecided voters, like Cambria County in Pennsylvania and Appleton, Wisconsin. In other words, a lot of people were online trying to get to the bottom of these crazy claims and conspiracy theories before casting their votes. Too often, what they found was more misinformation and Russian-directed propaganda.

Together, the effects of Comey's letter and the Russian attack formed a devastating combination. Silver concluded after the election that if it hadn't been for these two late-breaking factors, I likely would have won Florida, Michigan, Wisconsin, and Pennsylvania by about 2 points. Instead, I lost all four by less than 1 point on average, and Michigan by just two-tenths of a point.

What Explains Trump's Support?

All of this is depressing, infuriating, and ultimately unsatisfying. Outside interference may help explain why enough votes shifted in the final days to give the Electoral College to Trump. But it doesn't explain why the race was close to begin with, close enough that late movement in a few states could make the difference. It doesn't really explain how sixty-two million people—many of whom agreed Trump was unfit for the job—could vote for a man so manifestly unqualified to be President. This may be the more important question for understanding what's going on in our country right now.

Start with the 13.3 million Republicans who voted for Trump in the primaries. It's safe to say these are mostly hard-core supporters—the ones Trump was talking about when he said, "I could stand in the middle of Fifth Avenue and shoot somebody and I wouldn't lose voters." Thirteen million is a lot of people to strongly support someone most Americans think is unqualified and unfit, but they account for less than half of all Republican primary voters and less than 10 percent of all general election voters. It's a mistake to give those base voters more political weight than they deserve. More interesting and important is how Trump consolidated support among the much larger pool of voters beyond his base.

Besides antipathy toward me, probably the biggest factor pushing Trump skeptics into his camp was pure partisanship. There's an old saying that "Democrats fall in love, Republicans fall in line." That was proven true once again in 2016. I won 89 percent of Democratic voters. Despite the example of a few courageous "Never Trumpers," Trump won 90 percent of Republican voters. Many of them preferred a different candidate in the primaries. Many were surely disgusted by his outrageous behavior, including his treatment of women. Yet when it came down to it, the *R* next to his name was more important than anything else. Maybe this was about the Supreme Court, or the assumption that he would end up rubber-stamping the congressional GOP's agenda, especially big tax cuts for the rich. Maybe it reflects a deeper partisan element in our politics.

Either way, it stands in stark contrast to what happened in the French election in 2017, when conservatives and socialists alike crossed party lines and rallied behind centrist Emmanuel Macron to stop the extremist Marine Le Pen. In France, patriotism trumped partisanship. Some analysts say French voters watched what happened here and acted to stop it there. So did the Dutch in their election, defeating the right-wing nationalist Geert Wilders. Of course, it helps when the candidate who gets the most votes wins the election. What an idea! If our voters had known more about what Putin was doing on Trump's behalf, would it have made a difference? All I can say is that I believe Americans are just as patriotic as the French and the Dutch.

Partisanship is powerful, but it was far from the only factor fueling Trump's support. As I noted earlier, a desire for change was also important. Exit polls tell us that 39 percent of voters said the ability to bring change was the most important quality in a candidate, and 82 percent of them supported Trump. By comparison, 22 percent of voters said having the "right experience" was most important, and they went for me 90 to 7. The 20 percent who said "good judgment" was most important supported me 65 to 25. And the 15 percent who wanted a candidate who "cares about me" went 57 to 34 for me. In other words, "change" voters provided the bulk of Trump's support.

Change can mean different things to different people. But as I've noted, this was a challenge I grappled with from the very beginning. History shows how hard it is for a party to hold on to the White House for three terms, even after successful presidencies. I castigated Republican obstruction in Congress and offered lots of solutions to make the economy fairer and politics cleaner, but I never escaped being pigeonholed as the candidate of continuity rather than change. Certainly, if voters wanted to "shake things up" or "burn it all down," they were more likely to choose Donald Trump over me. They weren't in any mood to remember that great old Texas saying from Sam Rayburn, the former Speaker of the House: "Any jackass can kick down a barn. It takes a good carpenter to build one."

In polls throughout the campaign, we asked voters what they thought of President Obama and if they wanted to continue in the same direction or go in a fundamentally different direction. You might expect the answers to be linked. And yet, while voters consistently gave the President high marks—in fact, Obama's popularity continued to rise throughout 2016, as did economic forecasts—they just as consistently said they were ready for a new direction. That may show the power of the impulse for change, but it also shows how complicated this is. One might also ask: Why were the vast majority of members of Congress reelected? Incumbents have advantages and gerrymandering has given many of them safe seats, but if there was a real "throw the bums out" wave in this election, we would have seen it down ballot as well.

So, yes, a desire for change was an important factor, but to understand what this was really about we have to look deeper.

Economic Anxiety or Bigotry

Most postgame analysis has weighed two competing theories: either it was economic anxiety or it was bigotry. A lot of data point toward the latter, but ultimately this is a false choice that misses the complexity of the situation.

Let's start with this: the idea that the 2016 election was purely about economic anxiety just isn't supported by the evidence. There's a perception that Trump was the tribune of the working class while I was the candidate of the elites. And it's true that there was a big divide in this election between voters with a college degree and those without. But this doesn't line up neatly with income levels. There are a lot of middle- and upper-class people without a college degree. As the *Washington Post* explained in a piece titled, "It's Time to Bust the Myth: Most Trump Voters Were Not Working Class," nearly 60 percent of Trump supporters without a college degree were in the top half of the income distribution. The average income of a Trump voter during the primaries was $72,000, which is higher than for most Americans. And in the general election, voters with incomes below $50,000 preferred me by 12 points.

It's surely true that many blue-collar white voters in Rust Belt communities did like what Trump had to say on the economy. Exit polls found that voters who thought the national economy was in poor shape strongly supported Trump. But that wasn't necessarily their most compelling concern. The same exit polls found that voters who thought the economy was the most important issue in the election (52 percent nationwide) preferred me by a margin of 11 points. This was also true in the key battlegrounds. In Michigan, voters who cared most about the economy went for me 51 to 43. In Wisconsin, it was 53 to 42. In Pennsylvania, 50 to 46. To be fair, there are other ways to look at the numbers. Many Trump supporters who told pollsters they cared most passionately about other issues—especially terrorism and immigration—almost certainly preferred Trump on the economy as well. Nonetheless, the story on the economy is a lot more nuanced than the postelection narrative would have you believe.

Some supporters of Bernie Sanders have argued that if I had veered further left and run a more populist campaign we would have done better in the Rust Belt. I don't believe it. Russ Feingold ran a passionately populist campaign for Senate in Wisconsin and lost by much more than I did, while a champion of free trade, Senator Rob Portman, outperformed Trump in Ohio. Scott Walker, the right-wing Governor of Wisconsin, has won elections there by busting unions and catering to the resentments of conservative rural voters, not by denouncing trade deals and corporations. Sanders himself had a chance to test out his appeal during the primaries, and he ended up losing to me by nearly four million votes—including in Ohio and Pennsylvania. And that was without any pummeling by the Republican attack machine that would have savaged him in a general election.

That said, a small but still significant number of left-wing voters may well have thrown the election to Trump. Jill Stein, the Green Party candidate, called me and my policies "much scarier than Donald Trump" and praised his pro-Russia stance. This isn't surprising, considering that Stein sat with Putin and Michael Flynn at the infamous Moscow dinner in 2015 celebrating the Kremlin's propaganda network RT, and later said she and Putin agreed "on many issues." Stein wouldn't be worth mentioning, except for the fact that she won thirty-one thousand votes in Wisconsin, where Trump's margin was smaller than twenty-three thousand. In Michigan, she won fifty-one thousand votes, while Trump's margin was just over ten thousand. In Pennsylvania, she won nearly fifty thousand votes, and Trump's margin was roughly forty-four thousand. So in each state, there were more than enough Stein voters to swing the result, just like Ralph Nader did in Florida and New Hampshire in 2000. Maybe, like actress Susan Sarandon, Stein thinks electing Trump will hasten "the revolution." Who knows? By contrast, former Massachusetts Governor Bill Weld, a Republican who ran for Vice President on the Libertarian ticket topped by Gary Johnson, told his supporters toward the end that if they lived in swing states they should vote for me. If more third-party voters had listened to Bill Weld, Trump would not be President.

So, if arguments about the power of Trump's economic appeal are overstated, what about his exploitation of racial and cultural anxiety?

Since the election, study after study has suggested that these factors are essential to understanding what happened in the election.

In June 2017, the Voter Study Group, a consortium of academic researchers, published a major new survey that tracked the same eight thousand voters from 2012 to 2016. "What stands out most," concluded George Washington University professor John Sides, are "attitudes about immigration, feelings toward black people, and feelings toward Muslims." Data from the gold standard American National Election Studies also showed that resentment toward these groups was a better predictor of Trump support than economic concerns. And as I previously mentioned, exit polls found that Trump's victory depended on voters whose top concerns were immigration and terrorism, despite his lack of any national security experience and my long record. That's a polite way of saying many of these voters were worried about people of color—especially blacks, Mexicans, and Muslims—threatening their way of life. They believed that the political, economic, and cultural elites cared more about these "others" than about them.

I'm not saying that all Trump voters are racist or xenophobic. There are plenty of good-hearted people who are uncomfortable about perceived antipolice rhetoric, undocumented immigrants, and fast-changing norms around gender and sexual orientation. But you had to be deaf to miss the coded language and racially charged resentment powering Trump's campaign.

When I said, "You could put half of Trump's supporters into what I call the basket of deplorables," I was talking about well-documented reality. For example, the General Social Survey conducted by the University of Chicago found that in 2016, 55 percent of white Republicans believed that blacks are generally poorer than whites "because most just don't have the motivation or willpower to pull themselves up out of poverty." In the same survey, 42 percent of white Republicans described blacks as lazier than whites and 26 percent said they were less intelligent. In all cases, the number of white Democrats who said the same thing was much lower (although still way too high).

Generalizing about a broad group of people is almost always unwise. And I regret handing Trump a political gift with my "deplorables" comment. I know that a lot of well-intentioned people were insulted because they misunderstood me to be criticizing *all* Trump voters. I'm sorry about that.

But too many of Trump's core supporters *do* hold views that I find—there's no other word for it—deplorable. And while I'm sure a lot of Trump supporters had fair and legitimate reasons for their choice, it is an uncomfortable and unavoidable fact that everyone who voted for Donald Trump—all 62,984,825 of them—made the decision to elect a man who bragged about sexual assault, attacked a federal judge for being Mexican and grieving Gold Star parents who were Muslim, and has a long and well-documented history of racial discrimination in his businesses. That doesn't mean every Trump voter approved of those things, but at a minimum they accepted or overlooked them. And they did it without demanding the basics that Americans used to expect from all presidential candidates, from releasing tax returns to offering substantive policy proposals to upholding common standards of decency.

"Wait a minute," some critics will say, "President Obama won twice. How could race be a real factor here?"

The important thing to remember is that racial attitudes aren't static and they don't exist in a vacuum. As Christopher Parker, a political science professor at the University of Washington, has explained, the Obama years produced a backlash among white voters: "Every period of racial progress in this country is followed by a period of retrenchment. That's what the 2016 election was about." It's like in physics—every action has an equal and opposite reaction.

Cornell Belcher, a respected Democratic pollster, has studied changing racial attitudes in America extensively and documented this backlash in his book *A Black Man in the White House*. He described Obama's election as setting off anxiety among many white Americans that built over time. "After a significantly brief honeymoon in November 2008, racial aversion among Republicans climbed precipitously," Belcher wrote, "and stayed at that level until October 2014 when it again spiked—to an all-time high." It's not surprising that those spikes occurred around the two midterm elections, when Republican candidates were working double-time to demonize Obama and he wasn't on the ballot and fully engaged in fighting back.

Other academic researchers have studied a phenomenon they call "racial priming." Their findings show that when white voters are encouraged to view the world through a racial lens and to be more conscious of their own racial identity, they act and vote more conservatively. That's exactly what happened in 2016. John McCain and Mitt Romney made principled decisions not to make their campaigns about race. McCain famously stood up to one of his own voters at a town hall in October 2008 and assured the crowd that rumors about Obama being foreign were false. By contrast, Donald Trump rose to prominence by spreading the racist "birther" lie that President Obama was not born in the United States. Trump launched his campaign for President by calling Mexican immigrants rapists and criminals. And he continued to make racially charged attacks right up until Election Day. All this happened against the backdrop of police shootings and Black Lives Matter protests. It makes sense that by Election Day, more white voters may have been thinking about race and identity than in 2012, when those issues were rarely talked about on either side.

To be fair, I likely contributed to a heightened racial consciousness as well. I called out Trump's bigotry and his appeal to white supremacists and the so-called Alt-Right. In a speech in Reno, Nevada, in August 2016, I laid out a detailed case documenting Trump's history of racial discrimination in his business career and how he used a campaign based on prejudice and paranoia to take hate groups mainstream and help a radical fringe take over the Republican Party. I denounced his decision to hire Stephen Bannon, the head of Breitbart, as campaign CEO. I also spoke positively throughout the campaign about racial justice, immigration, and Muslims.

As a result, some white voters may have decided I wasn't on their side. For example, my meeting with Black Lives Matter activists and support for the Mothers of the Movement was seen by some white police officers as presuming their guilt, in spite of my long-standing support for more police on the street, community policing, and 9/11 first responders. I always said we needed to both reform policing *and* support police officers. It didn't seem to matter. But this is one issue on which I don't second-guess myself. No parent should fear for the life of an unarmed, law-abiding child when he walks out of the house. That's not "identity politics." It's simple justice.

But back to the question at hand. I find the data on all this to be compelling. Yet I believe that, in the end, the debate between "economic anxiety" and racism or "cultural anxiety" is a false choice. If you listen to many Trump voters talk, you start to see that all these different strands of anxiety and resentment are related: the decline of manufacturing jobs in the Midwest that had allowed white men without a college degree to provide their families with middle-class lives, the breakdown of traditional gender roles, anger at immigrants and other minorities for "cutting in line" and getting more than their "fair share," discomfort with a more diverse and cosmopolitan culture, worries about Muslims and terrorism, and a general sense that things aren't going the way they should and that life was better and easier for previous generations. In people's lives and worldviews, concerns about economics, race, gender, class, and culture all blend together.

The academics see this, too. According to the director of the Voter Study Group, which followed thousands of voters from 2012 to 2016, "Voters who experienced increased or continued economic stress were inclined to have become more negative about immigration and terrorism, demonstrating how economic pressures coincided with cultural concerns."

This isn't new. Back in 1984, Ronald Reagan won by a landslide by flipping formerly Democratic blue-collar whites. The term "Reagan Democrats" came out of a series of famous focus groups conducted in Macomb County, Michigan, by Stan Greenberg, who went on to become Bill's pollster in 1992. Stan found that many working-class white voters "interpreted Democratic calls for economic fairness as code for transfer payments to African-Americans," and blamed blacks "for almost everything that has gone wrong in their lives." After the 2016 election, Stan went back to Macomb County to talk to "Trump Democrats." He found pretty much all the sentiments you would expect—frustration with elites and a rigged political system, and a desire for fundamental change, but also anger at immigrants who compete with them for jobs and don't speak English, fear of Muslims, and resentment of minorities who are seen as collecting more than their fair share of government benefits. Some of the comments sounded like they were ripped straight from the 1984 focus groups.

Stan largely blames President Obama for turning working-class voters away from the Democratic Party by embracing free trade and "heralding economic progress and the bailout of the irresponsible elites, while ordinary people's incomes crashed and they continued to struggle financially." That's another reminder that, despite the heroic work President Obama did to get our economy back on the right track after the financial crisis, many Americans didn't feel the recovery in their own lives and didn't give Democrats credit. Stan also thought my campaign was too upbeat on the economy, too liberal on immigration, and not vocal enough about trade. Still, he notes that coming out of the third debate, I was poised to overperform with white working-class women compared with Obama in 2012 and perhaps achieve "historic numbers," until those voters broke away in the final week and went to Trump.

Stan thinks this happened because I "went silent on the economy and change." But that's baloney. I went back to look at what I said in my final rallies across the battlegrounds. The day before the election, I told a crowd in Grand Rapids, Michigan, "We've got to get the economy working for everybody, not just those at the top. If you believe, as I do, that America thrives when the middle class thrives, then you have to vote tomorrow!" I went on to pledge "the biggest investment in good paying jobs since World War Two," with an emphasis on infrastructure jobs that can't be outsourced, advanced manufacturing that pays high wages, stronger unions, a higher minimum wage, and equal pay for women. I also hit Trump for buying cheap Chinese steel and aluminum for his buildings and for wanting to cut taxes for millionaires, billionaires, and corporations. I spoke directly to "people in our country who feel like they've been knocked down, and nobody cares." I said, "If you give me the honor of being your President, I am going to do everything I can to get this country and everybody in it back up on our feet." I wouldn't call that going "silent on the economy and change."

That said, I do sometimes lie awake at night thinking about how we closed the campaign and if there was anything different we could have done that would have made a difference. It's true that before Comey's letter, I had planned to close with aggressive advertising reminding working families of my plans to change our country and their lives for the better. But after Comey's letter sent my numbers sliding, the consensus on my team was that our best strategy was to hit Trump hard and remind voters why he was an unacceptable choice. Was that a mistake? Maybe. But we were competing against wall-to-wall negative coverage of emails, plus the slime of fake news.

It's easy to second-guess. It's also easy to listen to the ugliest comments in Stan's focus groups and just get furious. But I try to hold on to my empathy. I still believe what I said immediately after my ill-fated comment about the "basket of deplorables," although this part didn't get much attention: many Trump supporters "are people who feel that the government has let them down, the economy has let them down, nobody cares about them, nobody worries about what happens to their lives and their futures, and they're just desperate for change . . . Those are people we have to understand and empathize with as well." Those were people I intended to help.

Voter Suppression

All of this played out against a landscape shaped by structural factors that didn't get enough scrutiny during the campaign. Most notable is the impact of voter suppression, through restrictive laws as well as efforts to discourage and depress turnout.

An unnamed senior Trump campaign official boasted to the press in late October 2016 that "we have three major voter suppression operations underway," aimed at white liberals, young women, and African

Americans. It's worth pausing on this for a moment and reflecting on the fact that they weren't even trying to hide that they were suppressing the vote. Most campaigns try to win by attracting more support. Trump actively tried to discourage people from voting at all. They used some of the same tactics as the Russians, including trafficking in fake news and under-the-radar Facebook attacks. Despicable stuff. After the election, Trump even thanked African Americans for not voting.

But whatever Trump was up to was just the latest in a long-term Republican strategy to discourage and disenfranchise Democratic-leaning voters.

The Supreme Court under Chief Justice John Roberts opened the floodgates by gutting the Voting Rights Act in 2013. When I was in the Senate, we voted to reauthorize the law 98 to 0 and President George W. Bush signed it. But Justice Roberts essentially argued that racism was a thing of the past, and therefore the country no longer needed key protections of the Voting Rights Act. It was one of the worst decisions the court has ever made. By 2016, fourteen states had new restrictions on voting, including burdensome ID requirements aimed at weeding out students, poor people, the elderly, and people of color. Republicans in many states also limited the number and hours of polling places, curtailed early voting and same-day registration, scrapped language assistance for non-English speakers, and purged large numbers of voters from the rolls, sometimes erroneously. Ohio alone has removed up to two million voters since 2011. Much of this national effort was coordinated by Kansas Secretary of State Kris Kobach, who runs a suppression initiative called the Interstate Voter Registration Crosscheck Program.

Kobach is the nation's leading voter suppression advocate and was recently fined for misleading a federal court. He is also the vice chairman of the new commission Trump has created to deal with the phantom epidemic of voting fraud. Studies have found that out of the more than a billion votes cast in the United States between 2000 and 2014, there were just 31 credible cases of voter impersonation. Yet Trump has claimed that millions of people voted illegally in 2016. A review by the *Washington Post* found only 4 documented instances of voter fraud out of 136 million votes cast in 2016—including an Iowa woman who voted twice for Trump. As Trump's own lawyers asserted in a Michigan court: "All available evidence suggests that the 2016 general election was not tainted by fraud or mistake." Nonetheless, Kobach and Republicans across the country continue to use false claims about fraud to justify curtailing voting rights.

Since the election, studies have documented how big an impact all this suppression had on the outcome. States with harsh new voting laws, such as Wisconsin, saw turnout dip 1.7 points, compared with a 1.3-point increase in states where the law didn't change. And the drop was particularly acute among black voters. Turnout was down 5 points in heavily African American counties in states with strict new ID laws, but down just 2.2 points in similar counties in states without the new laws.

In Wisconsin, where I lost by just 22,748 votes, a study from Priorities USA estimated that the new voter ID law helped reduce turnout by 200,000 votes, primarily from low-income and minority areas. We know for sure that turnout in the city of Milwaukee fell by 13 percent. By contrast, in neighboring Minnesota, which has similar demographics but did not impose arduous new restrictions on voting, turnout in heavily African American counties declined much less and overall turnout was essentially flat. In Illinois, where the state put in place new measures to make it easier to vote, not harder, turnout was up more than 5 percent overall. Among African Americans, turnout was 14 points higher in Illinois than in Wisconsin. The experience living under a deeply unpopular Trumpian governor there may also have motivated people to show up and reject the even worse national version. In short, voting laws matter. A lot. Before the election, one Republican state representative in Wisconsin predicted the new law would help Trump pull off an upset in the state. It turns out he was right.

The Associated Press profiled several Wisconsinites who were turned away or did not have their votes counted because they did not have the required identification, including a Navy veteran with an out-of-state driver's license, a recent college graduate whose student ID was disqualified because it lacked an expiration date, and a sixty-six-year old woman with chronic lung disease who lost her driver's license just before Election Day. She provided Social Security and Medicare cards and a government-issued bus pass with a photo, but her vote was still not counted. The AP reported that these disenfranchised citizens were "not hard to find."

Reading these stories is both eye-opening and infuriating. The right to vote is the foundation of our free society, and protecting that right is the single most important thing we can do to strengthen our democracy. Yet in state after state, Republicans are still at it. President Trump's obsession to root out nonexistent voter fraud is just cover for further suppression. Already in 2017, more states have imposed new restrictions on voting than in 2015 and 2016 combined. Nearly a hundred bills have been introduced in thirty-one states. This is a problem that will grow only more pervasive and urgent in future elections.

Where Do Democrats Go from Here?

Republicans have another advantage: a powerful, permanent political infrastructure, particularly online. After Mitt Romney's defeat in 2012, and widespread praise for the Obama campaign's technology, Republicans vowed to catch up. Between 2013 and 2016, the Republican National Committee invested more than $100 million in data operations. Outside groups such as the Mercers and the Koch brothers also spent heavily.

By contrast, the Democratic National Committee was badly outgunned. Tom Perez, the new DNC chair, has said, "We've got to up our game on technology." He's right. Perez pledged to "do a better job of building the data analytics platform that will enable us not only to succeed in elections today but to be the state of the art for decades to come." That's crucial.

If we want to win in the future, Democrats need to catch up and leapfrog ahead. And this isn't just about data. We need an "always-on" content distribution network that can match what the right-wing has built. That means an array of loosely connected Facebook pages, Instagram accounts, Twitter feeds, Snapchat stories, and Reddit communities churning out memes, graphics, and videos. More sophisticated data collection and analysis can support and feed this network. I'm no expert in these matters, but I know enough to understand that most people get their news from screens, so we have to be there 24/7.

There are other lessons I hope Democrats learn from 2016. Since the election, the party has been debating how best to set ourselves up to win in the future, starting with the midterms in 2018. I think most of the perceived drama between the center-left and the left-left on this question is overblown. We're far closer together than any of us are to Trump and the Republicans, who just keep getting more extreme. Bernie Sanders and I wrote the 2016 platform together, and he called it the most progressive one in history. We share many of the same values and most of our differences over policy are relatively minor compared to the stark divide between the two parties.

You'd also be hard pressed to find any Democrat who doesn't agree that we need to continue sharpening our economic pitch and that we should make a sustained effort to win back voters who switched from Obama to Trump. We'll have to convince them that Democrats respect them, care about them, and have a plan to make life better, not just in big cities but also in small towns and rural areas. That might become easier as voters watch Trump break his populist promises and embrace a congressional Republican agenda that tilts the playing field even more toward the wealthy and powerful at the expense of working families. So far, their health care debate is about whether they're going to take it away from 22 million Americans to fund tax cuts for the wealthy!

So yes, we need to compete everywhere, and we can't afford to write off any voter or any state. But it's not all kumbaya in the Democratic Party. We're hearing a lot of misguided rhetoric and analysis that could lead us in the wrong direction.

One argument is about whether pursuing the Russia investigation is distracting from making the case to voters about health care and the economy. This is another false choice. It makes all the sense in the world for congressional candidates to focus on pocketbook issues, and the disastrous Republican health care legislation should be front and center. But that doesn't mean Democrats already in Congress should stop doing their jobs. They should continue providing rigorous oversight and hold the Trump administration accountable. I have confidence that Democrats can walk and chew gum at the same time. Plus, the ever-growing Russia scandal is showing Americans that Trump is a liar, and that will help us convince them that he's lying about health care and jobs, too. And don't underestimate how, if left unchecked, Russia's covert operations can easily be used again in the future to defeat other Democrats. That torrent of misinformation helped drown out my message and steal my voice. It gave Trump cover to escape his own problems. This can all happen again if we don't stop it. Oh, and for any Democratic members of Congress feeling squeamish about pushing too hard, just ask yourselves what Republicans would be doing if the situation were reversed.

Here's another misguided argument. Some of the same people who say that the reason I lost was because I didn't have an economic message now insist that all Democrats need to do to win in the future is talk more about jobs, and then—poof!—all those Trump voters will come home. Both the premise and conclusion are false. Yes, we need to talk as much as we possibly can about creating more jobs, raising wages, and making health care and college more affordable and accessible. But that's exactly what I did throughout 2016. So it's not a silver bullet and it can't be the only thing we talk about.

Democrats have to continue championing civil rights, human rights, and other issues that are part of our march toward a more perfect union. We shouldn't sacrifice our principles to pursue a shrinking pool of voters who look more to the past than the future.

My loss doesn't change the fact that the Democrats' future is tied to America's in a fast-changing world where our ability to make progress depends an increasingly diverse, educated, young electorate. Even when the headlines are bad, there's reason to be optimistic about the trend lines. I was the first Democrat since FDR to win Orange County, California. I made historic gains in the suburbs of Atlanta, Houston, Dallas, and Charlotte, as well as in other traditionally Republican areas across the Sun Belt. Latino turnout jumped nearly 5 percent in Florida and rose in other key areas as well.

It wasn't enough this time, but these trends hold the key to our future. That's why the Republicans have worked so hard to keep young people and people of color away from the polls, and to gerrymander districts that protect incumbents. Democrats will have to work even harder to fight for voting rights, fair redistricting, and high turnout not just in presidential elections, but also in local, state, and federal midterm elections where the people who make the voting laws and draw congressional districts are selected.

I know we can do it. There are enough vulnerable Republican congressional seats in districts I won for Democrats to be well on their way to retaking the House in 2018, many of them in Sun Belt suburbs. And if we can flip some Midwestern blue-collar districts that went for Trump but are now disillusioned by his performance in office, all the better. We need a strategy that puts us in a position to catch a wave if it forms, and compete and win all over the country.

I do believe it's possible to appeal to all parts of our big, diverse nation. We need to get better at explaining to all Americans why a more inclusive society with broadly shared growth will be better and more prosperous for everyone. Democrats must make the case that expanding economic opportunity and expanding the rights and dignity of all people can never be either/or, but always go hand in hand. I tried to do this in 2016. That was the whole point of "Stronger Together." And it's why I emphasized my commitment to help create jobs in every zip code, in neglected urban neighborhoods *and* in small Appalachian towns. That vision did win the popular vote by nearly three million (yes, I'm going to keep mentioning that). Unfortunately, zero-sum resentment proved more powerful than positive-sum aspiration in the places where it mattered most. But that doesn't mean we give up. It means we have to keep making the case, backed up by bold new policy ideas and renewed commitment to our core values.

As for me, I'm sure I'll keep replaying in my head for a long time what went wrong in this election. As I said in my concession speech, it's going to be painful for quite a while. None of the factors I've discussed here lessen the responsibility I feel or the aching sense that I let everyone down. But I'm not going to sulk or disappear. I'm going to do everything I can to support strong Democratic candidates everywhere. If you're reading this book, I hope you'll do your part, too.

If our expectations—if our fondest prayers and dreams are not realized—then we should all bear in mind that the greatest glory of living lies not in never falling, but in rising every time you fall.

—Nelson Mandela

Resilience

Three things in human life are important. The first is to be kind. The second is to be kind. And the third is to be kind.

—Henry James

Love and Kindness

Politics has always been a rough business. Thomas Jefferson and John Adams hurled insults at each other that would make today's nastiest politicians blush. It's just how the game is played: Every campaign seeks to draw contrasts with opponents and the media want to cover conflict. So it's not surprising that two words you don't hear very often in our knock-down, drag-out political brawls are *love* and *kindness*. But you heard them from our campaign.

It started as something I'd occasionally mention at the end of speeches, how our country needed compassion and a spirit of community in a time of division. It eventually became a rallying cry: "Love trumps hate!" Partly this was because the race felt ugly and mean and we wanted to be an antidote to that. But partly it was because I've been thinking for a long time about how our country needs to become kinder and all of us need to become more connected to one another.

That's not just a sweet thought. It's serious to me. If I had won the election, this would have been a quiet but important project of my presidency.

A few weeks after the election, I picked up a copy of a sermon called "You Are Accepted" by Paul Tillich, the Christian theologian of the mid-twentieth century. I remembered sitting in my church basement in Park Ridge years ago as our youth minister, Don Jones, read it to us. "Grace strikes us when we are in great pain and restlessness . . . Sometimes at that moment, a wave of light breaks into our darkness, and it is as though a voice were saying: 'You are accepted.'" Years later, when my marriage was in crisis, I called Don. Read Tillich, he said. I did. It helped.

Tillich says about grace: "It happens; or it does not happen. And certainly it does not happen if we try to force it upon ourselves." This stuck with me. "Grace happens. Grace happens." In other words, be patient, be strong, keep going, and let grace come when it can.

Now I was sixty-nine and reading Tillich again. There was more here than I remembered. Tillich says sin is separation and grace is reconciliation—it's "being able to look frankly into the eyes of another . . . understanding each other's words . . . not merely the literal meaning of the words, but also that which lies behind them, even when they are harsh or angry." After a divisive election, this resonated in a new way. A lot of Americans were estranged from one another. Reconciliation seemed far away. The whole country was seething. Before the election, it felt as if half the people were angry and resentful, while the other half was still fundamentally hopeful. Now pretty much everyone is mad about something.

Tillich published his sermon the year after I was born. Sometimes people describe the postwar years as a golden age in America. But even then, he sensed a "feeling of meaninglessness, emptiness, doubt, and cynicism—all expressions of despair, of our separation from the roots and the meaning of our life." That could just as easily be America in 2016. How many shrinking small towns and aging Rust Belt cities did I visit over the past two years where people felt abandoned, disrespected, invisible? How many young men and women in neglected urban neighborhoods told me they felt like strangers in their own land because of the color of their skin? The alienation cut across race, class, geography. Back in 1948, Tillich was concerned that technology had removed "the walls of distance, in time and space" but strengthened "walls of estrangement between heart and heart." If only he could have seen the internet!

How are we supposed to love our neighbors when we feel like this? How are we supposed to find the grace that Tillich says comes with reconciliation and acceptance? How can we build the trust that holds a democracy together?

Underneath these questions are ones I've been wrestling with and writing and speaking about for decades.

It started in college. Like a lot of kids, I felt stifled by the conservative, dollar-crazed conformity of the *Mad Men* era. That scene in *The Graduate* where an older man pulls Dustin Hoffman aside and, with great seriousness, shares the secret of life in one word—"Plastics"—made all of us groan. It's no wonder so many of us were looking for meaning and purpose wherever we could find them. As I put it in my Wellesley graduation speech, we were "searching for more immediate, ecstatic, and penetrating modes of living." (Yes, I'm aware of how idealistic that sounds, but that's how we talked!) I didn't know quite how to put it into words, but what many of us wanted was an integrated life that blended and balanced family, work, service, and a spiritual connection all together. We wanted to feel like we were part of something bigger than ourselves—certainly something bigger than "plastics."

Surprisingly, I found some of what I was looking for not in a New Age manifesto but in a very old book.

In one of my political science classes, I read *Democracy in America* by Alexis de Tocqueville. He came from France and traveled across the United States in the 1830s trying to understand what made our young nation work. He was amazed by the social and economic equality and mobility he saw here, unheard of in aristocratic Europe, and by what he called our "habits of the heart," the everyday values and customs that set Americans apart from the rest of the world. He described a nation of volunteers and problem solvers who believed that their own self-interest was advanced by helping one another. Like Benjamin Franklin, they formed volunteer fire departments, because they realized that if your neighbor's house is on fire, it's your problem, too. Middle-class women—including a lot of Methodists—went into the most danger-ous nineteenth-century slums to help poor children who had no one else standing up for them. Those early Americans came together, in-spired by religious faith, civic virtue, and common decency, to lend a hand to those in need and improve their communities. They joined clubs and congregations, civic organizations and political parties, all kinds of groups that bound a diverse country together. De Tocqueville thought that spirit made America's great democratic experiment pos-sible.

Those "habits of the heart" felt distant to me in the turmoil of the 1960s. Instead of pitching in to raise a barn or sew a quilt—or clean up a park or build a school—Americans seemed always to be at one another's throats. And a pervasive loss of trust was undermining the democracy de Tocqueville had celebrated 130 years before. Reading his observations helped me realize that my generation didn't need to totally reinvent America to fix the problems we saw and find the meaning we sought, we just had to reclaim the best parts of our national character. That started, I told my classmates in my graduation speech, with "mutuality of respect between people," another clunky phrase but still a pretty good message.

Fast-forward twenty years, to early 1991. I'd gotten what I'd always dreamed of—a loving family, a fulfilling career, and a life of service to others—plus more that I had never imagined. I was the First Lady of Arkansas. Every part of that statement would have surprised my college-age self. Now my husband was thinking about running for President of the United States. I didn't know if he could win—George H. W. Bush's approval rating surpassed 90 percent after winning the Gulf War—but I was sure the country needed him to try. The Reagan years had rebuilt America's confidence but sapped its soul. Greed was good. Instead of a nation defined by "habits of the heart," we had become a land of "sink or swim." Bush had said some of the right things, calling for a "kinder, gentler" country and celebrating the generosity of our civil society as "a thousand points of light." But conservatives used that as an excuse for government to do even less to help the less fortunate. It's easy to forget what this was like. Now that the Republican Party has moved so far to the extreme right in the years since, the 1980s have taken on a retrospective halo of moderation by comparison. And it's true that Reagan gave amnesty to undocumented immigrants, and Bush raised taxes and signed the Americans with Disabilities Act. But their trickle-down economic policies exploded the deficit and hurt working families. I thought they were wrong on most issues, and still do.

In those days, I still read *Life* magazine, and in the February 1991 issue, I came across something that caught me totally by surprise. It was an article by Lee Atwater, the Republican mastermind who'd helped

elect Reagan and Bush with slash-and-burn campaigns that played to
our country's worst impulses and ugliest fears. He was the man behind
the infamous race-baiting "Willie Horton" ad in 1988, the man who
believed in winning at any cost. He was also mortally ill with brain
cancer and not yet forty years old.

Atwater's piece in *Life* magazine read like a death-bed conver-
sion. The bare-knuckled political brawler was having an attack of
conscience. And despite coming from someone with whom I disagreed about virtually everything, it was like reading my own thoughts
printed out on the page. Here's what he wrote that made such a big
impression on me:

> Long before I was struck with cancer, I felt something stir-
> ring in American society. It was a sense among the people of
> the country, Republicans and Democrats alike, that something
> was missing from their lives—something crucial. I was trying
> to position the Republican Party to take advantage of it. But
> I wasn't exactly sure what it was. My illness helped me to see
> that what was missing in society is what was missing in me. A
> little heart, a lot of brotherhood.
>
> The '80s were about acquiring—acquiring wealth, power,
> prestige. I know. I acquired more wealth, power, and prestige
> than most. But you can acquire all you want and still feel empty.
> What power wouldn't I trade for a little more time with my
> family? What price wouldn't I pay for an evening with friends?
> It took a deadly illness to put me eye-to-eye with that truth,
> but it is a truth that the country, caught up in its ruthless ambi-
> tions and moral decay, can learn on my dime.
>
> I don't know who will lead us through the '90s, but they
> must be made to speak to this spiritual vacuum at the heart of
> American society—this tumor of the soul.

This was exactly how I felt! Atwater was getting to a question that had been gnawing at me for years. Why, I wondered, in the wealthiest, most powerful country on earth, with the oldest, most successful democracy, did so many Americans feel like we lacked meaning in our individual lives and in our collective national life? What was missing, it seemed to me, was a sense that our lives were part of some greater effort, that we were all connected to one another and that each of us had a place and a purpose.

This was part of why I thought Bill should run for President. Filling America's "spiritual vacuum" wasn't a job for government, but it would help to have strong, caring leadership. Bill was starting to think about how to root a campaign in the values of opportunity, responsibility, and community. Eventually he'd call it a "new covenant," a biblical concept. He hoped it would speak to this feeling, articulated so well by Atwater, that something important was missing in the heart of American life.

I cut out the *Life* magazine article and showed it to Bill.

(I wonder what Lee Atwater would say about Donald Trump. Would he admire the chutzpah of a campaign that stopped blowing dog whistles and spoke its bigotry in plain English for all to hear? Or would he see Trump as the embodiment of everything he hated about the eighties: one big tumor of the American soul?)

Fast-forward again, this time to April 1993. My eighty-two-year-old father was lying in a coma in St. Vincent's Hospital in Little Rock. It had been two weeks since he suffered a massive stroke. All I wanted to do was keep sitting by his bedside, hold his hand, smooth his hair, and wait and hope for him to open his eyes or squeeze my fingers. But nobody knew how long his coma would last, and Chelsea had to get back to school in Washington. For reasons passing understanding, I also had a commitment I couldn't get out of: a speech to fourteen thousand people at the University of Texas at Austin.

I was, to put it mildly, a wreck. On the plane to Austin, I leafed through the little book I keep of quotations, Scripture, and poems, trying to figure out what I could possibly say. Then I turned the page and saw the cutout from Lee Atwater's *Life* article. Something missing from our lives, a spiritual vacuum—this is what I would talk about. It wouldn't be the most articulate or coherent speech I'd ever given, but at least it would come straight from my wounded heart. I began sketching out a new appeal for the "mutuality of respect" I'd talked about in my graduation speech at Wellesley, a return to de Tocqueville's "habits of the heart."

When I got to Texas, I spoke about the alienation, despair, and hopelessness I saw building just below the surface of American life. I quoted Atwater. And to his question—"Who will lead us out of this spiritual vacuum?"—I answered, "all of us." We needed to improve government and strengthen our institutions, and that's what the new Clinton administration was trying to do, but it wouldn't be enough. "We need a new politics of meaning," I said, "a new ethos of individual responsibility and caring." And that would take all of us doing our part to build "a society that fills us up again and makes us feel that we are part of something bigger than ourselves." I cited de Tocqueville and talked about the importance of networks of family, friendship, and communities that are the glue that hold us together.

There had been so much change in our country, a lot of it positive but also much of it profoundly unsettling. The social and cultural upheaval of the 1960s and 1970s, followed by the economic and technological shifts of the 1980s and 1990s, with the rise of automation, income inequality, and the information economy, all of it seemed to be contributing to a spiritual hollowing out. "Change will come whether we want it or not, and what we have to do is to try and make change our friend, not our enemy," I said.

> The changes that will count the most are the millions and millions of changes that take place on the individual level as people reject cynicism; as they are willing to take risks to meet the challenges they see around them; as they truly begin to try to see other people as they wish to be seen and to treat them as they wish to be treated; to overcome all of the obstacles we have erected around ourselves that keep us apart from one another, fearful and afraid, not willing to build the bridges necessary; to fill that spiritual vacuum that Lee Atwater talked about.

People in politics don't normally talk this way. Neither do First Ladies. I soon discovered why.

The day after my speech, my father died. I returned to Washington and found that many in the press had hated my attempt to talk unguardedly about what I thought was wrong in the country. The *New York Times Magazine* put me on the cover with the mocking headline "Saint Hillary." The writer described the Texas speech as "easy, moralistic preaching couched in the gauzy and gushy wrappings of New Age jargon."

I learned my lesson. Over the next few years, I kept thinking about a "new ethos of individual responsibility and caring," but I didn't talk about it much. I read as much as I could, including a new article by Harvard professor Bob Putnam, which later became a bestselling book titled *Bowling Alone*. Putnam used declining membership in bowling leagues as an evocative example of the breakdown in America's social capital and civil society—the same problems I'd been worrying about.

I decided to write a book of my own. It would speak to these concerns in a less "gauzy and gushy" way than my Texas speech and offer a practical, kitchen-table vision for what we could do about it. The focus would be the responsibility we all had to help create a healthy, nurturing community for children. I'd call it *It Takes a Village*, after an African proverb that captured something I had long believed.

I wrote about how frantic and fragmented American life had become for many people, especially stressed-out parents. Extended families didn't provide the support they used to. Crime was still a big problem in a lot of communities, making neighborhood streets places of danger rather than support and solidarity. We were spending more time in our cars and in front of the television and less time participating in civic associations, houses of worship, unions, political parties, and, yes, bowling leagues.

I believed we needed to find new ways to support one another. "Our challenge is to arrive at a consensus of values and a common vision of what we can do today, individually and collectively, to build strong families and communities," I wrote. "Creating that consensus in a democracy depends on seriously considering other points of view, resisting the lure of extremist rhetoric, and balancing individual rights and freedoms with personal responsibility and mutual obligations."

Once again, the response from some quarters was brutal. Republicans caricatured my appeal for stronger families and communities as more big-government liberalism, even "crypto-totalitarianism" in one magazine's words. "We are told that it takes a village, that is collective, and thus the state, to raise a child," Bob Dole said, his voice dripping with disdain, in his acceptance speech at the 1996 Republican National Convention. "I am here to tell you it does not take a village to raise a child. It takes a family to raise a child." The crowd went wild.

You might think it's a little odd for the nominee of a major political party to take time out of the most important speech of the campaign to take a swipe at a book about children written by the First Lady—and you would be right.

It was becoming painfully clear that there was no room in our poli-tics for the kind of discussion I wanted to have. Or maybe I was the wrong messenger. Either way, this wasn't working.

I found more receptive audiences overseas. In a speech at the World Economic Forum in Davos, Switzerland, in 1998, I tried to explain how my "village" concept fit together with a broader global agenda of political and economic reform. I used the metaphor of a three-legged stool, which I'd come back to many times in the years that followed. An open and thriving economy was one leg. A stable and responsive democratic government was a second leg. And the third, too often undervalued in serious foreign policy discussions, was civil society. "It is the stuff of life," I said. "It is the family, it is the religious belief and spirituality that guide us. It is the voluntary association of which we are a member. It is the art and culture that makes our spirits soar."

Another twenty years went by. Now I was running for President in a time of deep division and smoldering anger. On the news, there was a seemingly endless series of terrorist attacks and mass shootings. Young black men kept getting killed by police. A candidate for President called Mexican immigrants rapists and encouraged violence at his rallies. On the internet, women were harassed frequently, and it was impossible to have a conversation about politics without enduring a blizzard of invective.

In late May 2015, I was campaigning in Columbia, South Caro-lina. In between events, we squeezed in a quick stop at the Main Street Bakery so I could get a cupcake and shake some hands. There was only one customer in the place, an older African American gentleman sit-ting alone by the window, engrossed in a book. I was reluctant to dis-turb him, but we made eye contact. I walked over to say hello and ask what he was reading.

The man looked up and said, "First Corinthians 13."

I smiled. "Love is patient, love is kind," I said, "it does not envy, it does not boast, it is not proud."

His name was Donnie Hunt, and he was a minister at the First Calvary Baptist Church, getting ready for the day's Bible study. He invited me to sit down.

He told me how rewarding he found it to read these familiar lines again and again. "You always learn something," he said.

"Well, it's alive," I replied. "It's the living word."

We sat and talked for a long time—about books, his church, the local schools, racial tensions in the community, his hope to one day visit the Holy Land. "It's on my bucket list," he told me.

A few weeks later, I was back in South Carolina. This time it was Charleston. I visited a technical college and talked with apprentices hoping their training would lead to a good job and a happy life. It was a diverse group—black, white, Hispanic, Asian—all young, all incredibly hopeful. I listened to their stories and heard the pride in their voices.

I got on a plane for Nevada and didn't hear the news until I landed. A young white man trying to start a race war had massacred nine black worshippers at an evening Bible study at Mother Emanuel Church in Charleston. *Emanuel* means "God with us," but the news made it hard to feel that way. Nine faithful women and men, with families and friends and so much left to do and contribute in their lives, cut down as they prayed. What is wrong with us? I thought. How did we let this happen in our country? How did we still allow guns to fall into the hands of people whose hearts were filled with hate?

Two days later, police brought the murderer into court. One by one, grieving parents and siblings stood up and looked into his blank eyes, this young man who had taken so much from them, and they said:

"I forgive you." In its way, their acts of mercy were more stunning than his act of cruelty.

A friend of mine sent me a note. "Think about the hearts and values of those men and women of Mother Emanuel," he said.

"A dozen people gathered to pray. They're in their most intimate of communities, and a stranger who doesn't look or dress like them joins in. They don't judge. They don't question. They don't reject. They just welcome. If he's there, he must need something: prayer, love, community, something. During their last hour, nine people of faith welcomed a stranger in prayer and fellowship."

My friend said it reminded him of the words of Jesus in Matthew: "I was hungry and you gave me food. I was thirsty and you gave me drink. I was a stranger and you welcomed me."

In a speech in San Francisco, I read my friend's note out loud. Then I looked up, and I said what I was feeling in that moment: "I know it's not usual for somebody running for President to say what we need more of in this country is love and kindness. But that's exactly what we need."

"Love and kindness" became a staple for me on the campaign trail. Never the core message of the day, never a full-fledged "new politics of meaning" call to arms, but something I'd come back to again and again, and that audiences nearly always responded to, as if they were thirsty for it. With all the rotten news on television and all the negativity in the race, a lot of people wanted to be reassured about the basic goodness of our country and our hope for a better, kinder future. When we started using the phrase "love trumps hate," it caught on like wildfire among our supporters. There were times when I listened to huge crowds chanting those words, and for a minute I'd get swept up in the swell of positive energy and think it might really carry us all the way.

I've spent many hours since the election wondering whether there was more we could have done to get that message through to an angry electorate in a cynical time. There's been so much said and written about the economic hardships and declining life expectancy of the working-class whites who embraced Donald Trump. But why should they be more angry and resentful than the millions of blacks and Latinos who are poorer, die younger, and have to contend every day with entrenched discrimination? Why were many people who were enchanted by Barack Obama in 2008 so cynical in 2016 after he saved the economy and extended health care to millions who needed it?

I went back to de Tocqueville. After studying the French Revolution, he wrote that revolts tend to start not in places where conditions are worst, but in places where expectations are most unmet. So if you've been raised to believe your life will unfold a certain way—say, with a steady union job that doesn't require a college degree but does provide a middle-class income, with traditional gender roles intact and everyone speaking English—and then things don't work out the way you expected, that's when you get angry. It's about loss. It's about the sense that the future is going to be harder than the past. Fundamentally, I believe that the despair we saw in so many parts of America in 2016 grew out of the same problems that Lee Atwater and I were worried about twenty-five years ago. Too many people feel alienated from one another and from any sense of belonging or higher purpose. Anger and resentment fill that void and can overwhelm everything else: tolerance, basic standards of decency, facts, and certainly the kind of practical solutions I spent the campaign offering.

Do I feel empathy for Trump voters? That's a question I've asked myself a lot. It's complicated. It's relatively easy to empathize with hardworking, warmhearted people who decided they couldn't in good conscience vote for me after reading that letter from Jim Comey . . . or who don't think any party should control the White House for more than eight years at a time . . . or who have a deeply held belief in limited government, or an overriding moral objection to abortion. I also feel sympathy for people who believed Trump's promises and are now terrified that he's trying to take away their health care, not make it better, and cut taxes for the superrich, not invest in infrastructure. I get it. But I have no tolerance for intolerance. None. Bullying disgusts me. I look at the people at Trump's rallies, cheering for his hateful rants, and I wonder: Where's *their* empathy and understanding? Why are *they* allowed to close their hearts to the striving immigrant father and the grieving black mother, or the LGBT teenager who's bullied at school and thinking of suicide? Why doesn't the press write think pieces about Trump voters trying to understand why most Americans rejected *their* candidate? Why is the burden of opening our hearts only on half the country?

And yet I've come to believe that for me personally and for our country generally, we have no choice but to try. In the spring of 2017, Pope Francis gave a TED Talk. Yes, a TED Talk. It was amazing. This is the same pope whom Donald Trump attacked on Twitter during the campaign. He called for a "revolution of tenderness." What a phrase! He said, "We all need each other, none of us is an island, an autonomous and independent 'I,' separated from the other, and we can only build the future by standing together, including everyone." He said that tenderness "means to use our eyes to see the other, our ears to hear the other, to listen to the children, the poor, those who are afraid of the future."

On all my long walks in the woods and quiet days at home, when I'm not losing my mind about something I've read in the newspaper or on Twitter, this is what I'm thinking about. I'm coming around to the idea that what we need more than anything at this moment in America is what you might call "radical empathy."

This isn't too different from the "mutuality of respect" I hoped for at Wellesley all those years ago. I'm older now. I know how hard this is and how cruel the world can be. I'm under no illusions that we'll start agreeing on everything or stop having fierce debates about the future of our country—nor should we. But if 2016 taught us anything, it should be that we have an urgent imperative to recapture a sense of common humanity.

Each of us must try to walk in the shoes of people who don't see the world the way we do. President Obama put it very well in his farewell address. He said white Americans need to acknowledge "that the effects of slavery and Jim Crow didn't suddenly vanish in the sixties; that when minority groups voice discontent, they're not just engaging in reverse racism or practicing political correctness; that when they wage peaceful protest, they're not demanding special treatment but the equal treatment our Founders promised." And, for people of color, it means understanding the perspective of "the middle-aged white man who from the outside may seem like he's got all the advantages, but who's seen his world upended by economic, cultural, and technological change."

And, practicing "radical empathy" means more than trying to reach across divides of race, class, and politics, and building bridges *between* communities. We have to fill the emotional and spiritual voids that have opened up *within* communities, within families, and within ourselves as individuals. That can be even more difficult, but it's essential. There's grace to be found in those relationships. Grace and meaning and that elusive sense that we're all part of something bigger than ourselves.

I know this isn't the language of politics, and some will roll their eyes again, just as they always have. But I believe as strongly as I ever have that this is what our country needs. It's what we all need as human beings trying to make our way in changing times. And it's the only way I see forward for myself. I can carry around my bitterness forever, or I can open my heart once more to love and kindness. That's the path I choose.

Concern yourself not with what you tried and failed in, but with what is still possible to do.

—Pope John XXIII

Onward Together

One day a few months after the election, I called some friends and suggested we make a pilgrimage to Hyde Park, New York. I was feeling restless and needed an emotional boost. I thought it might help to visit Val-Kill, Eleanor Roosevelt's cottage, which is one of my favorite historical sites. That's where Eleanor went when she wanted to think, write, entertain, and plan for the future. Maybe I'd be inspired. If nothing else, it would be a nice day out with friends.

It was a cold but clear March day when we arrived. The cottage, simple and unpretentious, was just as I remembered: the rustic "sleeping porch" with its narrow single bed, some of Eleanor's favorite books, her radio, the portrait of her husband she kept over the mantel. A historian who joined us for the tour was kind enough to share some of Eleanor's letters. Reading the mix of adoring fan mail and nasty, cutting diatribes was a reminder of the love-hate whiplash that women who challenge society's expectations and live their lives in the public eye often receive.

I'd been thinking about Eleanor a lot lately. She put up with so much vitriol, and she did it with grace and strength. People criticized her voice and appearance, the money she made speaking and writing, and her advocacy for women's rights, civil rights, and human rights. An overzealous director of the FBI put together a three-thousand-page file on her. One vituperative national columnist called her "impudent, presumptuous, and conspiratorial," and said that "her withdrawal from public life at this time would be a fine public service." Sound familiar?

There were plenty of people hoping that I, too, would just disappear. But here I am. As Bill likes to say, at this point in our lives, we have more yesterdays than tomorrows. There is no way I am going to waste the time I have. I know there is more good to do, more people to help, and a whole lot of unfinished business.

I can only hope to come close to the example Eleanor had set. After her husband died and she left the White House, in 1945, she grew even more outspoken. She became a stateswoman on the world stage, leading the global movement to write and adopt the Universal Declaration of Human Rights. At the same time, she was an active player in national and local Democratic politics, fighting for the soul of her party and her country in a postwar era marked by fear and demagoguery. When she died in 1962, the *New York Times* obituary described how she outlasted ridicule and bitter resentment to become "the object of almost universal respect."

Her friends and supporters clamored for Eleanor to run for Senate, Governor, even President, but she decided instead to pour her energy into helping elect others. Her favorite was Adlai Stevenson, the Governor of Illinois who ran for President unsuccessfully in 1952 and 1956. His losses hurt. "Though one may doubt the wisdom of the people," Eleanor wrote in a newspaper column after the second defeat to Dwight Eisenhower, "it is always best to trust that in time the wisdom of the majority of the people will be greater and more dependable and those who are in the minority must accept their defeat with grace." She was right, of course. But I would have loved to have heard her response if Adlai had ended up winning the popular vote but losing the Electoral College. She would have found just the right way to capture the absurdity of it all.

As we walked through the cottage, I tried to picture Eleanor in her chair writing, or holding court at the table, surrounded by friends and comrades in arms. She was, until the end, her own person, despite all the demands and constraints the world placed on her—true to herself and her values. That's a surprisingly rare and special thing.

Back in 1946, when Eleanor was charting her post-FDR course, she said something that resonates with me now as it never has before. "During a long life, I have always done what, for one reason or another, was the thing which was incumbent upon me to do without any consideration as to whether I wished to do it or not," she wrote. "That no longer seems to be a necessity, and for my few remaining years, I hope to be free!"

That's the future I want, too. As Eleanor showed, it's there for the taking.

"What do we do now?" That's the question a lot of Democrats asked me in the first months after Trump's victory and inauguration. Many of my campaign staff, donors, and volunteers were eager—desperate, even—to find new ways to keep up the fight for the progressive values we all shared. People came up to me in restaurants, airports, and theaters, asking for direction. They wanted to help but didn't know the best way to do it. Should they be giving everything they could to the American Civil Liberties Union and others trying to stop Trump's travel ban in court? Or throw themselves into the handful of special elections that would fill open House seats in 2017? What about diving into new efforts to fight gerrymandering and voter suppression? Should they run for office themselves? There were so many causes, groups, and candidates looking for support, it was hard to know where to begin. Frankly, I was asking the same questions.

At first, I had intended to keep relatively quiet. Former Presidents and former nominees often try to keep a respectful distance from the front lines of politics, at least for a while. I always admired how both George H. W. Bush and George W. Bush avoided criticizing Bill and Barack, and how Bill ended up working with George H. W. on tsunami relief in Asia and Katrina recovery on the Gulf Coast. And with George W. in Haiti after the earthquake in 2011. That's how it's supposed to work. But these weren't ordinary times, and Trump wasn't an ordinary President.

The Russia scandal was getting more disturbing by the day. Polls showed that respect for the United States around the world was collapsing. The understaffed, overpoliticized Trump administration was consumed by crises of their own making, but I shuddered to think about how they would handle a real emergency, whether it was a clash with nuclear-armed North Korea, a major terrorist attack, a natural disaster like Hurricane Katrina, or a cyberattack on a nuclear power plant. At home, instead of investing in infrastructure and jobs, the new administration was busy rolling back protections for civil rights, worker's rights, and clean air and water. I watched with horror as Republicans in Congress moved methodically to dismantle the Affordable Care Act, which would strip tens of millions of Americans of their health care. Soon it became clear their target was much bigger than Obamacare. They wanted to strike a major blow against Medicaid, too. I had no doubt that Medicare and Social Security would soon be on the chopping block as well. It was a full-on ideological assault on the legacy of the Great Society and the New Deal. They don't just want to erase Barack Obama from the history books—they're coming for LBJ and FDR, too. Hardworking families I'd met across the country were going to pay the price. They needed help getting ahead but instead they were getting stabbed in the back. Watching all this unfold in the early months of the Trump presidency, I knew there was no way I could sit quietly on the sidelines.

Not long after I got back from my Val-Kill visit, I was trying to figure out what to say to a conference of businesswomen in California and I came up with a phrase that was a little silly, but it felt right: "Resist, insist, persist, enlist." It became a mantra of sorts for me over the next few months.

Ever since the Women's March in January, *resistance* had become the watchword for everyone opposed to Trump and all the protests, large and small, spreading across the country. Mitch McConnell had unintentionally made "persistence" a rallying cry as well, after he tried to justify his outrageous silencing of Elizabeth Warren on the Senate floor by saying, "She was warned. She was given an explanation. Nevertheless, she persisted." That last part was now showing up on signs, T-shirts, and hashtags. Chelsea even decided to write a children's book about thirteen inspiring women who shaped American history called *She Persisted*.

My new mantra celebrated all that energy and activism, but I thought its most important word was the last one: *enlist*. Unless people stay engaged and find ways to translate protests into political power, we aren't going to stop Trump's agenda or win future elections. To do that, we need to invest in political infrastructure: rebuilding the Democratic Party, training new candidates and staffers, improving our data and social media operations, beating back efforts to restrict voting rights, and more.

I know there are a lot of people—including a lot of Democrats—who are not eager to see me leading such an effort. They feel burned by my defeat, tired of defending me against relentless right-wing attacks, and ready for new leaders to emerge. Some of that sentiment is totally reasonable. I, too, am hungry for new leaders and ideas to reinvigorate our party. But if Al Gore, John Kerry, John McCain, and Mitt Romney can find positive ways to contribute after their own election defeats, so can I. That doesn't mean I'll ever run for office again—although I was amused and surprised by the brief but fervent speculation over whether I would run for Mayor of New York. It does mean I will speak out on the causes I care about, campaign for other Democrats, and do whatever I can to build the infrastructure we need to succeed.

My thinking on all this crystalized in the spring of 2017 during a series of conversations with Howard Dean, the former Vermont Governor. As a presidential candidate in 2004, Howard pioneered many of the online organizing and fund-raising tactics that would later help elect Barack Obama. As chair of the Democratic National Committee, he led a "fifty-state strategy" that extended the party's organizing into red states that had been neglected for too long. That experience made him the perfect person to talk to about the work Democrats needed to do now and how I could help.

Howard shared my enthusiasm for supporting the next generation of Democratic organizers, and he told me about the growing number of grassroots groups sprouting up in the wake of the election. Letting a thousand flowers bloom was great, he said, but it would be important to help the most promising groups find funding and focus. I agreed, and we decided to start a new organization that would identify and support up-and-coming groups and leaders who might not otherwise get the resources they deserved. We recruited a few like-minded colleagues and got to work.

We did a lot of research and met with many young leaders, which itself was both fun and fascinating. I listened to their presentations and peppered them with questions: What inspired you to start this organization? What are your strategic imperatives? What's the one thing you wish you could do with additional resources? They gave smart, thoughtful answers. I walked out of those meetings feeling more hopeful and optimistic than I had in a long time.

After some tough deliberation, we landed on five initial groups to support with fund-raising and advice. Some were already hard at work helping channel a surge of grassroots energy opposing Trump's attempt to repeal Obamacare and offering practical advice for how people could most effectively make their voices heard on Capitol Hill. Others were mobilizing volunteers in swing districts with the goal of taking back the House in 2018 and recruiting and training talented, diverse Democratic women and young people to run for office and win.

The working name of our new umbrella organization was Our American Future. We created a logo and a website and prepared to go public. Luckily, a friend of mine pointed out that the acronym of Our American Future would be OAF. I imagined the headlines: "Hillary Clinton Lurches Out of the Woods: Here Comes OAF." We needed a new name, stat! After a quick brainstorm, we came up with a better option that combined my campaign slogan, Stronger Together, with "Onward!" the exhortation I'd been using to close personal notes for years. (What can I say? I'm a sentimentalist.) The logo and website got a quick makeover, and we were ready to launch Onward Together.

I hope you'll join us in this effort. Check it out at OnwardTogether .org. Become a member and help us support these fantastic groups and the future of Democratic grassroots organizing.

There are many other ways to resist, insist, persist, and enlist. Register to vote. Help your friends and family do the same. You have to vote in every election, not just during presidential years. It matters. For one, your right to vote is protected or undermined by state and local officials who oversee and conduct elections. Bring as many other people as you can to the polls with you.

Get involved in a cause that matters to you. Just pick one, start somewhere. Women's rights, LGBT rights, workers' rights, voting rights, the environment, health care, campaign finance reform, public education—they all deserve attention. Don't just think about it or talk about it: support a cause with your money, your time, and your talents. Find an organization that's doing work you believe in. It may be a long-standing organization or a newer or smaller one. If it doesn't exist, build it.

Local issues are every bit as important as national and global ones. If you see a problem in your community that needs fixing or an injustice that needs correcting, and you think, "Someone ought to do something about that," guess what? That someone could easily be you. Show up at a city council or school board meeting and suggest a solution. If a problem is affecting your life, it's probably affecting someone else's—and that person might just be willing to join you.

Try to get to know your elected officials at every level and learn where they stand. If you disagree with them, challenge them. Learn when they're holding their next town hall and show up. Don't forget to support and contribute to candidates who will fight for your values and interests. Better yet, run for office yourself.

If you've been keeping your opinions to yourself, try speaking out—whether that's on social media, in a letter to the editor, or in conversations with friends, family, and neighbors. Your views are every bit as valuable as everyone else's. You'll be surprised by how satisfying it can be to express yourself. And chances are, once you take a stand, you'll find you're not standing alone for long. If all else fails, make a sign and show up at a protest.

One of my supporters, Katy from Bellevue, Washington, sent me her five-step plan, which I think is a great road map for anyone looking to make a difference:

1) I have set up a monthly contribution to the ACLU and I will stand by, ready to take action as needed.

2) I'm looking ahead to 2018. I know the Democrats have a rough road ahead, with many seats to defend, but I'm ready to start now. I will become more active in my local Democratic Party.

3) I will join a church or a synagogue (I grew up Methodist and my husband is Jewish) as an avenue for public service and to give my sons a greater sense of community.

4) I am a high school history teacher, but because my older son has autism and requires a lot of therapy I am on leave this year. While on leave, I will volunteer at a local school for a few hours a week so that I can continue educating the next generation.

5) I will be more proactive about teaching my sons to love ALL people. We will have conversations about racism and misogyny. I will help them to understand their privilege and to understand that privilege makes them responsible for others.

There's an African proverb I've always loved: "If you want to go quickly, go alone. If you want to go far, go together." If ever there was a moment to channel that spirit, it's now. We have a long road ahead, and we'll only get there together.

In the spring of 2017, I received a letter from a group called Wellesley Women for Hillary. Thousands of current and former students from my alma mater had worked their hearts out during the campaign. They were crushed by the outcome, but the group stayed together, supporting and encouraging one another. Now they wanted my advice about what to do next.

Around the same time, I got an invitation from Wellesley's new President, Dr. Paula A. Johnson, to speak at the college's graduation at the end of May. This would be the third pivotal moment in my life when I addressed a Wellesley graduation. It had been nearly a half century since the first time—at my own graduation in 1969—and doing so again in 2017, in the middle of this long, strange year of regret and resistance, felt fitting. I could try to answer the question posed by the Wellesley Women for Hillary—What do we do now?—for the class of 2017, for our country, and for myself.

I love going back to campus. It's more built up than it used to be but still beautiful and full of memories: swimming in Lake Waban . . . staying up late arguing about the war and civil rights . . . being told by my French teacher, "Mademoiselle, your talents lie elsewhere" . . . placing a panicked collect call back to Park Ridge because I didn't think I was smart or sophisticated enough to cut it at Wellesley, and hearing my father say, "Okay, come home," only to have my mother insist, "There aren't quitters in our family."

Over the years, I've had a chance to spend time with several generations of Wellesley students, and it's always a tonic. They're so smart, engaged, and eager to make their marks on the world. It energizes me, and reminds me of the fire and ambition I felt all those years ago.

In the dizzying, depressing days after my defeat, that's what I needed. I needed to remember who I was, where I came from, what I believed, and why I fought so hard and so long for it. Wellesley helped me find myself as a young woman. Maybe it could help me again now chart my path.

The second time I spoke at a Wellesley graduation was in 1992, during the heat of Bill's first run for the White House. I was trying to adjust to the bright glow of the national spotlight (actually, it often felt more like a scorching flame)—and still smarting from the "cookies and tea" fiasco—but also feeling exhilarated by the passion and optimism of our campaign. It was one of the most remarkable years of my life, and I wanted to share what I'd learned and how it felt with my fellow Wellesley grads. In my speech, I urged the class of '92 to defy the barriers and expectations they still faced as strong, independent women, and focus instead on finding fulfillment in their own unique balance of family, work, and service. I reminded them of Wellesley's Latin motto, *Non Ministrari sed Ministrare*, which means "Not to be ministered unto, but to minister." That sentiment always appealed to my Methodist sensibilities, and it resonated even more in a year when Bill and I were crisscrossing the country talking about a new birth of responsibility, opportunity, and community.

Since I was speaking at an academic event, I reached for a lofty source of wisdom to give a little oomph to my heartfelt advice about serving others: Václav Havel, the dissident Czech playwright and activist who had recently become his country's first freely elected President. Later, as First Lady, I would meet Havel, and he would take me on a mesmerizing moonlit walk through the old city of Prague. But in 1992 I knew him only through his writing, which was eloquent and compelling. Only "by throwing yourself over and over again into the tumult of the world, with the intention of making your voice count—only thus will you really become a person," he wrote. That's what I wanted those Wellesley graduates to understand and act on. It was a time of hope and change, and they belonged at the vanguard of a rising generation.

Boy, did 2017 feel different. The hope so many of us felt in 1992 was gone, and in its place was a creeping dread about the future. Every day, the new Trump administration was disgracing our country, undermining the rule of law, and telling such bald-faced lies that it seemed as if it really had no shame at all. (According to the *New York Times*, Trump lied or dissembled at least once every day for the first 40 days of his presidency. The *Washington Post* counted 623 false and misleading statements he had made over his first 137 days.)

In 1969, my classmates and I had worried about the loss of trust in our leaders and institutions. Those fears were back at full force, amplified for the internet age, when it's so easy to live in echo chambers that shut out contrary voices and inconvenient truths. Our leaders now have tools at their disposal to exploit fear, cynicism, and resentment that were unimaginable in 1969.

And as for me, I had thrown myself "into the tumult of the world," but it had left me bruised and gasping for air. What could I possibly say to the Wellesley class of 2017 in a moment like this?

I thought about Havel. He had persevered through much worse. He and all of Soviet-dominated Eastern Europe had lived for decades under what Havel called "a thick crust of lies." He and other dissidents had managed to punch through those lies and ultimately tear down the authoritarian regimes that propagated them. I went back and re-read one of his essays, "The Power of the Powerless," which explains how individuals can wield truth like a weapon, even when they lack all political influence. Havel understood that authoritarians who rely on lies to control their people are fundamentally not that different from neighborhood bullies. They're more fragile than they look. He wrote, "The moment someone breaks through in one place, when one person cries out, 'The emperor is naked!'—when a single person breaks the rules of the game, thus exposing it as a game—everything suddenly appears in another light."

This felt like the right message for 2017. I could warn the Wellesley graduates that they were becoming adults during an all-out assault on truth and reason, especially from a White House specializing in "alternative facts." I could explain how the administration's attempts to distort reality were an affront to the Enlightenment values our country was founded on, including the belief that an informed citizenry and free and open debate are the foundations of a healthy democracy. But Havel's words gave reason to hope. Every one of us has a role to play in defending our democracy and standing up for rational thought. I could remind the graduates of what I'd said in my concession speech:

that they are valuable and powerful, and that the skills and values they learned at Wellesley had given them everything they would need to fight back.

It drove me crazy that since the election, pundits had fetishized stereotypical Trump supporters to such a degree that they had started dismissing anyone who lived on the coasts and had a college education as irrelevant and out of touch. I wanted to assure the Wellesley grads that this was nonsense. Their capacity for critical thinking, their commitment to inclusiveness and pluralism, their ethic of serving others— that's precisely what we needed in America in 2017. My advice would be simple: Don't let the bastards get you down. Stay true to yourself and your values. Most of all, keep going.

I woke up early on May 26. I had spent the previous evening with Bill and a few former campaign aides, eating Thai food, drinking white wine, and working on my speech. I wanted this one to be good. It would be my first big speech since the concession, and I knew a lot of my supporters across the country were eager to hear from me. Many were scared, angry, and hungry for inspiration. Most of all, the graduates deserved a memorable graduation.

It was raining in Chappaqua, and the weather report said it was drizzling in Boston, too. I felt for all the families at Wellesley who surely had been hoping for a perfect day. I had graduated under a brilliantly clear New England sky. Oh well; some people say rain on a wedding day is good luck. Maybe the same is true for graduations.

I got dressed in Wellesley blue, had a cup of coffee, and found a sweet note from Bill. He had stayed up to all hours reading the latest speech draft and scribbled on the top of the page, "H—I like this speech. Hope these suggestions help make it better—wake me and we'll go over it—I love you." I thought for the ten millionth time how glad I was that I had married my best friend and biggest cheerleader. And yes, like always, his edits made my speech better.

Puttering, I turned on the news and quickly regretted it. Overnight, a Republican congressional candidate in Montana who had body-slammed a reporter for asking tough questions about health care had won his special election. At the NATO summit across the Atlantic, Donald Trump had shoved the prime minister of Montenegro out of the way so he could get a better spot in a group photo. I watched the clip several times, like rubbernecking at a car wreck. It was hard not to see the two stories as related, both symbols of our degraded national life in the Age of Trump. I sighed, turned off the television, gathered my things, headed to the airport, and flew to Massachusetts.

Even in the rain, seeing the old redbrick buildings of Wellesley made me feel better. The campus was humming with the familiar rituals of graduation. Parents and grandparents were fawning over their embarrassed children. Younger siblings were soaking in everything, imagining when it would be their turn. Some of the grads had decorated their mortarboards with flower crowns and rainbow flags. Others sported "I'm With Her" stickers and "Love Trumps Hate" pins, which made me smile. By tradition, every Wellesley class is assigned a color. As it happened, both 1969 and 2017 were green classes. As a result, it felt a little like Saint Patrick's Day all over campus.

President Johnson, whom I knew and admired for her work in medicine and on public health issues, met me and brought me to the aptly named Green Hall, a lovely old Gothic building. There I found my academic robes and tasseled cap. As a general rule, I don't wear silly hats in public, but this was an exception. I resolved to see it as jaunty.

To my delight, before the graduation ceremony began, I was able to steal a few minutes with an old friend. When I was a student at Wellesley, Rev. Paul Santmire was the college chaplain and became an important mentor for me. In my '69 commencement speech, I cited him as a model of integrity at a time when we didn't trust authority figures and hardly anyone at all over thirty. Now, in his early eighties, Paul was as sharp and humane as ever. We embraced, and he told me that he'd driven up to New Hampshire in the fall to go door-to-door for my campaign. We reminisced about the old days when I was a wide-eyed student activist, and he mentioned my favorite line from John Wesley, the call to "Do all the good you can." I assured him it was closer to my heart than ever and that my faith had been a rock in this period when everything else felt topsy-turvy.

I also had a chance to visit briefly with a young woman named Lauren, who was the president of the Wellesley Republicans club—a post I had held as a student myself before realizing my evolving views and values were taking me in a different direction. Lauren seemed to be going through similar soul-searching. Wellesley was a lonely place to be a conservative, but she told me her classmates had been eager to talk through their differences in an open and supportive way. Lauren wasn't a Trump fan and was torn about what to do after he won the nomination. The Wellesley Republicans withheld its endorsement. But like most people, Lauren assumed Trump would lose and things would go back to normal. Now she was wrestling with what it all meant. Join the club, I thought. (Or, quit it! Seriously, if anyone is thinking of quitting the Republican Party, now would be a good time.)

There was one more person to meet. Tala Nashawati was chosen by her classmates to be the student speaker at graduation, just as I was in 1969. The American daughter of Syrian immigrants living in Ohio, she was graceful and poised, with a warm smile. Like so many Wellesley students, Tala was ridiculously accomplished and well rounded: a Middle Eastern Studies major, sought-after kickboxing instructor, and soon-to-be medical student. The night before my graduation speech in 1969, I had stayed up all night writing, pacing, and thinking, and in the morning, I was still in a barely controlled panic. But Tala appeared calm. She had been up late putting the finishing touches on her speech, but she had known for a long time what she wanted to say. And now she was ready.

Tala had brought a photo for me to sign. It was from 1969. There I was, standing at the podium, leaning ever so slightly in toward the microphone, my hair swept back into a bun that I remember thinking was very grown up, big glasses perched on my nose. So young. Behind me, a row of gray-haired faculty and trustees looking very serious. Some of them were probably wondering why President Ruth Adams had allowed a student to speak at graduation at all, something that had never happened before. Or they were struggling to follow my passionate but somewhat incoherent remarks. At the bottom of the photo was printed a quote from my speech: "The challenge now is to practice politics as the art of making what appears to be impossible, possible."

I had borrowed that line from a poem written by a friend. It captured the idealism so many of us felt, despite the war and assassinations and unrest all around us. We really believed we could change the world. Forty-seven years later, I had planned to use the line again in the victory speech I hoped to deliver on election night. "I'm older now. I'm a mother and a grandmother," I would have said. "But I still believe with all my heart that we can make the impossible, possible. Look at what we're celebrating tonight."

But in the end, there was nothing to celebrate. The glass ceiling held. The impossible remained so. I looked at Tala. We had never met before this moment, but in so many ways, I felt like I had been fighting for her and millions like her my entire career. And I had let them all down.

Yet here she was, bright-eyed and full of spirit, asking me to sign this black-and-white photo. It meant something to her. So did those words. Despite my defeat, she still believed in making the impossible possible.

It was time to go. There was a long walk through the snaking halls of the old academic building to get out to the tent where the graduation ceremony would be held. President Johnson and I lined up behind the college's trustees, and the procession began.

We turned a corner and saw young women in black robes lining both sides of the hall. They began to clap and cheer wildly. Around another corner were more students. They went on and on, hundreds of them, the entire senior class, lined up like an honor guard. Their cheers were deafening. It was like they were letting months of pent-up feelings pour out—all the hope and hurt they'd felt since November or perhaps since long before. I felt loved and lifted, carried aloft on a wave of emotion.

Finally, we emerged out into the misty air, with waiting parents and news cameras and all the pomp and circumstance of a college commencement. Sitting on the stage, I tried to compose myself, but my heart was still beating fast. Soon Tala was standing at the podium, just like me in the photo. She looked great up there, and her speech was graceful and heartfelt.

Noting that green was the 2017 color, she compared her classmates to emeralds. "Like us, emeralds are valuable, rare, and pretty durable," she said. "But there's something else emeralds are known for: their flaws. I know it's hard to admit, especially as Wellesley students, but we all have a lot of flaws. We are incomplete, scratched up in some places, jagged around the edges."

I leaned in, curious. This is not what I had expected to hear.

"Flawed emeralds are sometimes even better than flawless ones," Tala went on, "because the flaws show authenticity and character."

There was that word again, *authenticity*. But she was using it as a balm instead of a bludgeon. *Flawed*. How often had I heard that word over the past two years. "Flawed Hillary." But here was Tala defiantly reclaiming the word, insisting on the beauty and strength of imperfection.

Now her classmates were leaning in, too. They snapped their fingers instead of clapping, as Tala smiled and built to her close.

"In the words of Secretary Clinton, never doubt that you are valuable and powerful and deserving of every chance in the world to pursue your dreams," she told the class of 2017. "You are rare and unique. Let yourself be flawed. Go proudly and confidently into the world with your blinding hues to show everyone who's boss and break every glass ceiling that still remains."

Now the snaps gave way to cheers. I was among the loudest. I stood and applauded and felt hope and pride rising in my heart. If this was the future, then everything had been worth it.

Things are going to be hard for a long time. But we are going to be okay. All of us.

The rain was ending. It was my turn to speak.

"What do we do now?" I said. There was only one answer: "Keep going."

Acknowledgments

I dedicated this book to the team that stood with me in 2016.

I will always be grateful to Barack and Michelle Obama and their staffs for all their support before, during, and after the campaign; Tim Kaine, Anne Holton, and their family; everyone who spent endless days and nights working in our Brooklyn headquarters; the state directors and state staffs, field and advance teams, coordinated campaign staff, volunteers, interns, and fellows in all fifty states; our consultants, contractors, and vendors; the team at the DNC; our lawyers at Perkins Coie; House and Senate Democrats, Governors, Mayors, and their staffs; and all the friends and surrogates who poured their hearts into our campaign. I wish I could thank each and every one of you. In fact, I asked the publisher whether we could print all your names here—more than 6,500—but they said it would make this book twice as long. Please know that you are written in my heart, now and always.

What Happened wouldn't have happened without the help and support of another great team. This process has been intensely personal, but there's no way I could have done it alone. I'm grateful to everyone who lent a hand in big ways and small. They proved yet again that we really are stronger together.

This starts with Dan Schwerin, Megan Rooney, and Tony Carrk, who spent many hours with me around my kitchen table in Chappaqua, reliving memories and helping me discover what this book would be.

Dan walked into my Senate office a dozen years ago as a young staffer and has been with me ever since. He helped me with my last book, *Hard Choices*, led my speechwriting team in 2016, and signed on again with this book. I could not have done this and so much else without him. His keen intellect and superior organizational skills are unmatched. He wrestled to the ground reams of facts and arguments to help me make my case. And he's a calm, steady presence in the midst of crisis, and good company all the rest of the time.

Megan Rooney was part of my team at the State Department and came back as a speechwriter for the campaign. She dove into the rigors of this book with thoughtful intelligence, wit, and a well-honed skill at storytelling, all of which made this better than I could have done alone. She was my partner in feminist mind melds and brought her good humor, mischievous smile, and twinkling eyes to many long nights when we all needed a lift.

She and Dan continued their long writing partnership and I loved watching them sitting side by side on my couch, computers on their laps, working on a piece of text, not talking but understanding each other and the task perfectly.

Tony Carrk joined me on my 2008 campaign as a researcher, and in 2016 took charge of that critical team. Through intense pressure and stressful days, he was the go-to guy who knew whatever we needed.

His dedication and decency are evident to all. And he did it while becoming the father of a little girl, Celia, during the campaign and a little boy, Diego, during the book writing.

Huma Abedin, Nick Merrill, Cheryl Mills, Philippe Reines, Heather Samuelson, and Jake Sullivan have been by my side for years, through triumph and heartbreak. As they have so many times before, they supported this project and me with wise advice and perspective.

I'm indebted to everyone who shared memories and insights, offered advice, helped review pages and facts, and supported me and my work throughout this process, including Emily Aden, John Anzalone, Charlie Baker, Kris Balderston, De'Ara Balenger, Shannon Beckham, Daniel Benaim, Joel Benenson, Jonathan Berkon, David Binder, Allida Black, Sid Blumenthal, Susie Buell, Glen Caplin, Dennis Cheng, Corey Ciorciari, Brian Cookstra, Brynne Craig, Jon Davidson, Howard Dean, Karen Dunn, Marc Elias, YJ Fischer, Oren Fliegelman, Oscar Flores, Tina Flournoy, Danielle Friedman, Ethan Gelber, Teddy Goff, Jorie Graham, Shane Hable, Tyler Hagenbuch, Maya Harris, Trevor Houser, Jill Iscol, Jay Jacobs, Beth Jones, Elizabeth Kanick, Grady Keefe, Ron Klain, Jen Klein, Harold Koh, Elan Kriegel, Amy Kuhn, David Levine, Jenna Lowenstein, Bari Lurie, Moj Mahdara, Jim Margolis, Capricia Marshall, Marlon Marshall, Garry Mauro, Michael McFaul, Judith McHale, Kelly Mehlenbacher, Craig Minassian, Robby Mook, Minyon Moore, Lissa Muscatine, Navin Nayak, Kevin O'Keefe, Ann O'Leary, Jennifer Palmieri, Maura Pally, Adam Parkhomenko, Matt Paul, Lauren Peterson, John Podesta, Jacob Priley, Amy Rao, Ed Rendell, Mary Kate Rooney, Emmy Ruiz, Rob Russo, Sheryl Sandberg, Marina Santos, Kristina Schake, Oren Schur, Ella Serrano, Meredith Shepherd, Bill Shillady, David Shimer, Anne-Marie Slaughter, Craig Smith, Burns Strider, Donna Tartt, Mario Testino, Opal Vadhan, Lona Valmoro, Jon Vein, Melanne Verveer, Mike Vlacich, Rachel Vogelstein, Diane von Fürstenberg, Don Walker and the Harry Walker Agency,

Maggie Williams, Graham Wilson, Theresa Vargas Wyatt, and Julie Zuckerbrod.

Thanks as well to all the experts and academics who helped me develop the policies mentioned in this book and many more that comprised the most progressive Democratic platform in history. Those policies continue to offer a road map for building a better future. You can read more about them at www.hillaryclinton.com/issues.

I couldn't have gotten through the election and its aftermath without my friends. They kept me sane, took me to the theater, came for visits, went on walks, made me laugh, sustained my spirit, and endured an occasional venting session. I'm so looking forward to spending more time with all of you.

I'm indebted to Simon & Schuster, especially Chief Executive Officer Carolyn Reidy, and my editors Jonathan Karp and Priscilla Painton, all of whom spent many hours advising me and reviewing drafts. Thanks to their team: Tamara Arellano, Phil Bashe, Eloy Bleifuss, Alice Dalrymple, Amar Deol, Lisa Erwin, Jonathan Evans, Tiffany Frarey, Megan Gerrity, Cary Goldstein, Megan Hogan, John Paul Jones, Ruth Lee-Mui, Kristen Lemire, Dominick Montalto, Laura Ogar, Anne Tate Pearce, Emily Remes, Richard Rhorer, Jackie Seow, Elisa Shokoff, Laura Tatham, and Dana Trocker.

Thanks to my attorneys: Bob Barnett, debate prep sparring partner and publishing sage; David Kendall, who lived through the email craziness with me; and their team at Williams and Connolly—Tanya Abrams, Tom Hentoff, Deneen Howell, Michael O'Connor, Adam Perlman, Ana Reyes, Amy Saharia, Katherine Turner, and Steve Wohlgemuth.

To the men and women of the United States Secret Service, thank you for always having my back. Your professionalism and courage are an inspiration.

And to the 65,844,610 Americans who voted for me, thank you for your trust and confidence. We didn't get there this time, but I hope you never lose faith in the vision we share for a better America.

The poet Max Ehrmann says, "Whatever your labors and aspirations, in the noisy confusion of life, keep peace with your soul." My peace is only possible because of the love and support of Bill, Chelsea, Marc, Charlotte, Aidan, and our entire family. Thank you for being the greatest editors, sounding boards, stress relievers, and joy givers in the world. And thanks for being excited that I'm around a lot more these days.

Index

Permissions

About the Author

HILLARY RODHAM CLINTON is the first woman in U.S. history to become the presidential nominee of a major political party. She served as the 67th Secretary of State—from January 21, 2009, until February 1, 2013—after nearly four decades in public service advocating on behalf of children and families as an attorney, First Lady, and Senator. She is a wife, mother, and grandmother.